KU-272-021

THEORIES OF SOCIAL ORDER

edited by

MICHAEL HECHTER

and

CHRISTINE HORNE

THEORIES OF SOCIAL ORDER

A READER

STANFORD SOCIAL SCIENCES
An Imprint of Stanford University Press

Stanford University Press
Stanford, California

© 2003 by the Board of Trustees of the
Leland Stanford Junior University. All rights reserved.

Chapter 1: Excerpts from *The Nature of Social Science*,
copyright © 1967 by George C. Homans,
reprinted by permission of Harcourt, Inc.

Printed in the United States of America
on acid-free, archival-quality paper.

Library of Congress Cataloging-in-Publication Data

Theories of social order : a reader / edited by Michael Hechter
and Christine Horne.
    p.   cm.
  Includes bibliographical references and index.
   ISBN 0-8047-4675-3 (cloth : alk. paper)—
ISBN 0-8047-4611-7 (pbk. : alk. paper)
   1. Social structure. 2. Sociology. I. Hechter, Michael.
II. Horne, Christine.
HM706. T54 2003
301—dc21   2002155746

Original Printing 2003
Last figure below indicates year of this printing:
12 11 10 09 08 07 06

Designed by James P. Brommer
Typeset by TBH Typecast in 10.5/14 and 10.5/18 Garamond

TO OUR TEACHERS

CONTENTS

CONTENTS

PREFACE

Most introductory courses in sociological theory aspire to provide students with an overview of the intellectual history of the discipline. This approach has a number of implications. It ensures that the main organizing principle of a course consists of *theorists* rather than *theories*. Dutiful students learn what a Marxian, Durkheimian, and Weberian approach to sociology entails. Because the ideas of all theorists who are worth their salt (such as those featured in these pages) develop over the course of their careers, this labeling invariably bowdlerizes: early Marx differs in important respects from late Marx, early Durkheim from late, early Weber from late, and so forth. Attempts to force a false consistency to each theorist ring hollow and mislead.

More importantly, because the focus is on theorists rather than questions, students never have the opportunity to compare the kinds of explanations that theorists provide. Newcomers to social theory are ill equipped to draw out common analytical threads. And there is no common substantive focus that would facilitate this kind of intellectual effort.

Further, the standard historical approach leads naturally to a division of classical from contemporary sociological theory. Naturally, there is ample justification for such a division. It is difficult to understand any given theorist's contribution unless it is placed in its historical context. How can one fully appreciate the contributions of Marx or Durkheim without first knowing those of Rousseau? But just as the focus on theorists rather than on questions hinders the development of students' analytical understanding, historical divisions also serve to obscure the connections that may hold between theorists. For example, it is difficult to fully understand control theory (Hirschi 1969), a theory much discussed by contemporary criminologists, without considering what Émile Durkheim, a preeminently classical theorist, had to say about the causes of suicide. Adherence to a strict distinction between classical and contemporary theory makes it difficult for students to appreciate how, and to what extent, theoretical knowledge has cumulated in sociology.

Not only is there little coherence in the substantive questions being addressed, but strong disputes about the concept of theory itself abound as well. Theory is variously seen as constituting explanation, the description of empirical regularities, or interpretation. Typically it is taught in isolation from classes in methods and particular substantive areas. Perhaps as a result, students often finish such courses wondering what implications theory has either for their own lives or for sociological research in general.

Unfortunately, the analytical weaknesses of the standard introductory theory course do not exist in isolation. These tendencies contribute to the benighted place that theory now occupies in the discipline today.[1] Although every sociology department in the world compels its students—both undergraduate and graduate—to undergo at least some instruction in sociological theory, this activity is more often viewed as a rite of passage than as an opportunity to acquire a set of tools that can help guide empirical research. Indeed, the importance of theory for the development of empirical research is all but obscured in the standard course format.

Theories of Social Order offers something different. By pairing theories with empirical applications, it aims to reveal the implications that different theories have for contemporary research. And by focusing on theor*ies* of one important question rather than on the theor*ists* of most everything, it facilitates the exploration of common analytical themes. The question addressed is the problem of social order.

Once widely regarded as the single most important problem in all of social

---

1. Indeed, one influential sociologist has characterized theory's marginal position in the discipline as nothing less than a scandal (Goldthorpe 2000; see also van den Berg 1998). For a less damning view of the state of theory in contemporary sociology, see Grusky and Di Carlo 2001.

theory,[2] in recent years social order has receded from view. This inattention has at least two independent sources. The first source is political. During the turbulent days of the late 1960s, a concern with social order was often perceived as a barely disguised conservative apology for an ethically dubious status quo. Students' interest shifted to matters of social transformation. Now many of those same students comprise the senior faculty in sociology departments around the globe. The second source is intellectual. Sociologists of the postwar generation who were devoted to grand theory wrote much about how values and culture resolved the problem of social order. Because these concepts are inherently ambiguous, however, too little of this work had any recognizable empirical implications.

But these are not good reasons to abandon a concern with social order. Although for some (Adorno 1976), grand theory's lack of empirical implications was taken as a badge of honor rather than a lacuna remaining to be filled, this was far from the mainstream view. As the emphasis on sound empirical research increased in sociology and the allied social sciences, many scholars and teachers found, and continue to find, precious little to admire in these highly abstract treatises. Further, dismissing social order as a concern of conservatives alone obscures the point that order is simply the flip side of conflict and change. A full explanation of social order requires an understanding of its transformation as well as its production.

No comparable intellectual rationale for sociological theory has ever superseded the problem of social order. Without social order, there can be no agriculture, no industry, no trade, no economic investment, no technological development, no justice, no art, no science, and no human advancement. Although it is frequently unacknowledged, the problem of social order underlies questions of central concern to sociologists in substantive areas as diverse as crime and deviance, social movements, organizations, politics, religion, international relations, and the family.

---

2. Thus, the most intellectually influential reader on sociological theory in the 1960s, *Theories of Society* (Parsons et al. 1961), was largely organized around the problem of social order.

Linking classical texts on social order, contemporary theoretical extensions, and recent empirical research, the present volume contends that the principal justification for theory in the social sciences lies in its fruitfulness for understanding real-world phenomena. The early sociological theorists dwelled on the problem of social order. Since the 1980s, new theoretical and empirical literatures have arisen that also address the issue. Articles and excerpts have been selected for this volume on the basis of their relevance to classical theoretical issues. We have aimed to include only well-written, nontechnical pieces that are accessible to a broad undergraduate readership. Moreover, in the introductions to each section, we endeavor to draw explicit links between the classical and modern texts.

Although we believe that the approach taken in this volume is analytically superior to that found in traditional volumes on sociological theory, it comes with its own limits. Obviously, *Theories of Social Order* is substantively narrow. It provides no biographical information about the discipline's founding fathers. Moreover, it conveys nothing of the history of theory in sociology. We make no effort to present the theories in chronological order; for instance, Hobbes, the seventeenth-century writer who first articulated the problem of social order in its modern form, does not make his appearance until after the introduction of late-nineteenth- and early-twentieth- century sociological theorists—many of whom explicitly reacted to Hobbes. Rather than present the history of theory, which necessarily is a tale of attack and counterattack, we have simplified the narrative by presenting the core solutions that have been advanced to resolve the problem of social order.

This reader gives students the opportunity to explore and compare the various factors and mechanisms that have been held responsible for social order. We think this strategy facilitates a deeper theoretical understanding. Moreover, by wedding these alternate explanations to empirical applications, *Theories of Social Order* helps students grasp the essential lesson that sociological theory must have empirical implications. This lesson makes it easier for students to appreciate the relevance of theory for their own lives, for the research enterprise, and for the development of better social policies.

REFERENCES

Adorno, Theodor W. 1976. *The Positivist Dispute in German Sociology*. London: Heinemann.

Goldthorpe, John H. 2000. *On Sociology*. Oxford: Oxford University Press.

Grusky, David B., and Matthew Di Carlo. 2001. "Should Sociologists Plod Along and Establish Descriptive Regularities or Seek a Grand Explanation for Them?" *European Sociological Review* 17:457–63.

Hirschi, Travis. 1969. *Causes of Delinquency*. Berkeley: University of California Press.

Parsons, Talcott, Edward Shils, Kaspar D. Naegele, and Jesse R. Pitts, editors. 1961. *Theories of Society: Foundations of Modern Sociological Theory*. New York: Free Press of Glencoe.

van den Berg, Axel. 1998. "Is Sociological Theory Too Grand for Social Mechanisms?" In *Social Mechanisms: An Analytical Approach to Social Theory,* edited by Peter Hedström and Richard Swedberg, 204–37. Cambridge: Cambridge University Press.

PART I WHAT IS THEORY?

A.

Theory Is Explanation

Several years ago, a reporter for National Public Radio had an idea. He considered the stock phrase "This may seem difficult, but it isn't rocket science!" and wondered how rocket scientists expressed the idea that some subjects were simply beyond their ability to comprehend. So he asked a rocket scientist how he would express this same notion. His informant told him that rocket scientists often said, "This may seem difficult, but it isn't theoretical physics!" Naturally, the reporter then posed the same question to a theoretical physicist. The response: "This may seem difficult, but it isn't sociology!"

Social phenomena are staggeringly complex—complex enough to seem bewildering to a theoretical physicist. Facts about social life are abundant—indeed, they are superabundant. How can we understand social phenomena when so many facts are potentially relevant?

Say that we discover (as Émile Durkheim did at the end of the nineteenth century) that some European countries have higher suicide rates than others. What kinds of factors might be responsible for this finding? Is this difference in suicide rates related to the nature of religion in these countries? Are there systematic economic differences between them? Maybe some countries are subject to greater political instability or have climates with low levels of sunshine. We can collect evidence about these factors and many more. Intuitively, we recognize that not all these factors are likely to be equally important in understanding cross-national variation in suicide rates. Why should we pay more attention to some factors as opposed to others? How can we tell which facts are key in accounting for these differences in suicide rates?

This is where theory comes in. Theories provide a way of identifying those facts that are important. Like a map used by a traveler, theories help us find our way. In principle, we could do without them. We could drive aimlessly around a new town, hoping to get to our destination eventually, and enjoying the ambience. But if we want to get from point A to point B, a map identifying a direct route will be helpful. As the traveler's task is made easier with the aid of a map, so it is more productive to explore social phenomena with the help of a theory.

Because they simplify reality, social theories are necessarily incomplete. A map does not identify every stop sign or strip mall; if it did, it would not be very useful. Similarly, a theory does not include every possible fact. Instead, it points only to those factors that are likely to be important in explaining a particular phenomenon. Thus theories can focus our thoughts—reducing the number of facts to which we must pay attention. This simplification improves our ability to understand our social world.

WHAT IS THEORY?

Just what kind of help does a theory provide? As George Homans emphasizes, all *theories are explanations* of observable phenomena. Good explanations consist of two different kinds of elements: statements about *causal relations,* and statements about *causal mechanisms.*

A causal relation asserts that some outcome Y depends on some factor X if by modifying X one can affect Y. For instance, Durkheim's theory of suicide states that the degree to which a group is integrated (factor X) is a cause of suicide rates in that group (factor Y). By *integration* Durkheim refers to social situations in which groups exert influence over individuals. According to Durkheim's theory, a lack of integration leads to higher rates of suicide. Thus variation in factor X (integration) is correlated with variation in factor Y (suicide).

But simply proposing that two factors are correlated does not fully answer the question of why suicide rates vary in different populations. To answer this question we must understand something about the *processes* by which one variable influences the other. These processes are the causal mechanisms. In other words, a causal mechanism tells us *how* X produces Y.

Homans's essay provides an example. When swimming in the ocean off the Massachusetts coast, he noticed that the water near the shore was warmer when the wind was blowing toward the shore than when the wind was blowing off-shore. Thus there was a causal relation between the direction of the wind and the temperature of the water. Why does this relation occur? Surface water tends to be warmer than deep water (because of the tendency of heat to rise as well as the influence of the sun). Because the wind acts more on surface than deep water, an onshore wind concentrates warmer water near the shore, whereas an offshore wind moves warmer water out to sea. When warmer water is blown to shore, the existing cooler water must move out to sea; when warmer water is blown away from the shore, it is replenished with colder water.

In this example, the causal variable (factor X) is wind direction. The outcome to be explained (factor Y) is water temperature. There are two mechanisms that help to explain why wind direction is related to water temperature near the shore. First, warm water rises.[1] Second, water seeks its own level. Because warm water rises, as wind direction (factor X) changes, it moves the warm surface water either toward or away from the shore. And because water seeks its own level, if more warm water is blown toward the shore, the existing cooler water must move somewhere else. These two mechanisms lead to a change in water temperature (factor Y). The causal factor, in conjunction with the two mechanisms, explains why the water temperature at the shore varies.

It is important to recognize that causal mechanisms usually make claims about a process occurring in units of analysis at a given level (such as groups or societies) by referring to events occurring at a lower level (such as individuals).[2] In this example, the causal variable (wind direction) and the outcome to be explained (water temperature) are both large-scale, aggregate phenomena. The mechanism responsible for variation in water temperature, however, occurs at the molecular level; wind direction affects water temperature at the shore in this way because heat rises.

---

1. Because warm water is less dense than cold water, it rises to the surface.

2. There is no consensual definition of causal mechanisms in the sociological literature. For some alternate views, see Parsons 1961, 66–70; Coleman 1990, chap. 1; Kiser and Hechter 1991; and Hedström and Swedberg 1998, chaps. 1 and 4.

The same explanatory framework holds in social science, despite its radically different substantive content. Durkheim's suicide rates—like water temperature—are *aggregate* phenomena. His explanation for the lower propensity of suicide among groups is based on the way that group integration affects *individuals,* who comprise the lowest-level units in social theory. Because more integrated groups provide their members with a greater sense of purpose, individuals are less likely to commit suicide. In turn, the rates of suicide in such groups will be lower. Thus Durkheim's theory predicts that integration (factor X) will affect suicide rates (factor Y) and explains why by referring to how integration, a group-level causal factor, affects individuals, and how individual behaviors in turn are translated into suicide rates, a group-level outcome.

WHICH THEORY IS BEST?

Simply developing an explanation of a phenomenon is not sufficient, however. Because theories shape our understanding of social life, they have important consequences for research as well as for social policies. This means that we have a strong interest in selecting superior theories and rejecting inferior ones. In practice, social scientists employ a variety of criteria in selecting between rival theories. Some select theories on the basis of familiarity, whereas others select on political grounds. Because these selection criteria have more to do with the properties of the chooser than the theory, however, there is no assurance that the preferred theory will provide the best explanation. Clearly, the most appropriate criterion for selecting between alternate theories is to choose the theory that provides us with the best explanation of the given phenomenon.

How do we know whether an explanation is the best one? Consider Durkheim's theory about the relation between group integration and suicide rates. At this quite abstract level, integration is not readily observable. But religious affiliation is. For reasons that Durkheim analyzed at length, Protestants are less socially integrated than Catholics. The theory therefore would predict that Protestants will commit suicide at higher rates than Catholics. Marital status is also observable. Single people are less socially integrated than married people. They are less attached to groups and therefore face fewer social demands and obligations. If, as Durkheim's theory says, the lack of social integration is a cause of suicide, then it follows that single people ought to have higher suicide rates than married people.

These two predictions about effects of religion and marital status on suicide rates are empirical implications of Durkheim's theory. All theories have empirical implications. Theories are tested by determining if these implications are consistent with events that are observed in the real world. More specifically, to test a theory, we must translate the abstract theoretical concepts—the purported causes and outcomes—into something that we can observe and measure. To the degree that measures of the outcome are correlated with different levels of the causal indicators, we gain confidence in the theory.

But simply finding that measures of causal factors and the outcome are correlated does not rule out alternate explanations. To increase our confidence in one theory over another, we must also consider causal order and spuriousness. Causal order refers to the possibility that the measure of Y may be determining the measure of X rather than the other way around. Durkheim's theory would be invalidated, for example, if the act of contemplating suicide led people to convert from Catholicism to Protestantism.

Spuriousness refers to the possibility that there is some third variable that was not measured that is causing change in both of the factors that the theory identifies. For example, it may be that both religion and suicide are affected by economic factors and that religion does not influence suicide rates at all. To determine whether religion influences suicide rates, we must account for the potential effects of this additional variable. We gain more confidence in a theory when the outcomes we observe are not determined by (spurious) variables that are neglected by the theory, and when the outcomes do not affect changes in the purported causal variable (Stinchcombe 1968).[3]

---

3. These requirements imply that the experiment is the best means for testing theories. Experiments allow researchers to rule out spurious effects and to manipulate causal factors, directly revealing their influence on outcomes. Most sociologists resort to statistical controls to estimate causality in nonexperimental data.

Our discussion emphasizes the importance of (1) causal relations and mechanisms and (2) empirical implications. One of the most fruitful ways of reading this book is to attempt to identify the respective causal relations and mechanisms proposed in each reading. This task is challenging for at least a couple of reasons. Because few of the following texts explicitly mention either causal relations or mechanisms, different readings may yield different interpretations of these elements. In addition, some of the sections are clearly less amenable to analysis in terms of mechanisms than are others.

A second useful exercise is to consider a theory's empirical implications. Although a particular theory may explicitly seek to explain suicide, or stratification, or cooperation, it may also be useful for explaining other social phenomena. Applying a theory to new settings and problems will help us to better understand the theory as well as its relevance for research and for appreciating the intricacies of social life.

REFERENCES

Coleman, James S. 1990. *Foundations of Social Theory*. Cambridge, Mass.: Belknap Press of Harvard University Press.

Hedström, Peter, and Richard Swedberg, editors. 1998. *Social Mechanisms: An Analytical Approach to Social Theory*. Cambridge: Cambridge University Press.

Kiser, Edgar, and Michael Hechter. 1991. "The Role of General Theory in Comparative-Historical Sociology." *American Journal of Sociology* 97:1–30.

Parsons, Talcott. 1961. "An Outline of the Social System." In *Theories of Society: Foundations of Modern Sociological Theory*, edited by Talcott Parsons, Edward Shils, Kaspar D. Naegele, and Jesse R. Pitts, 30–79. New York: Free Press of Glencoe.

Stinchcombe, Arthur L. 1968. *Constructing Social Theories*. New York: Harcourt Brace and World.

I.

Explanation in the Social Sciences

GEORGE C. HOMANS, 1967

THE NATURE OF EXPLANATION

Most people interested in comparing the social sciences with the natural sciences, especially those interested in making sure that social science *is* a natural science, emphasize the greater difficulty the social sciences face in establishing, against data, the empirical truth of its propositions. It is certainly less easy in the social sciences than in some physical and biological sciences to manipulate variables experimentally and to control the other variables entering into a concrete phenomenon, so that the relationship between those the scientist is interested in at the moment shall be, beyond question, unmasked and stand out clearly. It is less easy to control the variables because it is less easy to control men than things. Indeed it is often immoral to try to control them: men are not to be submitted to the indignities to which we submit, as a matter of course, things and animals. Hence the relative prominence in some of the social sciences, even increasingly in history, of other methods of controlling variables, methods thought somehow to be less satisfactory, such as the use of statistical techniques.

I shall have no more to say about this difference between the social sciences and the others. Admittedly it is important, but it is also rather well understood, and much intelligence of a high order has been devoted to finding methods of dealing with the problem. Moreover, some of the biological sciences, such as medicine, suffer from difficulties of control almost as much as do the social sciences. Much less well understood are the differences between the social and the other sciences in the matter of explanation.

Though stating and testing relationships between properties of nature is what makes a science, it is certainly not the only thing a science tries to do. Indeed we judge not the existence, but the success, of a science by its capacity to explain. If there is one thing I should like my students to learn but seldom teach them is what an explanation is—not that it is hard to do. Again, no "big" word is more often used in social science than the word "theory." Yet

Excerpts from *The Nature of Social Science,* copyright © 1967 by George C. Homans, reprinted by permission of Harcourt, Inc.

how seldom do we ask our students—or, more significantly, ourselves—what a theory is. But a theory of a phenomenon is an explanation of the phenomenon, and nothing that is not an explanation is worthy of the name of theory.

I am, of course, using "explanation" in the special sense of explaining why under given conditions a particular phenomenon occurs and not in one of the vaguer senses in which we use the word, as when we "explain" how to drive a car by telling a youngster what to do with the controls in various circumstances. In the special sense, the explanation of a finding, whether a generalization or a proposition about a single event, is the process of showing that the finding follows as a logical conclusion, as a deduction, from one or more general propositions under specified given conditions.[1] Thus we explain the familiar finding that there are two low and two high tides a day (actually a little longer than twenty-four hours) by showing that it follows logically from the law of gravitation under the given conditions that the earth is largely covered with water, that it rotates on its axis, and that the moon moves in orbit around it.

But let me go into more detail, using a humble example but one that in the past had good reason to interest me. As a boy swimming in the fundamentally rather chilly waters of Massachusetts Bay in summer, I discovered, as others had done before me, that for comfort in swimming, the water near the shore was apt to be warmer when the wind was blowing onshore—towards the shore—than when it was blowing offshore. By thoroughly unsystematic statistical methods I tested the discovery and found it true. But why should it be true? I shall try to give the essentials of what I believe to be the correct, though obvious, explanation, without spelling it out in all its logical, but boring, rigor.

Warm water tends to rise. The sun warms the surface water more than the depths. For both reasons, surface water tends to be warmer than deeper water. The wind acts more on the surface water than it does on the depths, displacing it in the direction of the wind. Accordingly an onshore wind tends to pile up the warmer water along the shore, while an offshore wind tends to move it away from the shore, where, by the principle that "water seeks its own level," it is continuously replaced by other water, which, since it can only come from the depths, must be relatively cold. Therefore water along the shore tends to be warmer when the wind is blowing onshore than when it is blowing offshore. Q.E.D.

Simple though it is, the characteristics of this explanation are those of all explanations. Each step of the argument is itself a proposition stating a relationship between properties of nature: between, for instance, the temperature

---

1. The view of explanation adopted here is, I think, that of R. B. Braithwaite, *Scientific Explanation* (Cambridge: Cambridge University Press, 1953) and of C. H. Hempel, *Aspects of Scientific Explanation* (New York: The Free Press, 1965), pp. 229–489.

of water and the direction of its movement, up or down. That is why propositions are so important. Some of the propositions are more general than others. In the example, some of the more general propositions are that warm water tends to rise and that water seeks its own level. They are more general in that they apply to all water and not just water along a coast. Some of the propositions state the effect of the given conditions, such as that the wind sometimes blows onshore and sometimes offshore. By calling them given conditions we mean simply that we do not choose to explain them in turn—we do not choose to explain why the wind sometimes blows onshore—though no doubt we could do so. And the proposition to be explained, the *explicandum*—in this case the difference in temperature of coastal water under onshore and offshore winds—is explained in the sense that it follows as a matter of logic from the general propositions under the specified given conditions. That is, the *explicandum* is deduced from, derived from, the other propositions, the whole set forming a "deductive system." The reason why orienting statements cannot play a part in explanation is that little in logic can be deduced from them.

Note that, if the *explicandum* can be deduced from the general propositions under the given conditions, the general propositions cannot be deduced in turn from the others in the set, any more than in the classic syllogism we can deduce that all men are mortal from the facts that Socrates is a man and that Socrates is mortal. That is, the process of deduction runs in one direction but not the other in the set of propositions. If it did both, the argument would be circular. On the other hand, the general propositions in our example can themselves be explained by, can themselves become the *explicanda* of, other deductive systems containing still more general propositions. That hot water rises is ultimately explained by propositions of thermodynamics relating the temperature of any substance to its volume and thus to its weight per unit volume. That water seeks its own level is ultimately explained by the law of gravitation. But as we move towards more and more general propositions, we reach, at any given time in the history of science, propositions that cannot themselves be explained. If we can judge from experience, this condition, for any particular proposition, is unlikely to last forever. Newton's law of gravitation stood unexplained for some two hundred years, but can now be shown to follow from Einstein's theory of relativity. Nevertheless at any given time there are always at least a few unexplainable propositions.

The explanation of the relation of water temperature to wind direction is also the theory of this phenomenon. But of course scientists generally use the word "theory" in a broader sense than this. They use it to refer, not just to an explanation of a single phenomenon, but to a cluster of explanations of related phenomena, when the explanations, the deductive systems, share some of the same general propositions. Thus someone might write a book called *The Theory of Water Temperatures,* which might explain the relations between variations in temperature and a number of other conditions besides the one chosen in our example, and which would apply, in doing so, a number of the same general propositions from thermodynamics and mechanics. Naturally any scholar is free to use the word "theory" in any way he likes, even for something different from what I call theory, provided he makes clear just how he is using it and does not, by slurring over the issue, claim for his kind of theory, by implication, virtues that belong to a different kind. All I submit here is that, normally in science, "theory" refers to the sort of thing I have described.

If we like, we can look on theory as a game. The winner is the man who can deduce the largest variety of empirical findings from the smallest number of general propositions, with the help of a variety of given conditions. Not everyone need get into the game. A man can be an admirable scientist and stick to empirical discovery, but most scientists do find themselves playing it sooner or later. It is fascinating in itself, and it has a useful ulterior result. A science whose practitioners have been good at playing it has achieved a great economy of thought. No longer does it face just one damn finding after another. It has acquired an organization, a structure. When Newtonian mechanics reached this sort of achievement it became the first thoroughly successful science, and other sciences have since become successful in the same way. But if theory is a game, it must like other games be played according to the rules, and the basic rules are that a player must state real propositions and make real deductions. Otherwise, no theory!

EXPLANATION IN SOCIAL SCIENCE

There are scholars who argue that, if social science is a science at all, it is a radically different kind of science from the others, and that it makes a mistake pretending to be the same sort of thing. I do not believe this in the least. The content of the propositions and explanations is naturally different in social science, because the subject matter is different, from what it is in the others, but the requirements for a proposition and an explanation are the same for both. And so long as the compulsion to be scientists does not rob us of our native wit and prevent our seeing what is there in nature to be seen, I believe that the social sciences should become more like the others rather than less. As we have come to accept, with all the difficulties that acceptance entails in our case, the standards of natural science for testing the truth of propositions, so we should take more seriously the standards of natural science in explanation. In that we have been laggard. Though the social sciences face special difficulties with explanation as they do with testing propositions, we can still do better than we have done.

It is not in its findings, which are now numerous and well attested, that social science gets into trouble, but in its explanations. The trouble takes somewhat different forms in different fields, but explanation, theory, is always its seat. Let me briefly take up some examples.

Most scholars would recognize that economics is the most advanced of the social sciences. It certainly possesses real theories, both in the micro- and the macro-fields. The question with economics is how general its theories are. The so-called laws of supply and demand are certainly not general. The demand for perfume, for instance, does not obey the law: the higher the price of a perfume, the greater the demand for it, at least up to a point. The question for economics is: What are the more general propositions from which, under different conditions, both the agreements with, and the exceptions to, economic laws may be deduced? Economists have, I think, acknowledged the pertinence of the question, but they have not reached agreement on an answer, perhaps because they have been successful enough in other ways not to feel the need of one.

History is at the opposite pole. It possesses an enormous range of empirical findings, findings, that is, of a rather low order of generality. It certainly claims to explain, but it pretends—or most historians pretend—to have no theories. A theory ought to include general propositions. The historians have looked for general propositions in their subject-matter, found none that they recognized as such, and concluded that they had no theories. I think they looked in the wrong place—but that is not quite fair. What they did was miss, as many of us do, the object hidden in plain sight. I think history does have general propositions, but history does not mention them, leaves them unstated.

If history has many explanations and no theories, sociology—and anthropology resembles it—sometimes appears to have many theories and no explanations. Certainly there are sociologists who claim to have very general theories, general enough indeed to encompass all the other social sciences. But when examined closely the theories often fail as explanations. They may consist of a matrix of definitions, and of nonoperating definitions at that. And when the theories try to state relationships between the properties defined, the statements may turn out to be orienting statements and not real propositions. On both counts they fail to qualify as deductive systems.

Besides theories, sociology possesses, as I have pointed out, a great many tested propositions. Again, most of them are of a low order of generality, and so cry out for the kind of organization that a good theory could provide. At this very point official sociological theory fails them. There is no science in which the rich and varied findings bear so little relation to the theories, in spite of endless pleas that they ought to be related. Indeed the faults of the theories, as theories, seem positively to get in the way of the organization of the findings. The theorists are always about to get into contact with the data, but never do; and the empirical researchers, while waiting in vain for help from on high, do not create their own theories because "theory" is a special field pre-empted by others.

Sociology and anthropology even possess some very general generalizations, the so-called "cultural universals," such as that all societies have incest taboos or, the one mentioned earlier, that all societies are stratified. Unfortunately it is not enough, in order to be useful in a theory, for a proposition to be general. It must also have explanatory power, and the cultural universals do not. From them alone one can derive only one kind of empirical proposition—propositions about single instances. These propositions refer to societies, and a society for them is a single instance. So if Xia is a society, it will be stratified—that is all one can say. This is a much lower degree of explanatory power than that possessed, for instance, by Newton's laws, from which a wide variety of propositions can be derived, not only propositions about individual instances, but also many propositions, like the one about the tides, that are themselves generalizations. Far from helping us explain anything, propositions like the one about stratification themselves demand explanation. Why indeed should all societies be stratified?

The characteristic problems of social science, compared with other sciences, are problems of explanation. Explanation is the deduction of empirical propositions from more general ones. Accordingly, in the matter of explanation, the problems of social science are two in number. What are its general propositions? And can empirical propositions be reliably deduced from them?

B.

Motives and Mechanisms

We have argued that mechanisms are an essential component of theories. Now we will say more about them. As we have already discussed, theories explain the relation between a higher-level social cause and social outcome by referring to mechanisms that link the two. Thus theories must include statements telling how higher-level (or macro-level) phenomena affect lower-level (or micro-level) individual units, why individual units act in particular ways, and how individual actions combine to produce new higher-order outcomes. In other words, explanations of social phenomena require an understanding of the reasons that individuals act the way they do.

But the reasons for individual action often are unclear.[1] Although people may know their own state of mind,[2] outside observers do not. Sometimes, siblings or best friends know each other well enough to gauge each other's moods and intentions. Social scientists can have no comparable insight, however. It is very hard to peer inside people's heads to discern their motives and goals. Further, people are complicated; they may be driven by many, sometimes inconsistent, motivations. As a result, we cannot include everything about them in a single theory. How then can we incorporate individual actors into our explanations of social phenomena?

The solution is to make *simplifying assumptions*. That is, if we want to predict social outcomes, then we need to make assumptions about how actors are affected by social conditions and about the *predominant* motivations of the

---

1. This difficulty is magnified many times over when we consider social action that is far removed from us in time, space, and culture.

2. Even this is uncertain. Often we are influenced by emotion, for example, without being consciously aware of the fact.

actors in the group. Of course, these assumptions are always fairly unrealistic: they do a poor job of describing the complexity of what's inside people's heads and how this governs what people actually do. But even though assumptions that simplify are faulty, they can be useful in predicting the behaviors of large numbers of individuals. This is because when we consider the actions of large numbers of people, many individual idiosyncratic motives and actions are likely to cancel one another out. Those that are common to the individuals in the group or society are both simpler and more general than those of any particular individual. These simple assumptions likely will not produce accurate predictions of any *particular individual's* behavior, but they can produce accurate predictions of *group-level* outcomes.

Theories, then, rely on assumptions about individuals in order to link social causes to individual internal states, internal states to action, and those individual actions in turn to social outcomes. The general framework is illustrated in Figure B.I.[3]

SITUATIONAL MECHANISMS

As Figure B.I reveals, there are three different types of mechanisms. The first, situational mechanisms, explain how macro-level social phenomena affect individuals.[4] The social environment may affect what people believe, what they know, what they want, what consequences they expect to result from action, and so forth. To make an argument about the connection between external conditions and these internal states, the theorist must make assumptions about the actors. For example, if we assume that people like knowing their limits, then we can argue that in conditions in which there are no regulations providing such limits, people will experience emotional distress. Or if we assume that people are emotionally affected by social interaction, then we can predict that in large crowds people may be more easily moved to passion than

---

3. The framework is associated with Coleman 1990, chap. 1. An earlier, less developed version can be found in McClelland 1961, 47.

4. This term comes from Hedström and Swedberg 1998.

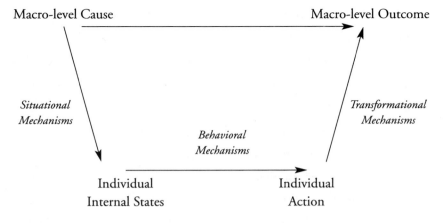

Macro-level Cause   Macro-level Outcome

Situational
Mechanisms

Transformational
Mechanisms

Behavioral
Mechanisms

Individual   Individual
Internal States   Action

FIGURE B.I   Three Types of Mechanisms in Social Explanation

when they are alone. Some of the explanations in this book rely heavily on situational mechanisms. In particular, the sections on meaning and values provide possible explanations for internal states.

BEHAVIORAL MECHANISMS

Behavioral mechanisms tell us how people act given their internal states. Peoples' beliefs and the information that they have will affect their behavior. But simply having ideas about how people see their world is not enough to predict what they will do. We also need to make some assumptions about what motivates them.[5] What kinds of motivations might theorists rely on? In this section's reading by Max Weber, four possibilities are distinguished: instrumental rationality, value rationality, affect, and tradition. Weber makes a key distinction that separates the first orientation, *instrumental rationality,* from the other three. Instrumentalism alone is shaped by the anticipated *consequences* of individual action. Individuals who act instrumentally calculate the costs and benefits of the courses of action open to them at any given time

---

5. One possible behavioral assumption (Rousseau [1754] 1952) is that human nature is basically malleable, dependent on social structure rather than something fixed that exists apart from it. Note that the Rousseauian conception of human nature, which influenced both Marx and Durkheim, among others, effectively does away with the causal status of internal states in explanations of social order.

and choose the one they believe will produce the best consequences for them—that is, their most preferred goal with the least cost or effort. Star athletes like the baseball player Alex Rodriguez act instrumentally when they change teams, often antagonizing their fans in order to reap much higher salaries.

By contrast, none of the other orientations assumes that actors are motivated by consequences. Agents who behave in a *value-rational* manner choose a course of action because they believe in it "for its own sake . . . independently of its prospects of success" (see p. 22). A good example of value rationality is presented in the movie *A Man for All Seasons,* in which Sir Thomas More, formerly England's chief legal officer, chooses to be executed by Henry VIII rather than approve the king's establishment of a national church, an act More considers to be illegal. More expresses his disagreement with the establishment of such a church—even though he has little hope of actually affecting the king's decision—simply because he believes it is the right thing to do.

Agents act *affectively* when their behavior is driven by emotion rather than by rational calculation; for example, think of a crime of passion. Last, agents act in a *traditional* manner when their behavior is not the result of deliberate calculation, value commitments, or emotion but of habit. Most people in this country shake hands when they are first introduced to someone; this is a traditional act in this sense of the term.

Each action orientation leads us to behave differently in the same social situation. Consider what an academically ambitious student might do on a typical Saturday afternoon during the school year. If she is instrumentally oriented, she will want to do well in her courses to maximize her opportunities after college. Therefore she will spend much of her free time studying. To the degree that her orientation is value rational, a strong commitment to a value (say, political activism) will take pride of place, and some studying time will be sacrificed. If she is in the throes of early love, her affective orientation will be sky high and her studies will suffer correspondingly. If she has a traditional orientation and always spends Saturday afternoons shopping, then her studying will be deferred to another day.

Of course, she may be motivated by more than one of these orientations.[6] Weber points out that all four action orientations may characterize our behavior over the course of time. If we always acted instrumentally, we would never fall in love. If we were always value rational, we would soon run out of food and shelter. Continuous affective action surely would land us in a series of feuds over love objects, and traditional action would leave us in the lurch whenever we needed to adapt to new social situations. Thus any individual experiences a variety of motivations, which makes for endless complexity.

As we have discussed, however, theories can simplify this complexity. Behavioral assumptions are among the most important simplifying assumptions used in social science. The most common behavioral assumption is *rational egoism*. Rational egoists are like Weber's instrumentally motivated actors. They are purposive, self-regarding agents. If we know the rational egoist's most preferred goal, and we know her social situation and the choices it provides, then we can predict her behavior. She will choose the course of action that she believes will yield the greatest net benefit: the action that provides the most preferred goal with the least cost or effort.[7] At the same time, we know that everyone is not rational all of the time. Individuals might also be acting according to values, emotion, habit, or some other motivation. But if many people are instrumentally motivated to some degree at least some of the time, then this assumption can produce accurate predictions of social outcomes (Hechter 1994). You will find that many of the theories in this book rely on the behavioral assumption that people are rational egoists, either explicitly or implicitly.

6. Because our behavioral repertoire includes (at least) all four of these orientations to action, it is no surprise that social institutions try to shape our behavior by affecting our orientations. A college that prides itself on its students' achievements will try to stimulate an instrumental orientation, perhaps by placing great emphasis on grades and avoiding grade inflation. A social movement will work hard to increase its followers' value rationality by continually promulgating its ideology. Lovers will attempt to maintain one another's affective intensity by gift giving and other courting behavior, and so forth.

7. The reasoning underlying this prediction is formally known as expected utility theory (Dawes 1988). For a discussion of the limits of this assumption, see Mansbridge 1990.

Finally, to predict social outcomes, we must explain how individual actions combine to produce group-level phenomena.[8] Sometimes (as in most U.S. elections) this is a matter of simple aggregation. We can merely add up the number of people who voted for a particular candidate to determine the winner. But at other times it is more complicated. This is because people do not only respond to external conditions; they also may react to the decisions of others.

For example, we might be able to explain the popularity of a social movement by assuming that people share the beliefs and goals of the movement and by arguing that those movements with the most popular causes will attract the largest number of adherents. People are not always familiar with social issues, however. In such situations they may look to see if their friends belong before making a decision about participating themselves. In this case, we cannot simply aggregate individual reactions to a condition—the popularity of a movement's cause. Instead we must incorporate into our theory an explanation about how people's decisions are affected by the behavior of others. That is, not only do we need to know the appeal of a particular social movement but also we must make assumptions about how choices are affected by the number of people who are already members. Many theorists emphasize situational or behavioral mechanisms and merely rely on aggregation to explain the relation between individual behaviors and group-level outcomes. Others, particularly those represented in the section of readings that discuss spontaneous order, focus on how individual actions combine in more complex ways to produce new social outcomes.

The types of mechanisms that theorists choose and the assumptions that they make about human beings determine the kinds of theories that they develop. In this book, we focus on theories that seek to explain social order. As the readings illustrate, theorists differ fundamentally in the mechanisms on which they rely and in the explanations of order that they propose.

8. The term in this heading comes from Hedström and Swedberg 1998.

REFERENCES

Coleman, James. 1990. *Foundations of Social Theory*. Cambridge, Mass.: Belknap Press of Harvard University Press.

Dawes, Robyn M. 1988. *Rational Choice in an Uncertain World*. San Diego: Harcourt Brace and Jovanovich.

Hechter, Michael. 1994. "The Role of Values in Rational Choice Theory." *Rationality and Society* 6:318–33.

Hedström, Peter, and Richard Swedberg. 1998. "Social Mechanisms: An Introductory Essay." In *Social Mechanisms: An Analytical Approach to Social Theory*, edited by Peter Hedström and Richard Swedberg, 1–31. Cambridge: Cambridge University Press.

Mansbridge, Jane J., editor. 1990. *Beyond Self-Interest*. Chicago: University of Chicago Press.

McClelland, David C. 1961. *The Achieving Society*. New York: Free Press.

Rousseau, Jean-Jacques. [1754] 1952. *A Discourse on the Origin of Inequality*. Translated by G. D. H. Cole. Chicago: Encyclopaedia Britannica.

2.

Types of Social Action

MAX WEBER, 1921-1922

Social action, like all action, may be oriented in four ways. It may be:

1. *instrumentally rational (zweckrational)*, that is, determined by expectations as to the behavior of objects in the environment and of other human beings; these expectations are used as "conditions" or "means" for the attainment of the actor's own rationally pursued and calculated ends;

2. *value-rational (wertrational)*, that is, determined by a conscious belief in the value for its own sake of some ethical, aesthetic, religious, or other form of behavior, independently of its prospects of success;

3. *affectual* (especially emotional), that is, determined by the actor's specific affects and feeling states;

4. *traditional*, that is, determined by ingrained habituation.

1. Strictly traditional behavior, like the reactive type of imitation discussed above, lies very close to the borderline of what can justifiably be called meaningfully oriented action, and indeed often on the other side. For it is very often a matter of almost automatic reaction to habitual stimuli which guide behavior in a course which has been repeatedly followed. The great bulk of all everyday action to which people have become habitually accustomed approaches this type. Hence, its place in a systematic classification is not merely that of a limiting case because . . . attachment to habitual forms can be upheld with varying degrees of self-consciousness and in a variety of senses. In this case the type may shade over into value rationality (*Wertrationalität*).

2. Purely affectual behavior also stands on the borderline of what can be considered "meaningfully" oriented, and often it, too, goes over the line. It

Reprinted with permission of the University of California Press, from *Economy and Society,* by Max Weber, edited by Guenther Roth and Claus Wittich. Copyright © 1978 by The Regents of the University of California. Reprinted also with the permission of J. C. B. Mohr (Paul Siebeck) Tübingen.

may, for instance, consist in an uncontrolled reaction to some exceptional stimulus. It is a case of sublimation when affectually determined action occurs in the form of conscious release of emotional tension. When this happens it is usually well on the road to rationalization in one or the other or both of the above senses.

3. The orientation of value-rational action is distinguished from the affectual type by its clearly self-conscious formulation of the ultimate values governing the action and the consistently planned orientation of its detailed course to these values. At the same time the two types have a common element, namely that the meaning of the action does not lie in the achievement of a result ulterior to it, but in carrying out the specific type of action for its own sake. Action is affectual if it satisfies a need for revenge, sensual gratification, devotion, contemplative bliss, or for working off emotional tensions (irrespective of the level of sublimation).

Examples of pure value-rational orientation would be the actions of persons who, regardless of possible cost to themselves, act to put into practice their convictions of what seems to them to be required by duty, honor, the pursuit of beauty, a religious call, personal loyalty, or the importance of some "cause" no matter in what it consists. In our terminology, value-rational action always involves "commands" or "demands" which, in the actor's opinion, are binding on him. It is only in cases where human action is motivated by the fulfillment of such unconditional demands that it will be called value-rational. This is the case in widely varying degrees, but for the most part only to a relatively slight extent. Nevertheless . . . the occurrence of this mode of action is important enough to justify its formulation as a distinct type; though it may be remarked that there is no intention here of attempting to formulate in any sense an exhaustive classification of types of action.

4. Action is instrumentally rational (*zweckrational*) when the end, the means, and the secondary results are all rationally taken into account and weighed. This involves rational consideration of alternative means to the end, of the relations of the end to the secondary consequences, and finally of the relative importance of different possible ends. Determination of action either in affectual or in traditional terms is thus incompatible with this type. Choice between alternative and conflicting ends and results may well be determined in a value-rational manner. In that case, action is instrumentally rational only in respect to the choice of means. On the other hand, the actor may, instead of deciding between alternative and conflicting ends in terms of a rational orientation to a system of values, simply take them as given subjective wants and arrange them in a scale of consciously assessed relative urgency. He may then orient his action to this scale in such a way that they are satisfied as far as possible in order of urgency, as formulated in the principle of "marginal utility."

Value-rational action may thus have various different relations to the instrumentally rational action. From the latter point of view, however, value-rationality is always irrational. Indeed, the more the value to which action is oriented is elevated to the status of an absolute value, the more "irrational" in this sense the corresponding action is. For, the more unconditionally the actor devotes himself to this value for its own sake, to pure sentiment or beauty, to absolute goodness or devotion to duty, the less is he influenced by considerations of the consequences of his action. The orientation of action wholly to the rational achievement of ends without relation to fundamental values is, to be sure, essentially only a limiting case.

5. It would be very unusual to find concrete cases of action, especially of social action, which were oriented *only* in one or another of these ways. Furthermore, this classification of the modes of orientation of action is in no sense meant to exhaust the possibilities of the field, but only to formulate in conceptually pure form certain sociologically important types to which actual action is more or less closely approximated or, in much the more common case, which constitute its elements. The usefulness of the classification . . . can only be judged in terms of its results.

PART II   SOLUTIONS TO THE PROBLEM OF SOCIAL ORDER

C.

The Problem of Social Order

Social order is a core theoretical issue in the social sciences. The problem arises because human beings are both individual and social. If we were each living alone on a private planet, we could do whatever we wanted and would never have to worry about anyone else. Or, if each of us were attached to one group mind, we would have no individual impulses and urges. But we are both. Every individual inhabits a separate physical body and thus each has his or her own experiences, information, feelings, and ambitions. Yet we are not completely independent. Stories of people living in isolation—neglected children, prisoners in solitary confinement—tell us that we need social contact to be physically and emotionally healthy, and simply to stay alive.

So the question is: How can a collection of individuals manage to live together? At its root, the problem of order concerns the means by which the demands of the group and those of the individual are reconciled. Do people follow the rules? Do they do things that help others or hurt them? The more that individual behavior is collectively oriented, the higher the level of order.

The social insects—ants, wasps, and bees—have long provided an example of an ordered society to social theorists.[1] Ants manage to coordinate their activities to obtain food, deal with garbage, and dispose of their dead (Johnson 2001). They also behave in self-sacrificing ways. The worker caste—females subservient to the needs of their mother—are content to surrender their own reproduction in order to raise sisters and brothers. Not only do worker ants give up the prospect of having their own offspring, but they also risk their lives

---

1. As the poet Alexander Pope put it in *An Essay on Man* (Pope [1733–34] 1994, 65), much can be gained if we "Learn each small people's genius, policies, / The ant's republic, and the realm of bees."

on behalf of the colony. Just leaving the nest to search for food is to choose danger over safety. Some ant species have been observed to suffer a death rate of 6 percent per hour when they hunt for food. Virtual suicide is the fate of workers of *Cataglyphis bicolor,* a scavenger of dead insects and other arthropods in the North African desert (Hölldobler and Wilson 1994). Ant societies appear to be superorganisms that can attain vast geographic and numerical scope: one European supercolony of an Argentine species of ants extends for at least six thousand kilometers and consists of millions of nests comprising billions of workers (Giraud, Pedersen, and Keller 2002).[2]

Of course, human societies also have a strong capacity for order—sometimes under difficult circumstances. This was amply demonstrated in New York City after the destruction of the World Trade Center in 2001. The city did not fall into chaos. Instead, New Yorkers listened to the news for information and instructions, and went to work. In the midst of scenes of devastation unprecedented in American history, volunteers flooded the Ground Zero site in lower Manhattan offering their help, restaurants gave away food to rescuers and victims, and celebrities raised funds for the victims in telethons.

Societies may not always be so resilient, however. Thomas Hobbes provides a famous description of social disorder in *Leviathan,* written in 1651 in the midst of the gory English Civil War:

> There is no place for Industry; because the fruit thereof is uncertain: and consequently no Culture of the Earth; no Navigation, nor use of the commodities that may be imported by Sea; no commodious Building; no Instruments of moving, and removing such things as require much force; no Knowledge of the face of the Earth; no account of Time; no Arts; no Letters; no Society; and which is worst of all, continuall feare, and danger of violent death; And the life of man, solitary, poore, nasty, brutish, and short (see p. 173).[3]

---

2. The leading explanation of this high level of social cooperation among these insects is genetic relatedness (Dawkins 1989). This explanation, however, does not account for the most important variations in social order found among human societies.

3. Much the same story emerges from descriptions of the civil war in Yugoslavia in 1991. Although each of the former Yugoslav republics had a dominant ethnic group, substantial minority populations also resided in Serbia, Croatia, and Bosnia-Herzegovina. Once the

The degree of disorder often is not as extreme as that depicted in Hobbes's colorful prose. The reading by Edward Banfield in this section describes an Italian village, circa 1950, in which there is relatively little social order. Although the village has inadequate schools, bad medical facilities, and poor roads—conditions that harm everyone—the residents do not cooperate politically to pressure the various government agencies that conceivably might remedy these problems. Underlying this inability to cooperate is an utter lack of public-spiritedness. Indeed, the very idea of public-spiritedness is so incomprehensible in Montegrano that Banfield has to explain the meaning of the concept to a local teacher. Not only is public-spiritedness unknown in this village, but there is a pervasive desire to keep others from getting ahead.

Societies with high levels of social order are able to cope with social challenges like those faced in Montegrano. Of course, more order is not necessarily better. Very high levels of social order may impose great costs on individuals. None of us would be likely to choose to live in an ant-like community. Thus in this book we make no claims about the level of order that is desirable. Rather, we focus on explanations of how social order is actually achieved.

For social order to arise and be maintained, two separate problems must be overcome. First, society must be reasonably predictable. Individuals must be able to *coordinate* their activity. This requires that they develop stable expectations about others' behavior. When driving down the road, for example, it is helpful to know whether others are likely to drive on the right or the left side of the road.

These stable expectations can be upset by rapid economic and political changes. For example, in eighteenth-century England, handloom cotton weavers and spinners were a mainstay of the occupational structure. After the invention of machines for weaving and cotton spinning, however, handloom weaving ceased being economically viable. As a result, the lives of this large

central government disintegrated, many people became insecure. If a Serb family living in Croatia were attacked, would the Croat police protect them? Would the Serbian police protect Croats in the same situation? After the collapse of central authority, the demand for security led to the rise of warlords, newfound celebrities of the Balkans, who engaged in prolonged and bloody campaigns of ethnic cleansing (Ignatieff 1993).

group of workers were thrown into disarray. Those who managed to become employed in factories faced a radically different work situation:

> The introduction of machinery implied for the first time a complete separation from the means of production; the worker became a "hand." . . . The machine imposed a new discipline. No longer could the spinner turn her wheel and the weaver throw his shuttle at home, free of supervision, both in their own good time. Now the work had to be done in a factory, at a pace set by tireless, inanimate equipment, as part of a large team that had to begin, pause, and stop in unison—all under the close eye of overseers, enforcing assiduity by moral, pecuniary, occasionally even physical means of compulsion. The factory was a new kind of prison; the clock a new kind of jailer. (Landes 1969, 43)

But many other handloom workers had neither the opportunity nor the ability to adapt. These displaced workers formed the core of the Luddites, machine-breakers who stormed the factories to sabotage the new technology.

We can have stable expectations and still not much social order, however. Contemporary Afghanistan, for example, is a society visited by frequent interethnic violence, highly unequal relations between the genders and age grades, and a meager standard of living. Yet Afghan society also exhibits high predictability. Because most Afghans expect to be living under these conditions, they act according to their expectations and therefore are able to carry on. But life is hard. It is predictable but not what we would call orderly. Something else is required for social order to be maintained.

If people are to live together, they must not only be able to coordinate their activities but also to interact productively—to do things that help rather than hurt others. Thus highly ordered societies have a remarkable capacity to sustain *cooperation*. To explain social order, therefore, we must understand why individuals behave in prosocial ways.

Prosocial behavior is not necessarily automatic. Sometimes behaving cooperatively imposes costs on the individual. Everyone thinks it's a good idea to spend money on education, but nobody wants to pay more property taxes. We appreciate National Public Radio, but we change stations when it's fund-raising time. In many situations, then, the interests of the individual and the group are at odds. Sometimes individuals fail to contribute to the group—they don't volunteer at the local school, don't donate money to National Public Radio, and don't give to people when help is needed. They hope that others will work to improve the community. They would prefer to enjoy the benefits without having to make too much effort themselves.[4] At other times, people may do things that impose harm on the group—take others' property, pollute, or cheat. They do what they want regardless of the effects of their actions on others. If order is to be maintained, these natural human tendencies must be overcome.

How can this be done? Under what conditions are people able both to coordinate their activities and to cooperate? Through what mechanisms is social order achieved? Theories of social order explain how order is produced and maintained, and why some groups, towns, and societies have more order than others. These theories do so by focusing on one or both of the problems—coordination and cooperation—described previously. The remaining sections of this volume are devoted to the five most important solutions that have been proposed for the problem of social order—meaning, values and norms, power and authority, spontaneous interaction, and networks and groups. Each solution seeks to explain social order. The solutions differ depending on the conditions that are identified as causing social order and on the mechanisms by which this order is produced.

If we think back a bit to the earlier discussion of mechanisms, it is easy to see how different behavioral mechanisms lead to different types of explanations. Yet, as later sections of this book reveal, it turns out that the same behavioral mechanism can lead to quite different explanations of social order. Perhaps the single most common question about social order revolves around behavioral mechanisms, and the assumption of rational egoism in particular. If people are for the most part rational egoists, how is a viable social order sustained?

---

4. This syndrome has come to be known in social science as the free-rider problem (Olson 1965).

Dawkins, Richard. 1989. *The Selfish Gene*. Oxford: Oxford University Press.

Giraud, Tatiana, Jes S. Pedersen, and Laurent Keller. 2002. "Evolution of Supercolonies: The Argentine Ants of Southern Europe." *Proceedings of the National Academy of Science* 99:6075–79.

Hölldobler, Bert, and Edward O. Wilson. 1994. *Journey to the Ants: A Story of Scientific Exploration*. Cambridge, Mass.: Belknap Press of Harvard University Press.

Ignatieff, Michael. 1993. *Blood and Belonging: Journeys into the New Nationalism*. New York: Farrar, Straus and Giroux.

Johnson, Steven. 2001. *Emergence: The Connected Lives of Ants, Brains, Cities, and Software*. New York: Scribner's.

Landes, David S. 1969. *The Unbound Prometheus: Technological Change and Industrial Development in Western Europe from 1750 to the Present*. Cambridge: Cambridge University Press.

Olson, Mancur. 1965. *The Logic of Collective Action*. Cambridge, Mass.: Harvard University Press.

Pope, Alexander. [1733–34] 1994. *An Essay on Man and Other Poems*. New York: Dover Publications.

3.

The Moral Basis of a Backward Society

EDWARD C. BANFIELD, 1958

Americans are used to a buzz of activity having as its purpose, at least in part, the advancement of community welfare. For example, a single issue of the weekly newspaper published in St. George, Utah (population 4,562), reports a variety of public-spirited undertakings. The Red Cross is conducting a membership drive. The Business and Professional Women's Club is raising funds to build an additional dormitory for the local junior college by putting on a circus in which the members will be both clowns and "animals." The Future Farmers of America (whose purpose is "to develop agricultural leadership, cooperation, and citizenship through individual and group leadership") are holding a father-son banquet. A local business firm has given an encyclopedia to the school district. The Chamber of Commerce is discussing the feasibility of building an all-weather road between two nearby towns. "Skywatch" volunteers are being signed up. A local church has collected $1,393.11 in pennies for a children's hospital 350 miles away. The County Farm Bureau is flying one of its members to Washington, 2,000 miles away, to participate in discussions of farm policy. Meetings of the Parent Teachers Associations are being held in the schools. "As a responsible citizen of our community," the notice says, "you belong in the PTA."

Montegrano, a commune of 3,400 persons, most of them poor farmers and laborers, in the province of Potenza in southern Italy, presents a striking contrast. The commune consists of a town, lying like a white beehive against the top of a mountain, and twenty-seven square miles of surrounding fields and forests. One-third of the Montegranesi live on scattered farms at the base of the mountain and in the valley around it. The others live in the town, but since they are mostly farmers and laborers, their waking hours are spent in the fields below the town or on the footpaths that wind between town and country.

No newspaper is published in Montegrano or in any of the thirteen other towns lying within view on nearby hilltops. Occasional announcements of

Reprinted with the permission of The Free Press, an imprint of Simon & Schuster Adult Publishing Group, from *The Moral Basis of a Backward Society* by Edward C. Banfield. Copyright © 1958 by The Free Press; copyright renewed 1985 by Edward C. Banfield.

public interest—"there are fish for sale in the *piazza* at 100 *lire* per *chilo*"—are carried by a town crier wearing an official cap, who toots a brass horn to attract attention. Official notices are posted in the salt and tobacco store, a government monopoly, and on a bulletin board in the town hall. Several copies of three or four newspapers published in Rome, Naples, and Potenza come into town by bus every day or two, but these of course do not deal much with local affairs and they are read by very few.

Twenty-five upper class men constitute a "circle" and maintain a clubroom where members play cards and chat. Theirs is the only association. None of the members has ever suggested that it concern itself with community affairs or that it undertake a "project."

The merchants of Montegrano are well aware of the importance to them of good roads. They would not, however, expect to be listened to by the authorities who decide which roads are to be improved. A Montegrano man might write a letter to the provincial authorities in Potenza or to the newspaper there, but it is unlikely that his doing so would make any difference. In fact, the officials would be likely to resent what they would consider interference in their affairs.

There are no organized voluntary charities in Montegrano. An order of nuns struggles to maintain an orphanage for little girls in the remains of an ancient monastery, but this is not a local undertaking. The people of Montegrano contribute nothing to the support of it, although the children come from local families. The monastery is crumbling, but none of the many half-employed stone masons has ever given a day's work to its repair. There is not enough food for the children, but no peasant or landed proprietor has ever given a young pig to the orphanage.

There are two churches in town and two priests, one the son of a Sicilian peasant and the other the son of a prosperous Montegrano merchant. The churches do not carry on charitable or welfare activities, and they play no part at all in the secular life of the community. Even in religious matters their influence is not very extensive. The life of the town goes on very much as usual on Sunday mornings: the artisans are at work on a new building as usual at seven o'clock, the stores are all open, and the country people are on their way down the mountainside with their donkeys. Of the 3,400 people in the commune, not more than 350 hear mass on Sunday. These are mostly women. The few men who go to mass remain standing near the door as if to signify that they are not unduly devout. When the collection plate is passed, many people give nothing and few give more than a half a cent (five or ten *lire*). By tradition the men of Montegrano are anti-clerical. The tradition goes back a century or more to a time when the church had vast holdings in southern Italy and was callous and corrupt. Today it owns only one small farm in Montegrano, and the village priests are both known to be kindly and respectable men. Nevertheless priests in general—so many Montegranesi insist—are money-grubbers, hypocrites, and worse.

When members of the upper class are asked who is known as particularly public-spirited—what private persons are apt to take the initiative in dealing with matters which involve the public welfare—a few mention the Baron di Longo and Colonel Pienso, both of whom live in Rome and are believed to have great influence there. Most people, however, say that no one in Montegrano is particularly public-spirited, and some find the idea of public-spiritedness unintelligible. When an interviewer explained to a young teacher that a "public-spirited" person is one who acts for the welfare of the whole community rather than for himself alone, the teacher said:

> No one in town is animated by a desire to do good for all of the population. Even if sometimes there is someone apparently animated by this desire, in reality he is interested in his own welfare and he does his own business.
>
> Even the saints, for all their humility, looked after themselves. And men, after all, are only made of flesh and spirit.

Another teacher said that not only is public-spiritedness lacking, but many people positively want to prevent others from getting ahead.

> Truly, I have found no one who interests himself in the general welfare. On the contrary, I know there is tremendous envy of either money or intelligence.

In some southern Italian towns the gentry are said to be indifferent to the misery of the peasants and consumed with hatred for each other. This is not the case in Montegrano. The leading families there get along well together, and many upper class people view the peasant's plight with evident sympathy. These people are not led by their sympathy to try to change things, however.

The affairs of the commune are conducted by a mayor and elected council and by the provincial civil service which is headed by a prefect in Potenza. The mayor and council propose, but it is the prefect who disposes. Even to buy an ashtray for the city hall requires approval from Potenza; ordinarily, after a certain amount of delay, the decisions of the local elected officials are approved, but this is not always the case and, of course, approval can never be counted upon.

The prefect is represented in Montegrano by the secretary of the commune, a career civil servant assigned from Potenza. With the assistance of two clerks, the secretary transacts all of the routine business of the town. This includes especially the maintenance of tax records, of vital statistics, and the making of disbursements on order of the higher authorities.

The mayor is elected for a four-year term and receives no salary. He represents the commune on all official occasions, supervises the municipal officers, is the legal representative of the commune in dealings with third parties, and has certain powers of certification. In practice, the elected council has little power. In fact, it is seldom possible to get a quorum of its members together at the mayor's call.

The elected officials are office-workers, artisans, and prosperous farmers rather than persons of the highest status. The mayor, for example, is a retired non-commissioned army officer and petty landowner. His council includes as deputy mayor a retired non-commissioned officer in the *carabinieri* police, four artisans or storekeepers, five office-workers, five teachers, two farmers, and a lawyer. The lawyer is the only one who is an "upper-upper," and even he is not of the very highest status.

The officials of the commune have nothing to do with the schools. A director of schools, independently responsible to Potenza, resides in Montegrano and has jurisdiction over the elementary schools of several communes. Public works, another important function, is also administered altogether apart from the elected local government.

The police (*carabinieri*) also are under a separate authority, the Ministry of Justice in Rome. The officer in charge locally (the "*maresciallo*") cooperates closely with the local authorities, but he is in no sense "their man." As a matter of policy, he is not a native of the town to which he is assigned, and he and his men are under instructions not to fraternize much with the townspeople. The attitude of the *carabinieri* towards all classes is generally good-tempered, businesslike, and aloof.

Although the constitution of Italy guarantees that every child will receive schooling through the age of 14, in Montegrano, as in many other places in Italy, only five grades of school are taught. Unless his family can afford to send him away to school, the Montegrano child normally completes his education at the age of 11 or 12.

One-third of the men and two-thirds of the women who were 21 years of age or over in 1954 had attended less than five grades of school. Only five percent of the men and less than two percent of the women had attended more than five grades.

Children attend school four hours each morning six days a week from the middle of September until the middle of June. Schools are poorly equipped, teachers are poorly paid, and the pupil's and sometimes even the teacher's attendance is irregular. After finishing the fifth grade some pupils can barely read and write or do simple sums. A few years after leaving school, peasant children have often completely forgotten what little they learned. According to a Montegrano school official, one-third of the graduates are illiterate several years after graduation. For the most part these are women. Since 1948, however, a night school for adults has been attended by 12 men a year. Thus in eight years 96 men—two thirds of them farmers or laborers and the other artisans—had learned, or re-learned, to read and write.

Until recently a large proportion of the children living on outlying farms were unable to go to school at all. Country schools have been built, and their hours adjusted to the convenience of the farm people (in some country schools classes begin at 6 A.M. and end at 10 A.M.). Few children nowadays are prevented from going to school by distance.

Nevertheless, there are many who do not attend regularly. The school authorities, the priests, and the police make joint efforts to persuade parents to send their children to school, and, if all else fails, a parent may be fined if his child is a chronic truant. Some of the farm people, perhaps because they see no use in five grades of schooling when there is no opportunity for more, send their children to school willingly only so long as they are too young to work in the fields.

Both because the schools are poor and irregularly attended and because during the war the operation of the school system was badly disrupted, nearly 30 percent of those 10–40 years of age were illiterate in 1951. The rate of illiteracy was highest (44%) among farm people living on outlying farms.

An artisan's child who completes five grades of school is usually apprenticed. However, if he is to become more than a third- or fourth-rate craftsman in one of the traditional crafts (tailoring, barbering, carpentry, stone masonry, and blacksmithing) he must either go to a newly established trade school in a nearby town or serve an apprenticeship in one of the big cities. If he goes away he may learn to be an automobile mechanic, a welder, a typewriter repairer or the like— skills which would enable him eventually to migrate to the north. But this possibility is not within the reach of many; there are very few artisans who can support their children away from home. Even at the government-run vocational school it is necessary to pay board. And for a Montegrano boy to find a place as an apprentice in a big city is next to impossible unless he has relatives there.

Those few boys and girls who go to "*media*" school (grades 6–8) must also leave town. The nearest *media* is in Basso. Basso is not far away, but the bus schedule does not permit commuting. To go to boarding school is very expensive by Montegrano standards. Boarding schools are run by the urban middle class for the urban middle class: a boy must have a *corredo* of six sheets and pillowcases, two blankets of specified quality, two pairs of "ordinary" and one pair of "dress" shoes, and so on. The *corredo*, a Montegrano mother estimated, costs about $80; other expenses amount to about $25 a month. The curriculum of the *media* emphasizes Latin, French (English is not taught even at the

University of Naples), history, literature, and government to the virtual exclusion of scientific and technical subjects. Most of those who go to *media* expect eventually to become teachers, lawyers, government clerks, or physicians.

Political parties are of little importance in Montegrano. The Fascists held an occasional rally there to which everyone (except the peasants, most of whom escaped to their fields before dawn) was required to come. Political parties in the usual sense did not exist until after the Second World War, however, and even now they are neither strong nor stable.

The Communist Party, for example, got 157 votes in the last (1956) election, but it has no cell in Montegrano. Its local representative is a tailor who reads *L'Unità,* the Communist daily, but has no other regular connection with the hierarchy. His views are far from orthodox.

> We Communists are not really bad people [he explains]. We want only bread and work. We exist because we stand opposed to the injustices of this town. Some people worked full-time building the new town hall. They worked from the day the job began until the day it ended. Others asked for a few days work to earn enough to buy bread and got nothing. This was an injustice. Packages used to come to the town officials from America. Some people always got a share. Others never did. That was an injustice.

America made a big mistake at the end of the war, the Communist tailor thinks. "When America occupied Italy, she should have stayed. It would have been much better for us."

Farmuso, the director of the school district, is a Communist and was once the Communist mayor of another town. He engages in private, informal discussions, but because of his official position does not take a formal part in party affairs in Montegrano. At election times, Communist speakers come from Basso, a larger town where there are paid organizers.

The most influential leader of the extreme left is the physician, Dr. Gino, a Nenni Socialist. Like many doctors in southern Europe, he is a materialist and a socialist by inheritance as well as by training and conviction. (His father is said to have baptized him Franco *Marx* Gino and to have had him dressed for the ceremony in a red rather than a white gown.) Dr. Gino is the owner of one of the few vineyards in Montegrano—only several acres, but enough to make him one of the town's principal proprietors.

As a doctor and as a landed proprietor, Dr. Gino has done favors for many people. He is, moreover, the leading upper class exponent of an ideology which demands the leveling of class differences and the division of wealth. Consequently he has a certain following or clientele among the peasants and artisans. There are some who feel that if any upper class person has their welfare at heart, it is he. Others owe him for professional services or want to get work at his vineyard. If he saw fit, he could enlarge his following and turn it to political account. He is too proud, however, and too individualistic to subject himself to the inconveniences and annoyances which serious political activity would entail. "There is a lot of falsity in politics," he explains. "You must make more friends than you want and you must act like a friend to many people you don't want to be friendly with. This is so because you must always be thinking of how to build up the party and win friends for it." He would hate the feeling of *having* to attend meetings for the party, and he would hate even more to be reprimanded for saying something out of turn. "I would feel like telling them, 'Go fry an egg.'"

Immediately after the war, in 1945, Dr. Gino overcame his distaste for politics sufficiently to try to organize a branch of the Socialist Party in Montegrano. About one hundred people turned out in the *piazza* at his call and voted to join the party. But when the application forms arrived and it was realized that a few *lire* in dues would be required, all interest died. Dr. Gino paid out of his own pocket for the memberships that had been applied for and never tried to organize anything again. "I was trying to get the workers together and to get a labor union started . . . or at least a group that could act to get what it wanted. But there is no spirit. There is no feeling of working together," he said afterward.

If the presence of a patron like Dr. Gino tends to call a clientele into existence, the presence of a potential clientele also tends to call a patron into existence. Just as some of the Roosevelt family have always found it advantageous to be on the Democratic side, so at least one professional man in every southern Italian town finds satisfaction in taking the part of the workers. A man who would have to compete with many others to make himself influential as a Christian Democrat may have the field to himself as a left-wing socialist.

The strongest party in Montegrano is the Christian Democratic (DC) party—"the party of the priests," as the peasants say. The Montegrano priests are in fact extremely active politically both in the pulpit and out. (One of them even became involved in a fist-fight at an election-eve rally.) Other leading figures include the lawyer, an amiable young man who is one of the most thoughtful people in town, and two retired petty officers of the army and the *carabinieri*, respectively, who are mayor and vice-mayor. In view of widespread anti-clericalism, there is reason to suppose that many voters support the Christian Democratic party despite its connection with the church rather than because of it.

Just before elections the Christian Democratic party distributes small packages of *pasta*, sugar, and clothing to the voters. These are called gifts from the Vatican. The voter would be no less willing to accept gifts from any other quarter. "If the Russians sent over 25 bushels of grain," a defeated candidate remarked after the last election, "the people would vote the Christian Democrats out of office tomorrow."

The Monarchist Party is the only right-wing group of importance. It is supported by the Baron di Longo and other landlord proprietors and by a scattering of individuals in all other social classes. The secretary of the party is a retired petty officer of the *carabinieri* who runs a bar. The Monarchist Party, he says, stands for order, peace, lower taxes, and no revolution. By "order" he means "respect," "not too much criticism," and "giving what is expected in all cases."

A monarchy is the best kind of government because the king is then the owner of the country. Like the owner of a house, when the wiring is wrong, he fixes it. He looks after his people like a father. If you have a child, always you love him more and do more for him than you would for others. It is in this way that the king looks after his people. He wants them to love him. He loves them. In a republic, the country is like a house that is rented. If the lights go out, well, that's all right . . . it's not his house. If the wall chips, well, it's not his house. The renter does not fix it. So with the men who govern a republic. They are not interested in fixing things. If something is not quite right and if they are turned out for it, well, meanwhile they have filled their pocketbooks.

The moderate socialist party (PSDI) has little strength in Montegrano. The so-called neo-fascist party (MSI) is of no importance.

In Montegrano it is not unusual for party officials to change their allegiances suddenly. Six months after he had made the statement quoted above, the secretary of the Monarchist Party announced that he had become a Communist. A few weeks later he was a Monarchist again.

The variability in the voters' behavior is also striking. There are eleven towns in the election district of which Montegrano is a part. Some are poorer than others, and in some land ownership is more widely diffused than in others. To the casual eye, however, these differences do not seem crucial—all of the towns have in common extreme poverty and isolation. The voting behavior of the towns differs greatly, however. . . . [T]he Communist vote in them in 1953 ranged from two to forty-six percent and from two to seventy-nine percent in 1956.

Variability in voting behavior exists not only from town to town but from election to election within the same town.

In Montegrano and nearby towns an official is hardly elected before the voters turn violently against him. As soon as he gets into office, his supporters say— often with much justice—he becomes arrogant, self-serving, and corrupt. At the next election, or sooner if possible, they will see that he gets what is coming to him. In Montegrano there is no better way to lose friends than to be elected to office.

In the following letter, written by a lower class Montegranese to a friend abroad, the village political style appears in its characteristic form:

It is true that the Mayor, Vincenzo Spomo, has resigned. That was nearly two months ago. But it was not by his own wish; it was at the prompting of the Council.

As you know, the Council had two factions. Among the Christian Democrats, that is, there were two factions with different ideas, factions which had never agreed from the beginning. Spomo, always in character, wanted to command things for his own purposes. He thought it was as it used to be in the old administration, but this time he had to deal with people who were college graduates . . . who really had some brains. It was not as he thought.

Every now and then the Council met. When he brought up something the members did not like, they would oppose him once, twice, three times, until he was beaten. But one night at a Council meeting he was forced to resign.

Now I want to tell you a little about Spomo. The people were always unhappy with him. He pleased himself. He helped only those he wished to help. All the circulars that came he locked up in his drawer and would not even inform the Council members of them. It was not so much his own will as that of his followers that carried him along, and if the Christian Democrats lost votes it was on account of him personally.

As I said, the Council was divided in two factions. Seven were in favor of Spomo and eleven were in favor of the present mayor. When Spomo heard how the voting went and that he was beaten, he got up without saying a word to anyone and left. Naturally, the new mayor got to his feet and began to thank all those who had voted for him, and the crowd applauded him and acclaimed him until he had to stay the applause with his hands . . . so long did the applause last.

The people are happier because this new mayor is on the side of everyone, listens to everyone, answers everyone, and wants the mass of the workers to be protected.

We will wait and see.

You know what I think about it? I am glad that Spomo no longer governs. He ended up by commanding with the haughtiness of a marshal of the army, just as if he were commanding his soldiers. It was the way he thought—that he was commanding the people of Montegrano. Those he liked he would raise to the stars and those he did not like he would crush. His tongue was for nothing but scolding, and he believed himself a superman. He gave the impression that we were living in the era of the feudal lords.

As for the people, what they think depends upon who they are. If they received favors, they are followers. Those who received neither good nor evil from him, they just repeat what they hear. The majority of those who talk are peasants and laborers.

One morning a jitney driver and a peasant were in the bar. The driver said that one could not find the equal of Spomo as the head of the administration for this town. The other said, "Perhaps so when it came to presumption and promises, but when it came to something positive, the mayor had nothing." Then the driver said that besides being good and fine the mayor had a lot of support—"the support of many influentials, especially the Minister of Agriculture, the prefect, and others. If the Mayor falls [this was before he did fall], the prefect will send a commissioner and the town will see that it will have to pay $5.00 a day [for the support of the commissioner] and in the end Spomo, who is the secretary of the Christian Democratic party, will be appointed commissioner . . . so you will see that he will be not only mayor but also commissioner and you will have to pay him."

The peasant answered that in any event we will pay less than the vacations he has had and the waste he has made have cost during his administration. The argument came very short of ending in blows.

I don't even mention the dissatisfaction of Nino's peasants who had been promised electricity in their zone and heard nothing about it since. Now they don't want to hear or know anything about it. They say that at the next elections they are not going to vote for anyone at all because they [the politicians] are all in it for themselves only.

Of this new mayor one can say nothing as yet because he has not been in very long. I can say only one thing with accuracy—that so persistent were Councilmen Viva and Lasso that we have been given—and it has already got underway—a winter work project which will last two months and employ forty workers a day. They will repair the roads and walls of the town.

As regards the gentry, naturally one knows nothing. Or, to say it better, they are reserved and don't let you hear anything.

These impressions of political behavior in Montegrano raise a number of questions.

What accounts for the absence of organized action in the face of pressing local problems? Why, for example, is nothing done about the schools? To the peasants, many of whom are desperately anxious for their children to get ahead, the lack of educational opportunity is one of the bitterest facts of life. Upper class people are affected too; some of them would like to live in Montegrano and cannot do so because it would cost too much to send their children away to a boarding school. One might think, then, that improvement of the local school would be an important local issue—one on which people would unite in political parties or otherwise. Failing to persuade the government to build a *media* school, upper class volunteers might teach an additional grade or two. Or, if this is too much to expect, the bus schedule might be changed so that the Montegrano children could commute to nearby Basso for the higher grades. However, such possibilities have not been considered.

The nearest hospital is in Potenza, five hours away by automobile. For years Montegrano people have complained that the state has not built a hospital in the village. The doctor and two or three other people have written letters to Rome urging that one be built, but that is as far as the effort to get one has gone. Candidates for local office do not campaign on the hospital "issue," and there has been no organized effort to bring pressure to bear upon the government. Nor has there been any consideration of stopgap measures such as might be taken locally—for example, equipping an ambulance to carry emergency cases from Montegrano and other nearby towns to Potenza.

These, of course, are only two of many possible examples of needs which would give rise to community action in some countries, but about which nothing is done in Montegrano.

The question of why nothing is done raises other questions. Why are the political parties themselves so unconcerned with local issues? Why is there no political "machine" in Montegrano, or even any stable and effective party organization? What explains the marked differences in the appeal of left, center, and right from town to town among towns that on the surface seem so much alike? What explains the erratic behavior of the electorate in a single town from one election to the next? And why do those elected to office at once lose credit with their supporters?

. . . [W]hat accounts for the political incapacity of the village?

D.

Meaning

We have argued that solving the problem of social order requires an under-standing of the mechanisms that lead to successful coordination and coopera-tion. One necessary ingredient is that individuals must be able to communi-cate with one another. Ants, for example, communicate through the use of chemical signals. They manage to attain extremely high levels of cooperation by reacting to pheromones that distinguish not only friend from foe but among individuals in the same colony. Presumably, cooperation in an ant col-ony would unravel were these chemical signals to be denatured.

In human societies, communication occurs through language (Berger and Luckmann 1967). In the absence of a common understanding of verbal sig-nals, therefore, cooperation is more difficult. Eighteenth-century English writ-ers were fond of stories about shipwrecked sailors landing on deserted islands. Put yourself in the shoes of Robinson Crusoe or Gulliver and imagine what an encounter with the indigenous population might be like. Even if you and they both prefer peace to conflict, would cooperation be a likely outcome of your first interaction? If Crusoe intends no harm but simply wants to chop wood to make a fire, he has to be able to tell the locals what he wants in terms that they can understand. And vice versa. In other words, each party must find words that convey the intended *meaning* to the other's mind.[1]

In this view, shared concepts and beliefs are a prerequisite for successful communication. We may not be consciously aware of the understandings and beliefs that underlie our interactions, but they are essential for communication

---

1. Goffman 1983 offers a description of some of the verbal cues that people engage in to facilitate this kind of communication.

to occur nonetheless. Thus if people had different understandings of fundamental concepts such as time, space, cause, and number, social order might be impossible. Take the shared but taken-for-granted concept of temporal regularity. It would be difficult to plan our lives were we to be totally in the dark as to what might take place when, how often, in what order, and how long. Imagine what life would be like if time suddenly weren't divided into weeks. Because we think of and reckon time in weekly units, we would tend to confuse one day with another. No doubt we would miss many of our appointments. Social order would be threatened by the disappearance of the week (Zerubavel 1981).

If common concepts and beliefs have such implications for the attainment of social order, then it becomes a pressing issue to determine their sources. Just where do these common concepts and beliefs come from? The selections in this section suggest some possible answers.

In "The Production of Consciousness," the young Karl Marx locates their genesis in humanity's productive activities—those by which we produce food, shelter, and other material necessities. As his renowned phrase puts it, "It is not consciousness that determines life, but life that determines consciousness" (see p. 51). Thus, for example, there ought to be more of an emphasis on the concept of fair sharing in societies dominated by big game hunters and whalers—whose members must cooperate so as to obtain their subsistence—than in those in which subsistence can largely be attained merely by individual effort. Marx therefore sees human productive activities as the source of common conceptions and beliefs. Moreover, he suggests that those in advantaged positions in society will attempt to ensure that their view of the world is accepted by all—including those in the lower classes.

Émile Durkheim has quite another view of these matters.[2] In his study of Australian aborigines, Durkheim seeks to explain how some objects come to be seen as sacred. Whereas Marx argues for the primacy of productive activities in generating common concepts and beliefs, Durkheim argues that these

---

2. For a comprehensive discussion of Durkheim's theories, see Lukes 1972.

elements are determined by social interactions. In conditions of rapid change or disaster, people interact more frequently, producing a situation of "collective effervescence." People feel heightened passions and attribute those passions to supernatural forces. Religious beliefs are born out of such intensity. They represent social relations by expressing, symbolizing, or dramatizing these ongoing relationships. Once in place, religion fosters social order by strengthening the bonds that attach individuals to their society.

Although Durkheim interpreted general cognitive concepts of space, time, and religious beliefs as social constructions, he drew the line sharply at science. Like Marx—who wrapped his own intellectual contribution in the guise of "scientific materialism"—Durkheim too thought of himself as a man of science. He advocated the discipline of sociology as the science of "social facts." Unlike theories, which are inherently speculative, he regarded facts as definite, permanent, and independent of subjective interpretations by scientists.

Ludwik Fleck, a physician born in Poland, focuses on one kind of belief—our confidence in scientific facts. Fleck was the first writer who questioned the view that scientific facts exist independent from social life. In "Genesis and Development of a Scientific Fact," he argues that research findings become accepted as facts only through a complex process of social negotiation. This negotiation leads to what Fleck terms a thought style, that is, a social product formed within a collective as the result of social forces. To demonstrate this, Fleck recounts the history of the venereal disease syphilis. Today, we know (owing to research conducted in the early years of the twentieth century) that syphilis is caused by the bacterium *Spirochaeta pallida*. When the disease was first noted, however, due to an outbreak at the end of the fifteenth century, it was attributed to an astrological circumstance—the conjunction of Saturn and Jupiter under the sign of Scorpio and the house of Mars on November 25, 1484. Fleck argues that "Sixteenth-century physicians were by no means at liberty to replace the mystical-ethical concept of syphilis with one based upon natural science and pathogenesis. A stylistic bond exists between many, if not all, concepts of a period, based on their mutual influence. We can therefore speak of a thought style which determines the formulation of every concept"

(1979, 9). A "scientific" explanation is only given credence if it is consistent with the current thought style. Thus so-called facts are not as objective as we often like to think; instead, they are socially constructed.

Even though Fleck's insistence on the social sources of scientific facts initially was ignored, in recent years it has gained much influence.[3] One historian even claims that conceptions of something as taken for granted as differences between the sexes have changed radically in Western culture over time. The "one-sex" model, which was dominant in the West from the Greeks until the eighteenth century, postulated that there was only one type of body, a male one. Although females obviously differed anatomically, they were thought to have the same reproductive organs. These organs, however, were turned inside out in the female. In this conception, females are not considered to be profoundly different from men. The "two-sex" model, which posits that the bodies of males and females are radically different from each other, only came to prominence a mere two centuries ago (Laqueur 1990).

It is perhaps not so difficult to appreciate that common concepts and beliefs must have social roots. Yet the claims of meaning theorists go much deeper than this. For George Herbert Mead, our understanding of our role in the world is forged in the process of interaction. If for Shakespeare all the world is a stage, for Mead social life is a game in which we all learn to play designated roles. In baseball, the game can only proceed smoothly if everyone knows the rules. For this to happen, people must take on themselves the attitudes of the entire group toward their own individual behavior and toward group endeavors. The batter must anticipate the actions of the pitcher, the shortstop those of the first baseman. More generally, the teacher must do the same for the student, the doctor for the patient, and so forth. According to Mead,

> the complex co-operative processes and activities and institutional functionings of organized human society are . . . possible only in so far as every individual involved in them or belonging to that society can take the general attitudes of all other such individuals with reference to these

---

3. Most notably, in Kuhn 1970.

processes and activities and institutional functionings, and to the organized social whole of experiential relations and interactions thereby constituted—and can direct his own behavior accordingly. (see p. 66)

According to meaning theorists, then, shared concepts and beliefs are the foundation of social life. Is there any empirical evidence to support these strong claims? Dov Cohen and Joe Vandello present a wide range of evidence about the different meanings that are attributed to the concept of violence. Comparing findings in the American South and North, they demonstrate in the reading presented here that the meaning of violence varies strongly across different cultures. These differences in meaning are associated with "distinct rituals for precipitating conflict and for resolving it" (see p. 80). Thus rates of violent behavior reflect communities' understanding of insults and violence.

REFERENCES

Berger, Peter L., and Thomas Luckmann. 1967. *The Social Construction of Reality: A Treatise in the Sociology of Knowledge.* New York: Doubleday.

Fleck, Ludwik. 1979. *Genesis and Development of a Scientific Fact.* Chicago: University of Chicago Press.

Goffman, Erving. 1983. "Felicity's Condition." *American Journal of Sociology* 89:1–53.

Kuhn, Thomas S. 1970. *The Structure of Scientific Revolutions.* Chicago: University of Chicago Press.

Laqueur, Thomas Walter. 1990. *Making Sex: Body and Gender from the Greeks to Freud.* Cambridge, Mass.: Harvard University Press.

Lukes, Steven. 1972. *Émile Durkheim; His Life and Work, A Historical and Critical Study.* New York: Harper and Row.

Zerubavel, Eviatar. 1981. *Hidden Rhythms: Schedules and Calendars in Social Life.* Chicago: University of Chicago Press.

4.

The Production of Consciousness

KARL MARX, 1845–46

The presuppositions with which we begin are not arbitrary ones, not dogmas, but are real presuppositions from which one can abstract only in one's imagination. We begin with real individuals, together with their actions and their material conditions of life, those in which they find themselves, as well as those which they have created through their own efforts. These presuppositions can, in other words, be confirmed in a purely empirical way.

The first presupposition of all human history is naturally the existence of living human individuals. The first fact to be established is thus the physical organisation of these individuals and, arising out of this, their relationship to the rest of nature. Naturally we cannot deal here with the physical constitution of the human being nor with the natural conditions in which mankind is placed, the geologic, orohydrographic, climatic, and other conditions. All historiography must proceed on the basis of these natural conditions and their modifications through the actions of men in the course of history.

Men can be distinguished from the animals by consciousness, by religion, or by whatever one wants. They begin to distinguish themselves from the animals as soon as they begin to *produce* their means of life, a step which is determined by their physical organisation. In producing their means of life they indirectly produce their material life itself.

The manner in which men produce their means of life depends in the first instance on the character of these means themselves, as they are found ready at hand and have to be reproduced. This form of production is not to be considered solely as a reproduction of the physical existence of the individuals. Rather it is a distinctive form of activity of these individuals, a distinctive form of expressing their life, a distinctive *form of life* of those very individuals. As individuals express their life, so they are. What they are, therefore, coincides

Excerpts from "The German Ideology" by Karl Marx in *Marx: Early Political Writings,* edited and translated by Joseph O'Malley with Richard A. Davis. © Cambridge University Press 1994. Reprinted with the permission of Cambridge University Press.

with their production, both with *what* they produce and with *how* they produce. Thus, what individuals are depends on the material conditions of their production.

This production first appears along with an *increase in population*. It itself presupposes a commerce, a communication among individuals. The form of this commerce is in turn determined by production.

The facts are as follows: determinate individuals who are productive in determinate ways enter into determinate social and political relationships. In each case empirical observation has to demonstrate, empirically and without any mystification and speculation, the connection of the social and political structure with production. The social structure and the state continuously issue forth out of the life process of given individuals—not as they may appear in their own or in others' imagination, but as they *really* are, i.e., as they function, produce materially, in short as they are active within certain limits, presupposed circumstances, and determinate material conditions, independent of their will.

The production of ideas, of concepts, of consciousness is at first directly interwoven with men's material activity and commerce: it is the language of real life. Here, conceptualising, thinking, the intellectual intercourse of men still appear to emanate directly from their material conduct and relations. The same holds true of intellectual production as it is represented in the language of politics, of the laws, of morality, religion, metaphysics, etc. Men are the producers of their notions and ideas, etc., but they are real, active men, conditioned by a definite development of their productive forces and by the relations that correspond to these forces, up to and including their most extended forms. Consciousness can never be anything other than the conscious being, and the being of men is their real life process. If, in all ideology, men and their relationships appear upside down, as in a *camera obscura,* then this phenomenon stems just as much from their historical life process as the inversion of objects on the retina stems from the process of direct physical life.

In complete contrast to German philosophy, which descends from heaven to earth, the procedure here will be to move from earth to heaven. That is, we will not proceed on the basis of what men say and imagine about themselves, nor on the basis of imagined and conceptualised men, in order to arrive from there at flesh and blood men; we will begin with real, active men, and from their real life process we will expose the development of the ideological reflections and echoes of this life process. The shadowy pictures in the human brain are also necessary sublimations of men's material life process, empirically verifiable and tied to material presuppositions. Consequently, morality, religion, metaphysics, and the other ideological constructs and forms of consciousness that correspond to them no longer retain the appearance of independence. They have no history, they have no development, but rather the men who develop their material production and commerce also alter, with this facet of their reality, their thinking and the products of their thinking. It is not consciousness that determines life, but life that determines consciousness. In the first way of looking at things one begins with consciousness regarded as the living individual; in the second, which corresponds to real life, one begins with the actual living individuals themselves, and regards consciousness only as *their* consciousness.

This way of looking at things is not without presuppositions. It proceeds on the basis of presupposed real circumstances and does not depart from them for one instant. Its presuppositions are human beings, not taken in some sort of imaginary isolation or fixed abstraction, but rather in their real, empirically observable process of development under definite conditions. As soon as this active life process is represented, history ceases to be a collection of dead facts, as it is with abstract empiricists, or an imagined action of imagined subjects, as it is with the idealists.

Where speculation ceases—in real life—there real, positive science begins, the representation of practical activity, of the practical process of development of men. The phrases about consciousness cease, and real knowledge takes their place. With the presentation of reality, independent philosophy loses its medium of existence. At most a recapitulation of the most general results may take its place, results which can be abstracted out of a consideration of the historical development of men. In themselves, apart from real history, these abstractions have no value whatsoever. They can serve only to simplify the ordering of the historical material, to indicate the sequence of its several layers. By no means, however, do they give, as philosophy does, any recipe or scheme for neatly arranging the epochs of history. On the contrary, the difficulty first arises when one begins to study and to classify the material, to really analyse it, whether it has to do with past epochs or the present. Removing these difficulties depends on presuppositions which cannot in any event be indicated here, because they result from a study of the real process of life and the actions of individuals of each epoch.

5.

The Origin of Beliefs

ÉMILE DURKHEIM, 1912

The central notion of totemism is that of a quasi-divine principle that is immanent in certain categories of men and things and thought of in the form of an animal or plant. In essence, therefore, to explain this religion is to explain this belief—that is, to discover what could have led men to construct it and with what building blocks.

It is manifestly not with the feelings the things that serve as totems are capable of arousing in men's minds. . . . [T]hese are often insignificant. In the sort of impression lizards, caterpillars, rats, ants, frogs, turkeys, breams, plum trees, cockatoos, and so forth make upon man (to cite only the names that come up frequently on lists of Australian totems), there is nothing that in any way resembles grand and powerful religious emotions or could stamp upon them a quality of sacredness. The same cannot be said of stars and great atmospheric phenomena, which do have all that is required to seize men's imaginations. As it happens, however, these serve very rarely as totems; indeed, their use for this purpose was probably a late development. Thus it was not the intrinsic nature of the thing whose name the clan bore that set it apart as the object of worship. Furthermore, if the emotion elicited by the thing itself really was the determining cause of totemic rites and beliefs, then this thing would also be the sacred being par excellence, and the animals and plants used as totems would play the leading role in religious life. But we know that the focus of the cult is elsewhere. It is symbolic representations of this or that plant or animal. It is totemic emblems and symbols of all kinds that possess the greatest sanctity. And so it is in totemic emblems and symbols that the religious source is to be found, while the real objects represented by those emblems receive only a reflection.

The totem is above all a symbol, a tangible expression of something else. But of what?

Reprinted with the permission of The Free Press, an imprint of Simon & Schuster Adult Publishing Group, from *The Elementary Forms of the Religious Life* by Emile Durkheim, translated with an introduction by Karen E. Fields. Translation and introduction, Copyright © 1995 by Karen E. Fields.

It follows from the same analysis that the totem expresses and symbolizes two different kinds of things. From one point of view, it is the outward and visible form of what I have called the totemic principle or god; and from another, it is also the symbol of a particular society that is called the clan. It is the flag of the clan, the sign by which each clan is distinguished from the others, the visible mark of its distinctiveness, and a mark that is borne by everything that in any way belongs to the clan: men, animals, and things. Thus, if the totem is the symbol of both the god and the society, is this not because the god and the society are one and the same? How could the emblem of the group have taken the form of that quasi-divinity if the group and the divinity were two distinct realities? Thus the god of the clan, the totemic principle, can be none other than the clan itself, but the clan transfigured and imagined in the physical form of the plant or animal that serves as totem.

How could that apotheosis have come about, and why should it have come about in that fashion?

Society in general, simply by its effect on men's minds, undoubtedly has all that is required to arouse the sensation of the divine. A society is to its members what a god is to its faithful. A god is first of all a being that man conceives of as superior to himself in some respects and one on whom he believes he depends. Whether that being is a conscious personality, like Zeus or Yahweh, or a play of abstract forces as in totemism, the faithful believe they are bound to certain ways of acting that the nature of the sacred principle they are dealing with has imposed upon them. Society also fosters in us the sense of perpetual dependence. Precisely because society has its own specific nature that is different from our nature as individuals, it pursues ends that are also specifically its own; but because it can achieve those ends only by working through us, it categorically demands our cooperation. Society requires us to make ourselves its servants, forgetful of our own interests. And it subjects us to all sorts of restraints, privations, and sacrifices without which social life would be impossible. And so, at every instant, we must submit to rules of action and thought that we have neither made nor wanted and that sometimes are contrary to our inclinations and to our most basic instincts.

If society could exact those concessions and sacrifices only by physical constraint, it could arouse in us only the sense of a physical force to which we have no choice but to yield, and not that of a moral power such as religions venerate. In reality, however, the hold society has over consciousness owes far less to the prerogative its physical superiority gives it than to the moral authority with which it is invested. We defer to society's orders not simply because it is equipped to overcome our resistance but, first and foremost, because it is the object of genuine respect.

An individual or collective subject is said to inspire respect when the representation that expresses it in consciousness has such power that it calls forth or inhibits conduct automatically, *irrespective of any utilitarian calculation of helpful or harmful results.* When we obey someone out of respect for the moral authority that we have accorded to him, we do not follow his instructions because they seem wise but because a certain psychic energy intrinsic to the idea we have of that person bends our will and turns it in the direction indicated. When that inward and wholly mental pressure moves within us, respect is the emotion we feel. We are then moved not by the advantages or disadvantages of the conduct that is recommended to us or demanded of us but by the way we conceive of the one who recommends or demands that conduct. This is why a command generally takes on short, sharp forms of address that leave no room for hesitation. It is also why, to the extent that command is command and works by its own strength, it precludes any idea of deliberation or calculation, but instead is made effective by the very intensity of the mental state in which it is given. That intensity is what we call moral influence.

The ways of acting to which society is strongly enough attached to impose them on its members are for that reason marked with a distinguishing sign that calls forth respect. Because these ways of acting have been worked out in common, the intensity with which they are thought in each individual mind finds resonance in all the others, and vice versa. The representations that translate them within each of us thereby gain an intensity that mere private states of consciousness can in no way match. Those ways of acting gather strength from the countless individual representations that have served to form each of them. It is society that speaks through the mouths of those who affirm them in our presence; it is society that we hear when we hear them, and the voice of all itself has a tone that an individual voice cannot have. The very forcefulness with which society acts against dissidence, whether by moral censure or physical repression, helps to strengthen this dominance, and at the same time forcefully proclaims the ardor of the shared conviction. In short, when something is the object of a state of opinion, the representation of the thing that each individual has draws such power from its origins, from the conditions in which it originated, that it is felt even by those who do not yield to it. The mental representation of a thing that is the object of a state of opinion has a tendency to repress and hold at bay those representations that contradict it; it commands instead those actions that fulfill it. It accomplishes this not by the reality or threat of physical coercion but by the radiation of the mental energy it contains. The hallmark of moral authority is that its psychic properties alone give it power. Opinion, eminently a social thing, is one source of authority. Indeed, the question arises whether authority is not the daughter of opinion. Some will object that science is often the antagonist of opinion, the errors of which it combats and corrects. But science can succeed in this task only if it has sufficient authority, and it can gain such authority only from opinion itself. All the scientific demonstrations in the world would have no influence if a people had no faith in science. Even today, if it should happen that science resisted a very powerful current of public opinion, it would run the risk of seeing its credibility eroded.[1]

Because social pressure makes itself felt through mental channels, it was bound to give man the idea that outside him there are one or several powers, moral yet mighty, to which he is subject. Since they speak to him in a tone of command, and sometimes even tell him to violate his most natural inclinations, man was bound to imagine them as being external to him. The mythological interpretations would doubtless not have been born if man could easily see that those influences upon him come from society. But the ordinary observer cannot see where the influence of society comes from. It moves along channels that are too obscure and circuitous, and uses psychic mechanisms that are too complex, to be easily traced to the source. So long as scientific analysis has not yet taught him, man is well aware that he is acted upon but not by whom. Thus he had to build out of nothing the idea of those powers with which he feels connected. From this we can begin to perceive how he was led to imagine those powers in forms that are not their own and to transfigure them in thought.

A god is not only an authority to which we are subject but also a force that buttresses our own. The man who has obeyed his god, and who for this reason thinks he has his god with him, approaches the world with confidence and a sense of heightened energy. In the same way, society's workings do not stop at demanding sacrifices, privations, and efforts from us. The force of the

---

1. I hope this analysis . . . will put an end to an erroneous interpretation of my ideas, which has more than once led to misunderstanding. Because I have made constraint the *external feature* by which social facts can be most easily recognized and distinguished from individual psychological ones, some have believed that I consider physical constraint to be the entire essence of social life. In reality, I have never regarded constraint as anything more than the visible, tangible expression of an underlying, inner fact that is wholly ideal: *moral authority*. The question for sociology—if there can be said to be *one* sociological question—is to seek, throughout the various forms of external constraint, the correspondingly various kinds of moral authority and to discover what causes have given rise to the latter. Specifically, the main object of the question treated in the present work is to discover in what form the particular kind of moral authority that is inherent in all that is religious was born, and what it is made of. Further, it will be seen below that in making social pressure one of the distinguishing features of sociological phenomena, I do not mean to say that this is the only one. I will exhibit another aspect of collective life, virtually the opposite of this one, but no less real. . . .

collectivity is not wholly external; it does not move us entirely from outside. Indeed, because society can exist only in and by means of individual minds, it must enter into us and become organized within us. That force thus becomes an integral part of our being and, by the same stroke, uplifts it and brings it to maturity.

This stimulating and invigorating effect of society is particularly apparent in certain circumstances. In the midst of an assembly that becomes worked up, we become capable of feelings and conduct of which we are incapable when left to our individual resources. When it is dissolved and we are again on our own, we fall back to our ordinary level and can then take the full measure of how far above ourselves we were. History abounds with examples. Suffice it to think about the night of August 4, when an assembly was suddenly carried away in an act of sacrifice and abnegation that each of its members had refused to make the night before and by which all were surprised the morning after. For this reason all parties—be they political, economic, or denominational—see to it that periodic conventions are held, at which their followers can renew their common faith by making a public demonstration of it together. To strengthen emotions that would dissipate if left alone, the one thing needful is to bring all those who share them into more intimate and more dynamic relationship.

In the same way, we can also explain the curious posture that is so characteristic of a man who is speaking to a crowd—if he has achieved communion with it. His language becomes high-flown in a way that would be ridiculous in ordinary circumstances; his gestures take on an overbearing quality; his very thought becomes impatient of limits and slips easily into every kind of extreme. This is because he feels filled to overflowing, as though with a phenomenal oversupply of forces that spill over and tend to spread around him. Sometimes he even feels possessed by a moral force greater than he, of which he is only the interpreter. This is the hallmark of what has often been called the demon of oratorical inspiration. This extraordinary surplus of forces is quite real and comes to him from the very group he is addressing. The feelings he arouses as he speaks return to him enlarged and amplified, reinforcing his own to the same degree. The passionate energies that he arouses reecho in turn within him, and they increase his dynamism. It is then no longer a mere individual who speaks but a group incarnated and personified.

Apart from these passing or intermittent states, there are more lasting ones in which the fortifying action of society makes itself felt with longer-term consequences and often with more striking effect. Under the influence of some great collective shock in certain historical periods, social interactions become much more frequent and active. Individuals seek one another out and come together more. The result is the general effervescence that is characteristic of revolutionary or creative epochs. The result of that heightened activity is a general stimulation of individual energies. People live differently and more intensely than in normal times. The changes are not simply of nuance and degree; man himself becomes something other than what he was. He is stirred by passions so intense that they can be satisfied only by violent and extreme acts: by acts of superhuman heroism or bloody barbarism. This explains the Crusades, for example, as well as so many sublime or savage moments in the French Revolution. We see the most mediocre or harmless bourgeois transformed by the general exaltation into a hero or an executioner. And the mental processes are so clearly the same as those at the root of religion that the individuals themselves conceived the pressure they yielded to in explicitly religious terms. The Crusaders believed they felt God present among them, calling on them to go forth and conquer the Holy Land, and Joan of Arc believed she was obeying celestial voices.

This stimulating action of society is not felt in exceptional circumstances alone. There is virtually no instant of our lives in which a certain rush of energy fails to come to us from outside ourselves. In all kinds of acts that express the understanding, esteem, and affection of his neighbor, there is a lift that the man who does his duty feels, usually without being aware of it. But that lift sustains him; the feeling society has for him uplifts the feeling he has for himself. Because he is in moral harmony with his neighbor, he gains new confidence, courage, and boldness in action—quite like the man of faith who believes he feels the eyes of his god turned benevolently toward him. Thus is produced what amounts to a perpetual uplift of our moral being. Since it varies according to a multitude of external conditions—whether our relations with the social groups that surround us are more or less active and what those groups are—we cannot help but feel that this moral toning up has an external cause, though we do not see where that cause is or what it is. So we readily conceive of it in the form of a moral power that, while immanent in us, also represents something in us that is other than ourselves. This is man's moral consciousness and his conscience. And it is only with the aid of religious symbols that most have ever managed to conceive of it with any clarity at all.

In addition to those free forces that continuously renew our own, there are other forces congealed in the techniques we use and in traditions of all kinds. We speak a language we did not create; we use instruments we did not invent; we claim rights we did not establish; each generation inherits a treasury of knowledge that it did not itself amass; and so on. We owe these varied benefits of civilization to society, and although in general we do not see where they come from, we know at least that they are not of our own making. It is these things that give man his distinctiveness among all creatures, for man is man only because he is civilized. Thus he could not escape the sense of mighty causes existing outside him, which are the source of his characteristic nature and which, like benevolent forces, help and protect him and guarantee him a privileged fate. He naturally accorded to those powers a respect commensurate with the great value of the benefits that he attributed to them.

Thus the environment in which we live seems populated with forces at once demanding and helpful, majestic and kind, and with which we are in touch. Because we feel the weight of them, we have no choice but to locate them outside ourselves, as we do for the objective causes of our sensations. But from another point of view, the feelings they provoke in us are qualitatively different from those we have for merely physical things. So long as these perceptions are no more than the empirical characteristics that ordinary experience makes manifest, and so long as the religious imagination has not yet transfigured them, we feel nothing like respect for them, and they have nothing of what it takes to lift us above ourselves. Therefore the representations that express them seem to us very different from those that collective influences awaken in us. The two sorts of representation form two kinds of mental state, and they are as separate and distinct as the two forms of life to which they correspond. As a result, we feel as though we are in touch with two distinct sorts of reality with a clear line of demarcation between them: the world of profane things on one side, the world of sacred things on the other.

Furthermore, now as in the past, we see that society never stops creating new sacred things. If society should happen to become infatuated with a man, believing it has found in him its deepest aspirations as well as the means of fulfilling them, then that man will be put in a class by himself and virtually deified. Opinion will confer on him a grandeur that is similar in every way to the grandeur that protects the gods. This has happened to many sovereigns in whom their epochs had faith and who, if not deified outright, were looked upon as direct representatives of the godhead. A clear indication that this apotheosis is the work of society alone is that society has often consecrated men whose personal worth did not warrant it. Moreover, the routine deference that men invested with high social positions receive is not qualitatively different from religious respect. The same movements express it: standing at a distance from a high personage; taking special precautions in approaching him; using a different language to speak with him and gestures other than those that will do for ordinary mortals. One's feeling in these circumstances is so closely akin to religious feeling that many do not distinguish between them. Sacredness is ascribed to princes, nobles, and political leaders in order to account for the special regard they enjoy. In Melanesia and Polynesia, for example, people say that a man of influence possesses mana and impute his influence to this mana. It is clear, nonetheless, that his position comes to him only from the importance that opinion gives him. Thus, both the moral power conferred by opinion and the moral power with which sacred beings are invested are of fundamentally the same origin and composed of the same elements. For this reason, one word can be used to designate both.

Just as society consecrates men, so it also consecrates things, including ideas. When a belief is shared unanimously by a people, to touch it—that is, to deny or question it—is forbidden, for the reasons already stated. The prohibition against critique is a prohibition like any other and proves that one is face to face with a sacred thing. Even today, great though the freedom we allow one another may be, it would be tantamount to sacrilege for a man wholly to deny progress or to reject the human ideal to which modern societies are attached. Even the peoples most enamored of free thinking tend to place one principle above discussion and regard it as untouchable, in other words, sacred: the principle of free discussion itself.

Nowhere has society's ability to make itself a god or to create gods been more in evidence than during the first years of the Revolution. In the general enthusiasm of that time, things that were by nature purely secular were transformed by public opinion into sacred things: Fatherland, Liberty, Reason. A religion tended to establish itself spontaneously, with its own dogma, symbols, altars, and feast days. It was to these spontaneous hopes that the Cult of Reason and the Supreme Being tried to give a kind of authoritative fulfillment. Granted, this religious novelty did not last. The patriotic enthusiasm that originally stirred the masses died away, and the cause having departed, the effect could not hold. But brief though it was, this experiment loses none of its sociological interest. In a specific case, we saw society and its fundamental ideas becoming the object of a genuine cult directly—and without transfiguration of any kind.

All these facts enable us to grasp how it is possible for the clan to awaken in its members the idea of forces existing outside them, both dominating and supporting them—in sum, religious forces. There is no other social group to which the primitive is more directly or tightly bound. The ties that bind him to the tribe are looser and less strongly felt. Although the tribe is certainly not foreign to him, it is with the people of his clan that he has most in common, and it is the influence of this group that he feels most immediately, and so it is also this influence, more than any other, that was bound to find expression in religious symbols.

6.

Genesis and Development
of a Scientific Fact

LUDWIK FLECK, 1935

Cognition is the most socially-conditioned activity of man, and knowledge is
the paramount social creation [*Gebilde*]. The very structure of language presents a compelling philosophy characteristic of that community, and even a
single word can represent a complex theory. To whom do these philosophies
and theories belong?

Thoughts pass from one individual to another, each time a little transformed, for each individual can attach to them somewhat different associations. Strictly speaking, the receiver never understands the thought exactly in
the way that the transmitter intended it to be understood. After a series of
such encounters, practically nothing is left of the original content. Whose
thought is it that continues to circulate? It is one that obviously belongs not to
any single individual but to the collective. Whether an individual construes it
as truth or error, understands it correctly or not, a set of findings meanders
throughout the community, becoming polished, transformed, reinforced, or
attenuated, while influencing other findings, concept formation, opinions,
and habits of thought. After making several rounds within the community, a
finding often returns considerably changed to its originator, who reconsiders
it himself in quite a different light. He either does not recognize it as his own
or believes, and this happens quite often, to have originally seen it in its present form. The history of the Wassermann reaction will afford us the opportunity to describe such meanderings in the particular case of a completely "empirical" finding.

This social character inherent in the very nature of scientific activity is not
without its substantive consequences. Words which formerly were simple
terms become slogans; sentences which once were simple statements become
calls to battle. This completely alters their socio-cognitive value. They no
longer influence the mind through their logical meaning—indeed, they often

Reprinted with the permission of The University of Chicago, from *Genesis and
Development of a Scientific Fact* by Ludwik Fleck, edited by Thaddeus J. Trenn and Robert
K. Merton, translated by Fred Bradley and Thaddeus J. Trenn. Copyright © 1979 by The
University of Chicago. All rights reserved.

act *against it*—but rather they acquire a magical power and exert a mental influence simply by being used. As an example, one might consider the effect of terms such as "materialism" or "atheism," which in some countries at once discredit their proponents but in others function as essential passwords for acceptability. This magical power of slogans, with "vitalism" in biology, "specificity" in immunology, and "bacterial transformation" in bacteriology, clearly extends to the very depth of specialist research. Whenever such a term is found in a scientific text, it is not examined logically, but immediately makes either enemies or friends.

New themes such as propaganda, imitation, authority, rivalry, solidarity, enmity, and friendship begin to appear—themes which could not have been produced by the isolated thought of any individual. Every such motif acquires epistemological importance, because the entire fund of knowledge as well as the intellectual interaction within the collective take part in every single act of cognition, which is indeed fundamentally impossible without them. Every epistemological theory is trivial that does not take this sociological dependence of all cognition into account in a fundamental and detailed manner. But those who consider social dependence a necessary evil and an unfortunate human inadequacy which ought to be overcome fail to realize that without social conditioning no cognition is even possible. Indeed, the very word "cognition" acquires meaning only in connection with a thought collective.

A kind of superstitious fear prevents us from attributing that which is the most intimate part of human personality, namely the thought process, also to a collective.[1] A thought collective exists wherever two or more people are actually exchanging thoughts. He is a poor observer who does not notice that a stimulating conversation between two persons soon creates a condition in which each utters thoughts he would not have been able to produce either by himself or in different company. A special mood arises, which would not otherwise affect either partner of the conversation but almost always returns whenever these persons meet again. Prolonged duration of this state produces, from common understanding and mutual misunderstanding, a thought structure [*Denkgebilde*] that belongs to neither of them alone but nevertheless is not at all without meaning. Who is its carrier and who its originator? It is neither more nor less than the small collective of two persons. If a third person joins in, a new collective arises. The previous mood will dissolve and with it the special creative force of the former small collective.

We could agree with anybody who calls the thought collective fictitious and the personification of a common result produced by interaction. But what is

---

1. Although nobody would refuse to attribute the creation of intellectual products such as language, folksongs, folklore, and others to a collective.

any personality if not the personification of many different momentary personalities and their common psychological Gestalt? A thought collective, by analogy, is composed of different individuals and also has its special rules of behavior and its psychological form. As an entity it is even more stable and consistent than the so-called individual, who always consists of contradictory drives.

The individual life of the human spirit contains incongruent elements, such as tenets of faith and superstition which, stemming from various individual complexes, muddy the purity of any theory or system. Both Kepler and Newton, who contributed so much to the modern concept of nature, were ritualistic and religious in their basic attitudes. Rousseau's ideas of education had much greater relevance to the thought collective than to his own individual life.

One individual belongs to several thought collectives at once. As a research worker he is part of that community with which he works. He may give rise to ideas and developments, often unconsciously, which soon become independent and frequently turn against their originator. As a member of a political party, a social class, a nation, or even a race, he belongs to other collectives. If he should chance to enter some other society, he soon becomes one of its members and obeys its rules. The individual can be examined from the viewpoint of a collective just as well as, conversely, the collective can be considered from that of the individual. Whether in the case of the individual personality or in that of the collective entity, that which specifies the one or the other is accessible only to adequate methods.

The history of science also records cases of independent—one might say personal—exploits. But their independence is only characterized by an absence of collaborators and helpers, or possibly of pioneers; that is, it manifests itself in the personal and independent concentration of historical and contemporary collective influence. In a manner corresponding closely to personal exploits in other areas of society, such scientific exploits can prevail only if they have a seminal effect by being performed at a time when the social conditions are right. The achievement of Vesalius as the originator of modern anatomy was just such an audacious and artistic feat. Had Vesalius lived in the twelfth or thirteenth century he would have made no impact. It is just as difficult to imagine him in that era, as it is, for instance, to imagine Napoleon before the French Revolution. Outside the appropriate social conditions, any development into historical greatness would have been denied to both. The futility of work that is isolated from the spirit of the age is shown strikingly in the case of that great herald of excellent ideas Leonardo da Vinci, who nevertheless left no positive scientific achievement behind.

This by no means implies that the individual must be ruled out as an epistemological factor. His sensory physiology and psychology are certainly very important. But a firm foundation for epistemology cannot be established without investigation of the thought community [*Denkgemeinschaft*]. Let me introduce a somewhat trivial analogy. If the individual may be compared to a soccer player and the thought collective to the soccer team trained for cooperation, then cognition would be the progress of the game. Can an adequate report of this progress be made by examining the individual kicks one by one? The whole game would lose its meaning completely.

The importance of sociological methods in the investigation of intellectual activities was already recognized by Auguste Comte. Recently it was stressed by Durkheim's school in France and by the philosopher Wilhelm Jerusalem among others in Vienna.

Durkheim speaks expressly of the force exerted on the individual by social structures both as objective specific facts and as controlled behavior. He also mentions the superindividual and objective character of ideas belonging to the collective. He describes that which is produced by the activities of the collective intellect, "as we encounter them in language, in religious and magic beliefs, in the existence of invisible powers, and in the innumerable spirits and demons which dominate the entire course of nature and the life of the tribe, and as we meet them in customs and habits."[2]

Lévy-Bruhl, a student of Durkheim, writes: "Ideas belonging to the collective follow laws of their own which, especially in primitive races, we cannot discover by studying the white, adult, and civilized individual. On the contrary, it is the study of those ideas belonging to the collective and their connections in primitive societies that throws some light on the origin of our own categories and logical principles."[3] "This approach will certainly lead to a new and positive epistemology based upon the comparative method."[4] Lévy-Bruhl contests the belief in "the identity of the human mind," "which at all times and in all places is supposed to have remained unchanged as far as logic is concerned."[5] He doubts whether "scientific use can at all be made of the idea of a human mind assumed to be untouched by any experience,"[6] because this concept "is just as chimerical as that of man before society."[7]

Gumplowicz expressed himself very poignantly on the importance of the collective. "The greatest error of individualistic psychology is the assumption that a *person* thinks. This leads to a continual search for the source of thought

---

2. According to Jerusalem, from his preface to the German edition of Lévy-Bruhl 1926, p. vii.

3. Lévy-Bruhl 1926, p. 1.

4. Ibid., p. 2.

5. Ibid., p. 5.

6. Ibid., p. 10.

7. Ibid., p. 11.

within the individual himself and for the reasons why he thinks in a particular way and not in any other. Theologians and philosophers contemplate this problem, even offer advice on how one ought to think. But this is a chain of errors. What actually thinks within a person is not the individual himself but his social community. The source of his thinking is not within himself but is to be found in his social environment and in the very social atmosphere he 'breathes.' His mind is structured, and necessarily so, under the influence of this ever-present social environment, and *he cannot think in any other way.*"[8]

... [T]hinkers trained in sociology and classics ... no matter how productive their ideas, commit a characteristic error. They exhibit an excessive respect, bordering on pious reverence, for scientific facts.

REFERENCES

Gumplowicz, Ludwig. *Grundriss der Soziologie.* Vienna, 1885; 2d ed., 1905.
Jerusalem, Wilhelm. "Die soziologische Bedingtheit des Denkens und der Denkformen." In *Versuche zu einer Soziologie des Wissens,* pp. 182–207, ed. Max Scheler. Leipzig and Munich: Duncker und Humblot, 1924.
Lévy-Bruhl, Lucien. *Das Denken der Naturvölker,* ed. Wilhelm Jerusalem. 2d ed. Vienna and Leipzig: Braumüller, 1926.

8. Gumplowicz 1905, p. 268, quoted according to Jerusalem 1924, p. 182. [The italics are Fleck's.—Eds.]

7.

Play, the Game, and the Generalized Other

GEORGE HERBERT MEAD, 1934

The fundamental difference between the game and play is that in the latter the child must have the attitude of all the others involved in that game. The attitudes of the other players which the participant assumes organize into a sort of unit, and it is that organization which controls the response of the individual. The illustration used was of a person playing baseball. Each one of his own acts is determined by his assumption of the action of the others who are playing the game. What he does is controlled by his being everyone else on that team, at least in so far as those attitudes affect his own particular response. We get then an "other" which is an organization of the attitudes of those involved in the same process.

The organized community or social group which gives to the individual his unity of self may be called "the generalized other." The attitude of the generalized other is the attitude of the whole community.[1] Thus, for example, in the case of such a social group as a ball team, the team is the generalized other in

Reprinted with the permission of The University of Chicago, from *Mind, Self, and Society* by George Herbert Mead. Edited and with an introduction by Charles W. Morris. Copyright © 1934 by The University of Chicago; Copyright © 1962 by Charles W. Morris. All rights reserved.

1. It is possible for inanimate objects, no less than for other human organisms, to form parts of the generalized and organized—the completely socialized—other for any given human individual, in so far as he responds to such objects socially or in a social fashion (by means of the mechanism of thought, the internalized conversation of gestures). Any thing—any object or set of objects, whether animate or inanimate, human or animal, or merely physical—toward which he acts, or to which he responds, socially, is an element in what for him is the generalized other; by taking the attitudes of which toward himself he becomes conscious of himself as an object or individual, and thus develops a self or personality. Thus, for example, the cult, in its primitive form, is merely the social embodiment of the relation between the given social group or community and its physical environment—an organized social means, adopted by the individual members of that group or community, of entering into social relations with that environment, or (in a sense) of carrying on conversations with it; and in this way that environment becomes part of the total generalized other for each of the individual members of the given social group or community.

so far as it enters—as an organized process or social activity—into the experience of any one of the individual members of it.

If the given human individual is to develop a self in the fullest sense, it is not sufficient for him merely to take the attitudes of other human individuals toward himself and toward one another within the human social process, and to bring that social process as a whole into his individual experience merely in these terms: he must also, in the same way that he takes the attitudes of other individuals toward himself and toward one another, take their attitudes toward the various phases or aspects of the common social activity or set of social undertakings in which, as members of an organized society or social group, they are all engaged; and he must then, by generalizing these individual attitudes of that organized society or social group itself, as a whole, act toward different social projects which at any given time it is carrying out, or toward the various larger phases of the general social process which constitutes its life and of which these projects are specific manifestations. This getting of the broad activities of any given social whole or organized society as such within the experiential field of any one of the individuals involved or included in that whole is, in other words, the essential basis and prerequisite of the fullest development of that individual's self: only in so far as he takes the attitudes of the organized social group to which he belongs toward the organized, co-operative social activity or set of such activities in which that group as such is engaged, does he develop a complete self or possess the sort of complete self he has developed. And on the other hand, the complex co-operative processes and activities and institutional functionings of organized human society are also possible only in so far as every individual involved in them or belonging to that society can take the general attitudes of all other such individuals with reference to these processes and activities and institutional functionings, and to the organized social whole of experiential relations and interactions thereby constituted—and can direct his own behavior accordingly.

It is in the form of the generalized other that the social process influences the behavior of the individuals involved in it and carrying it on, i.e., that the community exercises control over the conduct of its individual members; for it is in this form that the social process or community enters as a determining factor into the individual's thinking. In abstract thought the individual takes the attitude of the generalized other[2] toward himself, without reference to its

---

2. We have said that the internal conversation of the individual with himself in terms of words or significant gestures—the conversation which constitutes the process or activity of thinking—is carried on by the individual from the standpoint of the "generalized other." And the more abstract that conversation is, the more abstract thinking happens to be, the further removed is the generalized other from any connection with particular individuals. It is especially in abstract thinking, that is to say, that the

expression in any particular other individuals; and in concrete thought he takes that attitude in so far as it is expressed in the attitudes toward his behavior of those other individuals with whom he is involved in the given social situation or act. But only by taking the attitude of the generalized other toward himself, in one or another of these ways, can he think at all; for only thus can thinking—or the internalized conversation of gestures which constitutes thinking—occur. And only through the taking by individuals of the attitude or attitudes of the generalized other toward themselves is the existence of a universe of discourse, as that system of common or social meanings which thinking presupposes at its context, rendered possible.

The self-conscious human individual, then, takes or assumes the organized social attitudes of the given social group or community (or of some one section thereof) to which he belongs, toward the social problems of various kinds which confront that group or community at any given time, and which arise in connection with the correspondingly different social projects or organized co-operative enterprises in which that group or community as such is engaged; and as an individual participant in these social projects or co-operative enterprises, he governs his own conduct accordingly. In politics, for example, the individual identifies himself with an entire political party and takes the organized attitudes of that entire party toward the rest of the given social community and toward the problems which confront the party within the given social situation; and he consequently reacts or responds in terms of the organized attitudes of the party as a whole. He thus enters into a special set of social relations with all the other individuals who belong to that political party; and in the same way he enters into various other special sets of social relations, with various other classes of individuals respectively, the individuals of each of these classes being the other members of some one of the particular organized subgroups (determined in socially functional terms) of which he himself is a member within the entire given society or social community. In the most highly developed, organized, and complicated human social communities—those evolved by civilized man—these various socially functional classes or subgroups of individuals to which any given individual belongs (and with the other individual members of which he thus enters into a special set of social relations) are of two kinds. Some of them are concrete social classes or

---

conversation involved is carried on by the individual with the generalized other, rather than with any particular individuals. Thus it is, for example, that abstract concepts are concepts stated in terms of the attitudes of the entire social group or community; they are stated on the basis of the individual's consciousness of the attitudes of the generalized other toward them, as a result of his taking these attitudes of the generalized other and then responding to them. And thus it is also that abstract propositions are stated in a form which anyone—any other intelligent individual—will accept.

subgroups, such as political parties, clubs, corporations, which are all actually functional social units, in terms of which their individual members are directly related to one another. The other are abstract social classes or subgroups, such as the class of debtors and the class of creditors, in terms of which their individual members are related to one another only more or less indirectly, and which only more or less indirectly function as social units, but which afford or represent unlimited possibilities for the widening and ramifying and enriching of the social relations among all the individual members of the given society as an organized and unified whole. The given individual's membership in several of these abstract social classes or subgroups makes possible his entrance into definite social relations (however indirect) with an almost infinite number of other individuals who also belong to or are included within one or another of these abstract social classes or subgroups cutting across functional lines of demarcation which divide different human social communities from one another, and including individual members from several (in some cases from all) such communities. Of these abstract social classes or subgroups of human individuals the one which is most inclusive and extensive is, of course, the one defined by the logical universe of discourse (or system of universally significant symbols) determined by the participation and communicative interaction of individuals; for of all such classes or subgroups, it is the one which claims the largest number of individual members, and which enables the largest conceivable number of human individuals to enter into some sort of social relation, however indirect or abstract it may be, with one another—a relation arising from the universal functioning of gestures as significant symbols in the general human social process of communication.

I have pointed out, then, that there are two general stages in the full development of the self. At the first of these stages, the individual's self is constituted simply by an organization of the particular attitudes of other individuals toward himself and toward one another in the specific social acts in which he participates with them. But at the second stage in the full development of the individual's self that self is constituted not only by an organization of these particular individual attitudes, but also by an organization of the social attitudes of the generalized other or the social group as a whole to which he belongs. These social or group attitudes are brought within the individual's field of direct experience, and are included as elements in the structure or constitution of his self, in the same way that the attitudes of particular other individuals are; and the individual arrives at them, or succeeds in taking them, by means of further organizing, and then generalizing, the attitudes of particular other individuals in terms of their organized social bearings and implications. So the self reaches its full development by organizing these individual attitudes of others into the organized social or group attitudes, and by thus becoming an individual reflection of the general systematic pattern of social or group behavior in which it and the others are all involved—a pattern which enters as a whole into the individual's experience in terms of these organized group attitudes which, through the mechanism of his central nervous system, he takes toward himself, just as he takes the individual attitudes of others.

The game has a logic, so that such an organization of the self is rendered possible: there is a definite end to be obtained; the actions of the different individuals are all related to each other with reference to that end so that they do not conflict; one is not in conflict with himself in the attitude of another man on the team. If one has the attitude of the person throwing the ball he can also have the response of catching the ball. The two are related so that they further the purpose of the game itself. They are interrelated in a unitary, organic fashion. There is a definite unity, then, which is introduced into the organization of other selves when we reach such a stage as that of the game, as over against the situation of play where there is a simple succession of one role after another, a situation which is, of course, characteristic of the child's own personality. The child is one thing at one time and another at another, and what he is at one moment does not determine what he is at another. That is both the charm of childhood as well as its inadequacy. You cannot count on the child; you cannot assume that all the things he does are going to determine what he will do at any moment. He is not organized into a whole. The child has no definite character, no definite personality.

The game is then an illustration of the situation out of which an organized personality arises. In so far as the child does take the attitude of the other and allows that attitude of the other to determine the thing he is going to do with reference to a common end, he is becoming an organic member of society. He is taking over the morale of that society and is becoming an essential member of it. He belongs to it in so far as he does allow the attitude of the other that he takes to control his own immediate expression. What is involved here is some sort of an organized process. That which is expressed in terms of the game is, of course, being continually expressed in the social life of the child, but this wider process goes beyond the immediate experience of the child himself. The importance of the game is that it lies entirely inside of the child's own experience, and the importance of our modern type of education is that it is brought as far as possible within this realm. The different attitudes that a child assumes are so organized that they exercise a definite control over his response, as the attitudes in a game control his own immediate response. In the game we get an organized other, a generalized other, which is found in the nature of the child itself, and finds its expression in the immediate experience of the child. And it is that organized activity in the child's own nature controlling the particular response which gives unity, and which builds up his own self.

What goes on in the game goes on in the life of the child all the time. He is continually taking the attitudes of those about him, especially the roles of those who in some sense control him and on whom he depends. He gets the function of the process in an abstract sort of a way at first. It goes over from the play into the game in a real sense. He has to play the game. The morale of the game takes hold of the child more than the larger morale of the whole community. The child passes into the game and the game expresses a social situation in which he can completely enter; its morale may have a greater hold on him than that of the family to which he belongs or the community in which he lives. There are all sorts of social organizations, some of which are fairly lasting, some temporary, into which the child is entering, and he is playing a sort of social game in them. It is a period in which he likes "to belong," and he gets into organizations which come into existence and pass out of existence. He becomes a something which can function in the organized whole, and thus tends to determine himself in his relationship with the group to which he belongs. That process is one which is a striking stage in the development of the child's morale. It constitutes him a self-conscious member of the community to which he belongs.

Such is the process by which a personality arises. I have spoken of this as a process in which a child takes the role of the other, and said that it takes place essentially through the use of language. Language is predominantly based on the vocal gesture by means of which co-operative activities in a community are carried out. Language in its significant sense is that vocal gesture which tends to arouse in the individual the attitude which it arouses in others, and it is this perfecting of the self by the gesture which mediates the social activities that gives rise to the process of taking the role of the other. The latter phrase is a little unfortunate because it suggests an actor's attitude which is actually more sophisticated than that which is involved in our own experience. To this degree it does not correctly describe that which I have in mind. We see the process most definitely in a primitive form in those situations where the child's play takes different roles. Here the very fact that he is ready to pay out money, for instance, arouses the attitude of the person who receives money; the very process is calling out in him the corresponding activities of the other person involved. The individual stimulates himself to the response which he is calling out in the other person, and then acts in some degree in response to that situation. In play the child does definitely act out the role which he himself has aroused in himself. It is that which gives, as I have said, a definite content in the individual which answers to the stimulus that affects him as it affects somebody else. The content of the other that enters into one personality is the response in the individual which his gesture calls out in the other.

We may illustrate our basic concept by a reference to the notion of property. If we say "This is my property, I shall control it," that affirmation calls out a certain set of responses which must be the same in any community in which property exists. It involves an organized attitude with reference to property which is common to all the members of the community. One must have a definite attitude of control of his own property and respect for the property of others. Those attitudes (as organized sets of responses) must be there on the part of all, so that when one says such a thing he calls out in himself the response of the others. He is calling out the response of what I have called a generalized other. That which makes society possible is such common responses, such organized attitudes, with reference to what we term property, the cults of religion, the process of education, and the relations of the family. Of course, the wider the society the more definitely universal these objects must be. In any case there must be a definite set of responses, which we may speak of as abstract, and which can belong to a very large group. Property is in itself a very abstract concept. It is that which the individual himself can control and nobody else can control. The attitude is different from that of a dog toward a bone. A dog will fight any other dog trying to take the bone. The dog is not taking the attitude of the other dog. A man who says "This is my property" is taking an attitude of the other person. The man is appealing to his rights because he is able to take the attitude which everybody else in the group has with reference to property, thus arousing in himself the attitude of others.

What goes to make up the organized self is the organization of the attitudes which are common to the group. A person is a personality because he belongs to a community, because he takes over the institutions of that community into his own conduct. He takes its language as a medium by which he gets his personality, and then through a process of taking the different roles that all the others furnish he comes to get the attitude of the members of the community. Such, in a certain sense, is the structure of a man's personality. There are certain common responses which each individual has toward certain common things, and in so far as those common responses are awakened in the individual when he is affecting other persons he arouses his own self. The structure, then, on which the self is built is this response which is common to all, for one has to be a member of a community to be a self. Such responses are abstract attitudes, but they constitute just what we term a man's character. They give him what we term his principles, the acknowledged attitudes of all members of the community toward what are the values of that community. He is putting himself in the place of the generalized other, which represents the organized responses of all the members of the group. It is that which guides conduct controlled by principles, and a person who has such an organized group of responses is a man whom we say has character, in the moral sense.

It is a structure of attitudes, then, which goes to make up a self, as distinct from a group of habits. We all of us have, for example, certain groups of habits, such as the particular intonations which a person uses in his speech. This is a set of habits of vocal expression which one has but which one does not know about. The sets of habits which we have of that sort mean nothing to us; we do not hear the intonations of our speech that others hear unless we are paying particular attention to them. The habits of emotional expression which belong to our speech are of the same sort. We may know that we have expressed ourselves in a joyous fashion but the detailed process is one which does not come back to our conscious selves. There are whole bundles of such habits which do not enter into a conscious self, but which help to make up what is termed the unconscious self.

After all, what we mean by self-consciousness is an awakening in ourselves of the group of attitudes which we are arousing in others, especially when it is an important set of responses which go to make up the members of the community. It is unfortunate to fuse or mix up consciousness, as we ordinarily use that term, and self-consciousness. Consciousness, as frequently used, simply has reference to the field of experience, but self-consciousness refers to the ability to call out in ourselves a set of definite responses which belong to the others of the group. Consciousness and self-consciousness are not on the same level. A man alone has, fortunately or unfortunately, access to his own toothache, but that is not what we mean by self-consciousness.

I have so far emphasized what I have called the structures upon which the self is constructed, the framework of the self, as it were. Of course we are not only what is common to all: each one of the selves is different from everyone else; but there has to be such a common structure as I have sketched in order that we may be members of a community at all. We cannot be ourselves unless we are also members in whom there is a community of attitudes which control the attitudes of all. We cannot have rights unless we have common attitudes. That which we have acquired as self-conscious persons makes us such members of society and gives us selves. Selves can only exist in definite relationships to other selves. No hard-and-fast line can be drawn between our own selves and the selves of others, since our own selves exist and enter as such into our experience only in so far as the selves of others exist and enter as such into our experience also. The individual possesses a self only in relation to the selves of the other members of his social group; and the structure of his self expresses or reflects the general behavior pattern of this social group to which he belongs, just as does the structure of the self of every other individual belonging to this social group.

8.

Meanings of Violence

DOV COHEN and JOE VANDELLO, 1998

In his book *Southern Legacy*, Hodding Carter tells a revealing story. In the 1930s, Carter was the foreman on a jury in Louisiana hearing the case of a man accused of manslaughter. The man lived near a gas station and "had been for some time the butt of the station attendants' jokes. Despite his warnings that he had enough of their tomfoolery, and though aware of his short temper, they nevertheless persisted in badgering him."[1] One morning the man got truly fed up, got his gun, and opened fire, maiming one of the troublemakers, wounding another, and killing an innocent customer. The case was notable, Carter said, only because it was one of the few "passion killings" that went to a jury trial.

After hearing 3 days of testimony, the jury met to decide on a verdict. When Carter suggested a verdict of guilty, the jury room exploded. "Good God Almighty, bub. He ain't guilty. He wouldn't of been much of a man if he hadn't shot them fellows." All but Carter voted for acquittal, with one adding, "Son, you're a good boy but you got a lot to learn. You can't jail a man for standing up for his rights."[2]

As Carter's dissenting voice shows, there is not complete unanimity on this point. But the anecdote reflects something important about southern culture. In the South, insults have very serious meanings, and they must occasionally be answered with violence. This has been true historically, and as we will try to show, it is still true today. Our research has concentrated on the U.S. South, and we think our work can be used to help understand something about other violent cultures, with respect to the way honor and violence are conceived.[3]

73

Reprinted with the permission of The University of Chicago from "Meanings of Violence," *Journal of Legal Studies* 27, by Dov Cohen and Joe Vandello. Copyright © 1998 by The University of Chicago. All rights reserved.

Work on this article was supported in part by grants from the Russell Sage Foundation and the University of Illinois Research Board.

1. Hodding Carter, *Southern Legacy* 48 (1950).
2. Id. at 48–51.
3. Dov Cohen, Joe Vandello, and Adrian Rantilla, "The Sacred and the Social: Honor

The three points of this article are that (1) Southerners understand the meaning of the insult differently than Northerners do. (2) They have behavioral rituals that make allowances for this understanding. And (3) they live within social structures and systems that perpetuate these meanings and ideologies.

INSULTS IN CULTURES OF HONOR

Social status is important in all cultures. But over and above this, in many cultures around the world, men hold to what anthropologists call a "culture-of-honor" stance. This stance embraces the notion that a man's honor is tied up with physical prowess, toughness, and courage. Perhaps the best studied and most prototypical cultures of honor are found in the small villages of the Mediterranean.[4] But the stance is certainly not foreign to the United States.

This year, 20,000–25,000 Americans will die in homicides, with tens of thousands more injured in stabbings and gunfights that could easily have ended in death. A very large number of these incidents will begin over provocations that outsiders might call "trivial"—a small insult, a suspicious glance, a rude gesture, and so on. Yet, they are not so trivial to the participants in the conflicts, who act as if they are in a contest that carries a great deal of meaning about status and social position.

Such a culture-of-honor stance has been noted in our inner cities today.[5] But, the tradition in the United States goes back much further than this. Historians have argued that for the past few hundred years, whites in the U.S. South have acted as if they belonged to such a culture of honor. As Edward Ayers has commented, "[I]ronically, a white southern man from the 1830s or 1870s, whatever his class, would understand far better than most middle-class Americans of the twentieth century can the values of today's poor urban dweller, North and South."[6]

As we discuss below, there were probably good economic and ecological reasons why the culture-of-honor stance emerged in the Old South. But now, in the contemporary South, even after many of these original reasons have ceased to exist, the culture has remained. We argue that the culture-of-honor stance exists there today and that the social meanings of honor, insult, and vio-

---

and Violence in Cultural Context," in *Shame: Interpersonal Behavior, Psychopathology, and Culture* (Paul Gilbert and Bernice Andrews eds. 1998); Richard E. Nisbett and Dov Cohen, *Culture of Honor: The Psychology of Violence in the South* (1996).

4. David D. Gilmore, *Manhood in the Making* (1990); J. G. Peristiany, *Honour and Shame: The Values of Mediterranean Society* (1965).

5. Elijah Anderson, "The Code of the Streets," 5 *Atlantic Monthly* 81 (1994).

6. Edward L. Ayers, *Vengeance and Justice* 274 (1984).

lence for white Southerners have in fact persisted to some degree over the centuries.[7]

We do not claim that the South is typical of all or even most cultures of honor. Obviously, not everything we describe about the southern culture of honor generalizes to all others, as there are large variations across the world. But the U.S. South shares with other cultures of honor one central theme: a common conception of the insult as something that drastically reduces one's social standing and a belief that violence can be used to restore that standing once it has been jeopardized.[8]

THE FRONTIER SOUTH

From descriptions of historians, there can be little doubt that culture-of-honor norms were pervasive in the Old South. As Ayers has written, "In reconstructing the workings of southern honor and violence, it is crucial to understand that southern white men among all classes believed themselves 'honorable' men and acted on that belief. Honor did not reside only within the South's planter class. All knew that the failure to respond to insult marked them as less than real men, branded them, in the most telling epithets of the time, as 'cowards' and 'liars.' A coward tolerated insult, a liar attacked honor unfairly. To call a southern man either one was to invite attack."[9]

Aside from anything else it might mean, honor in the South meant toughness. As David Fischer noted of the southern backcountry, "[H]onor in this society meant a pride of manhood in masculine courage, physical strength, and warrior virtue."[10] And any man incapable of defending himself or his family dealt with "all the weight of shame that archaic society could muster."[11]

Origins of the Stance. There have been many proposals for why Southerners might have adopted this stance. But we believe that originally two conditions made this culture-of-honor ideology quite adaptive in the Old South.[12] The first was that the South was a herding economy.[13] Anthropologists note that herdsmen the world over tend to be quite vigilant against threats and encroachments because they are in a very precarious situation—that is, their

---

7. For a more extensive discussion of this cultural perpetuation, see Cohen, Vandello, and Rantilla, *supra* note 3.

8. Nisbett and Cohen, *supra* note 3.

9. Ayers, *supra* note 6, at 13.

10. David H. Fischer, *Albion's Seed* 690 (1989).

11. Bertram Wyatt-Brown, *Southern Honor* 53 (1982).

12. Nisbett and Cohen, *supra* note 3.

13. Grady McWhiney, *Cracker Culture* (1988).

livelihood can be rustled away from them instantly. Thus, to deter potential predators they adopt a tough, "don't mess with me" stance.

Second, such a posture becomes all the more important in places where people have to depend on themselves for their own protection and cannot rely on the state or effective law enforcement. And this was especially true of the frontier South, where as an old North Carolina proverb noted, "[E]very man should be sheriff on his own hearth."[14] (Later, of course, it would also be true of the West, which lacked adequate law enforcement and had in many areas a herding economy. And consistent with this, the West today also shows residuals of a culture-of-honor ideology.)

In such a situation where people are very vulnerable to theft and exploitation by others, people react not just to physical threats but to verbal affronts and insults as well because these are the probes by which one man tests another to see what he is made of. Letting infractions to honor go unanswered amounts to announcing that one is soft or can be walked over with impunity. Thus, "a man who absorbs insults is not a man at all."[15] As Martin Daly and Margo Wilson note in their book, *Homicide,* insults have a deeper meaning in this context:

> A seemingly minor affront is not merely a "stimulus" to action, isolated in time and space. It must be understood within a larger social context of reputations, face, relative social status, and enduring relationships. Men are known by their fellows as "the sort who can be pushed around" or "the sort who won't take any shit," as people whose word means action and people who are full of hot air, as guys whose girlfriends you can chat up with impunity or guys you don't want to mess with. In most social milieus, a man's reputation depends in part upon the maintenance of a credible threat of violence.[16]

Thus, in the Old South, Southerners displayed what seemed to Northerners to be a prickliness or hypersensitivity when it came to their honor, reacting to affronts that might appear quite "trivial." As one eighteenth-century observer of Virginia noted, fights occurred when one party "has in a merry hour called [the other] a Lubber or a thick-Skull or a Buckskin, or a Scotsman, or perhaps one has mislaid the other's hat, or knocked a peach out of his Hand, or offered him a dram without wiping the mouth of the Bottle; all these, and ten thousand more quite as trifling and ridiculous are thought and accepted as just Causes of immediate Quarrels in which every diabolical Stratagem for Mastery is allowed and practiced."[17]

---

14. Fischer, *supra* note 10, at 765.
15. Gilmore, *supra* note 4, at 67.
16. Martin Daly and Margo Wilson, *Homicide* 128 (1988).
17. Quote cited in Ayers, *supra* note 6, at 21.

And even as the herding economy and the frontier—the forces we believe gave rise to the culture of honor—have receded, the southern sense of honor has remained. If not to the same degree, Southerners today—as we will try to show—still retain a sense of the importance and meaning of the insult and of the redemptive power of violence.

Note on Terms. We must note that the data we describe below apply only to white Southerners and Northerners and mostly to white southern and north-ern males. We do not find regional differences with respect to violence for blacks for reasons that are discussed elsewhere.[18] Thus, we restrict our discus-sion to white Southerners and white Northerners and use the terms "northern" and "southern," accordingly, as shorthand labels.

THE CONTEMPORARY SOUTH

Survey Evidence

Attitude surveys show that Northerners have different views of when violence is acceptable compared with people from the South and, to a lesser extent, the West. When questions ask about violence in general or about violence not re-lated to culture-of-honor concerns, there is little difference among regions. However, when it comes to issues of self-protection and answering affronts, contemporary Southerners are far more likely to approve of violence than Northerners are. Thus, for example, Southerners are twice as likely as North-erners to say that it would be OK for a man to punch a drunk who bumped into the man and his wife on the street (15 percent vs. 8 percent). Or, for a more severe violation, they are also twice as likely as Northerners to endorse a man shooting another because that person sexually assaulted the man's 16-year-old daughter (47 percent vs. 26 percent). Such violence gets incorporated into the southern definition of manhood. Reminiscent of Carter's anecdote, almost one-quarter of all southern respondents would describe someone as "not much of a man" if he did not shoot the person who had assaulted his daughter. The comparable figure in the North was one in 10.[19] Such contem-porary attitudes seem to be a continuation of what historians have identified as two "vital principles" of justice in the Old South—"[1] the idea that order was a system of retributive violence and [2] that each individual was the guardian of his own interests in that respect."[20]

---

18. Nisbett and Cohen, *supra* note 3.

19. Dov Cohen and Richard Nisbett, "Self-Protection and the Culture of Honor: Explaining Southern Violence," 20 *Personality & Soc. Psychol. Bull.* 551 (1994).

20. Fischer, *supra* note 10, at 767; see also Ayers, *supra* note 6.

In addition to simple interpersonal violence, Southerners also seem to believe that violence for the purpose of macrolevel social control is more legitimate than Northerners do. They are more likely to endorse the statement that police should either shoot or shoot to kill when dealing with hoodlums causing trouble, students causing disturbances, or black people rioting in the cities.[21] The legitimacy of violence for social control probably has roots in the slave system, in which violence or the threat of it was used to keep between one-quarter to over half of the entire population enslaved, depending on the state.[22]

In addition, it is also possible that Southerners have extrapolated the principle that *violence in defense of self and honor is OK* to the principle that *violence in defense of the social order is OK*. In both the interpersonal and social control cases, the theme is that violence restores the world to its rightful state after it has been violated by "troublemakers."

There is a famous explanation for violence in the South. That is, there is more homicide in the South because "in the South, there's just more folks who need killing."[23] While this tongue-in-cheek remark is quite extreme, many Southerners probably would endorse a less harsh version of it. That is, there are situations in which violence is appropriate medicine for adults or times when a "good, hard" spanking is necessary for children.[24] In these cases, violence is seen as a necessary tool for restoring order, justice, and goodness in the world.[25]

Experimental Evidence

Such views are not merely symbolic statements of beliefs without consequences in the real world. Southerners act on their beliefs when they are affronted. In a series of experiments, we brought southern and northern subjects into the lab to see how they would respond when they were insulted by a confederate who was actually working with us. In these experiments, as the subject was walking down a narrow hallway, he attempted to pass our confederate, who was working at a file cabinet. As the subject approached, our

21. Monica D. Blumenthal et al., *Justifying Violence* (1972); Cohen and Nisbett, *supra* note 19.

22. Dov Cohen, "Law, Social Policy, and Violence: The Impact of Regional Cultures," 70 *J. Personality & Soc. Psychol.* 961 (1996).

23. J. Wright, "A Matter of Respect," *Reason* 62–64, 64 (February 1997).

24. Cohen and Nisbett, *supra* note 19.

25. Dov Cohen and Joe Vandello, "The Paradox of Politeness," in *The Cultural Shaping of Violence* (Myrdene Anderson ed., 1999); Fischer, *supra* note 10, at 765.

confederate slammed the file drawer shut, bumped into the subject, and then rudely called him an "asshole" after the collision. (In a control condition, the subject was obviously neither bumped nor called an "asshole.")

Northerners and Southerners showed profoundly different reactions to being insulted. First, Northerners tended to regard this incident as an occasion more for amusement than for anger (true of 65 percent of the northern subjects). Southerners, on the other hand, were far more angry than amused (true of 85 percent of southern subjects). Second, their cognitions—as well as their emotions—showed increased hostility. Thus, Southerners who were insulted were far more likely to complete a subsequent written scenario with violence than those Southerners who were not insulted (whereas insulted and uninsulted Northerners did not differ). Third, this increased hostility was actually acted out in subsequent meetings with people and in subsequent challenge situations. Southerners who were insulted became far more domineering when meeting another person (gave firmer handshakes, acted more dominantly) compared with uninsulted Southerners or with their northern counterparts. And insulted Southerners behaved far more aggressively when they encountered another subject (actually another confederate) who was walking down the center of the hallway and who they essentially had to play "chicken" with. This was no false show of bravado as our "chicken"—a 6-foot 3-inch, 250-pound, former college football player—was walking intimidatingly down the hall toward the subject at a good pace.

Perhaps most surprisingly, Northerners and Southerners showed different physiological reactions when they were insulted. Before and after the insulting incident, we measured subjects' levels of testosterone (a hormone associated with aggression, competition, and dominance) and cortisol (a hormone associated with stress and arousal) using saliva samples. Insulted Southerners showed the most dramatic rise for both hormones, compared to both uninsulted Southerners and insulted or uninsulted Northerners.

Finally, we have some indication that Southerners reacted with such aggression and hostility perhaps in part because the insult meant something to them in a way it did not for Northerners. In one of our experiments, subjects were insulted in front of another subject (again, actually a confederate of ours) who witnessed the incident. Under the guise of an interpersonal perception task, we asked our real subjects to guess what this other person thought of them. Northerners who were not insulted in front of this other person and Northerners who actually were insulted in front of this person did not believe they were perceived any differently. For Southerners, however, this was not true. Southerners who had been insulted in front of another person believed that this other person found them lacking in qualities such as courage, toughness, strength, and manliness. To them, the unanswered insult marked them as a "wimp" whose honor and reputation would perhaps be tainted until they could redeem themselves.[26] Their implicit understanding was that others who had witnessed the affront would think less of them. And with this understanding, it is easy to see how Southerners believe a response that restored their masculine standing would be called for.

RITUALS FOR CONFLICT AND RECONCILIATION

Given the meanings of insults and aggressive acts, it is not surprising that Southerners have carved out distinct rituals for precipitating conflict and for resolving it. Because Southerners know that anger is a dangerous thing and can bring hostility in return once it is expressed, we should find Southerners to be slower and less ready to engage in confrontational behaviors. This would square with what many anthropologists have described when they have shown that people in many of the world's most violent cultures are also incredibly friendly, polite, and hospitable in everyday interaction.[27] Rituals of politeness, conflict avoidance, and, ultimately, conflict behaviors derive from people's shared understanding of affronts and the violence used to retaliate for them.[28]

Precipitating Conflict. Norms for congeniality and violence can actually reinforce each other. The price of politeness is that norms of forced friendliness drive conflicts under the surface, prevent people from negotiating the difficulty, and keep hostility bottled up until there is a very serious explosion. That is, surface politeness when people are angry may mask their true feelings and lead to miscommunication (intentional or unintentional) of their true emotions, tolerance thresholds, and intents. Thus, the threat of violence may cause politeness, but strict politeness norms can also lead to more explosive violence. In another lab study, we tried to show this pattern.

In this study, we brought male subjects into the lab and exposed them to a series of mild annoyances from another person. These were nothing like the unequivocal "asshole" insult above but more like small provocations that build

26. Dov Cohen et al., "Insult, Aggression, and the Southern Culture of Honor: An "Experimental Ethnography," 70 *J. Personality & Soc. Psychol.* 945 (1996).

27. Elizabeth Colson, *Tradition and Contract* (1975); Bruce M. Knauft, *Good Company and Violence* (1985).

28. The opposite phenomena is also possible. That is, cultures of honor can create norms for everyday belligerence instead of congeniality and friendliness. In terms of establishing norms for everyday social behavior, multiple equilibriums and multiple solutions to the problems that a culture of honor presents are obviously quite possible. For an extended discussion of this issue, see Cohen and Vandello, *supra* note 25. For an extended discussion of multiple equilibriums and social phenomena generally, see, for example, Timur Kuran, *Private Truths, Public Lies* (1995); Thomas Schelling, *Micromotives and Macrobehavior* (1978).

up and get under a person's skin over time. Thus, we brought subjects into the lab and presented the study under the guise that subjects were participating in a simulated "art therapy" session in which they were to draw pictures of childhood memories using crayons. However, as the experiment unfolded and the subject tried to bring himself "in touch with his inner child," another subject (actually a confederate of ours) began to annoy him when the two were left alone. The confederate repeatedly crumpled up his own drawings and threw them at the garbage, missing but hitting the subject instead. He kept calling the subject "Slick." He stole the subject's crayons. He hit the subject with more paper wads. He commented negatively on the subject's drawings, and so on.

We found the expected pattern of responses. Northern subjects who were in this situation were more confrontational and hostile than were Southerners in the beginning. Then, at some point, probably realizing that their actions were doing little to check the other person's behavior, Northerners began to level out in their anger and conflict behavior (as rated by our confederate and by an experimenter watching the tape on a video feed in another room). Southerners, however, showed a distinctly different pattern. They played it cool in the beginning, staying polite and absorbing the annoyances stoically. Then, after little sign of stirring, some critical point was reached, and they began to show jumps in anger that were far more intense, large, and unpredictable than Northerners had ever shown. Whereas they began the study betraying little emotion, they ended it with levels of conflict and aggression far more severe than Northerners ever showed.[29]

Southern hospitality and aggression go hand in hand. As one commentator observed, it is the tradition of the "iron fist in a velvet glove."[30] Thus, it is not surprising to find that outside the laboratory, in the real world, violence and friendliness go together. Indeed, we have some correlational evidence that in the South politeness and violence have different associations with each other than they do in the North.

We know of no data sets for how polite various cities are, but there is something close. Robert Levine and colleagues have collected data on how friendly and helpful various cities were as experimenters in various locales dropped their pens, asked for change for a quarter, pretended to be blind people needing help crossing the street, and so on.[31] We merged Levine's data with data on

---

29. Cohen and Vandello, *supra* note 25.

30. Rowland Nethaway, "Southern White Men on Honor," *Orlando Sentinel,* July 28, 1996, at G5; Lawrence Lessig, "The Regulation of Social Meaning," 62 *U. Chi. L. Rev.,* 943, 968–72 (1995); and Lawrence Lessig, "Social Meaning and Social Norms," 144 *U. Pa. L. Rev.* 2181, 2183 (1996).

31. Robert Levine et al., "Helping in 36 U.S. Cities," 67 *J. Personality & Soc. Psychol.* 69 (1994).

white male homicide offenders, ages 15–39, for the counties corresponding to Levine's sample. Not surprisingly, in the North, places with more helpfulness and friendliness had less violence. In the South, however, places with more friendliness and helpfulness tended to have slightly more lethal violence. It is important that this was true only for argument- and brawl-related homicides, which are likely to center on conflicts, affronts, and insults and end in the type of violent eruptions previously described. The pattern did not hold true for homicides that were felony related (that is, those that took place during the commission of another felony such as robbery or burglary—and thus would not be condoned or ritualized in the culture-of-honor system).[32] Consistent with what one might expect, for both the North and South, more friendliness was associated with less felony-related violence.

Resolving Conflict. Southerners also seem to have their own rituals for ending a conflict. Just as starting conflicts seems to follow a culturally prescribed script, so too does ending a conflict, and our "art therapy" study above helps illustrate this. At the end of the "art therapy" session—but before subjects were debriefed as to the true nature of the experiment and the confederate's role in it—the confederate went over and attempted to apologize to the subject. For both Southerners and Northerners, how willing subjects were to accept the apology depended tremendously on how the subject himself had behaved during the encounter. But the relationship between expressions of anger and acts of forgiveness was profoundly different for Southerners and Northerners. For Northerners, those who had stayed calm over the course of the study were most willing to shake the confederate's hand and most willing to accept the apology (as rated by the confederate). Northerners who had blown up were genuinely mad, remained so, and were more likely to refuse the apology and the handshake.

The opposite pattern was found for Southerners. Southerners who had absorbed the annoyances without "blowing up" appeared to still hold a grudge and were unaccepting of the confederate's offer of peace. On the other hand, Southerners who had blown up seemed to have expressed themselves and were quite able to forgive the confederate and accept his handshake. It was as if Southerners were following a cultural script that allowed forgiveness once the affronted person had been allowed to stand up for himself and once the provoker had apologized. The implicit script might be something like, "You were a jerk. I blew up at you. Let's shake hands and call it even."

These effects were not merely short-term. Six months later, we sent pictures of our confederates to our subjects and asked them to pick out the per-

---

32. Cohen and Vandello, *supra* note 25.

son who had been provoking them in the lab study. Social psychologists, as well as Freudian theorists, have argued that it is our unresolved, uncompleted conflicts that we remember best and that continue to vex us. And that seems to be what happened here. Few people forgot the person who had done this to them 6 months earlier. However, those who forgot were (*a*) Northerners who had stayed calm and (*b*) Southerners who had "blown up." It appears that people who resolved the conflict in the culturally appropriate way (that is, Northerners who were able to cognitively explain it away, and Southerners who vented their anger) were able to most effectively put the issue behind them.[33]

Caution is warranted because the cell sizes for those who "blew up" were quite small (between 3 and 7 people, depending on the measure. We purposely adopted a stringent criterion for "blow ups" so we could separate those who had actually expressed themselves from those who were only working themselves up to the point of explosion). Yet, across the long-term memory data, hand-shaking data, and acceptance of the apology data, the results appear quite consistent. The crucial point is that for Southerners, once a sufficiently serious provocation occurs, honor must be redeemed. If it is not, the wound is allowed to fester and the conflict may continue. Forgiveness may be given but only when it is asked for and only under the right conditions.

Apologies. As with many cultures of honor, the apology is extremely important in conflict resolution for Southerners.[34] Rather than time healing all wounds, it is the offending party who must attempt and be given the chance to do the healing. This is consistent with what Thomas Kernan noted in his famous essay on "The Jurisprudence of Lawlessness." That is, "Any man who traduces a virtuous woman's character may be shot with impunity by her, or by her husband, or by any near relative; but the offender must first be given an opportunity to deny and disprove the charge, or to retract and apologize."[35] And it also squares with what H. C. Brearley noted in many parts of the South of his day. He wrote that it was impossible to convict someone of murder if the killer had been insulted; but to be exonerated, the killer also had to have warned the victim of his intent to kill if the insult was not compensated for or retracted.[36] The practices showed an understanding both of the meaning of the insult and of a valid mechanism for conflict resolution. The instantiation

---

33. Cohen and Vandello, *supra* note 25.

34. John Gould, "Hiketeia," 43 *J. Hellenic Stud.* 74 (1973).

35. Thomas Kernan, "The Jurisprudence of Lawlessness." Report of the 29th Annual Meeting of the American Bar Association 452 (1906).

36. H. Brearley, "The Pattern of Violence," in *Culture in the South* (W. T. Couch ed. 1934).

of other such culture-of-honor norms in the laws, social policies, and institutions of South is the topic we turn to next.

INSTITUTIONS AS PERPETUATING FORCES

Until the 1960s or 1970s, there were four states where it was legal for a man to kill his wife's lover if he discovered the pair in bed together. Not surprisingly, three of these states were in the South or Southwest (Georgia, New Mexico, and Texas). The fourth was Utah.[37] Thus, understandings of the culture-of-honor stance are not held just at the interpersonal level but also at the level of collective representations. There are some salient examples in the field of law today.

Law and Social Policy

In the contemporary South and West, culture-of-honor ideologies still separate these regions from the North when it comes to self-defense law and gun laws. On the one hand, statutory and case law in 20 of 23 northern states adopts the retreat rule, forcing a person to exhaust all possible options of escape before using deadly force. On the other hand, only about 40 percent of southern and western states require retreat.[38] Thus, they are more likely to adopt the "true man" rule, following the logic of an Oklahoma court that "in free America . . . the wall is to every man's back. It is the wall of his rights; and when he is [assailed] at a place where he has a right to be . . . he may stand and defend himself."[39] In addition, southern and western statutes are also less likely than northern statutes to require an actor to refrain from using deadly force if he could avoid it "by surrendering possession of a thing to a person asserting a claim of right thereto or by complying with a demand that he abstain from any action which he has no duty to take."[40]

Consistent also with the strong ethic of self-protection, southern and western states are likely to have more lenient gun control laws, and southern and western legislators in Congress are more likely to oppose gun control than

37. Laurie J. Taylor, "Provoked Reason in Men and Women," 33 *UCLA L. Rev.* 1679, 1694 (1986).

38. Cohen, *supra* note 22.

39. "Fowler v. State," 126 *Pac. Rep.* 831 (1912), cited in Philip E. Mischke, "Criminal-Law-Homicide-Self-Defense-Duty to Retreat," 48 *Tenn. L. Rev.* 1000, 1007 (1981).

40. Cohen, *supra* note 22; Wayne LaFave and Austin W. Scott, Jr., *Substantive Criminal Law* 661 (1986).

their northern counterparts are.[41] This is no secret. Money from gun control lobbies is more likely to go to legislators of the North, whereas money from the National Rifle Association is more likely to go to legislators of the South and West. Indeed, the issue of guns is often seen in blatantly sectional terms. As one cover of *Southern Guns and Shooter* proclaimed, there is "The Threat from Up North—They're Still Trying to Take Our Guns Away."[42]

Further, the principle approving of violence in self-defense is again likely to be extrapolated to larger issues. Legislators from the South and, to a lesser extent, the West are likely to be more hawkish on military and national defense issues, over and above their conservatism on other matters.[43]

Not all the legitimation of violence can rightly be attributed to the culture of honor, however. It is important to note that, perhaps as a legacy of its history of slavery, southern (though not western) states are particularly likely to have laws more tolerant of coercive or punitive violence. Thus, the laws of the South are more lenient in regard to domestic violence offenders; the schools of the South are more likely to administer corporal punishment; and the justice systems of the South are more likely to actually execute criminals (as opposed to merely sentencing them to death). These last two findings are far more true of the slave South than the nonslave South, consistent with the notion that the slave system legitimized types of coercive violence over and above the sort of violence that a culture of honor might condone. (See also Dan Kahan's argument about the connection in the public's mind between slavery and the use of violence for punishment.)[44]

Media and Organizations

In addition to law, there are other collective representations or institutional forces that embody values about the appropriateness of violence. One that gets a lot of attention is the way the media depict violence, particularly when they present it as a legitimate problem-solving tool. Larry Baron and Murray Straus have shown that citizens in southern and western states are more likely to read violent magazines and watch violent television shows.[45] But, in addition to

---

41. Cohen, *supra* note 22.

42. John S. Reed, *Whistling Dixie* 69 (1990).

43. Cohen, *supra* note 22.

44. Id.; Dan M. Kahan, "What Do Alternative Sanctions Mean?" 63 *U. Chi. L. Rev.* 591, 607–17 (1996).

45. Larry Baron and Murray A. Straus, *Four Theories of Rape* (1989).

this, in one of our field experiments, we have shown that southern and western media (in this case, newspapers) present culture-of-honor-type violence in a more favorable light than do northern newspapers.

In this study, we sent a hypothetical fact sheet about a crime to college newspapers across the country. Reporters knew the facts were not from a real case, but they were asked to turn these facts into a story, for pay, as it might appear in their newspapers. The facts for one story concerned a prototypical culture-of-honor conflict: one man stabs another after being repeatedly provoked and taunted by him with a series of family insults. We content analyzed the stories that these reporters produced and found that the stories were told differently in different regions of the country. In the South and West, newspapers were more likely to play up mitigating circumstances of the crime, more likely to play down aggravating circumstances of the crime, and more likely to write a story that was understanding and sympathetic to the perpetrator. Thus, the way southern and western reporters made meaning of the facts of the case was different from the way their northern counterparts had. It is important to note that we also sent these newspapers facts for a control story involving a beating that happened during a 7-11 robbery. There were no regional differences on this control story, showing that the greater sympathy of southern and western reporters does not extend to all forms of violence but only to those that fall within culture-of-honor norms.[46]

In a second field experiment, we showed that organizations of the South and West are less likely than those of the North to impose extralegal sanctions and stigmatization on those who have committed crimes of violence. In this study, we sent application letters to employers all over the country. The letters—which employers thought were real—came from an "applicant" who described himself as a hard-working 27-year-old man. He had good job experiences but one blemish on his record. The blemish was that he had served time for manslaughter; he killed a man in a bar fight after the man had repeatedly provoked him, claiming that he had slept with the man's fiancée and embarrassing him in front of the rest of the bar's patrons.

In response to this letter, southern and western organizations were far more understanding, warmer, and more cooperative than were their northern counterparts. As one southern employer wrote back to the applicant, "As for your problem of the past, anyone could probably be in the situation you were in. It was just an unfortunate incident that shouldn't be held against you." It is im-

---

46. Dov Cohen and Richard Nisbett, "Field Experiments Examining the Culture of Honor: The Role of Institutions in Perpetuating Norms About Violence," 23 *Personality & Soc. Psychol. Bull.* 1188 (1997).

portant to note that such sympathy was not extended to all law breakers. A control letter was sent to different employers describing a man who had stolen some cars to get himself out of debt. In all regions of the country, this man was treated equally—thus, he tended to get better treatment than the killer from northern employers and worse treatment than the killer from southern employers.

Given the obvious constraints on employers in this situation, the differences in stigmatization are probably even greater in more everyday situations in the North and South. We expect that we might find even more dramatic regional differences if we looked at how people who have committed crimes of violence are treated in informal settings and in normal social interactions where people have much greater discretion in their associations and behavior.[47]

SOCIAL MEANINGS AND SOCIAL ORGANIZATION

Because norms about violence and insult seem to suffuse so much of the South's and West's understanding of the world, one might actually make a counterintuitive prediction regarding violence and the level of social organization. It is a strong current of Western thought that people are naturally aggressive and that we need the "civilizing" forces of family, community, and religion to reign these in. The idea has a long history in political science (for example, the work of Thomas Hobbes) and psychology (the work of Sigmund Freud). Further, it is the basis of a major school of thought in sociology (the social disorganization perspective) and can often be heard in contemporary political rhetoric.

A cultural psychology perspective, however, suggests that this view is too simple and perhaps incorrect. When social meanings of honor, insult, and violence are shared as they are in the South and West, one might expect that the tighter, more cohesive, and more stable the society, the more violence one will see. Rather than reigning in aggressive impulses, tighter social organization in the South and West should reinforce culture-of-honor tendencies. In such a culture, as John Reed has suggested, "violence will emanate from the well-socialized, not just from marginal folk who don't know or care what's expected of them."[48]

And there is some very serious evidence to support this claim. For example, in looking at homicide rates, we have shown that there are distinctly different

47. Cohen and Nisbett, *supra* note 46.

48. John Reed, "Below the Smith and Wesson Line: Reflections on Southern Violence", in *Perspective on the American South* 12 (Merle Black and John Reed eds. 1981).

associations in the North, South, and West between violence and social organization. We measured community stability in terms of the percent of people living in the same house or same county that they were 5 years ago. In the North, consistent with traditional views, counties with more stability had less argument- and brawl-related violence. In the South and West, stable communities actually tended to have more such argument- and brawl-related violence.

This was true for family stability indicators as well. In the North, counties with more stable, traditional nuclear family structures tended to have less argument- and brawl-related homicides. In the South and West, counties with more stable nuclear family arrangements tended to have more such violence.[49] The results suggest that, rather than dampening aggressive impulses, community and family stability may actually help reinforce culture-of-honor values and violence in the South.

The pattern holds true not just for lethal violence but for more tame forms of "legitimate violence" as well (for example, readership of violent magazines, viewership of violent television programs, production of college football players, expenditures on state national guard units, and so forth). Data on such indicators of violence consumption were collected by Baron and Straus.[50] And sorting states by their levels of social organization (again measured in terms of family stability, community stability, and religious affiliation), it can be shown that in the North, states with higher levels of social organization consume less such violence. In the South and West, however, states with higher levels of social organization actually consume slightly more such violence.[51]

Further, similar patterns exist for data collected at the individual level as well as the community level. Analyzing surveys done by the National Opinion Research Center, we have shown that Northerners who are in more traditional nuclear family arrangements and who are closer to their families tend to be relatively less endorsing of honor-related violence and relatively less likely to own guns, whereas Southerners and Westerners in close-knit traditional families tend to be relatively more likely to endorse honor-related violence and relatively more likely to own guns. It is important to note that these same Southerners and Westerners from close-knit families are not relatively more likely to endorse violence unrelated to culture-of-honor concerns.[52] Thus, cohesive social organization only makes them relatively more accepting of culture-of-honor-type violence, not violence in general.

---

49. Cohen, Vandello, and Rantilla, *supra* note 3; Dov Cohen, "Culture, Social Organization, and Patterns of Violence," *J. Personality & Soc. Psychol.* (1998).

50. Baron and Straus, *supra* note 45.

51. Cohen, Vandello, and Rantilla, *supra* note 3; Cohen, *supra* note 49.

52. Cohen, Vandello, and Rantilla, *supra* note 3.

Of all the methods we have used, public opinion surveys have usually shown the weakest regional effects.[53] And so as one might expect, the interaction effects described above for the attitude data were quite small. Yet, they were consistent in direction, consistent with the homicide and violence consumption data, and generally consistent with the notion that in a culture of honor where the meaning of the insult is understood as something that must be answered, it will be the "best socialized . . . who understand what's expected of them [and who] will be violent sometimes."[54]

LAWFUL VIOLENCE

Cultures continually evolve. The South is changing, and not everything we have described is true for all people throughout the South—it never has been and never will be. Yet throughout the last several centuries, there seems to be something of a common understanding Southerners have about the importance of honor, insult, and violence that shapes their attitudes, behaviors, conflict rituals, institutional arrangements, and collective representations.

In 1906, Kernan, of Baton Rouge, Louisiana, formulated the "fundamental rules" of a "jurisprudence of lawlessness" that "prevailed within the southern courts where he had long practiced." The first seven of his 10 cardinal rules can be summarized in about three principles: (*a*) Rape, adultery, seduction of an "innocent," and impugning a woman's chastity are all crimes punishable by death, usually at the hands of a male relative of the victim; (*b*) survivors of duels or fair fights must be acquitted; and (*c*) an insult is "equal to a blow . . . [and] justifies an assault."[55]

Whereas this was and is an exaggeration, there is something to Kernan's central point. That is, there is a coherent belief system about honor and violence that organizes southern attitudes and behaviors. In this context, violence takes on a different meaning for Southerners than it does for Northerners. As Reed has suggested, Southerners "actually don't *see* much of the violence around them, don't register it as 'lawlessness,' because it *isn't* 'lawless.' It is lawful violence in the sociological if not the legal sense: more-or-less predictable, more-or-less expected, (in consequence) more or less taken for granted. It's effectively invisible—something like wallpaper."[56]

---

53. For possible reasons, see discussion in Dov Cohen, "Ifs and Thens in Cultural Psychology," in *Advances in Social Cognition* (Robert S. Wyer, Jr., ed. 1997).

54. Reed, *supra* note 48, at 15.

55. Kernan, *supra* note 35, at 450–53; Ayers, *supra* note 6, at 266.

56. Reed, *supra* note 48, at 12.

In attitude surveys, it is not the case that Southerners are more likely to endorse violence in the abstract, nor are they more likely to view it as a positive thing. In fact, there is evidence that in the abstract Southerners are more likely to view violence as "bad," "unnecessary," "avoidable," and "worthless."[57] Yet, when it comes to violence specifically related to insults, threats, and affronts, southern and northern attitudes depart in the ways described above. Perhaps this is because—as Reed suggests—such actions are not violence or perhaps—as Kernan suggests—such actions are considered self-defense because insults and affronts themselves amount to blows. If violence to Southerners means an unjustified act of offensive aggression, then actions in response to affronts are not really violence under this way of conceiving the world.

To understand the greater rate of homicide in the South, we must understand the cultural meaning system that gives rise to it. Northerners and Southerners have different conceptions of the self, honor, and masculinity. They have different ideas about what affronts do to social identity and what insults mean. They have different rituals for negotiating, avoiding, and reconciling conflicts. They have different views about what makes a violent act legitimate or perhaps even what violence itself is. They have institutions, collective representations, and social systems that embody such understandings. And the tighter and more close-knit communities are, the more such ideologies are perpetuated. Perhaps this in itself is compelling evidence that southern violence is not just deviance and lawlessness. Rather, southern violence is a product of a coherent, complete meaning system that defines the self, insults, honor, rituals for conflict, and the tools and methods—occasionally including violence—that are to be used when order is disrupted.

---

57. Cohen and Nisbett, *supra* note 19, at 554.

E.
Values and Norms

Meaning theorists focus on the link between social conditions and individual internal states; their explanations include situational mechanisms. For these scholars, social conditions—productive activities, interaction, and so forth—produce order through their effects on meaning. Once people share common meanings, then presumably the problem of social order is solved. Conversely, the destruction of common meaning (as is associated with the Tower of Babel) leads to a breakdown of order. These theorists are probably on firm ground when they suggest that a common language and some shared general concepts are *necessary* for the evolution of cooperation and hence for social order.

At the same time, these elements evidently are *insufficient* to produce cooperation. Societies that share a common language and concepts can also have low levels of social order. Banfield's portrait of amoral familism in Montegrano is a perfect example. Cohen and Vandello's description of the American South, with its higher levels of violence than the North, is another. Indeed, one might just as well suppose that a common language and shared concepts are also requisites for sustained interpersonal and intergroup conflict rather than for social order. Thus we must look to other mechanisms to fully explain the emergence of order.

To cooperate, individuals not only have to be able to understand one another; they also must *agree* on one or more mutual ends or goals—and *act* accordingly. This is an old adage in team sports. How many times have you heard sports commentators proclaim that a group of unselfish basketball players committed to winning a league championship will be more successful than an equally skilled group of players who assiduously pad their individual scoring statistics and slough off on defense? If some people in a society drive on the left side of the road and others drive on the right, this is a recipe for the emergency room. If some people believe in obeying the law and others do not, this will increase criminal activity. If some people believe that government should be upheld and others seek to overthrow it, this bodes ill for future political stability.

All well and good, but where does the requisite consensus come from? And why do people behave in ways that are consistent with the consensus? One answer is values and norms. These are cultural phenomena that aid cooperation by prescribing and proscribing particular kinds of behavior. If norms and values contribute to order, then we need to understand how they work. Two questions in particular arise with regard to this solution to the problem of order. How do norms and values emerge? And what makes them effective?

VALUES

Although values and norms often are conflated by social scientists, it makes sense to distinguish between them. Values are internal criteria for evaluation.[1] Let's pick this definition apart. "Criteria for evaluation" refers to the criteria that we apply when we deem some actions or events more or less praiseworthy. And "internal" means that these evaluative criteria are located within the individual's mind rather than imposed from without. According to this definition, if we value fairness then we will evaluate outcomes—a grade on an exam, a decision in a court case, or the size of a piece of pie—in terms of how fair they are. Or if we value honesty, we will evaluate accordingly—disapproving of hypocritical politicians, and becoming angry with a lover who deceives us.

There are two kinds of values. *Individual* values consist of desires—the preference for chocolate over vanilla, Mozart over the Rolling Stones, vegeta-

---

1. Values are also thought to be general and relatively durable. *General* means that values cover a wide range of behaviors rather than a limited one. *Durable* means that values persist over long periods of the life course. Although values and preferences are both internal states, they differ as well. Preferences are more specific and transient than are values.

bles over beef, blondes over brunettes, and so forth—and emanate from some complex (and ill-understood) amalgam of our genetic endowment and personal experiences. In contrast, *social* values, which enable us to examine critically our desires and modify them according to ethical principles, emanate from outside of ourselves. Their source lies in the values and norms embodied by friends, associates, and the groups to which we belong or aspire to belong. When we adopt the values and norms of these other people and groups, in effect we "internalize" them in our own minds.

The readings on values explain order by describing how internalization occurs. Sigmund Freud's "Civilization and Its Discontents" offers a psychological explanation of the internalization process, a distinctive set of behavioral assumptions, and a conclusion about the precariousness of social order. According to Freud, social order is problematic because people are motivated by hedonism. The individual's relentless pursuit of pleasure necessarily brings him into conflict with his neighbors. People are not gentle creatures craving others' esteem; on the contrary, they are inherently aggressive. Freud goes so far as to say that man is a wolf to man. If this aggressiveness were to go unchecked, there would be little prospect of attaining any social order. But because there is a considerable amount of order—the early-twentieth-century Vienna of Freud's youth was one of the most cultured cities on earth—some mechanism must be responsible for its attainment.

What then makes social order possible? Freud's explanation begins with a condition of extreme dependence—infancy. At first, the infant has no conception of the self. He is unable to distinguish himself from the rest of the world. But as soon as the infant's desires are thwarted—the first time he cries out in need and no one appears—an awful realization dawns. The infant learns that he is powerless and utterly dependent on a parent for love and sustenance. This dependence makes him extremely vulnerable not only to the loss of love but also to parental punishment. These losses must be avoided at all costs, but by what means? The solution rests on a self-deception: the infant takes the parent into the self (literally, internalizing the parent) and allows this newly installed "parent," the superego, to monitor his behavior before it gets enacted. Only in this way can the fearsome sanctions of loss of love and punishment be avoided. Thus a condition (dependence) leads to an internal state (the superego).

The superego, in turn, motivates people to behave cooperatively. Civilized society contains aggressiveness with the help of this agency within the individual. The superego accomplishes this essential task by watching over the individual "like a garrison in a conquered city" (see p. 104). Although the superego is unobservable, Freud finds ample evidence for its existence in the pervasiveness of the sense of *guilt*. Guilt emanates from what is popularly known as the conscience. In the old Walt Disney children's film, Jiminy Cricket constantly reminds Gepetto's stubborn little wooden doll to let his conscience be his guide. Freud's own interpretation is considerably darker than that found in *Pinocchio*: conscience makes cowards of us all.

This particular solution to the problem of order therefore relies on two types of mechanisms. The condition of dependence leads to the development of the superego. The superego in turn is constantly on guard to deter antisocial actions. It fosters social order by transforming inherently aggressive individuals into relatively docile, cooperative beings.

Émile Durkheim offers a sunnier explanation. Although at first glance his discussion appears to have a much narrower scope than does Freud's essay, this impression is misleading. Durkheim explores the determinants of a behavior—suicide—that is severely frowned on in all Western societies. Because suicide is so pervasively discouraged, suicide rates serve as an indicator of social order more generally. Durkheim notes that these rates vary systematically across groups over time. He identifies different types of suicide and offers an explanation for each. His explanations rest on social values.

We have already discussed one type—egoistic suicide—in a previous section ("Theory Is Explanation"). Durkheim argues that egoistic suicide rates are affected by levels of social integration. In weakly integrated social groups—Protestants as against Catholics and Jews, single people as against married couples, families with no children as against those with children—individuals are insufficiently attached to their respective groups and have little sense of purpose. They therefore are prone to egoistic suicide.[2] This individual propensity aggregates to produce higher suicide rates for the group.

In the next reading, Durkheim explains another type of suicide—anomic suicide. This explanation relies on a different causal factor and different mechanisms. Durkheim argues that in eras of relative stability, society provides people with a very good idea about the kinds of lives they are destined to lead. This expectation is crucial because it serves to limit their aspirations. For instance, in England no commoner can ever hope to be king. But in situations of rapid change—as a result of technological progress, economic upturns and downturns, natural and military disasters, and so forth—society is in flux and no longer provides such limits. In the absence of regulation, expectations are unlimited, whereas the means of obtaining desired ends are invariably finite. Individuals experience a state of anomie.

This internal state is frustrating to say the least. Durkheim assumes that people can never be satisfied with their lives when they are experiencing this kind of uncertainty. People are wont to compare their means, or their ability to get what they want, with their expectations about what they ought to have. The wider the gap between their means and their expectations—which is at its peak during times of societal flux—the greater the dissatisfaction. In turn, this discomfort and dissatisfaction (an internal state) leads to suicide (an individual behavior). The more satisfied individuals are, the less likely they are to commit suicide; the more dissatisfied, the more they are at risk of taking their own lives. Thus in the absence of regulation, individuals are more likely to kill themselves.[3]

This propensity of individuals to take their own lives can be aggregated to predict suicide rates for various groups. The greater the number of dissatisfied

---

2. By the same token, people who belong to very highly integrated social groups—infantry platoons, police partnerships, primitive tribes—have such strong attachments that sometimes they are willing to commit *altruistic* suicide when they perceive this to be in the group's interest. If the cause of egoistic suicide is excessive individualism, the cause of altruistic suicide is excessive social integration.

3. If insufficient normative regulation is responsible for anomic suicide, Durkheim states (in a brief aside) that excessive regulation leads to a fourth type—fatalistic suicide.

people, the more the individual propensity toward suicide and the higher the actual rate of suicide. Note that this theory has at least one highly counterintuitive empirical implication: if Durkheim is right, then—all things equal—lottery winners ought to have a higher risk of suicide than losers.

As this discussion illustrates, Durkheim relies on the same three *types* of mechanisms to explain egoistic and anomic suicide, although the causal factors and assumptions about actors vary. These three types of mechanisms are as follows: a proposition about the kinds of social conditions that promote a particular internal state; an assumption about the way that internal state affects behavior; and a simple principle of aggregation that yields the social outcome. Relying on these mechanisms, Durkheim is able to explain variation in rates of suicide across different conditions.

Although both Freud and Durkheim view internalization as a solution to the problem of order, their explanations are quite different. For Freud, regulation is aversive; it makes people unhappy: "the price we pay for our advance in civilization is a loss of happiness through the heightening of guilt" (Freud [1930] 1961, 91). Because social order comes at such a personal cost in Freud's theory, it is an inherently precarious state, constantly at risk of subversion. By contrast, Durkheim argues that without regulation, people are distressed. Socially determined limits therefore contribute to satisfaction.

NORMS

In contrast to values, norms are external criteria for evaluation. Typically, they refer to behavior, telling us what people ought to do in a given situation. Unlike values, which are internal, norms are enforced externally. This distinction is vital: because norms are external, they must rest on sanctions generated outside of us to be effective.

Evidence about norms is abundant. Etiquette books inform us about proper behavior at weddings, funerals, baseball games, birthdays, and other kinds of social events. The advice offered in daily newspapers by the likes of

Ann Landers promulgates norms by telling us what we ought to do in specific circumstances.

Norms not only tell us how to behave, however. Violations have social repercussions. Consider the case of George O'Leary. In 2001, the University of Notre Dame embarked on a national search for a football coach. Notre Dame is the plum college football coaching job in this country, and the university had a plethora of able candidates from which to choose. After some deliberation, it hired the head coach at Georgia Tech, George O'Leary. O'Leary was by no means selected at random; he had achieved great success coaching the Yellow Jackets. Notre Dame greeted his appointment with fanfare, and it was featured prominently in the national media.

Soon after O'Leary was hired, however, a newspaper revealed that he had lied on his resumé about events that had occurred decades previously. The resumé falsely stated that O'Leary had earned a master's degree and three varsity letters as a college football player. Notre Dame asked O'Leary to resign. Five days after he was hired, O'Leary was out of a job. Months later, a similar fate befell two assistant coaches hired by O'Leary's successor at Georgia Tech, as well as the women's basketball coach at Vanderbilt University. Meanwhile, a prize-winning historian at Mount Holyoke College, Joseph Ellis, was excoriated in the national press and suspended from his teaching job for lying to his students about his participation in the Vietnam War.

All these people were performing at the top of their game. Nobody questioned their ability to do their jobs; the only thing that was questioned was their truthfulness. These cases indicate that a norm of truth telling exists in American universities and that this norm is enforced with strong sanctions. This academic norm probably evolved from norms in the early scientific academies that sought to protect the purity of scientific research from external influences and to promote a spirit of organized skepticism that helps deter scientific fraud (Merton 1957, chap. 15).[4] (Note further that our recounting of

---

4. When scientists are revealed to have falsified data, their careers are imperiled (see the journalistic accounts in Broad and Wade 1983, and Taubes 1993).

these stories in this volume constitutes yet another sanction of these individuals and simultaneously serves to reinforce the norm of truth telling.)

Where do such norms come from? In "Explaining the Emergence of Norms," Christine Horne describes two arguments. Whereas Freud and Durkheim explain how values, whatever they might be, are internalized, Horne explains how people come to evaluate particular behaviors negatively or positively. That is, she describes arguments that explain the *content* of rules.

One perspective suggests that norms reflect behavior that is common. A norm develops because as people observe a particular behavior more frequently, they come to attach a sense of oughtness to it. In this view, as divorce rates increase, we would expect people to be more accepting of divorce. Or, when students on college campuses perceive that binge drinking is frequent, they are less critical of such behavior. Explanations of this type focus on how the frequency of a behavior (a social condition) leads to individuals' evaluations of that behavior (an internal state).

The other perspective assumes that people are concerned with their treatment by others. Individuals will disapprove of actions that hurt them and encourage those that benefit them. For example, to the extent that loud partying makes it difficult for people in the rest of the neighborhood to sleep, a norm may emerge regarding the time of night at which people ought to quiet down. In this view, the consequences of actions produce evaluations of those actions. The underlying assumption here is that people are self-interested—preferring behaviors in others that benefit themselves.

Once an act is defined as normative, what makes it effective? Values are effective because they are internalized. But norms must rely on external enforcement. That is, people follow norms because they receive social encouragement for doing so. But if external sanctions are necessary for norms to affect behavior, then we must explain the existence of such reactions.

Under what conditions will sanctioning occur? Instrumental individuals will consider the consequences of engaging in enforcement activity. How much effort will it take? What will the outcome be? The more interested they are in seeing the other person stop a behavior, the more likely they are to take action. So, for example, a person dining in a restaurant will weigh the pleasure of a smoke-free dinner against the discomfort of asking a smoker at a nearby table to put out a cigarette. This suggests that norms are more likely to be enforced if doing so will provide benefits for group members with minimal effort for enforcement.

What empirical evidence is there for the role of values and norms in the production of social order? In "Behavior in Public Places," Erving Goffman describes some everyday norms that govern face-to-face encounters and argues that they facilitate interaction. Such norms reflect the view that, in Goffman's words, "the welfare of the individual ought not to be put in jeopardy through his capacity to open himself up for encounters. In the case of acquainted persons, a willingness to give social recognition saves the other from the affront of being overlooked; in the case of unacquainted persons, willingness to refrain from soliciting encounters saves the other from being exploited by inopportune overtures and requests" (see p. 140). Goffman's discussion is consistent with the argument that norms emerge in response to the consequences of particular behaviors. His description illustrates the extent to which norms govern our workaday life, highlighting norms of which we may not even be aware.

In "Altruistic Punishment in Humans," Ernst Fehr and Simon Gächter focus on explaining why people enforce norms. As Horne points out, many explanations assume that self-interested individuals will take into account the possible consequences of punishing deviant behavior. Fehr and Gachter disagree, however. They suggest that human beings feel negatively toward those who take advantage of other group members. Their experimental evidence suggests that norms are enforced because of something internal. Although internal states are not sufficient to ensure that individuals behave cooperatively, they are helpful in motivating people to enforce norms. This explanation of order relies on *both* norms and values. Individuals are self-interested enough to want to violate norms, but they have values that encourage them to punish deviance.

Both values and norms tell us what behaviors are appropriate or inappropriate, moral or immoral. But they differ in what makes them effective. Social values are internalized and enforced through guilt and self-control. By contrast, norms are enforced through external sanctions. People are more likely to follow norms when there are social consequences for their compliance or disobedience.

REFERENCES

Broad, William J., and Nicholas Wade. 1983. *Betrayers of the Truth.* New York: Simon and Schuster.
Freud, Sigmund. [1930] 1961. *Civilization and Its Discontents.* Translated by James Strachey. New York: W. W. Norton.
Merton, Robert King. 1957. *Social Theory and Social Structure.* Glencoe, Ill.: Free Press.
Taubes, Gary. 1993. *Bad Science: The Short Life and Weird Times of Cold Fusion.* New York: Random House.

9.

Civilization and Its Discontents

SIGMUND FREUD, 1930

. . . [M]en are not gentle creatures who want to be loved, and who at the most can defend themselves if they are attacked; they are, on the contrary, creatures among whose instinctual endowments is to be reckoned a powerful share of aggressiveness. As a result, their neighbour is for them not only a potential helper or sexual object, but also someone who tempts them to satisfy their aggressiveness on him, to exploit his capacity for work without compensation, to use him sexually without his consent, to seize his possessions, to humiliate him, to cause him pain, to torture and to kill him. *Homo homini lupus.* Who, in the face of all his experience of life and of history, will have the courage to dispute this assertion? As a rule this cruel aggressiveness waits for some provocation or puts itself at the service of some other purpose, whose goal might also have been reached by milder measures. In circumstances that are favourable to it, when the mental counter-forces which ordinarily inhibit it are out of action, it also manifests itself spontaneously and reveals man as a savage beast to whom consideration towards his own kind is something alien. Anyone who calls to mind the atrocities committed during the racial migrations or the invasions of the Huns, or by the people known as Mongols under Jenghiz Khan and Tamerlane, or at the capture of Jerusalem by the pious Crusaders, or even, indeed, the horrors of the recent World War—anyone who calls these things to mind will have to bow humbly before the truth of this view.

The existence of this inclination to aggression, which we can detect in ourselves and justly assume to be present in others, is the factor which disturbs our relations with our neighbour and which forces civilization into such a high expenditure [of energy]. In consequence of this primary mutual hostility of human beings, civilized society is perpetually threatened with disintegration.

From *Civilization and Its Discontents* by Sigmund Freud, translated by James Strachey. Copyright © 1961 by James Strachey, renewed 1989 by Alix Strachey. Used by permission of W. W. Norton & Company, Inc. Sigmund Freud © Copyrights, The Institute of Psychoanalysis and The Hogarth Press for permission to quote from *The Standard Edition of the Complete Psychological Works of Sigmund Freud,* translated and edited by James Strachey. Reprinted by permission of The Random House Group Limited.

The interest of work in common would not hold it together; instinctual passions are stronger than reasonable interests. Civilization has to use its utmost efforts in order to set limits to man's aggressive instincts and to hold the manifestations of them in check by psychical reaction-formations. Hence, therefore, the use of methods intended to incite people into identifications and aim-inhibited relationship of love, hence the restriction upon sexual life, and hence too the ideal's commandment to love one's neighbour as oneself—a commandment which is really justified by the fact that nothing else runs so strongly counter to the original nature of man. In spite of every effort, these endeavours of civilization have not so far achieved very much. It hopes to prevent the crudest excesses of brutal violence by itself assuming the right to use violence against criminals, but the law is not able to lay hold of the more cautious and refined manifestations of human aggressiveness. The time comes when each one of us has to give up as illusions the expectations which, in his youth, he pinned upon his fellow-men, and when he may learn how much difficulty and pain has been added to his life by their ill-will. At the same time, it would be unfair to reproach civilization with trying to eliminate strife and competition from human activity. These things are undoubtedly indispensable. But opposition is not necessarily enmity; it is merely misused and made an occasion for enmity.

The communists believe that they have found the path to deliverance from our evils. According to them, man is wholly good and is well-disposed to his neighbour; but the institution of private property has corrupted his nature. The ownership of private wealth gives the individual power, and with it the temptation to ill-treat his neighbour; while the man who is excluded from possession is bound to rebel in hostility against his oppressor. If private property were abolished, all wealth held in common, and everyone allowed to share in the enjoyment of it, ill-will and hostility would disappear among men. Since everyone's needs would be satisfied, no one would have any reason to regard another as his enemy; all would willingly undertake the work that was necessary. I have no concern with any economic criticisms of the communist system; I cannot enquire into whether the abolition of private property is expedient or advantageous. But I am able to recognize that the psychological premises on which the system is based are an untenable illusion. In abolishing private property we deprive the human love of aggression of one of its instruments, certainly a strong one, though certainly not the strongest; but we have in no way altered the differences in power and influence which are misused by aggressiveness, nor have we altered anything in its nature. Aggressiveness was not created by property. It reigned almost without limit in primitive times, when property was still very scanty, and it already shows itself in the nursery almost before property has given up its primal, anal form; it forms the basis of every relation of affection and love among people (with the single exception, perhaps, of the mother's relation to her male child). If we do away with personal rights over material wealth, there still remains prerogative in the field of sexual relationships, which is bound to become the source of the strongest dislike and the most violent hostility among men who in other respects are on equal footing. If we were to remove this factor, too, by allowing complete freedom of sexual life and thus abolishing the family, the germ-cell of civilization, we cannot, it is true, easily foresee what new paths the development of civilization could take; but one thing we can expect, and that is that this indestructible feature of human nature will follow it there.

It is clearly not easy for men to give up the satisfaction of this inclination to aggression. They do not feel comfortable without it. The advantage which a comparatively small cultural group offers of allowing this instinct an outlet in the form of hostility against intruders is not to be despised. It is always possible to bind together a considerable number of people in love, so long as there are other people left over to receive the manifestations of their aggressiveness. I once discussed the phenomenon that it is precisely communities with adjoining territories, and related to each other in other ways as well, who are engaged in constant feuds and in ridiculing each other—like the Spaniards and Portuguese, for instance, the North Germans and South Germans, the English and Scotch, and so on. I gave this phenomenon the name of 'the narcissism of minor differences', a name which does not do much to explain it. We can now see that it is a convenient and relatively harmless satisfaction of the inclination to aggression, by means of which cohesion between the members of the community is made easier. In this respect the Jewish people, scattered everywhere, have rendered most useful services to the civilizations of the countries that have been their hosts; but unfortunately all the massacres of the Jews in the Middle Ages did not suffice to make that period more peaceful and secure for their Christian fellows. When once the Apostle Paul had posited universal love between men as the foundation of his Christian community, extreme intolerance on the part of Christendom towards those who remained outside of it became the inevitable consequence. To the Romans, who had not founded their communal life as a State upon love, religious intolerance was something foreign, although with them religion was a concern of the State and the State was permeated by religion. Neither was it an unaccountable chance that the dream of a Germanic world-domination called for anti-Semitism as its complement; and it is intelligible that the attempt to establish a new, communist civilization in Russia should find its psychological support in the persecution of the bourgeois. One only wonders, with concern, what the Soviets will do after they have wiped out their bourgeois.

If civilization imposes such great sacrifices not only on man's sexuality but on his aggressivity, we can understand better why it is hard for him to be happy in that civilization. In fact, primitive man was better off in knowing no restrictions of instinct. To counterbalance this, his prospects of enjoying this happiness for any length of time were very slender. Civilized man has exchanged a portion of his possibilities of happiness for a portion of security.

Why do our relatives, the animals, not exhibit any such cultural struggle? We do not know. Very probably some of them—the bees, the ants, the termites—strove for thousands of years before they arrived at the State institutions, the distribution of functions and the restrictions on the individual, for which we admire them today. It is a mark of our present condition that we know from our own feelings that we should not think ourselves happy in any of these animal States or in any of the roles assigned in them to the individual. In the case of other animal species it may be that a temporary balance has been reached between the influences of their environment and the mutually contending instincts within them, and that thus a cessation of development has come about. It may be that in primitive man a fresh access of libido kindled a renewed burst of activity on the part of the destructive instinct. There are a great many questions here to which as yet there is no answer.

Another question concerns us more nearly. What means does civilization employ in order to inhibit the aggressiveness which opposes it, to make it harmless, to get rid of it, perhaps? . . . This we can study in the history of the development of the individual. What happens in him to render his desire for aggression innocuous? Something very remarkable, which we should never have guessed and which is nevertheless quite obvious. His aggressiveness is introjected, internalized; it is, in point of fact, sent back to where it came from—that is, it is directed towards his own ego. There it is taken over by a portion of the ego, which sets itself over against the rest of the ego as super-ego, and which now, in the form of 'conscience', is ready to put into action against the ego the same harsh aggressiveness that the ego would have liked to satisfy upon other, extraneous individuals. The tension between the harsh super-ego and the ego that is subjected to it, is called by us the sense of guilt; it expresses itself as a need for punishment. Civilization, therefore, obtains mastery over the individual's dangerous desire for aggression by weakening and disarming it and by setting up an agency within him to watch over it, like a garrison in a conquered city.

As to the origin of the sense of guilt, the analyst has different views from other psychologists; but even he does not find it easy to give an account of it. To begin with, if we ask how a person comes to have a sense of guilt, we arrive at an answer which cannot be disputed: a person feels guilty (devout people would say 'sinful') when he has done something which he knows to be 'bad'. But then we notice how little this answer tells us. Perhaps, after some hesitation, we shall add that even when a person has not actually *done* the bad thing but has only recognized in himself an *intention* to do it, he may regard himself as guilty; and the question then arises of why the intention is regarded as equal to the deed. Both cases, however, presuppose that one had already recognized that what is bad is reprehensible, is something that must not be carried out. How is this judgement arrived at? We may reject the existence of an original, as it were natural, capacity to distinguish good from bad. What is bad is often not at all what is injurious or dangerous to the ego; on the contrary, it may be something which is desirable and enjoyable to the ego. Here, therefore, there is an extraneous influence at work, and it is this that decides what is to be called good or bad. Since a person's own feelings would not have led him along this path, he must have had a motive for submitting to this extraneous influence. Such a motive is easily discovered in his helplessness and his dependence on other people, and it can best be designated as fear of loss of love. If he loses the love of another person upon whom he is dependent, he also ceases to be protected from a variety of dangers. Above all, he is exposed to the danger that this stronger person will show his superiority in the form of punishment. At the beginning, therefore, what is bad is whatever causes one to be threatened with loss of love. For fear of that loss, one must avoid it. This, too, is the reason why it makes little difference whether one has already done the bad thing or only intends to do it. In either case the danger only sets in if and when the authority discovers it, and in either case the authority would behave in the same way.

This state of mind is called a 'bad conscience'; but actually it does not deserve this name, for at this stage the sense of guilt is clearly only a fear of loss of love, 'social' anxiety. In small children it can never be anything else, but in many adults, too, it has only changed to the extent that the place of the father or the two parents is taken by the larger human community. Consequently, such people habitually allow themselves to do any bad thing which promises them enjoyment, so long as they are sure that the authority will not know anything about it or cannot blame them for it; they are afraid only of being found out. Present-day society has to reckon in general with this state of mind.

A great change takes place only when the authority is internalized through the establishment of a super-ego. The phenomena of conscience then reach a higher stage. Actually, it is not until now that we should speak of conscience or a sense of guilt. At this point, too, the fear of being found out comes to an end; the distinction, moreover, between doing something bad and wishing to do it disappears entirely, since nothing can be hidden from the super-ego, not even thoughts. It is true that the seriousness of the situation from a real point of view has passed away, for the new authority, the super-ego, has no motive that we know of for ill-treating the ego, with which it is intimately bound up;

but genetic influence, which leads to the survival of what is past and has been surmounted, makes itself felt in the fact that fundamentally things remain as they were at the beginning. The super-ego torments the sinful ego with the same feeling of anxiety and is on the watch for opportunities of getting it punished by the external world.

At this second stage of development, the conscience exhibits a peculiarity which was absent from the first stage and which is no longer easy to account for. For the more virtuous a man is, the more severe and distrustful is its behaviour, so that ultimately it is precisely those people who have carried saintliness furthest who reproach themselves with the worst sinfulness. This means that virtue forfeits some part of its promised reward; the docile and continent ego does not enjoy the trust of its mentor, and strives in vain, it would seem, to acquire it. The objection will at once be made that these difficulties are artificial ones, and it will be said that a stricter and more vigilant conscience is precisely the hallmark of a moral man. Moreover, when saints call themselves sinners, they are not so wrong, considering the temptations to instinctual satisfaction to which they are exposed in a specially high degree—since, as is well known, temptations are merely increased by constant frustration, whereas an occasional satisfaction of them causes them to diminish, at least for the time being. The field of ethics, which is so full of problems, presents us with another fact: namely that ill-luck—that is, external frustration—so greatly enhances the power of the conscience in the super-ego. As long as things go well with a man, his conscience is lenient and lets the ego do all sorts of things; but when misfortune befalls him, he searches his soul, acknowledges his sinfulness, heightens the demands of his conscience, imposes abstinences on himself and punishes himself with penances. Whole peoples have behaved in this way, and still do. This, however, is easily explained by the original infantile stage of conscience, which, as we see, is not given up after the introjection into the super-ego, but persists alongside of it and behind it. Fate is regarded as a substitute for the parental agency. If a man is unfortunate it means that he is no longer loved by this highest power; and, threatened by such a loss of love, he once more bows to the parental representative in his super-ego—a representative whom, in his days of good fortune, he was ready to neglect. This becomes especially clear where Fate is looked upon in the strictly religious sense of being nothing else than an expression of the Divine Will. The people of Israel had believed themselves to be the favourite child of God, and when the great Father caused misfortune after misfortune to rain down upon this people of his, they were never shaken in their belief in his relationship to them or questioned his power or righteousness. Instead, they produced the prophets, who held up their sinfulness before them; and out of their sense of guilt they created the overstrict commandments of their priestly religion. It is remarkable how differently a primitive man behaves. If he has met with a misfortune, he does not throw the blame on himself but on his fetish, which has obviously not done its duty, and he gives it a thrashing instead of punishing himself.

Thus we know of two origins of the sense of guilt: one arising from fear of an authority, and the other, later on, arising from fear of the super-ego. The first insists upon a renunciation of instinctual satisfactions; the second, as well as doing this, presses for punishment, since the continuance of the forbidden wishes cannot be concealed from the super-ego. We have also learned how the severity of the super-ego—the demands of conscience—is to be understood. It is simply a continuation of the severity of the external authority, to which it has succeeded and which it has in part replaced. We now see in what relationship the renunciation of instinct stands to the sense of guilt. Originally, renunciation of instinct was the result of fear of an external authority: one renounced one's satisfactions in order not to lose its love. If one has carried out this renunciation, one is, as it were, quits with the authority and no sense of guilt should remain. But with fear of the super-ego the case is different. Here, instinctual renunciation is not enough, for the wish persists and cannot be concealed from the super-ego. Thus, in spite of the renunciation that has been made, a sense of guilt comes about. This constitutes a great economic disadvantage in the erection of a super-ego, or, as we may put it, in the formation of a conscience. Instinctual renunciation now no longer has a completely liberating effect; virtuous continence is no longer rewarded with the assurance of love. A threatened external unhappiness—loss of love and punishment on the part of the external authority—has been exchanged for a permanent internal unhappiness, for the tension of the sense of guilt.

These interrelations are so complicated and at the same time so important that, at the risk of repeating myself, I shall approach them from yet another angle. The chronological sequence, then, would be as follows. First comes renunciation of instinct owing to fear of aggression by the *external* authority. (This is, of course, what fear of the loss of love amounts to, for love is a protection against this punitive aggression.) After that comes the erection of an *internal* authority, and renunciation of instinct owing to fear of it—owing to fear of conscience. In this second situation bad intentions are equated with bad actions, and hence come a sense of guilt and a need for punishment. The aggressiveness of conscience keeps up the aggressiveness of the authority. So far things have no doubt been made clear; but where does this leave room for the reinforcing influence of misfortune (of renunciation imposed from without) . . . and for the extraordinary severity of conscience in the best and most tractable people . . . ? We have already explained both these peculiarities of conscience, but we probably still have an impression that those explanations do not go to the bottom of the matter, and leave a residue still unexplained.

And here at last an idea comes in which belongs entirely to psycho-analysis and which is foreign to people's ordinary way of thinking. This idea is of a sort which enables us to understand why the subject-matter was bound to seem so confused and obscure to us. For it tells us that conscience (or more correctly, the anxiety which later becomes conscience) is indeed the cause of instinctual renunciation to begin with, but that later the relationship is reversed. Every renunciation of instinct now becomes a dynamic source of conscience and every fresh renunciation increases the latter's severity and intolerance. If we could only bring it better into harmony with what we already know about the history of the origin of conscience, we should be tempted to defend the paradoxical statement that conscience is the result of instinctual renunciation, or that instinctual renunciation (imposed on us from without) creates conscience, which then demands further instinctual renunciation.

The contradiction between this statement and what we have previously said about the genesis of conscience is in point of fact not so very great, and we see a way of further reducing it. In order to make our exposition easier, let us take as our example the aggressive instinct, and let us assume that the renunciation in question is always a renunciation of aggression. (This, of course, is only to be taken as a temporary assumption.) The effect of instinctual renunciation on the conscience then is that every piece of aggression whose satisfaction the subject gives up is taken over by the super-ego and increases the latter's aggressiveness (against the ego). This does not harmonize well with the view that the original aggressiveness of conscience is a continuance of the severity of the external authority and therefore has nothing to do with renunciation. But the discrepancy is removed if we postulate a different derivation for this first instalment of the super-ego's aggressivity. A considerable amount of aggressiveness must be developed in the child against the authority which prevents him from having his first, but none the less his most important, satisfactions, whatever the kind of instinctual deprivation that is demanded of him may be; but he is obliged to renounce the satisfaction of this revengeful aggressiveness. He finds his way out of this economically difficult situation with the help of familiar mechanisms. By means of identification he takes the unattackable authority into himself. The authority now turns into his super-ego and enters into possession of all the aggressiveness which a child would have liked to exercise against it. The child's ego has to content itself with the unhappy role of the authority—the father—who has been thus degraded. Here, as so often, the [real] situation is reversed: 'If I were the father and you were the child, I should treat you badly.' The relationship between the super-ego and the ego is a return, distorted by a wish, of the real relationships between the ego, as yet undivided, and an external object. That is typical, too. But the essential difference is that the original severity of the super-ego does not—or does not so much—represent the severity which one has experienced from it [the object], or which one attributes to it; it represents rather one's own aggressiveness towards it. If this is correct, we may assert truly that in the beginning conscience arises through the suppression of an aggressive impulse, and that it is subsequently reinforced by fresh suppressions of the same kind.

Which of these two views is correct? The earlier one, which genetically seemed so unassailable, or the newer one, which rounds off the theory in such a welcome fashion? Clearly, and by the evidence, too, of direct observations, both are justified. They do not contradict each other, and they even coincide at one point, for the child's revengeful aggressiveness will be in part determined by the amount of punitive aggression which he expects from his father. Experience shows, however, that the severity of the super-ego which a child develops in no way corresponds to the severity of treatment which he has himself met with. The severity of the former seems to be independent of that of the latter. A child who has been very leniently brought up can acquire a very strict conscience. But it would also be wrong to exaggerate this independence; it is not difficult to convince oneself that severity of upbringing does also exert a strong influence on the formation of the child's super-ego. What it amounts to is that in the formation of the super-ego and the emergence of a conscience innate constitutional factors and influences from the real environment act in combination. This is not at all surprising; on the contrary, it is a universal aetiological condition for all such processes.

It can also be asserted that when a child reacts to his first great instinctual frustrations with excessively strong aggressiveness and with a correspondingly severe super-ego, he is following a phylogenetic model and is going beyond the response that would be currently justified; for the father of prehistoric times was undoubtedly terrible, and an extreme amount of aggressiveness may be attributed to him. Thus, if one shifts over from individual to phylogenetic development, the differences between the two theories of the genesis of conscience are still further diminished. On the other hand, a new and important difference makes its appearance between these two developmental processes. We cannot get away from the assumption that man's sense of guilt springs from the Oedipus complex and was acquired at the killing of the father by the brothers banded together. On that occasion an act of aggression was not suppressed but carried out; but it was the same act of aggression whose suppression in the child is supposed to be the source of his sense of guilt. At this point I should not be surprised if the reader were to exclaim angrily: 'So it makes no difference whether one kills one's father or not—one gets a feeling of guilt in either case! We may take leave to raise a few doubts here. Either it is not true that the sense of guilt comes from suppressed aggressiveness, or else the whole story of the killing of the father is a fiction and the children of primaeval man did not kill their fathers any more often than children do nowadays. Besides, if it is not fiction but a plausible piece of history, it would be a case of something happening which everyone expects to happen—namely, of a person feeling guilty because he really has done something which cannot be justified. And of this event, which is after all an everyday occurrence, psycho-analysis has not yet given any explanation.'

That is true, and we must make good the omission. Nor is there any great secret about the matter. When one has a sense of guilt after having committed a misdeed, and because of it, the feeling should more properly be called *remorse*. It relates only to a deed that has been done, and, of course, it presupposes that a *conscience*—the readiness to feel guilty—was already in existence before the deed took place. Remorse of this sort can, therefore, never help us to discover the origin of conscience and of the sense of guilt in general. What happens in these everyday cases is usually this: an instinctual need acquires the strength to achieve satisfaction in spite of the conscience, which is, after all, limited in its strength; and with the natural weakening of the need owing to its having been satisfied, the former balance of power is restored. Psycho-analysis is thus justified in excluding from the present discussion the case of a sense of guilt due to remorse, however frequently such cases occur and however great their practical importance.

But if the human sense of guilt goes back to the killing of the primal father, that was after all a case of 'remorse'. Are we to assume that [at that time] a conscience and a sense of guilt were not, as we have presupposed, in existence before the deed? If not, where, in this case, did the remorse come from? There is no doubt that this case should explain the secret of the sense of guilt to us and put an end to our difficulties. And I believe it does. This remorse was the result of the primordial ambivalence of feeling towards the father. His sons hated him, but they loved him, too. After their hatred had been satisfied by their act of aggression, their love came to the fore in their remorse for the deed. It set up the super-ego by identification with the father; it gave that agency the father's power, as though as a punishment for the deed of aggression they had carried out against him, and it created the restrictions which were intended to prevent a repetition of the deed. And since the inclination to aggressiveness against the father was repeated in the following generations, the sense of guilt, too, persisted, and it was reinforced once more by every piece of aggressiveness that was suppressed and carried over to the super-ego. Now, I think, we can at last grasp two things perfectly clearly: the part played by love in the origin of conscience and the fatal inevitability of the sense of guilt. Whether one has killed one's father or has abstained from doing so is not really the decisive thing. One is bound to feel guilty in either case, for the sense of guilt is an expression of the conflict due to ambivalence, of the external struggle between Eros and the instinct of destruction or death. This conflict is set going as soon as men are faced with the task of living together. So long as the community assumes no other form than that of the family, the conflict is bound to express itself in the Oedipus complex, to establish the conscience and to create the first sense of guilt. When an attempt is made to widen the community, the same conflict is continued in forms which are dependent on the past; and it is strengthened and results in a further intensification of the sense of guilt. Since civilization obeys an internal erotic impulsion which causes human beings to unite in a closely-knit group, it can only achieve this aim through an ever-increasing reinforcement of the sense of guilt. What began in relation to the father is completed in relation to the group. If civilization is a necessary course of development from the family to humanity as a whole, then—as a result of the inborn conflict arising from ambivalence, of the eternal struggle between the trends of love and death—there is inextricably bound up with it an increase of the sense of guilt, which will perhaps reach heights that the individual finds hard to tolerate. One is reminded of the great poet's moving arraignment of the 'Heavenly Powers':—

Ihr führt in's Leben uns hinein.
Ihr lasst den Armen schuldig werden,
Dann überlasst Ihr ihn den Pein,
Denn jede Schuld rächt sich auf Erden.[1]

And we may well heave a sigh of relief at the thought that it is nevertheless vouchsafed to a few to salvage without effort from the whirlpool of their own feelings the deepest truths, towards which the rest of us have to find our way through tormenting uncertainty and with restless groping.

---

1. One of the Harp-player's songs in Goethe's *Wilhelm Meister*.

[To earth, this weary earth, ye bring us
To guilt ye let us heedless go,
Then leave repentance fierce to wring us:
A moment's guilt, an age of woe!

Carlyle's translation.

The first couplet appears as an association to a dream in Freud's short book *On Dreams* (1901a), *Standard Ed.*, 5, 637, and 639.]

10.

Egoistic Suicide

ÉMILE DURKHEIM, 1897

We have . . . set up the three following propositions:

> Suicide varies inversely with the degree of integration of religious society.
>
> Suicide varies inversely with the degree of integration of domestic society.
>
> Suicide varies inversely with the degree of integration of political society.

This grouping shows that whereas these different societies have a moderating influence upon suicide, this is due not to special characteristics of each but to a characteristic common to all. Religion does not owe its efficacy to the special nature of religious sentiments, since domestic and political societies both produce the same effects when strongly integrated. This, moreover, we have already proved when studying directly the manner of action of different religions upon suicide. Inversely, it is not the specific nature of the domestic or political tie which can explain the immunity they confer, since religious society has the same advantage. The cause can only be found in a single quality possessed by all these social groups, though perhaps to varying degrees. The only quality satisfying this condition is that they are all strongly integrated social groups. So we reach the general conclusion: suicide varies inversely with the degree of integration of the social groups of which the individual forms a part.

But society cannot disintegrate without the individual simultaneously detaching himself from social life, without his own goals becoming preponderant over those of the community, in a word without his personality tending to surmount the collective personality. The more weakened the groups to which he belongs, the less he depends on them, the more he consequently depends only on himself and recognizes no other rules of conduct than what are founded on his private interests. If we agree to call this state egoism, in which the individual ego asserts itself to excess in the face of the social ego and at its

Reprinted with the permission of The Free Press, an imprint of Simon & Schuster Adult Publishing Group from *Suicide: A Study in Sociology* by Emile Durkheim, translated by John A. Spaulding and George Simpson. Copyright © 1951, renewed 1979 by The Free Press.

expense, we may call egoistic the special type of suicide springing from excessive individualism.

But how can suicide have such an origin?

First of all, it can be said that, as collective force is one of the obstacles best calculated to restrain suicide, its weakening involves a development of suicide. When society is strongly integrated, it holds individuals under its control, considers them at its service and thus forbids them to dispose wilfully of themselves. Accordingly it opposes their evading their duties to it through death. But how could society impose its supremacy upon them when they refuse to accept this subordination as legitimate? It no longer then possesses the requisite authority to retain them in their duty if they wish to desert; and conscious of its own weakness, it even recognizes their right to do freely what it can no longer prevent. So far as they are the admitted masters of their destinies, it is their privilege to end their lives. They, on their part, have no reason to endure life's sufferings patiently. For they cling to life more resolutely when belonging to a group they love, so as not to betray interests they put before their own. The bond that unites them with the common cause attaches them to life and the lofty goal they envisage prevents their feeling personal troubles so deeply. There is, in short, in a cohesive and animated society a constant interchange of ideas and feelings from all to each and each to all, something like a mutual moral support, which instead of throwing the individual on his own resources, leads him to share in the collective energy and supports his own when exhausted.

But these reasons are purely secondary. Excessive individualism not only results in favoring the action of suicidogenic causes, but it is itself such a cause. It not only frees man's inclination to do away with himself from a protective obstacle, but creates this inclination out of whole cloth and thus gives birth to a special suicide which bears its mark. This must be clearly understood for this is what constitutes the special character of the type of suicide just distinguished and justifies the name we have given it. What is there then in individualism that explains this result?

It has been sometimes said that because of his psychological constitution, man cannot live without attachment to some object which transcends and survives him, and that the reason for this necessity is a need we must have not to perish entirely. Life is said to be intolerable unless some reason for existing is involved, some purpose justifying life's trials. The individual alone is not a sufficient end for his activity. He is too little. He is not only hemmed in spatially; he is also strictly limited temporally. When, therefore, we have no other object than ourselves we cannot avoid the thought that our efforts will finally end in nothingness, since we ourselves disappear. But annihilation terrifies us. Under these conditions one would lose courage to live, that is, to act and struggle, since nothing will remain of our exertions. The state of egoism, in other words, is supposed to be contradictory to human nature and, consequently, too uncertain to have chances of permanence.

In this absolute formulation the proposition is vulnerable. If the thought of the end of our personality were really so hateful, we could consent to live only by blinding ourselves voluntarily as to life's value. For if we may in a measure avoid the prospect of annihilation we cannot extirpate it; it is inevitable, whatever we do. We may push back the frontier for some generations, force our name to endure for some years or centuries longer than our body; a moment, too soon for most men, always comes when it will be nothing. For the groups we join in order to prolong our existence by their means are themselves mortal; they too must dissolve, carrying with them all our deposit of ourselves. Those are few whose memories are closely enough bound to the very history of humanity to be assured of living until its death. So, if we really thus thirsted after immortality, no such brief perspectives could ever appease us. Besides, what of us is it that lives? A word, a sound, an imperceptible trace, most often anonymous, therefore nothing comparable to the violence of our efforts or able to justify them to us. In actuality, though a child is naturally an egoist who feels not the slightest craving to survive himself, and the old man is very often a child in this and so many other respects, neither ceases to cling to life as much or more than the adult; indeed we have seen that suicide is very rare for the first fifteen years and tends to decrease at the other extreme of life. Such too is the case with animals, whose psychological constitution differs from that of men only in degree. It is therefore untrue that life is only possible by its possessing its rationale outside of itself.

Indeed, a whole range of functions concern only the individual; these are the ones indispensable for physical life. Since they are made for this purpose only, they are perfected by its attainment. In everything concerning them, therefore, man can act reasonably without thought of transcendental purposes. These functions serve by merely serving him. In so far as he has no other needs, he is therefore self-sufficient and can live happily with no other objective than living. This is not the case, however, with the civilized adult. He has many ideas, feelings and practices unrelated to organic needs. The roles of art, morality, religion, political faith, science itself are not to repair organic exhaustion nor to provide sound functioning of the organs. All this supra-physical life is built and expanded not because of the demands of the cosmic environment but because of the demands of the social environment. The influence of society is what has aroused in us the sentiments of sympathy and solidarity drawing us toward others; it is society which, fashioning us in its image, fills us with religious, political and moral beliefs that control our actions. To play our social role we have striven to extend our intelligence and it is still society that has supplied us with tools for this development by transmitting to us its trust fund of knowledge.

Through the very fact that these superior forms of human activity have a collective origin, they have a collective purpose. As they derive from society they have reference to it; rather they are society itself incarnated and individualized in each one of us. But for them to have a raison d'être in our eyes, the purpose they envisage must be one not indifferent to us. We can cling to these forms of human activity only to the degree that we cling to society itself. Contrariwise, in the same measure as we feel detached from society we become detached from that life whose source and aim is society. For what purpose do these rules of morality, these precepts of law binding us to all sorts of sacrifices, these restrictive dogmas exist, if there is no being outside us whom they serve and in whom we participate? What is the purpose of science itself? If its only use is to increase our chances for survival, it does not deserve the trouble it entails. Instinct acquits itself better of this role; animals prove this. Why substitute for it a more hesitant and uncertain reflection? What is the end of suffering, above all? If the value of things can only be estimated by their relation to this positive evil for the individual, it is without reward and incomprehensible. This problem does not exist for the believer firm in his faith or the man strongly bound by ties of domestic or political society. Instinctively and unreflectively they ascribe all that they are and do, the one to his Church or his God, the living symbol of the Church, the other to his family, the third to his country or party. Even in their sufferings they see only a means of glorifying the group to which they belong and thus do homage to it. So, the Christian ultimately desires and seeks suffering to testify more fully to his contempt for the flesh and more fully resemble his divine model. But the more the believer doubts, that is, the less he feels himself a real participant in the religious faith to which he belongs, and from which he is freeing hmself; the more the family and community become foreign to the individual, so much the more does he become a mystery to himself, unable to escape the exasperating and agonizing question: to what purpose?

If, in other words, as has often been said, man is double, that is because social man superimposes himself upon physical man. Social man necessarily presupposes a society which he expresses and serves. If this dissolves, if we no longer feel it in existence and action about and above us, whatever is social in us is deprived of all objective foundation. All that remains is an artificial combination of illusory images, a phantasmagoria vanishing at the least reflection; that is, nothing which can be a goal for our action. Yet this social man is the essence of civilized man; he is the masterpiece of existence. Thus we are bereft of reasons for existence; for the only life to which we could cling no longer corresponds to anything actual; the only existence still based upon reality no longer meets our needs. Because we have been initiated into a higher existence, the one which satisfies an animal or a child can satisfy us no more and the other itself fades and leaves us helpless. So there is nothing more for our efforts to lay hold of, and we feel them lose themselves in emptiness. In this sense it is true to say that our activity needs an object transcending it. We do not need it to maintain ourselves in the illusion of an impossible immortality; it is implicit in our moral constitution and cannot be even partially lost without this losing its raison d'être in the same degree. No proof is needed that in such a state of confusion the least cause of discouragement may easily give birth to desperate resolutions. If life is not worth the trouble of being lived, everything becomes a pretext to rid ourselves of it.

But this is not all. This detachment occurs not only in single individuals. One of the constitutive elements of every national temperament consists of a certain way of estimating the value of existence. There is a collective as well as an individual humor inclining peoples to sadness or cheerfulness, making them see things in bright or sombre lights. In fact, only society can pass a collective opinion on the value of human life; for this the individual is incompetent. The latter knows nothing but himself and his own little horizon; thus his experience is too limited to serve as a basis for a general appraisal. He may indeed consider his own life to be aimless; he can say nothing applicable to others. On the contrary, without sophistry, society may generalize its own feeling as to itself, its state of health or lack of health. For individuals share too deeply in the life of society for it to be diseased without their suffering infection. What it suffers they necessarily suffer. Because it is the whole, its ills are communicated to its parts. Hence it cannot disintegrate without awareness that the regular conditions of general existence are equally disturbed. Because society is the end on which our better selves depend, it cannot feel us escaping it without a simultaneous realization that our activity is purposeless. Since we are its handiwork, society cannot be conscious of its own decadence without the feeling that henceforth this work is of no value. Thence are formed currents of depression and disillusionment emanating from no particular individual but expressing society's state of disintegration. They reflect the relaxation of social bonds, a sort of collective asthenia, or social malaise, just as individual sadness, when chronic, in its way reflects the poor organic state of the individual. Then metaphysical and religious systems spring up which, by reducing these obscure sentiments to formulae, attempt to prove to men the senselessness of life and that it is self-deception to believe that it has purpose. Then new moralities originate which, by elevating facts to ethics, commend suicide or at least tend in that direction by suggesting a minimal existence. On their appearance they seem to have been created out of whole cloth by their makers who are sometimes blamed for the pessimism of their doctrines. In reality they are an effect rather than a cause; they merely symbolize in abstract language and systematic form the physiological distress of the body social. As these currents are collective, they have, by virtue of their origin, an authority which they impose upon the individual and they drive him more vigorously on the way to which he is already inclined by the state of moral distress directly aroused in him by the disintegration of society. Thus, at the very moment that, with excessive zeal, he frees himself from the social environment, he still submits to its influence. However individualized a man may be, there is always something collective remaining—the very depression and melancholy resulting from this same exaggerated individualism. He effects communion through sadness when he no longer has anything else with which to achieve it.

Hence this type of suicide well deserves the name we have given it. Egoism is not merely a contributing factor in it; it is its generating cause. In this case the bond attaching man to life relaxes because that attaching him to society is itself slack. The incidents of private life which seem the direct inspiration of suicide and are considered its determining causes are in reality only incidental causes. The individual yields to the slightest shock of circumstance because the state of society has made him a ready prey to suicide.

Anomic Suicide

ÉMILE DURKHEIM, 1897

No living being can be happy or even exist unless his needs are sufficiently proportioned to his means. In other words, if his needs require more than can be granted, or even merely something of a different sort, they will be under continual friction and can only function painfully. Movements incapable of production without pain tend not to be reproduced. Unsatisfied tendencies atrophy, and as the impulse to live is merely the result of all the rest, it is bound to weaken as the others relax.

In the animal, at least in a normal condition, this equilibrium is established with automatic spontaneity because the animal depends on purely material conditions. All the organism needs is that the supplies of substance and energy constantly employed in the vital process should be periodically renewed by equivalent quantities; that replacement be equivalent to use. When the void created by existence in its own resources is filled, the animal, satisfied, asks nothing further. Its power of reflection is not sufficiently developed to imagine other ends than those implicit in its physical nature. On the other hand, as the work demanded of each organ itself depends on the general state of vital energy and the needs of organic equilibrium, use is regulated in turn by replacement and the balance is automatic. The limits of one are those of the other; both are fundamental to the constitution of the existence in question, which cannot exceed them.

This is not the case with man, because most of his needs are not dependent on his body or not to the same degree. Strictly speaking, we may consider that the quantity of material supplies necessary to the physical maintenance of a human life is subject to computation, though this be less exact than in the preceding case and a wider margin left for the free combinations of the will; for beyond the indispensable minimum which satisfies nature when instinctive, a more awakened reflection suggests better conditions, seemingly desir-

Reprinted with the permission of The Free Press, an imprint of Simon & Schuster Adult Publishing Group from *Suicide: A Study in Sociology* by Emile Durkheim, translated by John A. Spaulding and George Simpson. Copyright © 1951, renewed 1979 by The Free Press.

able ends craving fulfillment. Such appetites, however, admittedly sooner or later reach a limit which they cannot pass. But how determine the quantity of well-being, comfort or luxury legitimately to be craved by a human being? Nothing appears in man's organic nor in his psychological constitution which sets a limit to such tendencies. The functioning of individual life does not require them to cease at one point rather than at another; the proof being that they have constantly increased since the beginnings of history, receiving more and more complete satisfaction, yet with no weakening of average health. Above all, how establish their proper variation with different conditions of life, occupations, relative importance of services, etc.? In no society are they equally satisfied in the different stages of the social hierarchy. Yet human nature is substantially the same among all men, in its essential qualities. It is not human nature which can assign the variable limits necessary to our needs. They are thus unlimited so far as they depend on the individual alone. Irrespective of any external regulatory force, our capacity for feeling is in itself an insatiable and bottomless abyss.

But if nothing external can restrain this capacity, it can only be a source of torment to itself. Unlimited desires are insatiable by definition and insatiability is rightly considered a sign of morbidity. Being unlimited, they constantly and infinitely surpass the means at their command; they cannot be quenched. Inextinguishable thirst is constantly renewed torture. It has been claimed, indeed, that human activity naturally aspires beyond assignable limits and sets itself unattainable goals. But how can such an undetermined state be any more reconciled with the conditions of mental life than with the demands of physical life? All man's pleasure in acting, moving and exerting himself implies the sense that his efforts are not in vain and that by walking he has advanced. However, one does not advance when one walks toward no goal, or—which is the same thing—when his goal is infinity. Since the distance between us and it is always the same, whatever road we take, we might as well have made the motions without progress from the spot. Even our glances behind and our feeling of pride at the distance covered can cause only deceptive satisfaction, since the remaining distance is not proportionately reduced. To pursue a goal which is by definition unattainable is to condemn oneself to a state of perpetual unhappiness. Of course, man may hope contrary to all reason, and hope has its pleasures even when unreasonable. It may sustain him for a time; but it cannot survive the repeated disappointments of experience indefinitely. What more can the future offer him than the past, since he can never reach a tenable condition nor even approach the glimpsed ideal? Thus, the more one has, the more one wants, since satisfactions received only stimulate instead of filling needs. Shall action as such be considered agreeable? First, only on condition of blindness to its uselessness. Secondly, for this pleasure to be felt and to temper and half veil the accompanying painful unrest, such unending motion must at least always be easy and unhampered. If it is interfered with only restlessness is left, with the lack of ease which it, itself, entails. But it would be a miracle if no insurmountable obstacle were never encountered. Our thread of life on these conditions is pretty thin, breakable at any instant.

To achieve any other result, the passions first must be limited. Only then can they be harmonized with the faculties and satisfied. But since the individual has no way of limiting them, this must be done by some force exterior to him. A regulative force must play the same role for moral needs which the organism plays for physical needs. This means that the force can only be moral. The awakening of conscience interrupted the state of equilibrium of the animal's dormant existence; only conscience, therefore, can furnish the means to re-establish it. Physical restraint would be ineffective; hearts cannot be touched by physio-chemical forces. So far as the appetites are not automatically restrained by physiological mechanisms, they can be halted only by a limit that they recognize as just. Men would never consent to restrict their desires if they felt justified in passing the assigned limit. But, for reasons given above, they cannot assign themselves this law of justice. So they must receive it from an authority which they respect, to which they yield spontaneously. Either directly and as a whole, or through the agency of one of its organs, society alone can play this moderating role; for it is the only moral power superior to the individual, the authority of which he accepts. It alone has the power necessary to stipulate law and to set the point beyond which the passions must not go. Finally, it alone can estimate the reward to be prospectively offered to every class of human functionary, in the name of the common interest.

As a matter of fact, at every moment of history there is a dim perception, in the moral consciousness of societies, of the respective value of different social services, the relative reward due to each, and the consequent degree of comfort appropriate on the average to workers in each occupation. The different functions are graded in public opinion and a certain coefficient of well-being assigned to each, according to its place in the hierarchy. According to accepted ideas, for example, a certain way of living is considered the upper limit to which a workman may aspire in his efforts to improve his existence, and there is another limit below which he is not willingly permitted to fall unless he has seriously demeaned himself. Both differ for city and country workers, for the domestic servant and the day-laborer, for the business clerk and the official, etc. Likewise the man of wealth is reproved if he lives the life of a poor man, but also if he seeks the refinements of luxury overmuch. Economists may protest in vain; public feeling will always be scandalized if an individual spends too much wealth for wholly superfluous use, and it even seems that this severity relaxes only in times of moral disturbance. A genuine regimen exists, therefore, although not always legally formulated, which fixes with relative precision the maximum degree of ease of living to which each social class may legitimately aspire. However, there is nothing immutable about such a scale. It changes with the increase or decrease of collective revenue and the changes occurring in the moral ideas of society. Thus what appears luxury to one period no longer does so to another; and the well-being which for long periods was granted to a class only by exception and supererogation, finally appears strictly necessary and equitable.

Under this pressure, each in his sphere vaguely realizes the extreme limit set to his ambitions and aspires to nothing beyond. At least if he respects regulations and is docile to collective authority, that is, has a wholesome moral constitution, he feels that it is not well to ask more. Thus, an end and goal are set to the passions. Truly, there is nothing rigid nor absolute about such determination. The economic ideal assigned each class of citizens is itself confined to certain limits, within which the desires have free range. But it is not infinite. This relative limitation and the moderation it involves make men contented with their lot while stimulating them moderately to improve it; and this average contentment causes the feeling of calm, active happiness, the pleasure in existing and living which characterizes health for societies as well as for individuals. Each person is then at least, generally speaking, in harmony with his condition, and desires only what he may legitimately hope for as the normal reward of his activity. Besides, this does not condemn man to a sort of immobility. He may seek to give beauty to his life; but his attempts in this direction may fail without causing him to despair. For, loving what he has and not fixing his desire solely on what he lacks, his wishes and hopes may fail of what he has happened to aspire to, without his being wholly destitute. He has the essentials. The equilibrium of his happiness is secure because it is defined, and a few mishaps cannot disconcert him.

But it would be of little use for everyone to recognize the justice of the hierarchy of functions established by public opinion, if he did not also consider the distribution of these functions just. The workman is not in harmony with his social position if he is not convinced that he has his deserts. If he feels justified in occupying another, what he has would not satisfy him. So it is not enough for the average level of needs for each social condition to be regulated by public opinion, but another, more precise rule, must fix the way in which these conditions are open to individuals. There is no society in which such regulation does not exist. It varies with times and places. Once it regarded birth as the almost exclusive principle of social classification; today it recognizes no other inherent inequality than hereditary fortune and merit. But in all these various forms its object is unchanged. It is also only possible, everywhere, as a restriction upon individuals imposed by superior authority, that is, by collective authority. For it can be established only by requiring of one or another group of men, usually of all, sacrifices and concessions in the name of the public interest.

Some, to be sure, have thought that this moral pressure would become unnecessary if men's economic circumstances were only no longer determined by heredity. If inheritance were abolished, the argument runs, if everyone began life with equal resources and if the competitive struggle were fought out on a basis of perfect equality, no one could think its results unjust. Each would instinctively feel that things are as they should be.

Truly, the nearer this ideal equality were approached, the less social restraint will be necessary. But it is only a matter of degree. One sort of heredity will always exist, that of natural talent. Intelligence, taste, scientific, artistic, literary or industrial ability, courage and manual dexterity are gifts received by each of us at birth, as the heir to wealth receives his capital or as the nobleman formerly received his title and function. A moral discipline will therefore still be required to make those less favored by nature accept the lesser advantages which they owe to the chance of birth. Shall it be demanded that all have an equal share and that no advantage be given those more useful and deserving? But then there would have to be a discipline far stronger to make these accept a treatment merely equal to that of the mediocre and incapable.

But like the one first mentioned, this discipline can be useful only if considered just by the peoples subject to it. When it is maintained only by custom and force, peace and harmony are illusory; the spirit of unrest and discontent are latent; appetites superficially restrained are ready to revolt. This happened in Rome and Greece when the faiths underlying the old organization of the patricians and plebeians were shaken, and in our modern societies when aristocratic prejudices began to lose their old ascendancy. But this state of upheaval is exceptional; it occurs only when society is passing through some abnormal crisis. In normal conditions the collective order is regarded as just by the great majority of persons. Therefore, when we say that an authority is necessary to impose this order on individuals, we certainly do not mean that violence is the only means of establishing it. Since this regulation is meant to restrain individual passions, it must come from a power which dominates individuals; but this power must also be obeyed through respect, not fear.

It is not true, then, that human activity can be released from all restraint. Nothing in the world can enjoy such a privilege. All existence being a part of the universe is relative to the remainder; its nature and method of manifestation accordingly depend not only on itself but on other beings, who consequently restrain and regulate it. Here there are only differences of degree and form between the mineral realm and the thinking person. Man's characteristic privilege is that the bond he accepts is not physical but moral; that is, social.

He is governed not by a material environment brutally imposed on him, but by a conscience superior to his own, the superiority of which he feels. Because the greater, better part of his existence transcends the body, he escapes the body's yoke, but is subject to that of society.

But when society is disturbed by some painful crisis or by beneficent but abrupt transitions, it is momentarily incapable of exercising this influence; thence come the sudden rises in the curve of suicides which we have pointed out above.

In the case of economic disasters, indeed, something like a declassification occurs which suddenly casts certain individuals into a lower state than their previous one. Then they must reduce their requirements, restrain their needs, learn greater self-control. All the advantages of social influence are lost so far as they are concerned; their moral education has to be recommenced. But society cannot adjust them instantaneously to this new life and teach them to practice the increased self-repression to which they are unaccustomed. So they are not adjusted to the condition forced on them, and its very prospect is intolerable; hence the suffering which detaches them from a reduced existence even before they have made trial of it.

It is the same if the source of the crisis is an abrupt growth of power and wealth. Then, truly, as the conditions of life are changed, the standard according to which needs were regulated can no longer remain the same; for it varies with social resources, since it largely determines the share of each class of producers. The scale is upset; but a new scale cannot be immediately improvised. Time is required for the public conscience to reclassify men and things. So long as the social forces thus freed have not regained equilibrium, their respective values are unknown and so all regulation is lacking for a time. The limits are unknown between the possible and the impossible, what is just and what is unjust, legitimate claims and hopes and those which are immoderate. Consequently, there is no restraint upon aspirations. If the disturbance is profound, it affects even the principles controlling the distribution of men among various occupations. Since the relations between various parts of society are necessarily modified, the ideas expressing these relations must change. Some particular class especially favored by the crisis is no longer resigned to its former lot, and, on the other hand, the example of its greater good fortune arouses all sorts of jealousy below and about it. Appetites, not being controlled by a public opinion become disoriented, no longer recognize the limits proper to them. Besides, they are at the same time seized by a sort of natural erethism simply by the greater intensity of public life. With increased prosperity desires increase. At the very moment when traditional rules have lost their authority, the richer prize offered these appetites stimulates them and makes them more exigent and impatient of control. The state of de-regulation or anomy is thus further heightened by passions being less disciplined, precisely when they need more disciplining.

But then their very demands make fulfillment impossible. Overweening ambition always exceeds the results obtained, great as they may be, since there is no warning to pause here. Nothing gives satisfaction and all this agitation is uninterruptedly maintained without appeasement. Above all, since this race for an unattainable goal can give no other pleasure but that of the race itself, if it is one, once it is interrupted the participants are left empty-handed. At the same time the struggle grows more violent and painful, both from being less controlled and because competition is greater. All classes contend among themselves because no established classification any longer exists. Effort grows, just when it becomes less productive. How could the desire to live not be weakened under such conditions?

This explanation is confirmed by the remarkable immunity of poor countries. Poverty protects against suicide because it is a restraint in itself. No matter how one acts, desires have to depend upon resources to some extent; actual possessions are partly the criterion of those aspired to. So the less one has the less he is tempted to extend the range of his needs indefinitely. Lack of power, compelling moderation, accustoms men to it, while nothing excites envy if no one has superfluity. Wealth, on the other hand, by the power it bestows, deceives us into believing that we depend on ourselves only. Reducing the resistance we encounter from objects, it suggests the possibility of unlimited success against them. The less limited one feels, the more intolerable all limitation appears. Not without reason, therefore, have so many religions dwelt on the advantages and moral value of poverty. It is actually the best school for teaching self-restraint. Forcing us to constant self-discipline, it prepares us to accept collective discipline with equanimity, while wealth, exalting the individual, may always arouse the spirit of rebellion which is the very source of immorality. This, of course, is no reason why humanity should not improve its material condition. But though the moral danger involved in every growth of prosperity is not irremediable, it should not be forgotten.

If anomy never appeared except, as in the above instances, in intermittent spurts and acute crisis, it might cause the social suicide-rate to vary from time to time, but it would not be a regular, constant factor. In one sphere of social life, however—the sphere of trade and industry—it is actually in a chronic state.

For a whole century, economic progress has mainly consisted in freeing industrial relations from all regulation. Until very recently, it was the function of a whole system of moral forces to exert this discipline. First, the influence of religion was felt alike by workers and masters, the poor and the rich. It consoled the former and taught them contentment with their lot by informing them of the providential nature of the social order, that the share of each class was assigned by God himself, and by holding out the hope for just compensation in a world to come in return for the inequalities of this world. It governed the latter, recalling that worldly interests are not man's entire lot, that they must be subordinate to other and higher interests, and that they should therefore not be pursued without rule or measure. Temporal power, in turn, restrained the scope of economic functions by its supremacy over them and by the relatively subordinate role it assigned them. Finally, within the business world proper, the occupational groups by regulating salaries, the price of products and production itself, indirectly fixed the average level of income on which needs are partially based by the very force of circumstances. However, we do not mean to propose this organization as a model. Clearly it would be inadequate to existing societies without great changes. What we stress is its existence, the fact of its useful influence, and that nothing today has come to take its place.

Actually, religion has lost most of its power. And government, instead of regulating economic life, has become its tool and servant. The most opposite schools, orthodox economists and extreme socialists, unite to reduce government to the role of a more or less passive intermediary among the various social functions. The former wish to make it simply the guardian of individual contracts; the latter leave it the task of doing the collective bookkeeping, that is, of recording the demands of consumers, transmitting them to producers, inventorying the total revenue and distributing it according to a fixed formula. But both refuse it any power to subordinate other social organs to itself and to make them converge toward one dominant aim. On both sides nations are declared to have the single or chief purpose of achieving industrial prosperity; such is the implication of the dogma of economic materialism, the basis of both apparently opposed systems. And as these theories merely express the state of opinion, industry, instead of being still regarded as a means to an end transcending itself, has become the supreme end of individuals and societies alike. Thereupon the appetites thus excited have become freed of any limiting authority. By sanctifying them, so to speak, this apotheosis of well-being has placed them above all human law. Their restraint seems like a sort of sacrilege. For this reason, even the purely utilitarian regulation of them exercised by the industrial world itself through the medium of occupational groups has been unable to persist. Ultimately, this liberation of desires has been made worse by the very development of industry and the almost infinite extension of the market. So long as the producer could gain his profits only in his immediate neighborhood, the restricted amount of possible gain could not much overexcite ambition. Now that he may assume to have almost the entire world as his customer, how could passions accept their former confinement in the face of such limitless prospects?

Such is the source of the excitement predominating in this part of society, and which has thence extended to the other parts. There, the state of crisis and anomy is constant and, so to speak, normal. From top to bottom of the ladder, greed is aroused without knowing where to find ultimate foothold. Nothing can calm it, since its goal is far beyond all it can attain. Reality seems valueless by comparison with the dreams of fevered imaginations; reality is therefore abandoned, but so too is possibility abandoned when it in turn becomes reality. A thirst arises for novelties, unfamiliar pleasures, nameless sensations, all of which lose their savor once known. Henceforth one has no strength to endure the least reverse. The whole fever subsides and the sterility of all the tumult is apparent, and it is seen that all these new sensations in their infinite quantity cannot form a solid foundation of happiness to support one during days of trial. The wise man, knowing how to enjoy achieved results without having constantly to replace them with others, finds in them an attachment to life in the hour of difficulty. But the man who has always pinned all his hopes on the future and lived with his eyes fixed upon it, has nothing in the past as a comfort against the present's afflictions, for the past was nothing to him but a series of hastily experienced stages. What blinded him to himself was his expectation always to find further on the happiness he had so far missed. Now he is stopped in his tracks; from now on nothing remains behind or ahead of him to fix his gaze upon. Weariness alone, moreover, is enough to bring disillusionment, for he cannot in the end escape the futility of an endless pursuit.

We may even wonder if this moral state is not principally what makes economic catastrophes of our day so fertile in suicides. In societies where a man is subjected to a healthy discipline, he submits more readily to the blows of chance. The necessary effort for sustaining a little more discomfort costs him relatively little, since he is used to discomfort and constraint. But when every constraint is hateful in itself, how can closer constraint not seem intolerable? There is no tendency to resignation in the feverish impatience of men's lives. When there is no other aim but to outstrip constantly the point arrived at, how painful to be thrown back! Now this very lack of organization characterizing our economic condition throws the door wide to every sort of adventure. Since imagination is hungry for novelty, and ungoverned, it gropes at random. Setbacks necessarily increase with risks and thus crises multiply, just when they are becoming more destructive.

Yet these dispositions are so inbred that society has grown to accept them and is accustomed to think them normal. It is everlastingly repeated that it is man's nature to be eternally dissatisfied, constantly to advance, without relief or rest, toward an indefinite goal. The longing for infinity is daily represented as a mark of moral distinction, whereas it can only appear within unregulated consciences which elevate to a rule the lack of rule from which they suffer. The doctrine of the most ruthless and swift progress has become an article of faith. But other theories appear parallel with those praising the advantages of instability, which, generalizing the situation that gives them birth, declare life evil, claim that it is richer in grief than in pleasure and that it attracts men only by false claims. Since this disorder is greatest in the economic world, it has most victims there.

Industrial and commercial functions are really among the occupations which furnish the greatest number of suicides. . . . Almost on a level with the liberal professions, they sometimes surpass them; they are especially more afflicted than agriculture, where the old regulative forces still make their appearance felt most and where the fever of business has least penetrated. Here is best recalled what was once the general constitution of the economic order. And the divergence would be yet greater if, among the suicides of industry, employers were distinguished from workmen, for the former are probably most stricken by the state of anomy. The enormous rate of those with independent means (720 per million) sufficiently shows that the possessors of most comfort suffer most. Everything that enforces subordination attenuates the effects of this state. At least the horizon of the lower classes is limited by those above them, and for this same reason their desires are more modest. Those who have only empty space above them are almost inevitably lost in it, if no force restrains them.

Anomy, therefore, is a regular and specific factor in suicide in our modern societies; one of the springs from which the annual contingent feeds. So we have here a new type to distinguish from the others. It differs from them in its dependence, not on the way in which individuals are attached to society, but on how it regulates them. Egoistic suicide results from man's no longer finding a basis for existence in life; altruistic suicide, because this basis for existence appears to man situated beyond life itself. The third sort of suicide, the existence of which has just been shown, results from man's activity's lacking regulation and his consequent sufferings. By virtue of its origin we shall assign this last variety the name of *anomic suicide*.

Certainly, this and egoistic suicide have kindred ties. Both spring from society's insufficient presence in individuals. But the sphere of its absence is not the same in both cases. In egoistic suicide it is deficient in truly collective activity, thus depriving the latter of object and meaning. In anomic suicide, society's influence is lacking in the basically individual passions, thus leaving them without a check-rein. In spite of their relationship, therefore, the two types are independent of each other. We may offer society everything social in us, and still be unable to control our desires; one may live in an anomic state without being egoistic, and vice versa. These two sorts of suicide therefore do not draw their chief recruits from the same social environments; one has its principal field among intellectual careers, the world of thought—the other, the industrial or commercial world.

12.

Explaining the Emergence of Norms

CHRISTINE HORNE, 2001

WHAT ARE NORMS?

The study of norms is a difficult undertaking, as is the evaluation of existing work, in part because scholars disagree about what norms are. To complicate matters, they use a variety of terms—custom, convention, role, identity, institution, culture, and so forth—to refer to concepts that are similar to or overlap with notions about norms. Furthermore, the word has various meanings depending on the focus of the researcher. On some occasions it is used as an umbrella term that refers to a variety of controls, including formal organizational rules and laws as well as informal social controls, whereas at other times it is used more narrowly.

Even when viewed simply as informal social controls, definitions vary. For some, norms are a system of meaning. According to Gary Alan Fine, they "constitute a 'frame' within which individuals interpret a given situation and from which they take direction for their responsibilities as actors in that domain" (2001). For these scholars, the problem of order is solved by mutual understanding—which norms provide (Durkheim 1915, 30). For others, norms are patterns of action. Game theorists, for example, view cooperative behavior as a general equivalent to any norm. Self-interested individuals act in their own interests rather than those of others. Norms encourage them to behave prosocially instead of merely for themselves. Therefore, cooperative behavior is normative, and by studying the emergence of patterns of cooperative behavior, scholars explain how norms emerge.

Probably the most widely accepted view of norms, however, is that they are statements that regulate behavior. For some, these statements identify expectations. Such "expectations that arise concerning habits emerging and crystallizing in the course of repeated interactions might be regarded as latent norms" (Wrong 1994, 48; see also Bicchieri 1997, 25, 27). More frequently, these rules

Excerpts from Christine Horne, "Sociological Perspectives on the Emergence of Norms" in *Social Norms,* edited by Michael Hechter and Karl-Dieter Opp. © 2001 Russell Sage Foundation, 112 East 64th Street, New York, New York 10021. Reprinted with permission.

are seen as "ought" statements (Homans 1961, 12). They are "verbal description[s] of a concrete course of action . . . regarded as desirable, combined with an injunction to make certain future actions conform to this course. An instance of a norm is the statement 'Soldiers should obey the orders of their commanding officers'" (Parsons 1937, 75; see also Williams 1970, 413; LaPiere 1954, 118; and Blake and Davis 1964, 456). Norms may give permission, proscribe, prescribe, discourage and so forth.

Norms are not, however, simply rules. Without some means of enforcement, rules serve merely as assertions of ideals. Scholars differ in their views on exactly what it is that makes norms effective. For some, norms must be internalized (see Durkheim 1915, 236–45, for a discussion of internalization). Individuals apply sanctions to their own behavior and respond to these internally generated rewards or punishments (Coleman 1990, 243; Elster 1989; Durkheim 1951). Norms also may be internalized when individuals come to value the behavior specified by a norm for its own sake: that is, they follow social norms because they want to. When seen in this way, the concept of internalized norms is consistent with the term "values" as used by others (for example, Hechter et al. 1999).

Whereas some focus on internalization as an enforcement mechanism, the majority of scholars emphasize the role of external sanctions. On this view, "norms are ordinarily enforced by sanctions, which are either rewards for carrying out those actions regarded as correct or punishments for carrying out those actions regarded as incorrect" (Coleman 1990, 242; see also Scott 1971; MacIver 1937; Blake and Davis 1964). Even those who rely heavily on the idea of internalization still recognize the importance of additional sources of enforcement. Talcott Parsons, for example, typically is associated with the view that social norms are internalized and, once internalized, control individual behavior. Yet he also acknowledges the role of external sanctions.

> There is always a double aspect of the expectation system. . . . On the one
> hand there are the expectations which concern and in part set standards for
> the behavior of the actor, ego, who is taken as the point of reference. . . . On
> the other hand there is a set of expectations relative to the contingently
> probable reactions of others ("alters")—these will be called sanctions, which
> in turn may be subdivided into positive and negative according to whether
> they are felt by ego to be gratification-promoting or depriving. The relation
> between role-expectations and sanctions then is clearly reciprocal. (Parsons
> 1952, 38; see also Durkheim [1903] 1953, 36, 43)

For Parsons, as for most sociologists, social enforcement is an essential component of norms.

In addition to enforcement, for a norm to exist there must be agreement among group members regarding the validity of the rule and the right of group members to enforce it. A rule advocated only by an individual is not a norm at all but merely a personal idiosyncrasy. Although the amount of acceptance is unspecified, it is generally argued that at least some level of consensus is necessary.

This brief discussion illustrates some of the disagreement and lack of clarity over precisely what norms are. Several key elements, however, are widely acknowledged as essential. Based on these elements I define norms as rules, about which there is at least some degree of consensus, that are enforced through social sanctions. Understanding the emergence of norms, then, requires explanations of norm content, enforcement, and distribution.

THE CONTENT OF NORMS

[At least two] general approaches to explaining the content of normative rules can be identified: those that focus on the actions of ego, and those that emphasize ego's reactions to alter's behavior.

Model 1: Focus on the Actions of Ego

One widely held view of norms is that they reflect existing patterns of action. Arguments of this kind begin by identifying or predicting ego's behavior. "An individual may change his behavior, especially his social actions, either to protect his interests under new external conditions or simply to promote them more effectively under existing conditions" (Weber 1978, 755; see also Opp 1982). Actors may actively calculate the course of action that is most likely to produce desired ends at the lowest cost; or they may more passively simply imitate those around them (Asch 1956; Sherif [1936] 1973). Thus, for example, American car manufacturers imitate the strategies of Japanese companies, activists adopt successful methods of earlier exemplars (Clemens 1993), and educational institutions worldwide exhibit striking similarities (Meyer, Ramirez, and Soysal 1992; Meyer, Scott, and Deal 1992). In addition to imitating others, actors may engage in trial and error, repeating those strategies that appear to produce positive outcomes (Macy 1993; Sumner 1979). Finally, individuals may recall norms successfully applied in other situations and behave similarly under new conditions (Dobbin 1994).

Whatever the reason for the initial action, when many people engage in the same behavior, that behavior comes to be associated with a sense of oughtness. Thus patterns of action emerge that then become normative (Opp 1982; Homans 1950, 266; Sumner 1979; Weber 1978, 754–55). Individuals, in turn, comply with the new norm both for the original reason that the behavior was appealing, and also because it is now socially enforced (Homans 1950, 266,

320). If conditions change so that the compliance with the norm becomes excessively costly, actors explore new strategies, and the emergence process begins once again. On this view, Jewish restrictions on eating pork, for example, are seen as the result of individuals making the association between pork and trichinosis and changing their dietary habits. When many people make this change, these new practices presumably become normative and therefore continue even when the original danger—trichinosis—is no longer a threat.

Research on teenage pregnancy provides an illustration of this process (Fernandez-Kelly 1995). In poor inner-city neighborhoods in which residents have few ties outside of the community, girls do not have access to conventional means of achieving adulthood—educational opportunities, good jobs, and marriage. Motherhood is the most readily available route. Girls, therefore, have good reasons to want to have babies, and, as one might expect, rates of pregnancy among unwed teens are high. When babies are born, young mothers receive positive attention from family and friends. Thus individual choices about motherhood produce high pregnancy rates among teens, and in turn childbearing on the part of unwed girls is generally accepted.

At least on their face, arguments such as this are appealing. There are, however, . . . difficulties with this kind of approach. How does behavior that is merely habitual becomes normative? How are changes in normative behavior brought about?

How Do Patterns of Behavior Become Normative? It has been argued that once certain behaviors are adopted they become associated with a sense of oughtness (Homans 1950, 122, 266, 412; see also Hardin 1995, 60–65, for a discussion of the is-ought relationship); but which behaviors? In his study of religion, Émile Durkheim (1915) attempts to explain why a group comes to identify an emblem as being sacred. He suggests that "it is by uttering the same cry, pronouncing the same word, or performing the same gesture in regard to some object that [individuals] become and feel themselves to be in unison. . . . It is the homogeneity of these movements that [makes the group] exist" (262–63). Durkheim's discussion emphasizes the importance of commonality but has little to say about why particular behaviors and objects, rather than others, become imbued with sacredness. Thus, it is not clear why some behaviors become normative and others do not. Are all activities that are widespread supported by social sanctions?

One possibility is that, indeed, any action that is observed comes to be expected. Because individuals value certainty, they will be upset by deviation from what is usual (Opp 1982). Thus all behaviors that are reasonably frequent or consistent will become normative. If this is the case, then norms are synonymous with what is typical—there is no distinction between the term as referring to patterns of behavior and as referring to a rule. To the extent that this is so, one might reasonably wonder whether the concept is useful. Surely it would be more straightforward simply to focus on behavior rather than complicate matters by bring in notions of norms.

It may be, however, that there is something different about behavior that is merely typical and that which has an additional normative component. For example, one takes off one's winter hat upon coming into the house because it is warm. One may remove one's hat in church, however, because one is expected to do so. "Taking off your hat to escape the heat is different from taking off your hat to satisfy an obligation. The former is a regularity and the latter is a norm" (Cooter 1996, 1656; see also Weber 1978, 34). There seems to be at least an intuitive distinction between behavior that is merely habitual and that which is normative.

Why is it that some behaviors are associated with a stronger sense of oughtness than others? One possibility is that the salience of a behavior—for example, the frequency with which it is observed—matters. Another is that actions that have greater effects on others may be more likely to be subject to disapproval than those that create only minimal externalities. Thus a co-worker who has to perform the tasks of tardy colleagues will respond more strongly to their lateness than to their clothing style. Finally, it may be that when individuals have a more intense personal preference for a behavior, the perceived negative consequences of others' deviance are greater (Opp 1982).

Scholars have suggested at least some potential mechanisms through which behavior that is typical may be distinguished from that which is normative. Although explanations have been proposed, however, they have not been fully developed. The ego-centered approach does not enable us to distinguish between those behaviors that become normative and those that do not.

Model 2: Focus on Ego's Reactions to Actions of Alter

A second approach to explaining the emergence of normative rules to a large extent overcomes this problem. These arguments focus on actors' concerns with the behavior of others (Demsetz 1967). On this view, individuals must do more than consider the consequences of their own actions; they also must pay attention to the behavior of other people. Individuals are likely to approve of actions that benefit them and to dislike those that bring them harm. Under certain conditions, actors develop strategies to encourage others to engage in desirable behavior (Coleman 1990, 243–244, 266). Norms thus emerge when behavior produces externalities, when people recognize a right to sanction such externality-producing behaviors, and when the group has the ability to enforce its decisions (see Horne 2001a for experimental evidence supporting this view).

Gerry Mackie's (1996) explanation of foot binding and female genital mutilation is consistent with this approach. He begins by assuming that individuals want to have and raise children and that, therefore, men desire assurances of paternity and women seek assurances of support. Men want to know that their wives can be trusted to be faithful and that the children they raise carry on their bloodlines. In stratified polygamous societies, wealthy men have difficulty keeping track of their many wives, and monitoring costs are, therefore, high. Foot binding and female genital mutilation reduce these costs by providing a signal of a woman's reliability. Because women want good husbands, they are willing to engage in behaviors that establish that reliability and increase the likelihood that successful men will choose them as marriage partners. Thus part of the argument is that men's interest in female behavior, and their ability to make and enforce demands for assurances of fidelity, have contributed to the emergence of norms constraining women—in this case, requiring the binding of young women's feet in China and the mutilation of their genitals in parts of Africa.

For scholars taking this approach, norms emerge in response to externalities produced by the behaviors of others (Coleman 1990). Thus people will approve of actions that result in positive outcomes for them and disapprove of those that have negative consequences. To the extent that people are damaged by others, they will favor norms that discourage antisocial behaviors; and to the extent that they benefit from others' behaviors, they will want norms that institutionalize those behaviors. The mere existence of externalities does not necessarily lead to the emergence of a normative rule, however.

If individuals are to object to behavior of others that produces negative effects, they must be able to link that behavior with the resulting damage. Dissemination of information, therefore, is likely to matter. Widespread disapproval of drunk driving, for example, emerged only after research was made public showing that alcohol-related car accidents were preventable. This knowledge led the public to make the link between the behavior and the resulting harm (McCarthy 1994). Connections of this sort, however, are not always obvious. In parts of Malawi, for example, puberty rites for girls include an initiation into sex. They are instructed to practice with the threat that if they do not, they will lose the ability. Malawi has the youngest population of any country in the world and has high rates of acquired immunodeficiency syndrome (AIDS). Yet the tradition continues. Apparently the negative consequences of sexual activity are not salient. In many situations, it seems, causal relations are not clear because actors do not have adequate information or do not receive it within an appropriate time frame.

Even if people are able to link consequences to underlying causes, however, their responses will be affected by the extent to which they perceive those consequences are harmful or beneficial; and unfortunately, their evaluations may be different from those of the researcher. What appears obviously harmful to an outside observer may be seen by group members as beneficial. In other words, discrepancies between what may be objectively identified as a cost and what is subjectively experienced as such may create difficulties for predicting the content of norms.

Focusing on the consequences of alter's behavior solves some of the problems of the first argument presented. Here it is clear which behaviors will become normative: those that create externalities will be evaluated by the group, and those that produce only personal consequences will not. Thus once researchers identify the externalities experienced by the group, norm content ought to be predictable. This approach is useful, however, only in situations in which costs and benefits of externalities are determinative; and . . . this is not always the case.

THE ENFORCEMENT OF NORMS

Of course, for norms to exist, the group must have the ability to enforce its rules. To the extent that normative rules are consistent with individual interests, little if any enforcement is necessary. When individual and group interests conflict, however, enforcement is crucial. In addition, when meaning encourages one action and interests another, then enforcement is necessary to encourage people to act in appropriate symbolic ways, even if such behaviors are not in their personal interest. Thus for norms to be effective, there must be some mechanism that translates rules into action.

The principle source of enforcement of social norms is informal sanctioning by group members (Coleman 1990; Hechter 1984; Scott 1971). Much sociological research focuses on the ways in which structures of interaction produce incentives encouraging compliance (the contributions of game theorists are particularly important here) and the conditions that increase the likelihood that individuals will affirmatively sanction deviance.

Social Sanctioning

Why do people punish deviance or reward exceptional behavior? Some scholars argue that individuals punish others unconsciously without necessarily being aware that they are doing so—thus, control is cheap (Pettit 1993, 327–31). In addition, under certain conditions, sanctioning occurs as a by-product of other self-interested behavior..

Most explanations, however, assume that sanctioning is costly (see, for example, Axelrod 1986; Heckathorn 1989; Yamagishi 1986, 1995; Yamagishi and

Takahashi 1994). Costs associated with punishing others include the risk of retaliation or at least the potential loss of relationship, the loss of time or money, emotional discomfort, and so forth. In the face of these costs, people are, arguably, more likely to sanction if they receive compensating benefits as a result. One source of benefit is the change in deviant behavior that results from the punishment. In other words, to the extent that another's behavior produces externalities, discouraging that behavior will reduce those externalities. For some people the benefits of this reduction outweigh the costs of sanctioning, and they will punish such behavior. Often, however, this incentive is too small to motivate individuals to sanction.

Scholars, therefore, identify another possible source of benefits—the reactions of others. These reactions constitute metanorms that encourage sanctioning (Axelrod 1986). This solution to the problem gives rise to the additional question of why individuals reward punishers. Again, two answers are possible. Rewarders may be interested in the benefits resulting from sanctioning (Coleman 1990)—that is, like sanctioners, they may pay attention to the benefits resulting from a change in the rate of externality-producing behavior. Alternatively, they may be motivated by the potential reactions of others, including the person imposing the punishment (Horne 2000). Here the focus is not on giving rewards to sanctioners to change rates of deviance but, rather, on the potential rewarder's relationships. Variations in these relationships—for example, the distribution of resources and people's dependence on one another—affects willingness to punish or reward. Thus sanctioning is motivated not just by norm content (an interest in a share of the benefit) but also by an interest in exchange relationships and the rewards that can be obtained from them. Structural factors like interdependency, therefore, affect reactions to norm-violating behavior (Horne 2001b).

The ability of groups to organize themselves to respond to deviance can have an effect as well (see Coleman 1990 for an argument that the structure of network ties matters; also see Sampson, Raudenbush, and Earls 1997; Sampson and Groves 1989; Shaw and McKay [1942] 1969 for evidence that social disorganization decreases informal control). For example, actors may need to engage in collective action in order to enforce a particular norm. That is, if one group benefits from a norm and others are constrained by it, the extent to which that norm will be accepted and enforced will be affected not only by the relative power of the two groups, but also by their ability to organize. Those in disadvantaged positions will benefit if they can unite to enforce their demands against a more powerful actor (Emerson 1962). They are unlikely to be successful in enforcing the norm they prefer, however, if they lack resources or the ability to organize (Coleman 1990, 266; McAdam, McCarthy, and Zald 1996, 8). Arguably, when a potential norm benefits some and constrains others, it will not be reinforced if the beneficiaries are weak, few in numbers, or unorganized relative to the targets of the potential norm.

REFERENCES

Asch, Solomon E. 1956. "Studies of Independence and Conformity: I. A Minority of One Against a Unanimous Majority." *Psychological Monographs* 70(9):1–70.

Axelrod, Robert. 1986. "An Evolutionary Approach to Norms." *American Political Science Review* 80(4):1095–1111.

Bicchieri, Cristina. 1997. "Learning to Cooperate." In *The Dynamics of Norms,* edited by Cristina Bicchieri, Richard Jeffry, and Brian Skyrms. New York: Cambridge University Press.

Blake, Judith, and Kingsley Davis. 1964. "Norms, Values, and Sanctions." In *Handbook of Modern Sociology,* edited by R. E. L. Faris. Skokie, Ill.: Rand McNally.

Clemens, Elisabeth S. 1993. "Organizational Repertoires and Institutional Change: Women's Groups and the Transformation of U.S. Politics, 1890–1920." *American Journal of Sociology* 98(4):755–98.

Coleman, James S. 1990. *Foundations of Social Theory.* Cambridge, Mass.: Belknap Press of Harvard University Press.

Cooter, Robert D. 1996. "Decentralized Law for a Complex Economy: The Structural Approach to Adjudicating the New Law Merchant." *University of Pennsylvania Law Review* 144(5):1643–96.

Demsetz, Harold. 1967. "Toward a Theory of Property Rights." *American Economic Review* 57(2):347–59.

Dobbin, Frank. 1994. *Forging Industrial Policy: The United States, Britain, and France in the Railway Age.* Cambridge: Cambridge University Press.

Durkheim, Émile. 1915. *The Elementary Forms of the Religious Life.* New York: Free Press.

———. 1951. *Suicide.* New York: Free Press.

———. [1903] 1953. "The Determination of Moral Facts." In *Sociology and Philosophy,* translated by D. F. Pocock. London: Cohen and West.

Elster, Jon. 1989. *The Cement of Society: A Study of Social Order.* New York: Cambridge University Press.

Emerson, Richard. 1962. "Power-Dependence Relations." *American Sociological Review* 27(1):31–41.

Fernandez-Kelly, M. P. 1995. "Social and Cultural Capital in the Urban Ghetto: Implications for the Economic Sociology of Immigration." In *The Economic Sociology of Immigration,* edited by Alejandro Portes. New York: Russell Sage Foundation.

Fine, Gary Alan. 2001. "Enacting Norms: Mushrooming and the Culture of Expectations and Explanations." In *Social Norms,* edited by Michael Hechter and Karl-Dieter Opp. New York: Russell Sage Foundation.

Hardin, Russell. 1995. *One for All: The Logic of Group Conflict.* Princeton: Princeton University Press.

Hechter, Michael. 1984. "When Actors Comply: Monitoring Costs and the Production of Social Order." *Acta Sociologica* 27(3):161–83.

Hechter, Michael, James Ranger-Moore, Guillermina Jasso, and Christine Horne. 1999. "Do Values Matter? An Analysis of Advance Directives for Medical Treatment." *European Sociological Review* 15(4):405-30.

Heckathorn, Douglas D. 1989. "Collective Action and the Second-Order Free Rider Problem." *Rationality and Society* 1(1):78–100.

Homans, George C. 1950. *The Human Group*. New York: Harcourt, Brace.

———. 1961. *Social Behavior: Its Elementary Forms*. New York: Harcourt, Brace.

Horne, Christine. 2000. "Community and the State: The Relationship Between Normative and Legal Controls." *European Sociological Review* 16(3):225–43.

———. 2001a. "The Contribution of Norms to Social Welfare: Grounds for Hope or Pessimism?" *Legal Theory* 7(1):159–77.

———. 2001b. "The Enforcement of Norms: Group Cohesion and Meta-Norms." *Social Psychology Quarterly* 64(3):253–66.

LaPiere, Richard. 1954. *A Theory of Social Control*. New York: McGraw-Hill.

MacIver, Robert M. 1937. *Society: A Textbook of Sociology*. New York: Farrar and Rinehart.

Mackie, Gerry. 1996. "Ending Footbinding and Infibulation: A Convention Account." *American Sociological Review* 61(6):999–1017.

Macy, Michael W. 1993. "Backward-Looking Social Control." *American Sociological Review* 58(6):819–36.

McAdam, Doug, John D. McCarthy, and Mayer N. Zald. 1996. *Comparative Perspectives on Social Movements: Political Opportunities, Mobilizing Structures, and Cultural Framings*. New York: Cambridge University Press.

McCarthy, John D. 1994. "Activists, Authorities and Media Framing of Drunk Driving." In *New Social Movements: From Ideology to Identity*, edited by Enrique Larana, Hank Johnston, and Joseph R. Gusfield. Philadelphia: Temple University Press.

Meyer, John, Francisco O. Ramirez, and Yasemin Nuhoglu Soysal. 1992. "World Expansion of Mass Education, 1870–1980." *Sociology of Education* 65(2):128–49.

Meyer, John, W. Richard Scott, and Terrence E. Deal. 1992. "Institutional and Technical Sources of Organizational Structure: Explaining the Structure of Educational Organizations." In *Organizational Environments: Ritual and Rationality*, edited by John Meyer and W. Richard Scott. Newbury Park, Calif.: Sage Publications.

Opp, Karl-Dieter. 1982. "The Evolutionary Emergence of Norms." *British Journal of Social Psychology* 21(2):139–49.

Parsons, Talcott. 1937. *The Structure of Social Action*. New York: McGraw-Hill.

———. 1952. *The Social System*. New York: Free Press.

Pettit, Philip. 1993. *The Common Mind: An Essay on Psychology, Society, and Politics*. New York: Oxford University Press.

Sampson, Robert J., and W. Byron Groves. 1989. "Community Structure and Crime: Testing Social Disorganization Theory." *American Journal of Sociology* 94(4):774–802.

Sampson, Robert J., Stephen W. Raudenbush, and Felton Earls. 1997. "Neighborhoods and Violent Crime: A Multilevel Study of Collective Efficacy." *Science* 227 (August 15, 1997):918–24.

Scott, John Finley. 1971. *Internalization of Norms: A Sociological Theory of Moral Commitment*. Englewood Cliffs, N.J.: Prentice-Hall.

Shaw, Clifford, and Henry D. McKay. [1942] 1969. *Juvenile Delinquency and Urban Areas*. Chicago: University of Chicago Press.

Sherif, Muzafer. [1936] 1973. *The Psychology of Social Norms*. New York: Octagon Books.

Sumner, William Graham. 1979. *Folkways*. New York: Arno Press.

Weber, Max. 1978. *Economy and Society*. Edited by Guenther Roth and Claus Wittich. Berkeley: University of California Press.

Williams, Robin M., Jr. 1970. *American Society: A Sociological Interpretation.* New York: Alfred A. Knopf.

Wrong, Dennis. 1994. *The Problem of Order: What Unites and Divides a Society.* New York: Free Press.

Yamagishi, Toshio. 1986. "The Provision of a Sanctioning System as a Public Good." *Journal of Personality and Social Psychology* 51(1):110–16.

——. 1995. "Social Dilemmas." In *Sociological Perspectives on Social Psychology,* edited by Karen S. Cook, Gary Alan Fine, and James S. House. Boston: Allyn and Bacon.

Yamagishi, Toshio, and Nobuyuki Takahashi. 1994. "Evolution of Norms Without Meta-Norms." In *Social Dilemmas and Cooperation,* edited by Ulrich Schulz, Wulf Albers, and Ulrich Mueller. New York: Springer-Verlag.

13.

Behavior in Public Places

ERVING GOFFMAN, 1963

[A] social order may be defined as the consequence of any set of moral norms that regulates the way in which persons pursue objectives. The set of norms does not specify the objectives the participants are to seek, nor the pattern formed by and through the coordination or integration of these ends, but merely the modes of seeking them. Traffic rules and the consequent traffic order provide an obvious example. Any social system or any game may be viewed quite properly as an instance of social order, although the perspective of social order does not allow us to get at what is characteristically systemic about systems or what is gamelike about games.

In this study I shall try to be concerned with one type of regulation only, the kind that governs a person's handling of himself and others during, and by virtue of, his immediate physical presence among them; what is called face-to-face or immediate interaction will be involved.

ENGAGEMENTS AMONG THE UNACQUAINTED

One might say, as a general rule, that acquainted persons in a social situation require a reason not to enter into a face engagement with each other, while unacquainted persons require a reason to do so. In these two rules, the same fundamental principle seems to be operative, namely, that the welfare of the individual ought not to be put in jeopardy through his capacity to open himself up for encounters. In the case of acquainted persons, a willingness to give social recognition saves the other from the affront of being overlooked; in the case of unacquainted persons, a willingness to refrain from soliciting encounters saves the other from being exploited by inopportune overtures and requests.

If the assumption is correct that a kind of tacit contract underlies communication conduct, then we must conclude that there are imaginable circum-

Reprinted with permission of The Free Press, an imprint of Simon & Schuster Adult Publishing Group from *Behavior in Public Places* by Erving Goffman. Copyright © 1963 by The Free Press.

stances when *any* two unacquainted persons can properly join each other in some kind of face engagement—circumstances in which one person can approach another—since it will always be possible to imagine circumstances that would nullify the implied danger of contact. I should like now to consider some of these circumstances under which some kind of engagement among the unacquainted is permissible, and sometimes even obligatory, in our American middle-class society.

1. Exposed Positions

Every social position can be seen as an arrangement which opens up the incumbent to engagement with certain categories of others. In some cases these others will be chiefly limited to persons with whom the individual is already acquainted or to whom he has just been introduced in the current engagement. In other positions, such as that of salesperson or receptionist, the individual will be obliged to hold himself ready to be approached by unacquainted others, providing this is in line of daily business. (This fact makes some persons enjoy performing the entailed role and others consider it as socially inferior.) We have here an important example of engagement among the unacquainted, and one that does not disturb social distances because there is a patent reason why properly mannered customers would desire to initiate such encounters.

There are social positions, however, that open up the incumbent to more than mere occupational-others. Thus, in cities, policemen, priests, and often corner newsstand vendors are approached by a wide variety of others seeking a wide variety of information and assistance, in part because it is believed to be clear that no one would seek to take advantage of these public figures. Policemen and priests are especially interesting, since they may be engaged by strangers merely initiating a greeting as opposed to a request for information.

Furthermore, there are broad statuses in our society, such as that of old persons or the very young,[1] that sometimes seem to be considered so meager in

---

1. Children in some towns may even be approached at will for small favors. On the other hand, again as one might expect, in some difficult cities such as Chicago, adults initiating a face engagement with strange children may be suspected of improper designs and so in some cases will be careful not to engage children gratuitously, even in passing. When a child is "with" an adult, the improper possibilities of the contact can be ruled out, thus reestablishing the right of the strange adult. We can understand, then, why a male's comment to a child can be employed as a way of initiating contact with the woman accompanying the child. Dogs, of course, being even more profane than children, provide another classic bridging device to their masters.

sacred value that it may be thought their members have nothing to lose through face engagement, and hence can be engaged at will. None of these persons, it may be noted, has the kind of uniform that can be taken off; none can be off duty during part of the day. Here, then, *persons* are exposed, not merely incumbents; they are "open persons."

There is still another general circumstance that opens up an individual for face engagements; namely, that he can be out of role. Given the assumption that the interests of the individual ought not to be prejudiced by forcing him into contact, and given the fact that these interests of his will be expressed through his playing his serious roles, we can expect that when he is not engaged in his own roles there will then be less reason to be careful with him as regards communication; and this, in fact, is the case. Thus, when an individual is visibly intoxicated, or dressed in a costume, or engaged in an unserious sport, he may be accosted almost at will and joked with, presumably on the assumption that the self projected through these activities is one from which the individual can easily dissociate himself, and hence need not be jealous of or careful with. Similarly, when an individual finds himself in a momentarily peculiar physical position, as when he trips, slips, or in other ways acts in an awkward, unbecoming fashion, he lays himself open for light comment, for he will need a demonstration from others that they see this activity as one that does not prejudice his adult self, and it is in his own interest to allow them to initiate a joking contact with him for this purpose. Thus, as might have been predicted, the first persons in America to drive Volkswagens laid themselves open to face engagements from all and sundry, since they did not seem to be seriously presenting themselves in the role of driver, at least as a driver of a serious car.[2]

I have considered in terms of the language of status and role some of the grounds on which the individual's usual right to be unmolested by overtures is set aside. There are still other times of license, but ones when the terminology of social role is not very suitable. Thus, if an individual is in patent need of help, and if this help is of little moment to the putative giver, then satisfying this "free need" provides a nonsuspect basis for initiating communication contact. For example, when an individual unknowingly drops something in the street, he momentarily becomes open for overtures, since anyone has a right to tell him what has happened. As current etiquette suggests:

> Women must thank all those, including strangers, who do them little services. For example, if a stranger, man or woman, opens a door for a woman,

---

2. See, for example, the report on a New York to Florida trip in 1955, "On the Florida Highroads in a Low Car," *The New York Times,* Sunday, January 30, 1955, by G. H. Glueck.

or picks up something she has dropped, a woman should not allow timidity or shyness to stop her from saying thank you in a pleasant impersonal way. If the stranger seems to be trying to start an unwelcome conversation, one can, still with politeness but with increasing firmness, refuse to converse. But it is more attractive to take for granted that the gesture was motivated by politeness only than it is immediately to suspect another motive.[3]

It should be added that in the past some writers have felt that the very threat of a lady being accosted in a public place, or even being seen to be alone, is sometimes cause enough for a pure-minded stranger to beat others to the draw:

> If a lady is going to her carriage, or is alone in any public place where it is usual or would be convenient for ladies to be attended, you should offer her your arm and service, even if you don't know her. To do so in a private room, as in the case mentioned, might be thought a liberty.[4]

A more contemporary version of this courtesy is found in the tack occasionally taken by a man passing a strange woman at night on a narrow isolated walk: instead of conspicuously according the female civil inattention, the man may proffer a fleeting word to show that, unlike a would-be assailant, he is willing to be identified.

A final basis of exposure may be mentioned. An individual's actions can create a need in others that exposes them to engagement. For example, if the others have been bumped into or tripped over (or in other ways deprived of their right to unmolested passage) by him, he can claim the right to engage them in order to convey assistance, explanation, apology, and the like, the others' need for such redress presumably outweighing their reluctance to being engaged by a stranger. The same holds true for potential, as well as actual, offenses. In a train compartment, for example, individuals may be asked by a fellow-passenger if it is all right if he smokes, or if he opens (or closes) a window. As these opening engagements are patently in the interests of those whose comfort might be affected, the offense or injury the individual might create by his inclinations thus exposes fellow-passengers to solicitous inquiries in advance.

2. Opening Positions

Having considered some circumstances under which persons become available to unacquainted others, we can examine the other side of the question: when does the individual have the right to initiate overtures to those with whom he

---

3. *Vogue's Book of Etiquette,* op. cit., p. 35.

4. Anon., *The Canons of Good Breeding* (Philadelphia: Lee and Blanchard, 1839), p. 66.

is unacquainted? Obviously, one answer is that he can do this when the other is in an exposed position. Another answer is that some of the persons who are defined as open tend also to be defined as "opening persons," as individuals who have a built-in license to accost others. Just as the intentions of those who accost them are not suspect, so, in some cases, their intentions in accosting others may not be suspect. Priests and nuns provide one kind of example; police, who presumably will be able to produce a legitimate reason for the engagement after initiating it, provide another. Those who have responsibility for managing, or for guarding the entrance to, social occasions provide still another example, since they are allowed, and often obliged, to initiate engagements of welcome with all who enter, whether acquainted with them or not. Shopkeepers, in those societies that define shops, more than we do, as the scene of a running social occasion, may often find themselves in the host's role, required to engage each entrant and leave-taker in a special salutation. Freya Stark provides an illustration from Arabia:

> In Kuwait you are still at leisure to notice what a charming thing good manners are.
>
> As you step into the ragged booths you will greet the owner with "Peace be upon you," and he and all who are within hearing will reply with no fanatic exclusion, but in full and friendly chorus to that most gracious of salutations, and will follow your departing steps with their "Fi aman Allah," the divine security. Their shops they treat as small reception-rooms where the visiting buyer is a guest—and sitting at coffee over their affairs will look with surprised but tolerant amusement at the rough Westerner who brushes by to examine saddle-bags or daggers, unconscious of the decent rules of behavior. . . . [5]

In our society, license to approach, like license to be approached, is taken (if not given) by individuals who for a period find themselves out of role. Here, license to initiate improper contact is merely part of the syndrome of license associated with anonymity, in the sense that an individual projecting an alien self is not fully responsible for the good conduct of that self. (In the same way, when he trips or slips, he projects a self from which he can dissociate his inner being.) Again we see a connection between exposed positions and opening ones, for the very alienation from his projected self that allows others to treat this self as approachable and expendable allows him to misbehave in its name. The falsely presented individual may, in fact, have a special need to make and to elicit overtures; in both cases he is able to transmit an appreciation that what he is appearing as is not his true self.

---

5. Freya Stark, *Baghdad Sketches* (New York: Dutton, 1938), p. 192.

Nor is it only when engagement is patently to the advantage of the person approached that emergency engagement with strangers occurs. In our society, as presumably in others, bonds between unacquainted persons are felt to be strong enough to support the satisfying of "free needs," even where the person receiving the service is the one who initiates the encounter that makes this possible. A patent unthreatening need appears to provide a guarantee of the good intentions of the person who is asking for assistance. Thus, in our society, an individual has a right to initiate requests for the time of day, for a light, for directions, and for coin change—although, given a choice in the matter, the accoster is under obligation to select the individual present whom he is least likely to be able to exploit.

Similarly, if an individual finds himself in a position where he badly needs his apologies or explanations to be accepted, he then has some right to engage others. Liberty to apologize for accidentally inconveniencing another is also a liberty to present oneself in a proper light, even at the expense of communication rules. Thus, to parallel an earlier example, a man walking around in the grass looking for a key he has dropped has a right to comment on his predicament to a lone passing stranger to demonstrate that he is not improperly involved in some occult activity. The same kind of license occurs when an individual feels he has been mistreated in some way by an unacquainted other, and initiates a complaint, threat, or caution. While defense of one's honor may work hardship upon the person against whom action is taken, the person who institutes such action is not suspect as far as communication rules are concerned.

3. Mutual Openness

I have considered some of the conditions in which an individual can properly become open for face engagement with those with whom he is unacquainted and some of the conditions in which he can initiate an encounter with strangers. I want now to consider circumstances under which unacquainted individuals can be mutually open to each other, each having the right to initiate and the duty to accept an encounter with the other.

An important basis of mutual accessibility resides in the element of informality and solidarity that seems to obtain between individuals who can recognize each other as being of the same special group, especially, apparently, if this group be one that is disadvantaged or ritually-profane. In American society, Negroes at bus stops often extend greetings to Negroes who are strangers to them, as do Orthodox Jews to one another, or men with beards who meet in "square" surroundings.[6] Sports car drivers on the road may do the same—especially when the car of each is of the same make, and a rare one. And, of course, when fellow-nationals meet in exotic lands they may feel obliged or privileged to initiate a state of talk.

Mutual accessibility also occurs when each of the two persons involved finds himself in a position that is at once exposed and opening. As one student has already suggested, when two persons unintentionally touch each other in passing on the street, both may take on the guilty role, with consequent mutual license to initiate an encounter for purposes of apology.[7] Even when it is clear that only one of the parties is at fault, mutual openness can occur. The offender can treat himself as an opening person, needful of setting the record right about himself, while treating the other as one in need of receiving assurances, and hence place himself in an exposed position. At the same time the offended person can feel that he has the right to initiate demands for apology, or to confirm that no offense has been taken. Similarly, when two pedestrians must pass each other on a narrow walk, or when a pedestrian and motorist pair are in doubt about a joint line of action, a mutually initiated meeting of the eyes can be employed to subtly apportion sides of the walk, or to subtly assure right-of-way to the other, or to ratify and consolidate an allocation that has been communicated.

Another important basis for mutual accessibility arises from what might be called "open regions"—physically bounded places where "any" two persons, acquainted or not, have a right to initiate face engagement with each other for the purpose of extending salutations. Open regions differ according to whether the right is also felt as an obligation, according to the character of the face engagement that is permitted, according to whether or not introductions form part of the consequence of the encounter, and according to the categories of participants that are excluded. I would like to describe briefly some of the kinds of open regions.

In Anglo-American society there exists a kind of "nod line" that can be drawn at a particular point through a rank order of communities according to size. Any community below the line, and hence below a certain size, will subject its adults, whether acquainted or not, to mutual greetings; any community above the line will free all pairs of unacquainted persons from this obligation. (Where the line is drawn varies, of course, according to region.) In the case of communities that fall above the nod line, even persons who cognitively recognize each other to be neighbors, and know that this state of mutual in-

6. The last example was suggested by David Sudnow.

7. J. Toby, "Some Variables in Role Conflict Analysis," *Social Forces,* 30 (1952), 325.

formation exists, may sometimes be careful to refrain from engaging each other. Perhaps this is done on the theory that, once acquaintanceship is established between persons living near one another, it might become difficult to keep sufficient distance in the relationship.

Villages, towns, and rural places that fall below the nod line do not, of course, put absolutely everyone on nodding terms. Thus, in Shetland Isle, there was a general feeling that strange seamen who sounded and looked British were to be brought within the circle of humanity, but not those from foreign ports. The latter tended to be walked past and looked at as if they were not social objects but, rather, physical ones; they tended to be treated as "nonpersons." In spite of these limits, however, we can still speak of these rural settlements as "open regions," where coming into the region makes one accessible to anyone else in the vicinity.

While rural and small town communities are perhaps the largest open regions, they are by no means the only ones. One instance, apparently, is the English sports field, as a report on the social life of American military personnel in Britain suggests:

> Some [American] airmen who have played golf at Davyhulme have been impressed with the friendliness of other players. "Why, they talked to us!" they say. The explanation that to the British a person's presence on a sports field is the equivalent of an introduction, and that one can talk to strangers then, is greeted with some disbelief. Other sports produce similarly friendly results—athletics, flying, and of course darts.[8]

In American society, bars, cocktail lounges, and club cars tend to be defined as open places, at least as between men (and although women are not free to engage men, certainly an overture from a male to a female in these settings is not much of a social delict, this fact constituting one of the important attributes of these settings). Something similar can be said about vacation resorts and about other highly bounded settings:

> A ship may be compared to a country hotel. It is good manners to greet other passengers in a friendly fashion without, however, making presumptuous overtures. You speak to the people next to you in deck chairs, but you do not force conversation upon them. In general, as in a friend's house, the roof is the introduction, but this does not mean you are expected to do more than bow in greeting to fellow passengers as you encounter them during the day.[9]

8. "The Americans in Our Midst," *The Manchester Guardian Weekly,* August 5, 1954.

9. A. Vanderbilt, *Amy Vanderbilt's Complete Book of Etiquette* (New York: Doubleday, 1958), p. 637.

And, as implied, social parties and gatherings in private homes bring into being open regions where participants have a right not only to engage anyone present but also to initiate face engagement with self-introductions, if the gathering is too large for the host or hostess to have already introduced them. As an early American etiquette manual puts it:

> If you meet any one whom you have never heard of before at the table of a gentleman, or in the drawing-room of a lady, you may converse with him with entire propriety. The form of "introduction" is nothing more than a statement by a mutual friend that two gentlemen are by rank and manners fit acquaintances for one another. All this may be presumed from the fact, that both meet at a respectable house. This is the theory of the matter. Custom, however, requires that you should take the earliest opportunity afterwards to be regularly presented to such an one.[10]

A contemporary source restates this theme:

> Nevertheless, it is still true that in a private house, or at any party, a guest may speak to any other guest without an introduction of any kind.[11]

Another illustration of the open regions provided by convivial occasions is carnivals. During these costumed street celebrations, a roof and its rights is by social definition spread above the streets, bringing persons into contact—a contact facilitated by their being out of role.

The assumption of mutual regard and good will built into open regions guarantees a rationale for discounting the potential nefariousness of contact among the unacquainted, this being one basis for sociable accessibility. There are other bases. During occasions of recognized natural disaster, when individuals suddenly find themselves in a clearly similar predicament and suddenly become mutually dependent for information and help, ordinary communication constraints can break down. Again, however, what is occurring in the situation guarantees that encounters aren't being initiated for what can be improperly gained by them. And to the extent that this is assured, contact prohibitions can be relaxed. (If the disaster is quite calamitous, everyone is likely to be forced out of role and hence into mutual accessibility.)

A final contingency that bears on mutual openness may be mentioned. Earlier in this report it was argued that the individual in our society has a right to receive civil inattention. It was also suggested that, when persons ratify each other for mutual participation in an encounter, the rule against looking fully at another is set aside. Typically, then, one person may legitimately begin to

---

10. *The Laws of Etiquette,* by "A Gentleman" (Philadelphia: Carey, Lee and Blanchard, 1836), p. 101.

11. *Vogue's Book of Etiquette,* op. cit., p. 60.

look fully at another a moment before he initiates an encounter, the legitimacy being imputed retroactively, after it is shown what the individual had been intending to do. If, then, persons find that they must stare at each other, they can try to cope with the matter by initiating a state of talk, the overture being excusable (however embarrassing) because of what can be handled by means of it.

There are standard conditions under which the rule about not staring gives rise to these problems. When a few persons find themselves in a small space, as in a European railway compartment, or around the entrance of a store that is not yet quite open, civil inattention is hard to manage tactfully. To not stare requires looking very pointedly in other directions, which may make the whole issue more a matter of consciousness than it was meant to be, and may also express too vividly an incapacity or a distaste for engagement with those present. A lengthy illustration may be taken from a very relevant essay by Cornelia Otis Skinner called "Where to Look:"

> Fortunately such where-to-look situations do not arise with any frequency. One which does, however, is the elevator one . . . both while in an elevator and while waiting for one. The act of waiting for an elevator brings out a suspicious streak in people. You arrive before the closed landing door and push a button. Another person comes along and after a glance of mutual appraisal, you both look quickly away and continue to wait, thinking the while uncharitable thoughts of one another. The new arrival suspecting you of not having pushed the button and you wondering if the new arrival is going to be a mistrusting old meanie and go give the button a second shove . . . an unspoken tension which is broken by one or the other of you walking over and doing just that. Then back to positions of waiting and the problem of where to look. To stare the other person in the eye seems forward and usually the eye doesn't warrant it. Shoes are convenient articles for scrutiny—your own or those of the other person—although if overdone, this may give the impression of incipient shoe fetishism.[12]

It [the where-to-look problem] continues even inside the elevator . . . especially in the crowded and claustrophobic boxes of the modern high buildings. Any mutual exchange of glances on the part of the occupants would add almost a touch of lewdness to such already over-cozy sardine formation. Some people gaze instead at the back of the operator's neck, others stare trance-like up at those little lights which flash the floors, as if safety of the trip were dependent upon such deep concentration.

A rather similar situation arises in a Pullman diner when one is obliged to sit opposite an unknown at a table for two. How to fill in the awkward wait

---

12. Cornelia Otis Skinner, "Where to Look," in *Bottoms Up!* (New York: Dodd, Mead, 1955), pp. 29–30. All ellipsis dots are the author's.

between writing out "Luncheon #4 with coffee" and the arrival and serving of same? If one is not the type who, given the slightest provocation, bursts into friendly chitchat with a stranger, the risk of getting conversationally involved with someone who is, brings out the furtive behavior of an escaped convict. Sometimes it becomes apparent that the other person feels the same way . . . a discovery which comes as a minor shock but no major solution. Two strangers sitting directly opposite each other at a distance of a foot and a half, and determined politely but firmly to avoid each other's eye, go in for a fascinating little game of "I don't spy." They re-read the menu, they fool with the cutlery, they inspect their own fingernails as if seeing them for the first time. Comes the inevitable moment when glances meet but they meet only to shoot instantly away and out the window for an intent view of the passing scene.

It may be added that during such difficult times, if the individual decides against contact, he may well have to find some activity for himself in which he can become visibly immersed, so as to provide the others present with a face-saving excuse for being unattended to. Here again we see the situational functions that newspapers and magazines play in our society, allowing us to carry around a screen that can be raised at any time to give ourselves or others an excuse for not initiating contact.

Airplane and long-distance bus travel have here underlined some interesting issues. Seatmates, while likely to be strangers, are not only physically too close to each other to make nonengagement comfortable, but are also fixed for a long period of time, so that conversation, once begun, may be difficult thereafter either to close or to sustain. In such cases, a strategy is to "thin out" the encounter by keeping it impersonal and by declining to exchange identifying names, thus guaranteeing that some kind of nonrecognition will be possible in the future. Amy Vanderbilt, in newspaper advice, illustrates this point:

> As for airplanes today, seatmates may not exchange a word in a trip across the continent. But plane conversation is in order if mutually desired and kept impersonal. As on trains, names need not be exchanged. And why should they? After all, it is relaxing to talk without identifying oneself.

Relationships with service personnel in our society, when talk is required, may be thinned out in the same way—a thinning, incidentally, that servers may attempt to counteract by asking the name of the customer and proffering their own.

14.

Altruistic Punishment in Humans

ERNST FEHR and SIMON GÄCHTER, 2002

Throughout evolution, crucial human activities like hunting big game, sharing meat, conserving common property resources, and warfare constituted a public good. In situations like these, every member of the group benefits from the 'good', including those who did not pay any costs of providing the good. This raises the question of why people regularly participate in costly cooperative activities like warfare and big-game hunting (Smuts et al. 1987; Richerson and Boyd 1998; Sober and Wilson 1998; Boyd and Richerson forthcoming). . . .

Punishment provides a solution to this problem. If those who free ride on the cooperation of others are punished, cooperation may pay (Sober and Wilson 1998; Clutton-Brock and Parker 1995; Axelrod and Hamilton 1981; Heckathorn 1989; Henrich and Boyd 2001; Ostrom et al. 1992). Yet this 'solution' begs the question of who will bear the cost of punishing the free riders. Everybody in the group will be better off if free riding is deterred, but nobody has an incentive to punish the free riders. Thus, the punishment of free riders constitutes a second-order public good. The problem of second-order public goods can be solved if enough humans have a tendency for altruistic punishment, that is, if they are motivated to punish free riders even though it is costly and yields no material benefits for the punishers.

We examined the question of whether humans engage in altruistic punishment and how this inclination affects the ability of achieving and sustaining cooperation. A total of 240 students participated in a 'public goods' experiment with real monetary stakes and two treatment conditions: punishment and no punishment. In both conditions, groups with four members played the

Reprinted by permission from *Nature,* vol. 415, pp. 137–40. Copyright © 2002 Macmillan Publishers Ltd.

Support by the MacArthur Foundation Network on Economic Environments and the Evolution of Individual Preferences and Social Norms, and the EU-TMR Research Network ENDEAR is gratefully acknowledged. We also thank R. Boyd, A. Falk, U. Fischbacher, H. Gintis and J. Henrich for comments, and M. Näf and D. Reding for research assistance. We are particularly grateful to U. Fischbacher for writing the computer software.

following public goods game. Each member received an endowment of 20 money units (MUs) and each one could contribute between 0 and 20 MUs to a group project. Subjects could keep the money that they did not contribute to the project. For every MU invested in the project, each of the four group members, that is, also those who invested little or nothing, earned 0.4 MUs. Thus, the investor's return from investing one additional MU in the project was 0.4 MUs, whereas the group return was 1.6 MUs. Because the cost of investing 1 MU in the project was exactly 1 MU, whereas the private return was only 0.4 MUs, it was always in the material self-interest of any subject to keep all MUs privately—irrespective of how much the other three subjects contributed. Yet, if all group members kept all MUs privately, each subject earned only 20 MUs, whereas if all of them invested their 20 MUs each subject would earn $0.4 \times 80 = 32$ MUs.

All the interactions in the experiment took place anonymously. Members were not informed of the identity of the others in the group. Subjects made their investment decisions simultaneously and, once the decisions were made, they were informed about the investments of the other group members. The only difference between the two conditions was that in the punishment condition, subjects could punish each of the other group members after they were informed about the others' investments. A punishment decision was implemented by assigning between 0 and 10 points to the punished member. Each point assigned cost the punished member 3 MUs and the punishing member 1 MU. All the punishment decisions were also made simultaneously.

Because we conjectured that the opportunity for punishing would have a larger impact if subjects could learn about the behaviour of other group members, we repeated the basic public goods game—with and without punishment opportunity, depending on the treatment—for six periods. To rule out that repetition created cooperation or punishment through direct reciprocity (Trivers 1971; Axelrod 1984; Axelrod 1986; Nowak et al. 1995) or reputation (Alexander 1987; Nowak and Sigmund 1998a; Nowak and Sigmund 1998b; Lotem et al. 1999; Wedekind and Milinski 2000; Leimar and Hammerstein 2001), the group composition changed from period to period such that no subject ever met another subject more than once. Moreover, our design ruled out any kind of reputation formation . . . , so purely selfish subjects will never cooperate or punish others, because cooperation and punishment are costly and yield no pecuniary benefits. Therefore, the selfish motives associated with theories of indirect reciprocity (Alexander 1987; Nowak and Sigmund 1998a; Nowak and Sigmund 1998b; Lotem et al. 1999; Wedekind and Milinski 2000; Leimar and Hammerstein 2001) or costly signaling (Zahavi 1977; Zahavi 1995; Gintis 2000) cannot explain cooperation and punishment in this environment.

However, punishment may well benefit the future group members of a punished subject, if that subject responds to the punishment by raising investments in the following periods. In this sense, punishment is altruistic. In the presence of altruistic punishers, even purely selfish subjects have a reason to cooperate in the punishment treatment.

ALTRUISTIC PUNISHMENT AND COOPERATION

Altruistic punishment took place frequently. In the ten sessions, subjects punished other group members a total of 1,270 times; 84.3% of the subjects punished at least once, 34.3% punished more than five times during the six periods, and 9.3% punished even more than ten times. Punishment also followed a clear pattern. Most (74.2%) acts of punishment were imposed on defectors (that is, below-average contributors) and were executed by cooperators (that is, above-average contributors), and punishment of the defectors was harsh. . . . For example, if a subject invested 14–20 MUs less than the average investment of the other group members during periods 5 and 6, the total group expenditures for punishing this subject were almost 10 MUs. Moreover, the more a subject's investment fell short of the average investment of the other three group members, the more the subject was punished. The pattern and strength of punishment was also stable across time. . . .

We examined how the group expenditures for the punishment of member i varied with the positive and the negative deviation of member i's cooperation from the average cooperation of the others. . . . This analysis indicates that an increase in the negative deviation of i from the others' average cooperation by 10 MUs increased the punishment expenditure of the others by 6.22 MUs (and, hence, the pay-off reduction imposed on i by 18.66 MUs), whereas an increase in the positive deviation of i by 10 MUs reduced the punishment expenditure by 1.49 MUs. This punishment pattern led to a hump-shaped relation between an individual's income and the deviation from the average cooperation of the other group members. The income was highest when the individual's investment was close to the average investment of the others. Both positive and negative deviations from the average investment decreased an individual's income.

The punishment of non-cooperators substantially increased the amount that subjects invested in the public good. In the five sessions where the punishment condition was the first treatment (Figure 14.1a), the average cooperation level was much higher in the punishment condition. . . . The average investment of 94.2% of the subjects was higher in the punishment condition. In fact, the average investment in the punishment condition was higher in each session and in each period than the average investment in any of the periods

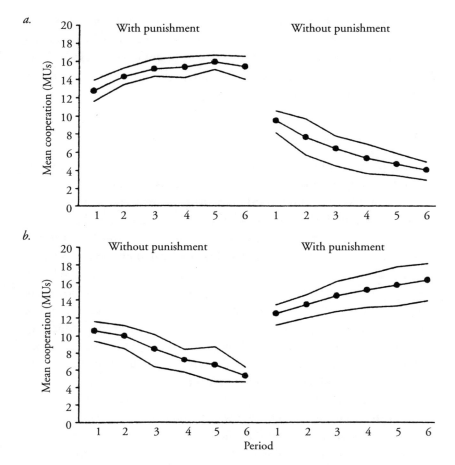

FIGURE 14.1 Time trend of mean cooperation together with the 95% confidence interval. *a.* During the first six periods, subjects have the opportunity to punish the other group members. Afterwards, the punishment opportunity is removed. *b.* During the first six periods, punishment of other group members is ruled out. Afterwards, punishment is possible.

and sessions of the no-punishment condition. The time trend of the average investment was also rather different in the two conditions (Figure 14.1a). Although cooperation increased over time in the punishment condition, it sharply decreased in the no-punishment condition. In the final period of the punishment condition, 38.9% of the subjects contributed their whole endowment and 77.8% contributed 15 MUs or more. In the final period of the no-punishment condition, 58.9% of the subjects contributed nothing and 75.6% contributed 5 MUs or less.

A very similar pattern emerged in the sessions where the no-punishment condition came first (Figure 14.1b). The average cooperation again was much higher in the punishment condition. . . . In the punishment condition, 91.4% of the subjects contributed more than in the no-punishment condition. In addition, although the average investment decreased in the no-punishment condition, it increased sharply in the punishment condition. Moreover, Figure 14.1b indicates that the punishment threat was immediately effective because there was a large upwards jump in investments when the punishment opportunity was made available to the subjects. It also turns out that the sequence of the treatments had no effect on cooperation. Investments in the punishment condition were similar, irrespective of whether this condition came first or second in a session. . . . The same held for the no-punishment condition. . . . Thus, we can use the data of all ten sessions to compare the average investments across conditions so that the differences are significant at a much higher level. . . .

It is not only the punishment opportunity (that is, the non-executed punishment threat) but also the actual punishment that raised cooperation levels. When a subject was punished before period 6, that subject raised investment in the next period on average by 1.62 MUs. Note, however, that this does not constitute an indirect material benefit of the act of punishment for an individual punisher, because the punishing subject never meets the same subjects again. The act of punishment does provide a material benefit for the future interaction partners of the punished subject but not for the punisher. Thus, the act of punishment, although costly for the punisher, provides a benefit to other members of the population by inducing potential non-cooperators to increase their investments. For this reason, the act of punishment is an altruistic act.

EMOTIONS AS A PROXIMATE MECHANISM

Given the pattern of punishment, the investment behaviour of subjects seems quite rational. To avoid punishment, subjects invested in accordance with the group norm. But we wondered why subjects punish free riders in a one-shot context when this is costly. With regard to the proximate source of the punishment, negative emotions may provide an explanation. Free riding may cause strong negative emotions among the cooperators and these emotions, in turn, may trigger their willingness to punish the free riders (Hirshleifer 1987; Frank 1988). If this conjecture is correct, we should observe particular emotional patterns in response to free riding. To elicit these patterns, the participants were confronted with the following two hypothetical investment scenarios after the final period of the second treatment (the numbers in brackets relate to the second scenario):

"You decide to invest 16 [5] francs to the project. The second group member invests 14 [3] and the third 18 [7] francs. Suppose the fourth member invests 2 francs to the project. You now accidentally meet this member. Please indicate your feeling toward this person."

After they had read a scenario, subjects had to indicate the intensity of their anger and annoyance towards the fourth person (the free rider) on a seven-point scale (1 = 'not at all' to 7 = 'very much'). The difference between scenarios 1 and 2 is that the other three persons in the group contribute relatively much in scenario 1 and relatively little in scenario 2. It turns out that a free rider triggered much anger among the other subjects if these subjects contributed a lot relative to the free rider (scenario 1). Forty-seven per cent of the subjects indicated an anger level of 6 or 7 and another 37% indicated an anger level of 5. If the deviation of the free rider's contribution from the other members' contribution was relatively small (scenario 2), the anger level was significantly lower. . . . but still considerable. In this case (scenario 2), 17.4% of the subjects indicated an anger level of 6 or 7 and 80.5% indicated a level of 4 or 5 in scenario 2. This shows that the intensity of negative emotions towards a free rider varies with the deviation from the others' average contribution.

Because we were also interested in the free riders' expectation of the other members' anger, we confronted subjects with a third and fourth hypothetical scenario (numbers in brackets relate to scenario 4):

"Imagine that the other three group members invest 14, 16 and 18 [3, 5 and 7] francs to the project. You invest 2 francs to the project and the others know this. You now accidentally meet one of the other members. Please indicate the feelings you expect from this member towards you."

In scenarios 3 and 4, the hypothetical free rider had to indicate the expected anger of the others on a seven-point scale. The anger that was expected by the free riders in scenario 3 was even greater than the actually expressed anger according to scenario 1. . . . In scenario 3, 74.5% of the subjects expected the anger level of others to be 6 or 7, and 22.5% expected an anger level of 5. In scenario 4, the deviation of the hypothetical free rider from the others' contribution was smaller than in scenario 3. This decrease in the deviation from the others caused significant differences in expected anger levels between scenarios 3 and 4. . . . Only 17.8% of the hypothetical free riders expected anger levels of 6 or 7 in scenario 4 and 80% expected levels of 4 or 5.

The low contributors in the no-punishment condition expected a higher intensity of negative emotions than the high contributors. This probably reflects the fact that the low contributors in the no-punishment condition experienced more sanctions in the punishment condition.

The same four scenarios were presented to 33 subjects that had not previously participated in our experiments, to check whether participating in the experiment affects the elicited emotions. The same emotional patterns that were expressed by our 240 experimental subjects were expressed by the 33 subjects who did not participate in our games.

Our results suggest that free riding causes strong negative emotions and that most people expect these emotions. Moreover, the above emotional pattern is consistent with the hypothesis that emotions trigger punishment for the following reasons. First, if negative emotions trigger punishment, most punishment acts would be expected to be executed by above-average contributors and imposed on below-average contributors. This is clearly the case in our experiments: 74.2% of all punishment acts follow this pattern. Second, punishment increased with the deviation of the free rider from the average investment of the other members. This is exactly what would be expected if negative emotions are the proximate cause of the punishment, because negative emotions became more intense as the free rider deviated further from the others' average investment. Third, if negative emotions cause punishment, the punishment threat is rendered immediately credible because most people are well aware that they trigger strong negative emotions when they free ride. Therefore, we should detect an immediate impact of the punishment opportunity on contributions at the switch points between the punishment and the no-punishment condition. This is what we observed. The introduction (or elimination) of the punishment opportunity led to an immediate rise (or fall) in investment (see Figure 14.1). Taken together, these observations are consistent with the view that emotions are an important proximate factor behind altruistic punishment.

Our evidence has profound implications for the evolutionary study of human behaviour. . . . By showing that altruistic punishment is a key force in the establishment of human cooperation, our . . . evidence suggests that the evolutionary study of human cooperation in large groups of unrelated individuals should include a focus on explaining altruistic punishment (Sober and Wilson 1998; Gintis et al. 2001; Sigmund et al. 2001). . . .

REFERENCES

Alexander, R. D. 1987. *The Biology of Moral Systems.* New York: Aldine de Gruyter.

Axelrod, R. 1984. *The Evolution of Cooperation.* New York: Basic Books.

Axelrod, R. 1986. "An evolutionary approach to norms." *Am. Pol. Sc. Rev.* 80:1095–11.

Axelrod, R., and W. D. Hamilton. 1981. "The evolution of cooperation." *Science* 211:1390–96.

Boyd, R., and P. Richerson. Forthcoming. In *Evolution and Culture,* edited by S. Levinson. Cambridge, Mass.: MIT Press.

Clutton-Brock, T. H., and G. A. Parker. 1995. "Punishment in animal societies." *Nature* 373:209–16.

Frank, R. 1988. *Passions Within Reason: The Strategic Role of the Emotions.* New York: Norton.

Gintis, H. 2000. "Strong reciprocity and human sociality." *J. Theor. Biol.* 206:169–79.

Gintis, H., E. Smith, and S. Bowles. 2001. "Costly signaling and cooperation." *J. Theor. Biol.* 213:103–19.

Heckathorn, D. D. 1989. "Collective action and the second-order free-rider problem." *Ration. Soc.* 1:78–100.

Henrich, J., and R. Boyd. 2001. "Why people punish defectors." *J. Theor. Biol.* 208:79–89.

Hirshleifer, J. 1987. In *The Latest on the Best: Essays on Evolution and Optimality,* edited by J. Dupré. Cambridge, Mass.: MIT Press.

Leimar, O., and P. Hammerstein. 2001. "Evolution of cooperation through indirect reciprocity." *Proc. R. Soc. Lond.* B 268:745–53.

Lotem, A., M. A. Fishman, and L. Stone. 1999. "Evolution of cooperation between individuals." *Nature* 400:226–27.

Nowak, M. A., R. M. May, and K. Sigmund. 1995. "The arithmetics of mutual help." *Sci. Am.* 272:76–81.

Nowak, M. A., and K. Sigmund. 1998a. "The dynamics of indirect reciprocity." *J. Theor. Biol.* 194:561–74.

Nowak, M. A., and K. Sigmund. 1998b. "Evolution of indirect reciprocity by image scoring." *Nature* 393:573–77.

Ostrom, E., J. Walker, and R. Gardner. 1992. "Covenants with and without a sword: self governance is possible." *Am. Pol. Sci. Rev.* 86:404–17.

Richerson, P., and R. Boyd. 1998. In *Ideology, Warfare, and Indoctrinability,* edited by I. Eibl-Eibesfeldt and F. Salter, 71–95. New York: Berghan Books.

Sigmund, K., C. Hauert, and M. A. Nowak. 2001. "Reward and punishment." *Proc. Natl. Acad. Sci. USA* 98:10757–761.

Smuts, B. B., D. L. Cheney, R. M. Seyfarth, R. W. Wrangham, and T. T. Struhsaker, editors. 1987. *Primate Societies.* Chicago: University of Chicago Press.

Sober, E., and D. S. Wilson. 1998. *Unto Others: The Evolution and Psychology of Unselfish Behaviour.* Cambridge, Mass.: Harvard University Press.

Trivers, R. 1971. "The evolution of reciprocal altruism." *Q. Rev. Biol.* 46:35–57.

Wedekind, C., and M. Milinski. 2000. "Cooperation through image scoring in humans." *Science* 288:850–52.

Zahavi, A. 1977. "The cost of honesty (further remarks on the handicap principle)." *J. Theor. Biol.* 67:603–5.

Zahavi, A. 1995. "Altruism as a handicap—the limitations of kin selection and reciprocity." *J. Avian. Biol.* 26:1–3.

F.
Power and Authority

For those who view norms and values as a source of order, social groups are able to regulate themselves informally, either through socializing their members so that values are internalized or by sanctioning those who engage in deviance. Although values and norms are widely viewed as solutions to the problem of order and are used to explain a range of social behavior, the difficulty is that antisocial behavior persists (Wrong 1961). Despite generally accepted rules to the contrary, people often engage in deviant activities. If values and norms were as effective as they are sometimes thought to be, we would all be good family and community citizens all of the time. Of course, we are not.

Under some conditions people seem willing to violate even the most deeply ingrained norms. For example, although the thought of eating human flesh horrifies us, under extreme conditions even civilized Westerners engage in cannibalism (Read 1974). Moreover, sometimes norms are unclear. Whereas normative obligations are often regarded as self-evident, in practice norms are always subject to a zone of interpretation. This affords individuals greater latitude in complying with them than is customarily recognized (Edgerton 1985; Fine 2001). Even when norms are followed, they may not contribute to social order. When groups such as urban gangs or the Mafia encourage behaviors like cheating, aggression, and retaliation, the likely consequence is social disorder. Mere observation thus suggests that values and norms alone do not guarantee social order.

Some theorists who doubt the sufficiency of values and norms regard a central authority as necessary for the emergence and maintenance of social order. Thomas Hobbes provides the most famous example, asserting that a strong central state is essential for the attainment of social order. He begins his argument by imagining a condition that has none of the common features of civilized societies—the state of nature. In this state of nature, there is no central authority. Further, people are fundamentally equal in their powers and capacities. This means that everyone has similar desires regarding what they want their lives to be like. Given these motivations, how will people behave?

Hobbes assumes that people are rational agents who calculate the expected benefits and costs of their actions and act so as to attain their most desired ends. The problem is that everyone wants the same things. Therefore, individuals must fight others both to get and to hold onto what they want. As Hobbes says, "if any two men desire the same thing, which nevertheless they cannot both enjoy, they become enemies; and in the way to their End . . . *endeavour to destroy, or subdue one an other*" (see p. 171; emphasis added).

The result is a war of all against all. People are totally free—they have untrammeled liberty. But they are also insecure. They live in fear of injury and death; there is no agriculture or industry because investment in enterprise is too risky. This is not the kind of life anyone wants to endure.

How is the desire for order translated into action? People cannot merely agree to live in peace. Such an approach is doomed to fail because individuals remain rational egoists who would renege on the agreement whenever it is to their advantage to do so. They are unrestrained by moral considerations and can be expected to use "force and fraud" to attain their ends. The solution then is for individuals to surrender their liberty to some person or body who can make the agreement stick. This agency is the state.

Once the state emerges, its capacity to enforce the agreement rests on military power "because the bonds of words are too weak to bridle mens ambition, avarice, anger, and other Passions, without the feare of some coërcive Power" (see p. 177). Social order triumphs over the state of nature by coercion: would-be rebels and miscreants are powerless against the military capacity of the government.

Hobbes's solution to the problem of order therefore relies on the emergence of a coercive force able to control self-interested individuals. The Marxian solution in the selected reading by Friedrich Engels is also coercive—it too rests on state power—but it focuses on collective actors. Instead of a world made up of *equal individuals,* Engels's starting point is a society made up of *unequal classes.*

A class is a group of people sharing a common relation to the means of production. The most important class distinction divides owners of the means of production from non-owners. Although a number of intermediate classes also exist in many types of societies, nearly every society has a dominant class that constitutes a small minority of the population.[1] This class owns the bulk of the productive resources. In feudal societies, where production is primarily agricultural, the dominant class is made up of that set of individuals who own the bulk of the productive land; in capitalist societies, the ruling class is composed of the individuals who own most of the capital; and so forth. The majority of the population in these societies, however, labors on behalf of the dominant class. In feudalism, this majority is the serfs; in capitalism it is the proletariat.

Class divisions are key because of how they affect individuals. As we saw in the Marx reading earlier in this book, people's characteristics—including modes of thought—depend crucially on their role in material production:

> As individuals express their life, so they are. What they are, therefore, coincides with their production, both with *what* they produce and with *how* they produce. Thus, what individuals are depends on the material conditions of their production.
>
> . . . In complete contrast to German philosophy, which descends from heaven to earth, the procedure here will be to move from earth to heaven. That is, we will not proceed on the basis of what men say and imagine about themselves, nor on the basis of imagined and conceptualised men, in order to arrive from there at flesh and blood men; we will begin with real, active men, and from their real life process we will expose the development of the ideological reflections and echoes of this life process. (see pp. 49–50)

People who are in the same life situations see the world in the same way. They all have the same beliefs and values. Thus individuals in a given class can be

---

1. Tribal societies that have communal property rights are the exception; Marx and Engels refer to these as "primitive communist" societies.

considered as identical, just as if they were sociological clones.[2] Those in different classes have different beliefs and interests.

The interests of the dominant and subordinate classes are directly at odds; their behavior reflects these opposing interests. On this view, then, societies are inherently prone to conflict. In "The Origin of the State," Engels argues that this conflict between the classes is responsible for the rise of the coercive state. The most powerful class (the owners) dominates the lower classes by controlling the government. Naturally, the coercive state rules in the interest of the upper class. Accordingly, in capitalist societies, the state can be seen as simply the executive committee of the bourgeoisie.[3]

For Engels, the state serves the function of maintaining order in class-divided societies. But how can such an institution, patently unjust as it is, ever be imposed and maintained? Hobbes says that coercive order provides benefits to the ruled. People are willing to accept the control of the state because they receive security in return. Engels offers no comparable mechanism. For Engels, the state coerces the lower classes and prevents them from pursuing their interests. Why do people in the lower classes go along with this oppression?

It is evident that coercion is at least partially responsible for social order. Every modern state has a police force charged with the responsibility and coercive capacity to uphold the law. Yet if coercion were solely responsible for social order, then there would have to be a cop on every corner, an Orwellian telescreen in every room. No complex society has ever approached this level of coercion; it is both ethically and economically unappealing. From an ethical view, as the nineteenth-century French anarchist Pierre-Joseph Proudhon noted,

> To be GOVERNED is to be watched, inspected, spied upon, directed,
> law-driven, numbered, regulated, enrolled, indoctrinated, preached at,
> controlled, checked, estimated, valued, censured, commanded, by

---

2. For a fuller discussion of Marx's behavioral assumptions, see Elster 1985.

3. A case in point is the recent controversy about campaign finance reform in the United States. The issue reflects a concern that wealthy individuals and corporations are buying elections, thereby subverting the popular will.

creatures who have neither the right nor the wisdom nor the virtue to do so. To be GOVERNED is to be at every operation, at every transaction noted, registered, counted, taxed, stamped, measured, numbered, assessed, licensed, authorized, admonished, prevented, forbidden, reformed, corrected, punished. It is, under pretext of public utility, and in the name of the general interest, to be placed under contribution, drilled, fleeced, exploited, monopolized, extorted from, squeezed, hoaxed, robbed; then, at the slightest resistance, the first word of complaint, to be repressed, fined, vilified, harrassed, hunted down, abused, clubbed, disarmed, bound, choked, imprisoned, judged, condemned, shot, deported, sacrificed, sold, betrayed; and to crown all, mocked, ridiculed, derided, outraged, dishonored. That is government; that is its justice; that is its morality. (Cited in Nozick 1974, 11)

From an economic point of view, coercion is simply too expensive to be the sole basis of social order. The government cannot afford to watch all of us all of the time. How then can it maintain its control?

Marx and Engels suggest that the disadvantaged are duped by the institutions and ideology of the ruling class. Religion, for example, functions as the opiate of the people (Marx and Engels 1964). A contemporary Marxist might note that this is no less true of print and broadcast media, which in many countries are owned by wealthy capitalists interested in maintaining the status quo. Even education, supposedly a ticket out of the working class, often serves the interests of the wealthy at the expense of the poor (Bowles and Gintis 1976).

A more complex answer is that the state must be seen as *legitimate*. For Max Weber, a defining feature of any social order is that rules are obeyed in the absence of coercion. In legitimate orders, people are willing to obey rules and laws of their own accord. To increase such voluntary compliance, therefore, every governance structure attempts to cultivate a belief in its own legitimacy.

In "The Types of Legitimate Domination," Weber identifies three kinds of authority structures—patrimonial, bureaucratic, and charismatic. Each type gets people to believe in its legitimacy in different ways. In patrimonial orders, which flourish in territories lacking advanced communications and transportation technology, the staff is tied to the ruler by personal loyalty. In return for their loyalty, the ruler grants the staff offices that they can exploit for their material benefit. In modern bureaucracies, however, the staff believes in the legality of enacted rules and the right of those placed in authority under these rules to issue commands. The salary that bureaucrats receive for their positions provides motivation to comply with their superiors' commands. Because it exploits the division of labor, and because recruitment to positions is based on expertise rather than personal dependence, bureaucracy is the most efficient means of exercising authority. In charismatic orders, authority is granted to the leader on the basis of his or her exceptional qualities; the leader is unable to compensate the staff for their loyalty.[4] Each type of authority thus relies on a different mechanism to produce loyalty in individuals. When authorities are successful, individuals see them as legitimate and behave accordingly.

In his ethnographic study of a secondary school in the English Midlands, Paul Willis provides an example of the kind of class conflict that Marx and Engels discuss in a situation in which authorities lack legitimacy. The school represents formal authority and is backed up by the police. Rather than obey this authority, the students view it as illegitimate and engage in constant challenges. They create their own counterculture that disparages teachers as well as the very idea of academic achievement. Students are bound to get the short end of the stick in this conflict, however. Because they view the system as illegitimate and rebel against it, they destroy any chance they may have of escaping to the university and more rewarding jobs. Their counterculture prepares them to step into their fathers' jobs and worlds. Thus, the students' behavior helps reproduce the very conditions of inequality that made them disaffected in the first place. Although the coercive power of the institution does not produce obedience, the students' rebellion facilitates the continued superior position and control of the upper class.

Each of the readings in this section argues that social order requires that some agency or group have greater power and authority than that held by other members of the society. Social order is produced and maintained when

---

4. For a recent discussion of Weber's thought, see Swedberg 1998.

a minority dominates a majority. The theorists differ, however, in their under-standing of the processes leading to such domination. They also differ in how they view the consequences. For Hobbes, state domination increases security and the quality of life. For Engels, by contrast, top-down controls are oppres-sive to large segments of society and limit individual development. Weber sug-gests that coercion is unlikely to sustain order without a leavening of legiti-macy. Willis's empirical evidence suggests that legitimation may be necessary for cooperation but not for predictability. He shows that the very illegitimacy of capitalist society in the eyes of working-class youth serves to reproduce the class structure from generation to generation.

REFERENCES

Bowles, Samuel, and Herbert Gintis. 1976. *Schooling in Capitalist America: Educational Reform and the Contradictions of Economic Life.* New York: Basic Books.

Edgerton, Robert. 1985. *Rules, Exceptions and Social Order.* Berkeley: University of California Press.

Elster, Jon. 1985. *Making Sense of Marx.* Cambridge: Cambridge University Press.

Fine, Gary Alan. 2001. "Enacting Norms: Mushrooming and the Culture of Expectations and Explanations." In *Social Norms,* edited by Michael Hechter and Karl-Dieter Opp, 139–64. New York: Russell Sage Foundation.

Marx, Karl, and Friedrich Engels. 1964. *On Religion.* New York: Schocken Books.

Nozick, Robert. 1974. *Anarchy, State, and Utopia.* New York: Basic Books.

Read, Piers Paul. 1974. *Alive: The Story of the Andes Survivors.* Philadelphia: Lippincott.

Swedberg, Richard. 1998. *Max Weber and the Idea of Economic Sociology.* Princeton: Princeton University Press.

Wrong, Dennis H. 1961. "The Oversocialized Conception of Man in Modern Sociology." *American Sociological Review* 26:183–93.

15.

Leviathan

THOMAS HOBBES, 1651

OF REASON, AND SCIENCE

Reason what it is.

When a man *Reasoneth,* hee does nothing else but conceive a summe totall, from *Addition* of parcels; or conceive a Remainder, from *Substraction* of one summe from another: which (if it be done by Words,) is conceiving of the consequence *from*[1] the names of all the parts, to the name of the whole; or from the names of the whole and one part, to the name of the other part. And though in some things, (as in numbers,) besides *Adding* and *Substracting,* men name other operations, as *Multiplying* and *Dividing*; yet they are the same; for Multiplication, is but Adding together of things equall; and Division, but Substracting of one thing, as often as we can. These operations are not incident to Numbers onely, but to all manner of things that can be added together, and taken one out of another. For as Arithmeticians teach to adde and substract in *numbers*; so the Geometricians teach the same in *lines, figures* (solid and superficiall,) *angles, proportions, times,* degrees of *swiftnesse, force, power,* and the like; The Logicians teach the same in *Consequences of words*; adding together *two Names,* to make an *Affirmation*; and *two Affirmations,* to make a *Syllogisme*; and *many Syllogismes* to make a *Demonstration*; and from the *summe,* or *Conclusion* of a *Syllogisme,* they substract one *Proposition,* to finde the other. Writers of Politiques, adde together *Pactions,* to find mens *duties*; and Lawyers, *Lawes,* and *facts,* to find what is *right* and *wrong* in the actions of private men. In summe, in what matter soever there is place for *addition* and *substraction,* there also is place for *Reason*; and where these have no place, there *Reason* has nothing at all to do.

Excerpts from *Leviathan* by Thomas Hobbes, edited by Richard Tuck. © in the Introduction and editorial matter Cambridge University Press 1991. Reprinted with the permission of Cambridge University Press.

1. *Syn.*: of

Reason defined.

Out of all which we may define, (that is to say determine,) what that is, which is meant by this word *Reason,* when wee reckon it amongst the Faculties of the mind. For REASON, in this sense, is nothing but *Reckoning* (that is, Adding and Substracting) of the Consequences of generall names agreed upon, for the *marking* and *signifying* of our thoughts; I say *marking* them, when we reckon by our selves; and *signifying,* when we demonstrate, or approve our reckonings to other men.

OF THE DIFFERENCE OF MANNERS

What is here meant by Manners.

By MANNERS, I mean not here, Decency of behaviour; as how one man should salute another, or how a man should wash his mouth, or pick his teeth before company, and such other points of the *Small Moralls*; But those qualities of man-kind, that concern their living together in Peace, and Unity. To which end we are to consider, that the Felicity of this life, consisteth not in the repose of a mind satisfied. For there is no such *Finis ultimus,* (utmost ayme,) nor *Summum Bonum,* (greatest Good,) as is spoken of in the Books of the old Morall Philosophers. Nor can a man any more live, whose Desires are at an end, than he, whose Senses and Imaginations are at a stand. Felicity is a continuall progresse of the desire, from one object to another; the attaining of the former, being still but the way to the later. The cause whereof is, That the object of mans desire, is not to enjoy once onely, and for one instant of time; but to assure for ever, the way of his future desire. And therefore the voluntary actions, and inclinations of all men, tend, not onely to the procuring, but also to the assuring of a contented life; and differ onely in the way: which ariseth partly from the diversity of passions, in divers men; and partly from the difference of the knowledge, or opinion each one has of the causes, which produce the effect desired.

A restlesse desire of Power, in all men.

So that in the first place, I put for a generall inclination of all mankind, a perpetuall and restlesse desire of Power after power, that ceaseth onely in Death. And the cause of this, is not always that a man hopes for a more intensive delight, than he has already attained to; or that he cannot be content with a moderate power: but because he cannot assure the power and means to live well, which he hath present, without the acquisition of more. And from hence it is, that Kings, whose power is greatest, turn their endeavours to the assuring it at home by Lawes, or abroad by Wars: and when that is done, there succeedeth a new desire; in some, of Fame from new Conquest; in others, of ease and sensuall pleasure; in others, of admiration, or being flattered for excellence in some art, or other ability of the mind.

Love of Contention from Competition.

Competition of Riches, Honour, Command, or other power enclineth to Contention, Enmity, and War: Because the way of one Competitor, to the attaining of his desire, is to kill, subdue, supplant, or repell the other. Particularly, competition of praise, enclineth to a reverence of Antiquity. For men contend with the living, not with the dead; to these ascribing more than due, that they may obscure the glory of the other.

Civil obedience from love of Ease. From feare of Death, or Wounds.

Desire of Ease, and sensuall Delight, disposeth men to obey a common Power: Because by such Desires, a man doth abandon the protection might be hoped for from his own Industry, and labour. Fear of Death, and Wounds, disposeth to the same; and for the same reason. On the contrary, needy men, and hardy, not contented with their present condition; as also, all men that are ambitious of Military command, are enclined to continue the causes of warre; and to stirre up trouble and sedition: for there is no honour Military but by warre; nor any such hope to mend an ill game, as by causing a new shuffle.

And from love of Arts.

Desire of Knowledge, and Arts of Peace, enclineth men to obey a common Power: For such Desire, containeth a desire of leasure; and consequently protection from some other Power than their own.

Love of Vertue from love of Praise.

Desire of Praise, disposeth to laudable actions, such as please them whose judgement they value; for of those men whom we contemn, we contemn also the Praises. Desire of Fame after death does the same. And though after death, there be no sense of the praise given us on Earth, as being joyes, that are either swallowed up in the unspeakable joyes of Heaven, or extinguished in the extreme torments of Hell: yet is not such Fame vain; because men have a present delight therein, from the foresight of it, and of the benefit that may redound thereby to their posterity: which though they now see not, yet they imagine; and any thing that is pleasure in the sense, the same also is pleasure in the imagination.

Hate, from difficulty of Requiting great Benefits.

To have received from one, to whom we think our selves equall, greater benefits than there is hope to Requite, disposeth to counterfeit love; but really secret hatred; and puts a man into the estate of a desperate debtor, that in declining the sight of his creditor, tacitely wishes him there, where he might never see him more. For benefits oblige; and obligation is thraldome; and unrequitable obligation, perpetuall thraldome; which is to ones equall, hatefull. But to have received benefits from one, whom we acknowledge for superiour, enclines to love; because the obligation is no new depression: and cheerfull acceptation, (which men call *Gratitude*,) is such an honour done to the obliger, as is taken generally for retribution. Also to receive benefits, though from an equall, or inferiour, as long as there is hope of requitall, disposeth to love: for in the intention of the receiver, the obligation is of ayd, and service mutuall; from whence proceedeth an Emulation of who shall exceed in benefiting; the most noble and profitable contention possible; wherein the victor is pleased with his victory, and the other revenged by confessing it.

And from Conscience of deserving to be hated.

To have done more hurt to a man, than he can, or is willing to expiate, enclineth the doer to hate the sufferer. For he must expect revenge, or forgivenesse; both which are hatefull.

Promptnesse to hurt, from Fear.

Feare of oppression, disposeth a man to anticipate, or to seek ayd by society: for there is no other way by which a man can secure his life and liberty.

Curiosity to know, from Care of future time. Naturall Religion, from the same.

Anxiety for the future time, disposeth men to enquire into the causes of things: because the knowledge of them, maketh men the better able to order the present to their best advantage.

Curiosity, or love of the knowledge of causes, draws a man from consideration of the effect, to seek the cause; and again, the cause of that cause; till of necessity he must come to this thought at last, that there is some cause, whereof there is no former cause, but is eternall; which is it men call God. So that it is impossible to make any profound enquiry into naturall causes, without being enclined thereby to believe there is one God Eternall; though they cannot have any Idea of him in their mind, answerable to his nature. For as a man that is born blind, hearing men talk of warming themselves by the fire, and being brought to warm himself by the same, may easily conceive, and assure himselfe, there is somewhat there, which men call *Fire,* and is the cause of the heat he feeles; but cannot imagine what it is like; nor have an Idea of it in his mind, such as they have that see it: so also, by the visible things of this world, and their admirable order, a man may conceive there is a cause of them, which men call God; and yet not have an Idea, or Image of him in his mind.

And they that make little, or no enquiry into the naturall causes of things, yet from the feare that proceeds from the ignorance it selfe, of what it is that hath the power to do them much good or harm, are enclined to suppose, and feign unto themselves, severall kinds of Powers Invisible; and to stand in awe of their own imaginations; and in time of distresse to invoke them; as also in the time of *unexpected*[2] good successe, to give them thanks; making the creatures of their own fancy, their Gods. By which means it hath come to passe, that from the innumerable variety of Fancy, men have created in the world innumerable sorts of Gods. And this Feare of things invisible, is the naturall Seed of that, which every one in himself calleth Religion; and in them that worship, or feare that Power otherwise than they do, Superstition.

And this seed of Religion, having been observed by many; some of those that have observed it, have been enclined thereby to nourish, dresse, and forme it into Lawes; and to adde to it of their own invention, any opinion of the causes of future events, by which they thought they should best be able to govern others, and make unto themselves the greatest use of their Powers.

OF THE NATURALL CONDITION OF MANKIND, AS CONCERNING THEIR FELICITY, AND MISERY

Men by nature Equall.

Nature hath made men so equall, in the faculties of body, and mind; as that though there bee found one man sometimes manifestly stronger in body, or of quicker mind then another; yet when all is reckoned together, the difference between man, and man, is not so considerable, as that one man can thereupon claim to himselfe any benefit, to which another may not pretend, as well as he.

---

2. *Syn.:* an expected.

For as to the strength of body, the weakest has strength enough to kill the strongest, either by secret machination, or by confederacy with others, that are in the same danger with himselfe.

And as to the faculties of the mind, (setting aside the arts grounded upon words, and especially that skill of proceeding upon generall, and infallible rules, called Science; which very few have, and but in few things; as being not a native faculty, born with us; nor attained, (as Prudence,) while we look after somewhat els,) I find yet a greater equality amongst men, than that of strength. For Prudence, is but Experience; which equall time, equally bestowes on all men, in those things they equally apply themselves unto. That which may perhaps make such equality incredible, is but a vain conceipt of ones owne wisdome, which almost all men think they have in a greater degree, than the Vulgar; that is, than all men but themselves, and a few others, whom by Fame, or for concurring with themselves, they approve. For such is the nature of men, that howsoever they may acknowledge many others to be more witty, or more eloquent, or more learned; Yet they will hardly believe there be many so wise as themselves: For they see their own wit at hand, and other mens at a distance. But this proveth rather that men are in that point equall, than un-equall. For there is not ordinarily a greater signe of the equall distribution of any thing, than that every man is contented with his share.

From Equality proceeds Diffidence.

From this equality of ability, ariseth equality of hope in the attaining of our Ends. And therefore if any two men desire the same thing, which neverthelesse they cannot both enjoy, they become enemies; and in the way to their End, (which is principally their owne conservation, and sometimes their delectation only,) endeavour to destroy, or subdue one an other. And from hence it comes to passe, that where an Invader hath no more to feare, than an other mans single power; if one plant, sow, build, or possesse a convenient Seat, others may probably be expected to come prepared with forces united, to dispossesse, and deprive him, not only of the fruit of his labour, but also of his life, or liberty. And the Invader again is in the like danger of another.

From Diffidence Warre.

And from this diffidence of one another, there is no way for any man to secure himselfe, so reasonable, as Anticipation; that is, by force, or wiles, to master the persons of all men he can, so long, till he see no other power great enough to endanger him: And this is no more than his own conservation requireth, and is generally allowed. Also because there be some, that taking pleasure in contemplating their own power in the acts of conquest, which they pursue farther than their security requires; if others, that otherwise would be glad to be at ease within modest bounds, should not by invasion increase their power, they would not be able, long time, by standing only on their defence, to subsist. And by consequence, such augmentation of dominion over men, being necessary to a mans conservation, it ought to be allowed him.

Againe, men have no pleasure, (but on the contrary a great deale of griefe) in keeping company, where there is no power able to over-awe them all. For every man looketh that his companion should value him, at the same rate he sets upon himselfe: And upon all signes of contempt, or undervaluing, naturally endeavours, as far as he dares (which amongst them that have no common power to keep them in quiet, is far enough to make them destroy each other,) to extort a greater value from his contemners, by dommage; and from others, by the example.

So that in the nature of man, we find three principall causes of quarrell. First, Competition; Secondly, Diffidence; Thirdly, Glory.

The first, maketh men invade for Gain; the second, for Safety; and the third, for Reputation. The first use Violence, to make themselves Masters of other mens persons, wives, children, and cattell; the second, to defend them; the third, for trifles, as a word, a smile, a different opinion, and any other signe of undervalue, either direct in their Persons, or by reflexion in their Kindred, their Friends, their Nation, their Profession, or their Name.

Out of Civil States, there is alwayes Warre of every one against every one.

Hereby it is manifest, that during the time men live without a common Power to keep them all in awe, they are in that condition which is called Warre; and such a warre, as is of every man, against every man. For WARRE, consisteth not in Battell onely, or the act of fighting; but in a tract of time, wherein the Will to contend by Battell is sufficiently known: and therefore the notion of *Time,* is to be considered in the nature of Warre; as it is in the nature of Weather. For as the nature of Foule weather, lyeth not in a showre or two of rain; but in an inclination thereto of many dayes together: So the nature of War, consisteth not in actuall fighting; but in the known disposition thereto, during all the time there is no assurance to the contrary. All other time is PEACE.

The Incommodities of such a War.

Whatsoever therefore is consequent to a time of Warre, where every man is Enemy to every man; the same is consequent to the time, wherein men live without other security, than what their own strength, and their own invention shall furnish them withall. In such condition, there is no place for Industry; because the fruit thereof is uncertain: and consequently no Culture of the Earth; no Navigation, nor use of the commodities that may be imported by Sea; no commodious Building; no Instruments of moving, and removing such things as require much force; no Knowledge of the face of the Earth; no account of Time; no Arts; no Letters; no Society; and which is worst of all, continuall feare, and danger of violent death; And the life of man, solitary, poore, nasty, brutish, and short.

It may seem strange to some man, that has not well weighed these things; that Nature should thus dissociate, and render men apt to invade, and destroy one another: and he may therefore, not trusting to this Inference, made from the Passions, desire perhaps to have the same confirmed by Experience. Let him therefore consider with himselfe, when taking a journey, he armes himselfe, and seeks to go well accompanied; when going to sleep, he locks his dores; when even in his house he locks his chests; and this when he knowes there bee Lawes, and publike Officers, armed, to revenge all injuries shall bee done him; what opinion he has of his fellow subjects, when he rides armed; of his fellow Citizens, when he locks his dores; and of his children, and servants, when he locks his chests. Does he not there as much accuse mankind by his actions, as I do by my words? But neither of us accuse mans nature in it. The Desires, and other Passions of man, are in themselves no Sin. No more are the Actions, that proceed from those Passions, till they know a Law that forbids them: which till Lawes be made they cannot know: nor can any Law be made, till they have agreed upon the Person that shall make it.

It may peradventure be thought, there was never such a time, nor condition of warre as this; and I believe it was never generally so, over all the world: but there are many places, where they live so now. For the savage people in many places of *America,* except the government of small Families, the concord whereof dependeth on naturall lust, have no government at all; and live at this day in that brutish manner, as I said before. Howsoever, it may be perceived what manner of life there would be, where there were no common Power to feare; by the manner of life, which men that have formerly lived under a peacefull government, use to degenerate into, in a civill Warre.

But though there had never been any time, wherein particular men were in a condition of warre one against another; yet in all times, Kings, and Persons of Soveraigne authority, because of their Independency, are in continuall jealousies, and in the state and posture of Gladiators; having their weapons pointing, and their eyes fixed on one another; that is, their Forts, Garrisons, and Guns upon the Frontiers of their Kingdomes; and continuall Spyes upon their neighbours, which is a posture of War. But because they uphold thereby, the Industry of their Subjects; there does not follow from it, that misery, which accompanies the Liberty of particular men.

In such a Warre, nothing is Unjust.

To this warre of every man against every man, this also is consequent; that nothing can be Unjust. The notions of Right and Wrong, Justice and Injustice have there no place. Where there is no common Power, there is no Law: where no Law, no Injustice. Force, and Fraud, are in warre the two Cardinall vertues. Justice, and Injustice are none of the Faculties neither of the Body, nor Mind. If they were, they might be in a man that were alone in the world, as well as his Senses, and Passions. They are Qualities, that relate to men in Society, not in Solitude. It is consequent also to the same condition, that there be no Propriety, no Dominion, no *Mine* and *Thine* distinct; but onely that to be every mans, that he can get; and for so long, as he can keep it. And thus much for the ill condition, which man by meer Nature is actually placed in; though with a possibility to come out of it, consisting partly in the Passions, partly in his Reason.

The Passions that incline men to Peace.

The Passions that encline men to Peace, are Feare of Death; Desire of such things as are necessary to commodious living; and a Hope by their Industry to obtain them. And Reason suggesteth convenient Articles of Peace, upon which men may be drawn to agreement. These Articles, are they, which otherwise are called the Lawes of Nature: whereof I shall speak more particularly. . . .

OF THE FIRST AND SECOND NATURALL LAWES,
AND OF CONTRACTS

Right of Nature what.

The RIGHT OF NATURE, which Writers commonly call *Jus Naturale,* is the Liberty each man hath, to use his own power, as he will himselfe, for the preservation of his own Nature; that is to say, of his own Life; and consequently, of doing any thing, which in his own Judgement, and Reason, hee shall conceive to be the aptest means thereunto.

Liberty what.

By LIBERTY, is understood, according to the proper signification of the word, the absence of externall Impediments: which Impediments, may oft take away part of a mans power to do what hee would; but cannot hinder him from using the power left him, according as his judgement, and reason shall dictate to him.

A Law of Nature what.
Difference of Right and Law.

A LAW OF NATURE, (*Lex Naturalis,*) is a Precept, or generall Rule, found out by Reason, by which a man is forbidden to do, that, which is destructive of his life, or taketh away the means of preserving the same; and to omit, that, by which he thinketh it may be best preserved. For though they that speak of this subject, use to confound *Jus,* and *Lex, Right* and *Law,* yet they ought to be distinguished; because RIGHT, consisteth in liberty to do, or to forbeare; Whereas LAW, determineth, and bindeth to one of them: so that Law, and Right, differ as much, as Obligation, and Liberty; which in one and the same matter are inconsistent.

Naturally every man has Right to every thing.
The Fundamentall Law of *Nature. To seek peace*

And because the condition of Man, (as hath been declared in the precedent Chapter) is a condition of Warre of every one against every one; in which case every one is governed by his own Reason; and there is nothing he can make use of, that may not be a help unto him, in preserving his life against his enemyes; It followeth, that in such a condition, every man has a Right to every thing; even to one anothers body. And therefore, as long as this naturall Right of every man to every thing endureth, there can be no security to any man, (how strong or wise soever he be,) of living out the time, which Nature ordinarily alloweth men to live. And consequently it is a precept, or generall rule of Reason, *That every man, ought to endeavour Peace, as farre as he has hope of obtaining it; and when he cannot obtain it, that he may seek, and use, all helps, and advantages of Warre.* The first branch of which Rule, containeth the first, and Fundamentall Law of Nature; which is, *to seek Peace, and follow it.* The Second, the summe of the Right of Nature; which is, *By all means we can, to defend our selves.*

The second Law of *Nature. Contract in way of peace*

From this Fundamentall Law of Nature, by which men are commanded to endeavour Peace, is derived this second Law; *That a man be willing, when others are so too, as farre-forth, as for Peace, and defence of himselfe he shall think it necessary, to lay down this right to all things; and be contented with so much liberty against other men, as he would allow other men against himselfe.* For as long as every man holdeth this Right, of doing any thing he liketh; so long are all men in the condition of Warre. But if other men will not lay down their Right, as well as he; then there is no Reason for any one, to devest himselfe of his: For that were to expose himselfe to Prey, (which no man is bound to) rather than to dispose himselfe to Peace. This is that Law of the Gospell; *Whatsoever you require that others should do to you, that do ye to them.* And that Law of all men, *Quod tibi fieri non vis, alteri ne feceris.*

What it is to lay down a Right.

To *lay downe* a mans *Right* to any thing, is to *devest* himselfe of the *Liberty,* of hindring another of the benefit of his own Right to the same. For he that re-nounceth, or passeth away his Right, giveth not to any other man a Right which he had not before; because there is nothing to which every man had not Right by Nature: but onely standeth out of his way, that he may enjoy his own originall Right, without hindrance from him; not without hindrance from an-other. So that the effect which redoundeth to one man, by another mans de-fect of Right, is but so much diminution of impediments to the use of his own Right originall.

Renouncing a Right what it is.
Transferring Right what. Obligation. Duty. Injustice.

Right is layd aside, either by simply Renouncing it; or by Transferring it to another. By *Simply* RENOUNCING; when he cares not to whom the benefit thereof redoundeth. By TRANSFERRING; when he intendeth the benefit thereof to some certain person, or persons. And when a man hath in either manner abandoned, or granted away his Right; then is he said to be OBLIGED, or BOUND, not to hinder those, to whom such Right is granted, or abandoned, from the benefit of it: and that he *Ought,* and it is his DUTY, not to make voyd that voluntary act of his own: and that such hindrance is INJUSTICE, and INJURY, as being *Sine Jure*; the Right being before renounced, or transferred. So that *Injury,* or *Injustice,* in the controversies of the world, is somewhat like to that, which in the disputations of Scholers is called *Absurdity.* For as it is there called an Absurdity, to contradict what one maintained in the Begin-ning: so in the world, it is called Injustice, and Injury, voluntarily to undo that, which from the beginning he had voluntarily done. The way by which a man either simply Renounceth, or Transferreth his Right, is a Declaration, or Signification, by some voluntary and sufficient signe, or signes, that he doth so Renounce, or Transferre; or hath so Renounced, or Transferred the same, to him that accepteth it. And these Signes are either Words onely, or Actions onely; or (as it happeneth most often) both Words, and Actions. And the same are the BONDS, by which men are bound, and obliged: Bonds, that have their strength, not from their own Nature, (for nothing is more easily broken than a mans word,) but from Feare of some evill consequence upon the rupture.

Not all Rights are alienable.

Whensoever a man Transferreth his Right, or Renounceth it; it is either in consideration of some Right reciprocally transferred to himselfe; or for some other good he hopeth for thereby. For it is a voluntary act: and of the voluntary acts of every man, the object is some *Good to himselfe*. And therefore there be some Rights, which no man can be understood by any words, or other signes, to have abandoned, or transferred. As first a man cannot lay down the right of resisting them, that assault him by force, to take away his life; because he cannot be understood to ayme thereby, at any Good to himself. The same may be sayd of Wounds, and Chayns, and Imprisonment; both because there is no benefit consequent to such patience; as there is to the patience of suffering another to be wounded, or imprisoned: as also because a man cannot tell, when he seeth men proceed against him by violence, whether they intend his death or not. And lastly the motive, and end for which this renouncing and transferring of Right is introduced, is nothing else but the security of a mans person, in his life, and in the means of so preserving life, as not to be weary of it. And therefore if a man by words, or other signes, seem to despoyle himselfe of the End, for which those signes were intended; he is not to be understood as if he meant it, or that it was his will; but that he was ignorant of how such words and actions were to be interpreted.

Covenants of Mutuall trust, when Invalid.

If a Covenant be made, wherein neither of the parties performe presently, but trust one another; in the condition of meer Nature, (which is a condition of Warre of every man against every man,) upon any reasonable suspition, it is Voyd: But if there be a common Power set over them both, with right and force sufficient to compell performance; it is not Voyd. For he that performeth first, has no assurance the other will performe after; because the bonds of words are too weak to bridle mens ambition, avarice, anger, and other Passions, without the feare of some coërcive Power; which in the condition of meer Nature, where all men are equall, and judges of the justnesse of their own fears, cannot possibly be supposed. And therefore he which performeth first, does but betray himselfe to his enemy; contrary to the Right (he can never abandon) of defending his life, and means of living.

But in a civill estate, where there is a Power set up to constrain those that would otherwise violate their faith, that feare is no more reasonable; and for that cause, he which by the Covenant is to perform first, is obliged so to do.

16.

The Origin of the State

FRIEDRICH ENGELS, 1884

The state arises on the ruins of the gentile constitution [in three main forms.]
Athens provides the purest, classic form; here the state springs directly and
mainly out of the class oppositions which develop within gentile society itself.
In Rome, gentile society becomes a closed aristocracy in the midst of the numerous *plebs* who stand outside it, and have duties but no rights, the victory
of *plebs* breaks up the old constitution based on kinship, and erects on its ruins the state, into which both the gentile aristocracy and the *plebs* are soon
completely absorbed. Lastly, in the case of the German conquerors of the Roman Empire, the state springs directly out of the conquest of large foreign territories, which the gentile constitution provides no means of governing. But
because this conquest involves neither a serious struggle with the original population nor a more advanced division of labor; because conquerors and conquered are almost on the same level of economic development, and the economic basis of society remains therefore as before—for these reasons the
gentile constitution is able to survive for many centuries in the altered, territorial form of the mark constitution and even for a time to rejuvenate itself in
a feebler shape in the later noble and patrician families, and indeed in peasant
families, as in Ditmarschen.

The state is therefore by no means a power imposed on society from without; just as little is it "the reality of the moral idea," "the image and the reality
of reason," as Hegel maintains. Rather, it is a product of society at a particular
stage of development; it is the admission that this society has involved itself in
insoluble self-contradiction and is cleft into irreconcilable antagonisms which
it is powerless to exorcise. But in order that these antagonisms, classes with
conflicting economic interests, shall not consume themselves and society in
fruitless struggle, a power, apparently standing above society, has become necessary to moderate the conflict and keep it within the bounds of "order"; and

Reprinted with permission of International Publishers, from *The Origin of the Family,
Private Property, and the State,* by Friedrich Engels. Copyright © 1942 International
Publishers Co., Inc.

this power, arisen out of society, but placing itself above it and increasingly alienating itself from it, is the state.

In contrast to the old gentile organization, the state is distinguished firstly by the grouping of its members *on a territorial basis*. The old gentile bodies, formed and held together by ties of blood, had, as we have seen, become inadequate largely because they presupposed that the gentile members were bound to one particular locality, whereas this had long ago ceased to be the case. The territory was still there, but the people had become mobile. The territorial division was therefore taken as the starting point and the system introduced by which citizens exercised their public rights and duties where they took up residence, without regard to gens or tribe. This organization of the citizens of the state according to domicile is common to all states. To us, therefore, this organization seems natural; but, as we have seen, hard and protracted struggles were necessary before it was able in Athens and Rome to displace the old organization founded on kinship.

The second distinguishing characteristic is the institution of a *public force* which is no longer immediately identical with the people's own organization of themselves as an armed power. This special public force is needed because a self-acting armed organization of the people has become impossible since their cleavage into classes. The slaves also belong to the population: as against the 365,000 slaves, the 90,000 Athenian citizens constitute only a privileged class. The people's army of the Athenian democracy confronted the slaves as an aristocratic public force, and kept them in check; but to keep the citizens in check as well, a police-force was needed, as described above. This public force exists in every state; it consists not merely of armed men, but also of material appendages, prisons and coercive institutions of all kinds, of which gentile society knew nothing. It may be very insignificant, practically negligible, in societies with still undeveloped class antagonism and living in remote areas, as at times and in places in the United States of America. But it becomes stronger in proportion as the class antagonisms with the state become sharper and as adjoining states grow larger and more populous. It is enough to look at Europe today, which class struggle and rivalry in conquest have brought the public power to a pitch that it threatens to devour the whole of society and even the state itself.

In order to maintain this public power, contributions from the state citizens are necessary—*taxes*. These were completely unknown to gentile society. We know more than enough about them today. With advancing civilization, even taxes are not sufficient; the state draws drafts on the future, contracts loans, *state debts*. Our old Europe can tell a tale about these, too.

In possession of the public power and the right of taxation, the officials now present themselves as organs of society standing *above* society. The free, willing respect accorded to the organs of the gentile constitution is not enough for them, even if they could have it. Representatives of a power which estranges them from society, they have to be given prestige by means of special decrees, which invest them with a peculiar sanctity and inviolability. The lowest police officer of the civilized state has more "authority" than all the organs of gentile society put together; but the mightiest prince and the greatest statesman or general of civilization might envy the humblest of the gentile chiefs the unforced and unquestioned respect accorded him. For the one stands in the midst of society; the other is forced to pose as something outside and above it.

As the state arose from the need to keep class antagonisms in check, but also arose in the thick of the fight between the classes, it is normally the state of the most powerful, economically ruling class, which by its means becomes also the politically ruling class, and so acquires new means of holding down and exploiting the oppressed class. The ancient state was, above all, the state of the slave-owners for holding down the slaves, just as the feudal state was the organ of the nobility for holding down the peasant serfs and bondsmen, and the modern representative state is the instrument for exploiting wage-labor by capital. Exceptional periods, however, occur when the warring classes are so nearly equal in forces that the state power, as apparent mediator, acquires for the moment a certain independence in relation to both. This applies to the absolute monarchy of the seventeenth and eighteenth centuries, which balances the nobility and the bourgeoisie against one another; and to the Bonapartism of the First and particularly of the Second French Empire, which played off the proletariat against the bourgeoisie and the bourgeoisie against the proletariat. The latest achievement in this line, in which ruler and ruled look equally comic, is the new German Empire of the Bismarckian nation; here the capitalists and the workers are balanced against one another and both of them fleeced for the benefit of the decayed Prussian cabbage Junkers.

Further; in most historical states the rights conceded to citizens are graded on a property basis, whereby it is directly admitted that the state is an organization for the protection of the possessing class against the non-possessing class. This is already the case in the Athenian and Roman property classes. Similarly in the medieval feudal state, in which the extent of political power was determined by the extent of land-ownership. Similarly, also, in the electoral qualifications in modern parliamentary states. This political recognition of property differences is, however, by no means essential. On the contrary, it marks a low stage in the development of the state. The highest form of the state, the democratic republic, which in our modern social conditions becomes more and more an unavoidable necessity and is the form of state in which alone the last decisive battle between proletariat and bourgeoisie can be fought out—the democratic republic no longer officially recognizes differences of property. Wealth here employs its power indirectly, but all the more surely. It does this in two ways: by plain corruption of officials, of which America is the classic example, and by an alliance between the government and the stock exchange, which is effected all the more easily the higher the state debt mounts and the more the joint-stock companies concentrate in their hands not only transport but also production itself, and themselves have their own center in the stock exchange. In addition to America, the latest French republic illustrates this strikingly, and honest little Switzerland has also given creditable performance in this field. But that a democratic republic not essential to this brotherly bond between government and stock exchange is proved not only by England, but also by the new German Empire, where it is difficult to say who scored most by the introduction of universal suffrage, Bismarck or the Bleichröder bank. And lastly the possessing class rules directly by means of universal suffrage. As long as the oppressed class—in our case, therefore, the proletariat—is not yet ripe for its self-liberation, so long will it, in its majority, recognize the existing order of society as the only possible one and remain politically the tail of the capitalist class, its extreme left wing. But in the measure in which it matures toward its self-emancipation, in the same measure it constitutes itself as its own party and votes for its own representatives, not those of the capitalists. Universal suffrage is thus the gauge of the maturity of the working class. It cannot and never will do anything more in the modern state; but that is enough. On the day when the thermometer of universal suffrage shows boiling-point among the workers, they as well as the capitalists will know where they stand.

The state, therefore, has not existed from all eternity. There have been societies, which have managed without it, which had no notion of the state or state power. At a definite stage of economic development, which necessarily involved the cleavage of society into classes, the state became a necessity because of this cleavage. We are now rapidly approaching a stage in the development of production at which the existence of these classes has not only ceased to be a necessity, but become a positive hindrance to production. They will fall as inevitably as they once arose. The state inevitably falls with them. The society which organizes production anew on the basis of free and equal association of the producers will put the whole state machinery where it will then belong—into the museum of antiquities, next to the spinning wheel and the bronze ax.

17.

The Types of Legitimate Domination

MAX WEBER, 1921-22

DOMINATION AND LEGITIMACY

Domination [is defined as] the probability that certain specific commands (or all commands) will be obeyed by a given group of persons. It thus does not include every mode of exercising "power" or "influence" over other persons. Domination ("authority") in this sense may be based on the most diverse motives of compliance: all the way from simple habituation to the most purely rational calculation of advantage. Hence every genuine form of domination implies a minimum of voluntary compliance, that is, an *interest* (based on ulterior motives or genuine acceptance) in obedience.

Not every case of domination makes use of economic means; still less does it always have economic objectives. However, normally the rule over a considerable number of persons requires a staff . . . , that is, a special group which can normally be trusted to execute the general policy as well as the specific commands. The members of the administrative staff may be bound to obedience to their superior (or superiors) by custom, by affectual ties, by a purely material complex of interests, or by ideal (*wertrationale*) motives. The quality of these motives largely determines the type of domination. Purely material interests and calculations of advantages as the basis of solidarity between the chief and his administrative staff result, in this as in other connexions, in a relatively unstable situation. Normally other elements, affectual and ideal, supplement such interests. In certain exceptional cases the former alone may be decisive. In everyday life these relationships, like others, are governed by custom and material calculation of advantage. But custom, personal advantage, purely affectual or ideal motives of solidarity, do not form a sufficiently reliable basis for a given domination. In addition there is normally a further element, the belief in *legitimacy.*

183

Reprinted with permission of the University of California Press from *Economy and Society* by Max Weber, edited by Guenther Roth and Claus Wittich. Copyright © 1978 by The Regents of the University of California. Reprinted also with the permission of J. C. B. Mohr (Paul Siebeck), Tübingen.

Experience shows that in no instance does domination voluntarily limit itself to the appeal to material or affectual or ideal motives as a basis for its continuance. In addition every such system attempts to establish and to cultivate the belief in its legitimacy. But according to the kind of legitimacy which is claimed, the type of obedience, the kind of administrative staff developed to guarantee it, and the mode of exercising authority, will all differ fundamentally. Equally fundamental is the variation in effect. Hence, it is useful to classify the types of domination according to the kind of claim to legitimacy typically made by each.

THE THREE PURE TYPES OF AUTHORITY

There are three pure types of legitimate domination. The validity of the claims to legitimacy may be based on:

1. Rational grounds—resting on a belief in the legality of enacted rules and the right of those elevated to authority under such rules to issue commands (legal authority).

2. Traditional grounds—resting on an established belief in the sanctity of immemorial traditions and the legitimacy of those exercising authority under them (traditional authority); or finally,

3. Charismatic grounds—resting on devotion to the exceptional sanctity, heroism or exemplary character of an individual person, and of the normative patterns or order revealed or ordained by him (charismatic authority).

In the case of legal authority, obedience is owed to the legally established impersonal order. It extends to the persons exercising the authority of office under it by virtue of the formal legality of their commands and only within the scope of authority of the office. In the case of traditional authority, obedience is owed to the *person* of the chief who occupies the traditionally sanctioned position of authority and who is (within its sphere) bound by tradition. But here the obligation of obedience is a matter of personal loyalty within the area of accustomed obligations. In the case of charismatic authority, it is the charismatically qualified leader as such who is obeyed by virtue of personal trust in his revelation, his heroism or his exemplary qualities so far as they fall within the scope of the individual's belief in his charisma.

LEGAL AUTHORITY: THE PURE TYPE

Legal authority rests on the acceptance of the validity of the following mutually inter-dependent ideas.

1. That any given legal norm may be established by agreement or by imposition, on grounds of expediency or value-rationality or both, with a claim to

obedience at least on the part of the members of the organization. This is, however, usually extended to include all persons within the sphere of power in question—which in the case of territorial bodies is the territorial area—who stand in certain social relationships or carry out forms of social action which in the order governing the organization have been declared to be relevant.

2. That every body of law consists essentially in a consistent system of abstract rules which have normally been intentionally established. Furthermore, administration of law is held to consist in the application of these rules to particular cases; the administrative process in the rational pursuit of the interests which are specified in the order governing the organization within the limits laid down by legal precepts and following principles which are capable of generalized formulation and are approved in the order governing the group, or at least not disapproved in it.

3. That thus the typical person in authority, the "superior," is himself subject to an impersonal order by orienting his actions to it in his own dispositions and commands. (This is true not only for persons exercising legal authority who are in the usual sense "officials," but, for instance, for the elected president of a state.)

4. That the person who obeys authority does so, as it is usually stated, only in his capacity as a "member" of the organization and what he obeys is only "the law." (He may in this connection be the member of an association, of a community, of a church, or a citizen of a state.)

5. In conformity with point 3, it is held that the members of the organization, insofar as they obey a person in authority, do not owe this obedience to him as an individual, but to the impersonal order. Hence, it follows that there is an obligation to obedience only within the sphere of the rationally delimited jurisdiction which, in terms of the order, has been given to him.

The following may thus be said to be the fundamental categories of rational legal authority:

(1) A continuous rule-bound conduct of official business.

(2) A specified sphere of competence (jurisdiction). This involves: (a) A sphere of obligations to perform functions which has been marked off as part of a systematic division of labor. (b) The provision of the incumbent with the necessary powers. (c) That the necessary means of compulsion are clearly defined and their use is subject to definite conditions. A unit exercising authority which is organized in this way will be called an "administrative organ" or "agency" (*Behörde*).

There are administrative organs in this sense in large-scale private enterprises, in parties and armies, as well as in the state and the church. An elected president, a cabinet of ministers, or a body of elected "People's Representatives" also in this sense constitute administrative organs. This is not, however, the place to discuss these concepts. Not every administrative organ is provided with compulsory powers. But this distinction is not important for present purposes.

(3) The organization of offices follows the principle of hierarchy; that is, each lower office is under the control and supervision of a higher one. There is a right of appeal and of statement of grievances from the lower to the higher. Hierarchies differ in respect to whether and in what cases complaints can lead to a "correct" ruling from a higher authority itself, or whether the responsibility for such changes is left to the lower office, the conduct of which was the subject of the complaint.

(4) The rules which regulate the conduct of an office may be technical rules or norms. In both cases, if their application is to be fully rational, specialized training is necessary. It is thus normally true that only a person who has demonstrated an adequate technical training is qualified to be a member of the administrative staff of such an organized group, and hence only such persons are eligible for appointment to official positions. The administrative staff of a rational organization thus typically consists of "officials," whether the organization be devoted to political, hierocratic, economic—in particular, capitalistic—or other ends.

(5) In the rational type it is a matter of principle that the members of the administrative staff should be completely separated from ownership of the means of production or administration. Officials, employees, and workers attached to the administrative staff do not themselves own the non-human means of production and administration. These are rather provided for their use, in kind or in money, and the official is obligated to render an accounting of their use. There exists, furthermore, in principle complete separation of the organization's property (respectively, capital), and the personal property (household) of the official. There is a corresponding separation of the place in which official functions are carried out—the "office" in the sense of premises—from the living quarters.

(6) In the rational type case, there is also a complete absence of appropriation of his official position by the incumbent. Where "rights" to an office exist, as in the case of judges, and recently of an increasing proportion of officials and even of workers, they do not normally serve the purpose of appropriation by the official, but of securing the purely objective and independent character of the conduct of the office so that it is oriented only to the relevant norms.

(7) Administrative acts, decisions, and rules are formulated and recorded in writing, even in cases where oral discussion is the rule or is even mandatory. This applies at least to preliminary discussions and proposals, to final decisions, and to all sorts of orders and rules. The combination of written docu-

ments and a continuous operation by officials constitutes the "office" (*Bureau*) which is the central focus of all types of modern organized action.

(8) Legal authority can be exercised in a wide variety of different forms which will be distinguished and discussed later. The following ideal-typical analysis will be deliberately confined for the time being to the administrative staff that is most unambiguously a structure of domination: "officialdom" or "bureaucracy."

In the above outline no mention has been made of the kind of head appropriate to a system of legal authority. This is a consequence of certain considerations which can only be made entirely understandable at a later stage in the analysis. There are very important types of rational domination which, with respect to the ultimate source of authority, belong to other categories. This is true of the hereditary charismatic type, as illustrated by hereditary monarchy, and of the pure charismatic type of a president chosen by a plebiscite. Other cases involve rational elements at important points, but are made up of a combination of bureaucratic and charismatic components, as is true of the cabinet form of government. Still others are subject to the authority of the chiefs of other organizations, whether their character be charismatic or bureaucratic; thus the formal head of a government department under a parliamentary regime may be a minister who occupies his position because of his authority in a party. The type of rational, legal administrative staff is capable of application in all kinds of situations and contexts. It is the most important mechanism for the administration of everyday affairs. For in that sphere, the exercise of authority consists precisely in administration.

The purest type of exercise of legal authority is that which employs a bureaucratic administrative staff. Only the supreme chief of the organization occupies his position of dominance (*Herrenstellung*) by virtue of appropriation, of election, or of having been designated for the succession. But even *his* authority consists in a sphere of legal "competence." The whole administrative staff under the supreme authority then consists, in the purest type, of individual officials (constituting a "monocracy" as opposed to the "collegial" type, which will be discussed below) who are appointed and function according to the following criteria:

(1) They are personally free and subject to authority only with respect to their impersonal official obligations.

(2) They are organized in a clearly defined hierarchy of offices.

(3) Each office has a clearly defined sphere of competence in the legal sense.

(4) The office is filled by a free contractual relationship. Thus, in principle, there is free selection.

(5) Candidates are selected on the basis of technical qualifications. In the most rational case, this is tested by examination or guaranteed by diplomas certifying technical training, or both. They are *appointed*, not elected.

(6) They are remunerated by fixed salaries in money, for the most part with a right to pensions. Only under certain circumstances does the employing authority, especially in private organizations, have a right to terminate the appointment, but the official is always free to resign. The salary scale is graded according to rank in the hierarchy; but in addition to this criterion, the responsibility of the position and the requirements of the incumbent's social status may be taken into account. . . .

(7) The office is treated as the sole, or at least the primary, occupation of the incumbent.

(8) It constitutes a career. There is a system of "promotion" according to seniority or to achievement, or both. Promotion is dependent on the judgment of superiors.

(9) The official works entirely separated from ownership of the means of administration and without appropriation of his position.

(10) He is subject to strict and systematic discipline and control in the conduct of the office.

This type of organization is in principle applicable with equal facility to a wide variety of different fields. It may be applied in profit-making business or in charitable organizations, or in any number of other types of private enterprises serving ideal or material ends. It is equally applicable to political and to hierocratic organizations. With the varying degrees of approximation to a pure type, its historical existence can be demonstrated in all these fields.

1. For example, bureaucracy is found in private clinics, as well as in endowed hospitals or the hospitals maintained by religious orders. Bureaucratic organization is well illustrated by the administrative role of the priesthood (*Kaplanokratie*) in the modern [Catholic] church, which has expropriated almost all of the old church benefices, which were in former days to a large extent subject to private appropriation. It is also illustrated by the notion of a [Papal] universal episcopate, which is thought of as formally constituting a universal legal competence in religious matters. Similarly, the doctrine of Papal infallibility is thought of as in fact involving a universal competence, but only one which functions "ex cathedra" in the sphere of the office, thus implying the typical distinction between the sphere of office and that of the private affairs of the incumbent. The same phenomena are found in the large-scale capitalistic enterprise; and the larger it is, the greater their role. And this is not less true of political parties, which will be discussed separately. Finally, the modern army is essentially a bureaucratic organization administered by that peculiar type of military functionary, the "officer."

2. Bureaucratic authority is carried out in its purest form where it is most clearly dominated by the principle of appointment. There is no such thing as a hierarchical organization of elected officials. In the first place, it is impossible to attain a stringency of discipline even approaching that in the appointed type, since the subordinate official can stand on his own election and since his prospects are not dependent on the superior's judgment. . . .

3. Appointment by free contract, which makes free selection possible, is essential to modern bureaucracy. Where there is a hierarchical organization with impersonal spheres of competence, but occupied by unfree officials—like slaves or *ministeriales,* who, however, function in a formally bureaucratic manner—the term "patrimonial bureaucracy" will be used.

4. The role of technical qualifications in bureaucratic organizations is continually increasing. Even an official in a party or a trade-union organization is in need of specialized knowledge, though it is usually developed by experience rather than by formal training. In the modern state, the only "offices" for which no technical qualifications are required are those of ministers and presidents. This only goes to prove that they are "officials" only in a formal sense, and not substantively, just like the managing director or president of a large business corporation. There is no question but that the "position" of the capitalistic entrepreneur is as definitely appropriated as is that of a monarch. Thus at the top of a bureaucratic organization, there is necessarily an element which is at least not purely bureaucratic. The category of bureaucracy is one applying only to the exercise of control by means of a particular kind of administrative staff.

5. The bureaucratic official normally receives a fixed salary. (By contrast, sources of income which are privately appropriated will be called "benefices" (*Pfründen*). . . . Bureaucratic salaries are also normally paid in money. Though this is not essential to the concept of bureaucracy, it is the arrangement which best fits the pure type. (Payments in kind are apt to have the character of benefices, and the receipt of a benefice normally implies the appropriation of opportunities for earnings and of positions.) There are, however, gradual transitions in this field with many intermediate types. Appropriation by virtue of leasing or sale of offices or the pledge of income from office are phenomena foreign to the pure type of bureaucracy. . . .

MONOCRATIC BUREAUCRACY

Experience tends universally to show that the purely bureaucratic type of administrative organization—that is, the monocratic variety of bureaucracy—is, from a purely technical point of view, capable of attaining the highest degree of efficiency and is in this sense formally the most rational known means of exercising authority over human beings. It is superior to any other form in precision, in stability, in the stringency of its discipline, and in its reliability. It thus makes possible a particularly high degree of calculability of results for the heads of the organization and for those acting in relation to it. It is finally superior both in intensive efficiency and in the scope of its operations, and is formally capable of application to all kinds of administrative tasks.

The development of modern forms of organization in all fields is nothing less than identical with the development and continual spread of bureaucratic administration. This is true of church and state, of armies, political parties, economic enterprises, interest groups, endowments, clubs, and many others. Its development is, to take the most striking case, at the root of the modern Western state. However many forms there may be which do not appear to fit this pattern, such as collegial representative bodies, parliamentary committees, soviets, honorary officers, lay judges, and what not, and however many people may complain about the "red tape," it would be sheer illusion to think for a moment that continuous administrative work can be carried out in any field except by means of officials working in offices. The whole pattern of everyday life is cut to fit this framework. If bureaucratic administration is, other things being equal, always the most rational type from a technical point of view, the needs of mass administration make it today completely indispensable. The choice is only that between bureaucracy and dilettantism in the field of administration.

The primary source of the superiority of bureaucratic administration lies in the role of technical knowledge which, through the development of modern technology and business methods in the production of goods, has become completely indispensable. In this respect, it makes no difference whether the economic system is organized on a capitalistic or a socialistic basis. Indeed, if in the latter case a comparable level of technical efficiency were to be achieved, it would mean a tremendous increase in the importance of professional bureaucrats.

When those subject to bureaucratic control seek to escape the influence of the existing bureaucratic apparatus, this is normally possible only by creating an organization of their own which is equally subject to bureaucratization. Similarly the existing bureaucratic apparatus is driven to continue functioning by the most powerful interests which are material and objective, but also ideal in character. Without it, a society like our own—with its separation of officials, employees, and workers from ownership of the means of administration, and its dependence on discipline and on technical training—could no longer function. The only exception would be those groups, such as the peasantry, who are still in possession of their own means of subsistence. Even in the case of revolution by force or of occupation by an enemy, the bureaucratic machinery will normally continue to function just as it has for the previous legal government.

The question is always who controls the existing bureaucratic machinery. And such control is possible only in a very limited degree to persons who are not technical specialists. Generally speaking, the highest-ranking career official is more likely to get his way in the long run than his nominal superior, the cabinet minister, who is not a specialist.

Though by no means alone, the capitalistic system has undeniably played a major role in the development of bureaucracy. Indeed, without it capitalistic production could not continue and any rational type of socialism would have simply to take it over and increase its importance. Its development, largely under capitalistic auspices, has created an urgent need for stable, strict, intensive, and calculable administration. It is this need which is so fateful to any kind of large-scale administration. Only by reversion in every field—political, religious, economic, etc.—to small-scale organization would it be possible to any considerable extent to escape its influence. On the one hand, capitalism in its modern stages of development requires the bureaucracy, though both have arisen from different historical sources. Conversely, capitalism is the most rational economic basis for bureaucratic administration and enables it to develop in the most rational form, especially because, from a fiscal point of view, it supplies the necessary money resources.

Along with these fiscal conditions of efficient bureaucratic administration, there are certain extremely important conditions in the fields of communication and transportation. The precision of its functioning requires the services of the railway, the telegraph, and the telephone, and becomes increasingly dependent on them. A socialistic form of organization would not alter this fact. It would be a question . . . whether in a socialistic system it would be possible to provide conditions for carrying out as stringent a bureaucratic organization as has been possible in a capitalistic order. For socialism would, in fact, require a still higher degree of formal bureaucratization than capitalism. If this should prove not to be possible, it would demonstrate the existence of another of those fundamental elements of irrationality—a conflict between formal and substantive rationality of the sort which sociology so often encounters.

Bureaucratic administration means fundamentally domination through knowledge. This is the feature of it which makes it specifically rational. This consists on the one hand in technical knowledge which, by itself, is sufficient to ensure it a position of extraordinary power. But in addition to this, bureaucratic organizations, or the holders of power who make use of them, have the tendency to increase their power still further by the knowledge growing out of experience in the service. For they acquire through the conduct of office a special knowledge of facts and have available a store of documentary material peculiar to themselves. While not peculiar to bureaucratic organizations, the concept of "official secrets" is certainly typical of them. It stands in relation to technical knowledge in somewhat the same position as commercial secrets do to technological training. It is a product of the striving for power.

Superior to bureaucracy in the knowledge of techniques and facts is only the capitalist entrepreneur, within his own sphere of interest. He is the only type who has been able to maintain at least relative immunity from subjection to the control of rational bureaucratic knowledge. In large-scale organizations, all others are inevitably subject to bureaucratic control, just as they have fallen under the dominance of precision machinery in the mass production of goods.

In general, bureaucratic domination has the following social consequences:

(1) The tendency to "levelling" in the interest of the broadest possible basis of recruitment in terms of technical competence.

(2) The tendency to plutocracy growing out of the interest in the greatest possible length of technical training. Today this often lasts up to the age of thirty.

(3) The dominance of a spirit of formalistic impersonality: "*Sine ira et studio,*" without hatred or passion, and hence without affection or enthusiasm. The dominant norms are concepts of straightforward duty without regard to personal considerations. Everyone is subject to formal equality of treatment; that is, everyone in the same empirical situation. This is the spirit in which the ideal official conducts his office.

The development of bureaucracy greatly favors the levelling of status, and this can be shown historically to be the normal tendency. Conversely, every process of social levelling creates a favorable situation for the development of bureaucracy by eliminating the office-holder who rules by virtue of status privileges and the appropriation of the means and powers of administration; in the interests of "equality," it also eliminates those who can hold office on an honorary basis or as an avocation by virtue of their wealth. Everywhere bureaucratization foreshadows mass democracy, which will be discussed in another connection.

The "spirit" of rational bureaucracy has normally the following general characteristics:

(1) Formalism, which is promoted by all the interests which are concerned with the security of their own personal situation, whatever this may consist in. Otherwise the door would be open to arbitrariness and hence formalism is the line of least resistance.

(2) There is another tendency, which is apparently, and in part genuinely, in contradiction to the above. It is the tendency of officials to treat their offi-

cial function from what is substantively a utilitarian point of view in the interest of the welfare of those under their authority. But this utilitarian tendency is generally expressed in the enactment of corresponding regulatory measures which themselves have a formal character and tend to be treated in a formalistic spirit. This tendency to substantive rationality is supported by all those subject to authority who are not included in the group mentioned above as interested in the protection of advantages already secured. The problems which open up at this point belong in the theory of "democracy."

TRADITIONAL AUTHORITY: THE PURE TYPE

Authority will be called traditional if legitimacy is claimed for it and believed in by virtue of the sanctity of age-old rules and powers. The masters are designated according to traditional rules and are obeyed because of their traditional status (*Eigenwürde*). This type of organized rule is, in the simplest case, primarily based on personal loyalty which results from common upbringing. The person exercising authority is not a "superior," but a personal master, his administrative staff does not consist mainly of officials but of personal retainers, and the ruled are not "members" of an association but are either his traditional "comrades" . . . or his "subjects." Personal loyalty, not the official's impersonal duty, determines the relations of the administrative staff to the master.

Obedience is owed not to enacted rules but to the person who occupies a position of authority by tradition or who has been chosen for it by the traditional master. The commands of such a person are legitimized in one of two ways:

a) partly in terms of traditions which themselves directly determine the content of the command and are believed to be valid within certain limits that cannot be overstepped without endangering the master's traditional status;

b) partly in terms of the master's discretion in that sphere which tradition leaves open to him; this traditional prerogative rests primarily on the fact that the obligations of personal obedience tend to be essentially unlimited.

Thus there is a double sphere:

a) that of action which is bound to specific traditions;

b) that of action which is free of specific rules.

In the latter sphere, the master is free to do good turns on the basis of his personal pleasure and likes, particularly in return for gifts—the historical sources of dues (*Gebühren*). So far as his action follows principles at all, these are governed by considerations of ethical common sense, of equity or of utilitarian expediency. They are not formal principles, as in the case of legal authority. The exercise of power is oriented toward the consideration of how far master and staff can go in view of the subjects' traditional compliance without arousing their resistance. When resistance occurs, it is directed against the master or his servant personally, the accusation being that he failed to observe the traditional limits of his power. Opposition is not directed against the system as such—it is a case of "traditionalist revolution."

In the pure type of traditional authority it is impossible for law or administrative rule to be deliberately created by legislation. Rules which in fact are innovations can be legitimized only by the claim that they have been "valid of yore," but have only now been recognized by means of "Wisdom" [the *Weistum* of ancient Germanic law]. Legal decisions as "finding of the law" (*Rechtsfindung*) can refer only to documents of tradition, namely to precedents and earlier decisions.

The master rules with or without an administrative staff. . . .

The typical administrative staff is recruited from one or more of the following sources:

(I) From persons who are already related to the chief by traditional ties of loyalty. This will be called patrimonial recruitment. Such persons may be
a) kinsmen,
b) slaves,
c) dependents who are officers of the household, especially *ministeriales,*
d) clients,
e) *coloni,*
f) freedmen;

(II) Recruitment may be extra-patrimonial, including
a) persons in a relation of purely personal loyalty such as all sorts of "favorites,"
b) persons standing in a relation of fealty to their lord (vassals), and, finally,
c) free men who voluntarily enter into a relation of personal loyalty as officials.

In the pure type of traditional rule, the following features of a bureaucratic administrative staff are absent:
a) a clearly defined sphere of competence subject to impersonal rules,
b) a rationally established hierarchy,
c) a regular system of appointment on the basis of free contract, and orderly promotion,
d) technical training as a regular requirement,
e) (frequently) fixed salaries, in the type case paid in money.
On a): In place of a well-defined functional jurisdiction, there is a conflicting series of tasks and powers which at first are assigned at the master's discretion. However, they tend to become permanent and are often traditionally

stereotyped. These competing functions originate particularly in the competition for sources of income which are at the disposal of the master himself and of his representatives. It is often in the first instance through these interests that definite functional spheres are first marked off and genuine administrative organs come into being.

At first, persons with permanent functions are household officials. Their (extra-patrimonial) functions outside the administration of the household are often in fields of activity which bear a relatively superficial analogy to their household function, or which originated in a discretionary act of the master and later became traditionally stereotyped. In addition to household officials, there have existed primarily only persons with *ad hoc* commissions.

The absence of distinct spheres of competence is evident from a perusal of the list of the titles of officials in any of the ancient Oriental states. With rare exceptions, it is impossible to associate with these titles a set of rationally delimited functions which have remained stable over a considerable period.

The process of delimiting permanent functions as a result of competition among and compromise between interests seeking favors, income, and other forms of advantage is clearly evident in the Middle Ages. This phenomenon has had very important consequences. The financial interests of the powerful royal courts and of the powerful legal profession in England were largely responsible for vitiating or curbing the influence of Roman and Canon law. In all periods the irrational division of official functions has been stereotyped by the existence of an established set of rights to fees and perquisites.

On b): The question of who shall decide a matter or deal with appeals— whether an agent shall be in charge of this, and which one, or whether the master reserves decision for himself—is treated either traditionally, at times by considering the provenience of certain legal norms and precedents taken over from the outside (*Oberhof-System*); or entirely on the basis of the master's discretion in such manner that all agents have to yield to his personal intervention.

Next to the traditionalist system of the [precedent-setting outside] "superior" court (*Oberhof*) we find the principle of Germanic law, deriving from the ruler's political prerogative, that in his presence the jurisdiction of any court is suspended. The *ius evocandi* and its modern derivative, chamber justice (*Kabinettsjustiz*), stem from the same source and the ruler's discretion. Particularly in the Middle Ages the *Oberhof* was very often the agency whose writ declared and interpreted the law, and accordingly the source from which the law of a given locality was imported.

On c): The household officials and favorites are often recruited in a purely patrimonial fashion: they are slaves or dependents (*ministeriales*) of the master. If recruitment has been extra-patrimonial, they have tended to be benefice-holders whom he can freely remove. A fundamental change in this situation is first brought about by the rise of free vassals and the filling of offices by a contract of fealty. However, since fiefs are by no means determined by functional considerations, this does not alter the situation with respect to a) and b) [the lack of definite spheres of competence and clearly determined hierarchical relationships]. Except under certain circumstances when the administrative staff is organized on a prebendal basis, "promotion" is completely up to the master's discretion. . . .

On d): Rational technical training as a basic qualification for office is scarcely to be found among household officials and favorites. However, a fundamental change in administrative practice occurs wherever there is even a beginning of technical training for appointees, regardless of its content.

For some offices a certain amount of empirical training has been necessary from very early times. This is particularly true of the art of reading and writing which was originally truly a rare "art." This has often, most strikingly in China, had a decisive influence on the whole development of culture through the mode of life of the literati. It eliminated the recruiting of officials from intra-patrimonial sources and thus limited the ruler's power by confronting him with a status group. . . .

On e): Household officials and favorites are usually supported and equipped in the master's household. Generally, their dissociation from the lord's own table means the creation of benefices, at first usually benefices in kind. It is easy for these to become traditionally stereotyped in amount and kind. In addition, or instead of them, the officials who live outside the lord's household and the lord himself count on various fees, which are often collected without any regular rate or scale, being agreed upon from case to case with those seeking favors. . . .

CHARISMATIC AUTHORITY

The term "charisma" will be applied to a certain quality of an individual personality by virtue of which he is considered extraordinary and treated as endowed with supernatural, superhuman, or at least specifically exceptional powers or qualities. These are such as are not accessible to the ordinary person, but are regarded as of divine origin or as exemplary, and on the basis of them the individual concerned is treated as a "leader." In primitive circumstances this peculiar kind of quality is thought of as resting on magical powers, whether of prophets, persons with a reputation for therapeutic or legal wisdom, leaders in the hunt, or heroes in war. How the quality in question would be ultimately judged from any ethical, aesthetic, or other such point of view is naturally entirely indifferent for purposes of definition. What is alone important is how the individual is actually regarded by those subject to charismatic authority, by his "followers" or "disciples."

For present purposes it will be necessary to treat a variety of different types as being endowed with charisma in this sense. It includes the state of a "berserk" whose spells of maniac passion have, apparently wrongly, sometimes been attributed to the use of drugs. In medieval Byzantium a group of these men endowed with the charisma of fighting frenzy was maintained as a kind of weapon. It includes the "shaman," the magician who in the pure type has to be subject to epileptoid seizures as a means of falling into trances. Another type is represented by Joseph Smith, the founder of Mormonism, who may have been a very sophisticated swindler (although this cannot be definitely established). Finally it includes the type of *littérateur*, such as Kurt Eisner, who is overwhelmed by his own demagogic success. Value-free sociological analysis will treat all these on the same level as it does the charisma of men who are the "greatest" heroes, prophets, and saviors according to conventional judgements.

I. It is recognition on the part of those subject to authority which is decisive for the validity of charisma. This recognition is freely given and guaranteed by what is held to be a proof, originally always a miracle, and consists in devotion to the corresponding revelation, hero worship, or absolute trust in the leader. But where charisma is genuine, it is not this which is the basis of the claim to legitimacy. This basis lies rather in the conception that it is the duty of those subject to charismatic authority to recognize its genuineness and to act accordingly. Psychologically this recognition is a matter of complete personal devotion to the possessor of the quality, arising out of enthusiasm, or of despair and hope.

No prophet has ever regarded his quality as dependent on the attitudes of the masses toward him. No elective king or military leader has ever treated those who have resisted him or tried to ignore him otherwise than as delinquent in duty. Failure to take part in a military expedition under such leader, even though the recruitment is formally voluntary, has universally met with disdain.

II. If proof and success elude the leader for long, if he appears deserted by his god or his magical or heroic powers, above all, if his leadership fails to benefit his followers, it is likely that his charismatic authority will disappear. This is the genuine meaning of the divine right of kings (*Gottesgnadentum*).

Even the old Germanic kings were sometimes rejected with scorn. Similar phenomena are very common among so-called primitive peoples. In China the charismatic quality of the monarch, which was transmitted unchanged by heredity, was upheld so rigidly that any misfortune whatever, not only defeats in war, but drought, floods, or astronomical phenomena which were considered unlucky, forced him to do public penance and might even force his abdication. If such things occurred, it was a sign that he did not possess the requisite charismatic virtue and was thus not a legitimate "Son of Heaven."

III. An organized group subject to charismatic authority will be called a charismatic community (*Gemeinde*). It is based on an emotional form of communal relationship (*Vergemeinschaftung*). The administrative staff of a charismatic leader does not consist of "officials"; least of all are its members technically trained. It is not chosen on the basis of social privilege nor from the point of view of domestic or personal dependency. It is rather chosen in terms of the charismatic qualities of its members. The prophet has his disciples; the warlord his bodyguard; the leader, generally, his agents (*Vertrauensmänner*). There is no such thing as appointment or dismissal, no career, no promotion. There is only a call at the instance of the leader on the basis of the charismatic qualification of those he summons. There is no hierarchy; the leader merely intervenes in general or in individual cases when he considers the members of his staff lacking in charismatic qualification for a given task. There is no such thing as a bailiwick or definite sphere of competence, and no appropriation of official powers on the basis of social privileges. There may, however, be territorial or functional limits to charismatic powers and to the individual's mission. There is no such thing as a salary or a benefice.

Disciples or followers tend to live primarily in a communistic relationship with their leader on means which have been provided by voluntary gift. There are no established administrative organs. In their place are agents who have been provided with charismatic authority by their chief or who possess charisma of their own. There is no system of formal rules, of abstract legal principles, and hence no process of rational judicial decision oriented to them. But equally there is no legal wisdom oriented to judicial precedent. Formally concrete judgments are newly created from case to case and are originally regarded as divine judgments and revelations. From a substantive point of view, every charismatic authority would have to subscribe to the proposition, "It is written . . . but I say unto you . . . " The genuine prophet, like the genuine military leader and every true leader in this sense, preaches, creates, or demands *new* obligations—most typically, by virtue of revelation, oracle, inspiration, or of his own will, which are recognized by the members of the religious, military, or party group because they come from such a source. Recognition is a duty. When such an authority comes into conflict with the competing authority of another who also claims charismatic sanction, the only recourse is to some kind of a contest, by magical means or an actual physical battle of the leaders. In principle, only one side can be right in such a conflict; the other must be guilty of a wrong which has to be expiated.

Since it is "extra-ordinary," charismatic authority is sharply opposed to rational, and particularly bureaucratic, authority, and to traditional authority, whether in its patriarchal, patrimonial, or estate variants, all of which are everyday forms of domination; while the charismatic type is the direct antithesis of this. Bureaucratic authority is specifically rational in the sense of being bound to intellectually analysable rules; while charismatic authority is specifically irrational in the sense of being foreign to all rules. Traditional authority is bound to the precedents handed down from the past and to this extent is also oriented to rules. Within the sphere of its claims, charismatic authority repudiates the past, and is in this sense a specifically revolutionary force. It recognizes no appropriation of positions of power by virtue of the possession of property, either on the part of a chief or of socially privileged groups. The only basis of legitimacy for it is personal charisma so long as it is proved; that is, as long as it receives recognition and as long as the followers and disciples prove their usefulness charismatically.

The above is scarcely in need of further discussion. What has been said applies to purely plebiscitary rulers (Napoleon's "rule of genius" elevated people of humble origin to thrones and high military commands) just as much as it applies to religious prophets or war heroes.

IV. Pure charisma is specifically foreign to economic considerations. Wherever it appears, it constitutes a "call" in the most emphatic sense of the word, a "mission" or a "spiritual duty." In the pure type, it disdains and repudiates economic exploitation of the gifts of grace as a source of income, though, to be sure, this often remains more an ideal than a fact. It is not that charisma always demands a renunciation of property or even of acquisition, as under certain circumstances prophets and their disciples do. The heroic warrior and his followers actively seek booty; the elective ruler or the charismatic party leader requires the material means of power. The former in addition requires a brilliant display of his authority to bolster his prestige. What is despised, so long as the genuinely charismatic type is adhered to, is traditional or rational everyday economizing, the attainment of a regular income by continuous economic activity devoted to this end. Support by gifts, either on a grand scale involving donation, endowment, bribery and honoraria, or by begging, constitute the voluntary type of support. On the other hand, "booty" and extortion, whether by force or by other means, is the typical form of charismatic provision for needs. From the point of view of rational economic activity, charismatic want satisfaction is a typical anti-economic force. It repudiates any sort of involvement in the everyday routine world. It can only tolerate, with an attitude of complete emotional indifference, irregular, unsystematic acquisitive acts. In that it relieves the recipient of economic concerns, dependence on property income can be the economic basis of a charismatic mode of life for some groups; but that is unusual for the normal charismatic "revolutionary."

The fact that incumbency of church office has been forbidden to the Jesuits is a rationalized application of this principle of discipleship. The fact that all the "virtuosi" of asceticism, the mendicant orders, and fighters for a faith belong in this category, is quite clear. Almost all prophets have been supported by voluntary gifts. The well-known saying of St. Paul, "If a man does not work, neither shall he eat," was directed against the parasitic swarm of charismatic missionaries. It obviously has nothing to do with a positive valuation of economic activity for its own sake, but only lays it down as a duty of each individual somehow to provide for his own support. This because he realized that the purely charismatic parable of the lilies of the field was not capable of literal application, but at best "taking no thought for the morrow" could be hoped for. On the other hand, in a case of a primarily artistic type of charismatic discipleship it is conceivable that insulation from economic struggle should mean limitation of those really eligible to the "economically independent"; that is, to persons living on income from property. This has been true of the circle of Stefan George, at least in its primary intentions.

V. In traditionalist periods, charisma is *the* great revolutionary force. The likewise revolutionary force of "reason" works from *without:* by altering the situations of life and hence its problems, finally in this way changing men's attitudes toward them; or it intellectualizes the individual. Charisma, on the other hand, *may* effect a subjective or *internal* reorientation born out of suffering, conflicts, or enthusiasm. It may then result in a radical alteration of the central attitudes and directions of action with a completely new orientation of all attitudes toward the different problems of the "world." In prerationalistic periods, tradition and charisma between them have almost exhausted the whole of the orientation of action.

THE ROUTINIZATION OF CHARISMA

In its pure form charismatic authority has a character specifically foreign to everyday routine structures. The social relationships directly involved are strictly personal, based on the validity and practice of charismatic personal qualities. If this is not to remain a purely transitory phenomenon, but to take on the character of a permanent relationship, a "community" of disciples or followers or a party organization or any sort of political or hierocratic organization, it is necessary for the character of charismatic authority to become radically changed. Indeed, in its pure form charismatic authority may be said to exist only *in statu nascendi*. It cannot remain stable, but becomes either traditionalized or rationalized, or a combination of both.

The following are the principal motives underlying this transformation: (a) The ideal and also the material interests of the followers in the continuation and the continual reactivation of the community, (b) the still stronger ideal and also stronger material interests of the members of the administrative staff, the disciples, the party workers, or others in continuing their relationship. Not only this, but they have an interest in continuing it in such a way that both from an ideal and a material point of view, their own position is put on a stable everyday basis. This means, above all, making it possible to participate in normal family relationships or at least to enjoy a secure social position in place of the kind of discipleship which is cut off from ordinary worldly connections, notably in the family and in economic relationships.

These interests generally become conspicuously evident with the disappearance of the personal charismatic leader and with the problem of *succession*. The way in which this problem is met—if it is met at all and the charismatic community continues to exist or now begins to emerge—is of crucial importance for the character of the subsequent social relationships. The following are the principal possible types of solution:

(a) The *search* for a new charismatic leader on the basis of criteria of the qualities which will fit him for the position of authority.

This is to be found in a relatively pure type in the process of choice of a new Dalai Lama. It consists in the search for a child with characteristics which are interpreted to mean that he is a reincarnation of the Buddha. This is very similar to the choice of the new Bull of Apis.

In this case the legitimacy of the new charismatic leader is bound to certain distinguishing characteristics; thus, to rules with respect to which a tradition arises. The result is a process of traditionalization in favor of which the purely personal character of leadership is reduced.

(b) *Revelation* manifested in oracles, lots, divine judgments, or other techniques of selection. In this case the legitimacy of the new leader is dependent on the legitimacy of the *technique* of his selection. This involves a form of legalization.

It is said that at times the *Shofetim* [Judges] of Israel had this character. Saul is said to have been chosen by the old war oracle.

(c) Designation on the part of the original charismatic leader of his own successor and his recognition on the part of the followers.

This is a very common form. Originally, the Roman magistracies were filled entirely in this way. The system survived most clearly into later times in the appointment of the *dictator* and in the institution of the *interrex*.

In this case legitimacy is *acquired* through the act of designation.

(d) Designation of a successor by the charismatically qualified administrative staff and his recognition by the community. In its typical form this process should quite definitely not be interpreted as "election" or "nomination" or anything of the sort. It is not a matter of free selection, but of one which is strictly bound to objective duty. It is not to be determined merely by majority vote, but is a question of arriving at the correct designation, the designation of the right person who is truly endowed with charisma. It is quite possible that the minority and not the majority should be right in such a case. Unanimity is often required. It is obligatory to acknowledge a mistake and persistence in error is a serious offense. Making a wrong choice is a genuine wrong requiring expiation. Originally it was a magical offence.

Nevertheless, in such a case it is easy for legitimacy to take on the character of an acquired right which is justified by standards of the correctness of the process by which the position was acquired, for the most part, by its having been acquired in accordance with certain formalities such as coronation.

This was the original meaning of the coronation of bishops and kings in the Western world by the clergy or the high nobility with the "consent" of the community. There are numerous analogous phenomena all over the world. The fact that this is the origin of the modern conception of "election" raises problems which will have to be gone into later.

(e) The conception that charisma is a quality transmitted by heredity; thus that it is participated in by the kinsmen of its bearer, particularly by his closest relatives. This is the case of *hereditary charisma*. The order of hereditary succession in such a case need not be the same as that which is in force for appropriated rights, but may differ from it. It is also sometimes necessary to select the proper heir within the kinship group by some of the methods just spoken of.

Thus in certain African states brothers have had to fight for the succession. In China, succession had to take place in such a way that the relation of the living group to the ancestral spirits was not disturbed. The rule either of seniority or of designation by the followers has been very common in the Orient. Hence, in the House of Osman, it used to be obligatory to kill off all other possible aspirants.

Only in Medieval Europe and in Japan, elsewhere sporadically, has the principle of primogeniture, as governing the inheritance of authority, become clearly established. This has greatly facilitated the consolidation of political groups in that it has eliminated struggle between a plurality of candidates from the same charismatic family.

In the case of hereditary charisma, recognition is no longer paid to the charismatic qualities of the individual, but to the legitimacy of the position he has acquired by hereditary succession. This may lead in the direction either of traditionalization or of legalization. The concept of divine right is fundamentally altered and now comes to mean authority by virtue of a personal right which is not dependent on the recognition of those subject to authority. Personal charisma may be totally absent.

Hereditary monarchy is a conspicuous illustration. In Asia there have been very numerous hereditary priesthoods; also, frequently, the hereditary charisma of kinship groups has been treated as a criterion of social rank and of eligibility for fiefs and benefices.

(f) The concept that charisma may be transmitted by ritual means from one bearer to another or may be created in a new person. The concept was originally magical. It involves a dissociation of charisma from a particular individual, making it an objective, transferrable entity. In particular, it may become the *charisma of office*. In this case the belief in legitimacy is no longer directed to the individual, but to the acquired qualities and to the effectiveness of the ritual acts.

The most important example is the transmission of priestly charisma by anointing, consecration, or the laying on of hands; and of royal authority, by anointing and by coronation. The *character indelebilis* thus acquired means that the charismatic qualities and powers of the office are emancipated from the personal qualities of the priest. For precisely this reason, this has, from the Donatist and the Montanist heresies down to the Puritan revolution, been the subject of continual conflicts. The "hireling" of the Quakers is the preacher endowed with the charisma of office.

18.

Learning to Labor

PAUL WILLIS, 1981

The most basic, obvious and explicit dimension of counter-school culture is entrenched general and personalised opposition to 'authority'. This feeling is easily verbalised by 'the lads' (the self-elected title of those in the counter-school culture).

[In a group discussion on teachers]

JOEY   (. . .) they're able to punish us. They're bigger than us, they stand for a bigger establishment than we do, like, we're just little and they stand for bigger things, and you try to get your own back. It's, uh, resenting authority I suppose.

EDDIE   The teachers think they're high and mighty 'cos they're teachers, but they're nobody really, they're just ordinary people ain't they?

BILL   Teachers think they're everybody. They are more, they're higher than us, but they think they're a lot higher and they're not.

SPANKSY   Wish we could call them first names and that . . . think they're God.

PETE   That would be a lot better.

PW[1]   I mean you say they're higher. Do you accept at all that they know better about things?

JOEY   Yes, but that doesn't rank them above us, just because they are slightly more intelligent.

BILL   They ought to treat us how they'd like us to treat them.

(. . .)

JOEY   (. . .) the way we're subject to their every whim like. They want something doing and we have to sort of do it, 'cos, er, er, we're just, we're under them like. We were with a woman teacher in here, and 'cos we all wear rings and one or two of them bangles, like he's got one on, and out of the blue, like, for no special reason, she says, 'take all that off'.

From *Learning to Labor* by Paul Willis. Copyright © 1981 Columbia University Press. Reprinted with the permission of the publisher.

1. PW refers to the author, Paul Willis.

PW   Really?

JOEY   Yeah, we says, 'One won't come off', she says, 'Take yours off as well'. I said, 'You'll have to chop my finger off first'.

PW   Why did she want you to take your rings off?

JOEY   Just a sort of show like. Teachers do this, like, all of a sudden they'll make you do your ties up and things like this. You're subject to their every whim like. If they want something done, if you don't think it's right, and you object against it, you're down to Simmondsy [the head], or you get the cane, you get some extra work tonight.

PW   You think of most staff as kind of enemies (. . .)?

—   Yeah.

—   Yeah.

—   Most of them.

JOEY   It adds a bit of spice to yer life, if you're trying to get him for something he's done to you.

This opposition involves an apparent inversion of the usual values held up by authority. Diligence, deference, respect—these become things which can be read in quite another way.

[In a group discussion]

PW   Evans [the Careers Master] said you were all being very rude (. . .) you didn't have the politeness to listen to the speaker [during a careers session]. He said why didn't you realise that you were just making the world very rude for when you grow up and God help you when you have kids 'cos they're going to be worse. What did you think of that?

JOEY   They wouldn't. They'll be outspoken. They wouldn't be submissive fucking twits. They'll be outspoken, upstanding sort of people.

SPANKSY   If any of my kids are like this, here, I'll be pleased.

This opposition is expressed mainly as a style. It is lived out in countless small ways which are special to the school institution, instantly recognised by the teachers, and an almost ritualistic part of the daily fabric of life for the kids. Teachers are adept conspiracy theorists. They have to be. It partly explains their devotion to finding out 'the truth' from suspected culprits. They live surrounded by conspiracy in its most obvious—though often verbally unexpressed—forms. It can easily become a paranoic conviction of enormous proportions.

As 'the lads' enter the classroom or assembly, there are conspiratorial nods to each other saying, 'Come and sit here with us for a laff', sidelong glances to check where the teacher is and smirking smiles. Frozen for a moment by a direct command or look, seething movement easily resumes with the kids moving about with that 'I'm just passing through, sir' sort of look to get closer to their mates. Stopped again, there is always a ready excuse, 'I've got to take my coat off sir', 'So and So told me to see him sir'. After assembly has started, the kid still marooned from his mates crawls along the backs of the chairs or behind a curtain down the side of the hall, kicking other kids, or trying to dismantle a chair with somebody on it as he passes.

'The lads' specialise in a caged resentment which always stops just short of outright confrontation. Settled in class, as near a group as they can manage, there is a continuous scraping of chairs, a bad tempered 'tut-tutting' at the simplest request, and a continuous fidgeting about which explores every permutation of sitting or lying on a chair. During private study, some openly show disdain by apparently trying to go to sleep with their head sideways down on the desk, some have their backs to the desk gazing out of the window, or even vacantly at the wall. There is an aimless air of insubordination ready with spurious justification and impossible to nail down. If someone is sitting on the radiator it is because his trousers are wet from the rain, if someone is drifting across the classroom he is going to get some paper for written work, or if someone is leaving class he is going to empty the rubbish 'like he usually does'. Comics, newspapers and nudes under half-lifted desks melt into elusive textbooks. A continuous hum of talk flows around injunctions not to, like the inevitable tide over barely dried sand and everywhere there are rolled-back eyeballs and exaggerated mouthings of conspiratorial secrets.

During class teaching a mouthed imaginary dialogue counterpoints the formal instruction: 'No, I don't understand, you cunt'; 'What you on about, twit?'; 'Not fucking likely.'; 'Can I go home now please?' At the vaguest sexual double meaning giggles and 'whoas' come from the back accompanied perhaps by someone masturbating a gigantic penis with rounded hands above his head in compressed lipped lechery. If the secret of the conspiracy is challenged, there are V signs behind the teacher's back, the gunfire of cracked knuckles from the side, and evasive innocence at the front. Attention is focused on ties, rings, shoes, fingers, blots on the desk—anything rather than the teacher's eyes.

In the corridors there is a foot-dragging walk, an overfriendly 'hello' or sudden silence as the deputy passes. Derisive or insane laughter erupts which might or might not be about someone who has just passed. It is as demeaning to stop as it is to carry on. There is a way of standing collectively down the sides of the corridor to form an Indian gauntlet run—though this can never be proved: 'We're just waiting for Spanksy, sir'.

Of course individual situations differ, and different kinds of teaching style are more or less able to control or suppress this expressive opposition. But the school conformists—or the 'ear'oles' for the lads—have a visibly different orientation. It is not so much that they support teachers, rather they support *the idea* of teachers. Having invested something of their own identities in the formal aims of education and support of the school institution—in a certain sense having foregone their own right to have a 'laff'—they demand that teachers should at least respect the same authority. There are none like the faithful for reminding the shepherd of his duty.

[In a group discussion with conformists at Hammertown Boys]

GARY   Well, I don't think they'm strict enough now (. . .) I mean like Mr Gracey, and some of the other teachers, I mean with Groucho, even the first years play him up (. . .) they [the lads] should be punished like, so they grow up not to be cheeky (. . .) Some of the others, you can get on with them all right. I mean from the very beginning with Mr Peters everybody was quiet and if you ain't done the work, you had to come back and do it. I mean some of the other teachers, say from the first years, they give you homework, say you didn't do it, they never asked for it, they didn't bother.

It is essentially what appears to be their enthusiasm for, and complicity with, immediate authority which makes the school conformists—or 'ear'oles' or 'lobes'—[a] target for 'the lads'. The term 'ear'ole' itself connotes the passivity and absurdity of the school conformists for 'the lads'. It seems that they are always listening, never *doing:* never animated with their own internal life, but formless in rigid reception. The ear is one of the least expressive organs of the human body: it responds to the expressivity of others. It is pasty and easy to render obscene. That is how 'the lads' liked to picture those who conformed to the official idea of schooling.

Crucially, 'the lads' not only reject but feel *superior* to the 'ear'oles'. The obvious medium for the enactment of this superiority is that which the 'ear'oles' apparently yield—fun, independence and excitement: having a 'laff'.

[In a group discussion]

PW   (. . .) why not be like the ear'oles, why not try and get CSEs?

—   They don't get any fun, do they?

DEREK   Cos they'm prats like, one kid he's got on his report now, he's got five As and one B.

—   Who's that?

DEREK   Birchall.

SPANKSY   I mean, what will they remember of their school life? What will they have to look back on? Sitting in a classroom, sweating their bollocks off, you know, while we've been . . . I mean look at the things we can look back on, fighting on the Pakis, fighting on the JAs [i.e. Jamaicans]. Some of the things we've done on teachers, it'll be a laff when we look back on it.

(. . .)

PERCE   Like you know, he don't get much fun, well say Spanksy plays about all day, he gets fun. Bannister's there sweating, sweating his bollocks off all day while Spanksy's doing fuck all, and he's enjoying it.

SPANKSY   In the first and second years I used to be brilliant really. I was in 2A, 3A you know and when I used to get home, I used to lie in bed think-ing, 'Ah, school tomorrow', you know, I hadn't done that homework, you know . . . 'Got to do it'.

—   Yeah, that's right, that is.

SPANKSY   But now when I go home, it's quiet, I ain't got nothing to think about, I say, 'Oh great, school tomorrow, it'll be a laff', you know.

WILL   You still never fucking come!

SPANKSY   Who?

WILL   You.

[Laughter]

(. . .)

—   You can't imagine . . .

—   You can't imagine [inaudible] going into the Plough and saying, 'A pint of lager please'.

FRED   You can't imagine Bookley goin' home like with the missus, either, and having a good maul on her.

—   I can, I've seen him!

—   He's got a bird, Bookley!

—   He has.

FRED   I can't see him getting to grips with her, though, like we do you know.

Opposition to staff and exclusive distinction from the 'ear'oles' is continuously expressed amongst 'the lads' in the whole ambience of their behaviour, but it is also made concrete in what we may think of as certain stylistic/symbolic dis-courses centering on the three great consumer goods supplied by capitalism and seized upon in different ways by the working class for its own purposes: clothing, cigarettes and alcohol. As the most visible, personalised and instantly understood element of resistance to staff and ascendancy over 'ear'oles' clothes have great importance to 'the lads'. The first signs of a lad 'coming out' is a fairly rapid change in his clothes and hairstyle. The particular form of this al-ternative dress is determined by outside influences, especially fashions current in the wider symbolic system of youth culture. At the moment the 'lads' look' includes longish well-groomed hair, platform-type shoes, wide collared shirt turned over waisted coat or denim jerkin, plus the still obligatory flared trousers. Whatever the particular form of dress, it is most certainly *not* school uniform, rarely includes a tie (the second best for many heads if uniform cannot be enforced), and exploits colours calculated to give the maximum distinction from institutional drabness and conformity. There is a clear stereotypical notion of what constitutes institutional clothes—Spike, for instance, trying to describe the shape of a collar: 'You know, like a teacher's!'

We might note the importance the wider system of commercial youth culture has here in supplying a lexicography of style, with already connoted meanings, which can be adapted by 'the lads' to express their own more located meanings. Though much of this style, and the music associated with it, might be accurately described as arising from purely commercial drives and representing no authentic aspirations of its adherents, it should be recognised that the way in which it is taken up and used by the young can have an authenticity and directness of personal expression missing from its original commercial generation.

It is no accident that much of the conflict between staff and students at the moment should take place over dress. To the outsider it might seem fatuous. Concerned staff and involved kids, however, know that it is one of their elected grounds for the struggle over authority. It is one of the current forms of a fight between cultures. It can be resolved, finally, into a question about the legitimacy of school as an institution.

Closely related with the dress style of 'the lads' is, of course, the whole question of their personal attractiveness. Wearing smart and modern clothes gives them the chance, at the same time as 'putting their finger up' at the school and differentiating themselves from the 'ear'oles', to also make themselves more attractive to the opposite sex. It is a matter of objective fact that 'the lads' do go out with girls much more than do any other groups of the same age and that, as we have seen, a good majority of them are sexually experienced. Sexual attractiveness, its association with maturity, and the prohibition on sexual activity in school is what valorises dress and clothes as something more than an artificial code within which to express an institutional/cultural identity. This double articulation is characteristic of the counter-school culture.

If manner of dress is currently the main apparent cause of argument between staff and kids, smoking follows closely. Again we find another distinguishing characteristic of 'the lads' against the 'ear'oles'. The majority of them smoke and, perhaps more importantly, are *seen* to smoke. The essence of schoolboy smoking is school gate smoking. A great deal of time is typically spent by 'the lads' planning their next smoke and 'hopping off' lessons 'for a quick drag'. And if 'the lads' delight in smoking and flaunting their impertinence, senior staff at least cannot ignore it. There are usually strict and frequently publicised rules about smoking. If, for this reason, 'the lads' are spurred, almost as a matter of honour, to continue public smoking, senior staff are incensed by what they take to be the challenge to their authority. . . .

Again, in a very typical conjunction of school-based and outside meanings cigarette smoking for 'the lads' is valorised as an act of insurrection before the school by its association with adult values and practices. The adult world, specifically the adult male working class world, is turned to as a source of material for resistance and exclusion.

As well as inducing a 'nice' effect, drinking is undertaken openly because it is the most decisive signal to staff and 'ear'oles' that the individual is separate from the school and has a presence in an alternative, superior and more mature mode of social being. Accounts of staff sighting kids in pubs are excitedly recounted with much more relish than mere smoking incidents, and inaction after being 'clocked boozing' is even more delicious proof of a traitor/sympathiser/weakling in the school camp than is the blind eye to a lighted 'fag'. . . .

In many respects the opposition [of the lads] can be understood as a classic example of the opposition between the formal and the informal. The school is the zone of the formal. It has a clear structure: the school building, school rules, pedagogic practice, a staff hierarchy with powers ultimately sanctioned—as we have seen in small way—by the state, the pomp and majesty of the law, and the repressive arm of state apparatus, the police. The 'ear'oles' invest in this formal structure, and in exchange for some loss in autonomy expect the official guardians to keep the holy rules—often above and beyond their actual call to duty. What is freely sacrificed by the faithful must be taken from the unfaithful.

Counter-school culture is the zone of the informal. It is where the incursive demands of the formal are denied—even if the price is the expression of opposition in style, micro-interactions and non-public discourses. In working class culture generally opposition is frequently marked by a withdrawal into the informal and expressed in its characteristic modes just beyond the reach of 'the rule'.

Even though there are no public rules, physical structures, recognised hierarchies or institutionalised sanctions in the counter-school culture, it cannot run on air. It must have its own material base, its own infrastructure. This is, of course, the social group. The informal group is the basic unit of this culture, the fundamental and elemental source of its resistance. It locates and makes possible all other elements of the culture, and its presence decisively distinguishes 'the lads' from the 'ear'oles'.

The importance of the group is very clear to members of the counter-school culture.

[In a group discussion]

WILL   (. . .) we see each other every day, don't we, at school (. . .)

JOEY   That's it, we've developed certain ways of talking, certain ways of acting, and we developed disregards for Pakis, Jamaicans and all different . . . for all the scrubs and the fucking ear'oles and all that (. . .) We're getting to know it now, like we're getting to know all the cracks, like, how to get out of lessons and things, and we know where to have a crafty smoke. You can come over here to the youth wing and do summat, and er'm . . . all your friends are here, you know, it's sort of what's there, what's always going to be there for the next year, like, and you know you have to come to school today, if you're feeling bad, your mate'll soon cheer yer up like, 'cos you couldn't go without ten minutes in this school, without having a laff at something or other.

PW   Are your mates a really big important thing at school now?

—   Yeah.

—   Yeah.

—   Yeah.

JOEY   They're about the best thing actually.

The essence of being 'one of the lads' lies within the group. It is impossible to form a distinctive culture by yourself. You cannot generate fun, atmosphere and a social identity by yourself. Joining the counter-school culture means joining a group, and enjoying it means being with the group. . . .

There is a universal taboo amongst informal groups on the yielding of incriminating information about others to those with formal power. Informing contravenes the essence of the informal group's nature: the maintenance of oppositional meanings against the penetration of 'the rule'. The Hammertown lads call it 'grassing'. Staff call it telling the truth. 'Truth' is the formal complement of 'grassing'. It is only by getting someone to 'grass'—forcing them to break the solemnest taboo—that the primacy of the formal organisation can be maintained. No wonder then, that a whole school can be shaken with paroxysms over a major incident and the purge which follows it. It is an atavistic struggle about authority and the legitimacy of authority. The school has to win, and someone, finally, has to 'grass': this is one of the ways in which the school itself is reproduced and the faith of the 'ear'-oles' restored. But whoever has done the 'grassing' becomes special, weak and marked. . . .

Membership of the informal group sensitises the individual to the unseen informal dimension of life in general. Whole hinterlands open up of what lies behind the official definition of things. A kind of double capacity develops to register public descriptions and objectives on the one hand, and to look behind them, consider their implications, and work out what will actually happen, on the other. This interpretative ability is felt very often as a kind of maturation, a feeling of becoming 'worldliwise', of knowing 'how things really work when it comes to it'. It supplies the real 'insider' knowledge which actually helps you get through the day.

PW   Do you think you've learnt anything at school, has it changed or moulded your values?

JOEY   I don't think school does fucking anything to you (. . .) It never has had much effect on anybody I don't think [after] you've learnt the basics. I mean school, it's fucking four hours a day. But it ain't the teachers who mould you, it's the fucking kids you meet. You'm only with the teachers 30 per cent of the time in school, the other fucking two-thirds are just talking, fucking pickin' an argument, messing about.

The group also supplies those contacts which allow the individual to build up alternative maps of social reality, it gives the bits and pieces of information for the individual to work out himself what makes things tick. It is basically only through the group that other groups are met, and through them successions of other groups. School groups coalesce and further link up with neighbourhood groups, forming a network for the passing on of distinctive kinds of knowledge and perspectives that progressively place school at a tangent to the overall experience of being a working class teenager in an industrial city. It is the infrastructure of the informal group which makes at all possible a distinctive kind of *class* contact, or class culture, as distinct from the dominant one.

CLASS FORM

The main emphasis so far has been upon the apparently creative and self-made forms of opposition and cultural style in the school. It is now time to contextualise the counter-school culture. Its points of contact with the wider working class culture are not accidental, nor its style quite independent, nor its cultural skills unique or special. Though the achievements of counter-school culture are specific, they must be set against the larger pattern of working class culture in order for us to understand their true nature and significance. This section is based on fieldwork carried out in the factories where 'the lads' get jobs after leaving school, and on interviews with their parents at home.

In particular, counter-school culture has many profound similarities with the culture its members are mostly destined for—shopfloor culture. Though one must always take account of regional and occupational variations, the central thing about the working class culture of the shopfloor is that, despite harsh conditions and external direction, people do look for meaning and impose frameworks. They exercise their abilities and seek enjoyment in activity, even where most controlled by others. Paradoxically, they thread through the dead experience of work a living culture which is far from a simple reflex of defeat. This is the same fundamental taking hold of an alienating situation that one finds in counter-school culture and its attempt to weave a tapestry of interest and diversion through the dry institutional text. These cultures are not simply layers of padding between human beings and unpleasantness. They are appropriations in their own right, exercises of skill, motions, activities applied towards particular ends.

The credentials for entry into shopfloor culture proper, as into the counter-school culture, are far from being merely one of the defeated. They are credentials of skill, dexterity and confidence and, above all, a kind of presence which adds to, more than it subtracts from, a living social force. A force which is *on the move*, not supported, structured and organised by a formal named institution, to which one may apply by written application.

[A] main theme of shopfloor culture—at least as I observed and recorded it in the manufacturing industries of the Midlands—is the massive attempt to gain informal control of the work process. Limitation of output or 'systematic soldiering' and 'gold bricking' have been observed from the particular perspective of management from Taylor (1972) onwards, but there is evidence now of a much more concerted—though still informal—attempt to gain control. It sometimes happens now that the men themselves to all intents and purposes actually control at least manning and the speed of production. Again this is effectively mirrored for us by working class kids' attempts, with the aid of the resources of their culture, to take control of classes, substitute their own unofficial timetables, and control their own routines and life spaces. Of course the limit to this similarity is that where 'the lads' can escape entirely, 'work' is done in the factory—at least to the extent of the production of the cost of subsistence of the worker—and a certain level of activity is seen as necessary and justified. Here is the father of one of 'the lads', a factory hand on a track producing car engines, talking at home:

> Actually the foreman, the gaffer, don't run the place, the men run the place. See, I mean you get one of the chaps says, 'Alright, you'm on so and so today'. You can't argue with him. The gaffer don't give you the job, they swop each other about, tek it in turns. Ah, but I mean the job's done. If the gaffer had gi'd you the job you would . . . They tried to do it one morning, gi'd a chap a job you know, but he'd been on it, you know, I think he'd been on all week, and they just downed tools (. . .) There's four hard jobs on the track and there's dozens that's . . . you know, a child of five could do it, quite honestly, but everybody has their turn. That's organised by the men.

Shopfloor culture also rests on the same fundamental organisational unit as counter-school culture. The informal group locates and makes possible all its other elements. It is the zone where strategies for wresting control of symbolic and real space from official authority are generated and disseminated. It is the massive presence of this informal organisation which most decisively marks off shopfloor culture from middle class cultures of work.

Amongst workers it is also the basis for extensive bartering, arranging 'foreigners' and 'fiddling'. These are expanded forms of the same thing which take place in school amongst 'the lads'.

The informal group on the shopfloor also shows the same attitude to conformists and informers as do 'the lads'. 'Winning' things is as widespread on the shopfloor as theft is amongst the lads, and is similarly endorsed by implicit informal criteria. Ostracism is the punishment for not maintaining the integrity of the world in which this is possible against the persistent intrusions of the formal. Here is the father of another of 'the lads' on factory life:

> A foreman is like, you know what I mean, they're trying to get on, they're trying to get up. They'd cut everybody's throat to get there. You get people like this in the factory. Course these people cop it in the neck off the workers, they do all the tricks under the sun. You know what I mean, they don't like to see anyone crawlin' (. . .) Course instead of taking one pair of glasses [from the stores] Jim had two, you see, and a couple of masks and about six pairs o'gloves. Course this Martin was watching and actually two days after we found out that he'd told the foreman see. Had 'im, Jim, in the office about it, the foreman did, and, (. . .) well I mean, his life hasn't been worth living has it? Eh, nobody speaks to him, they won't give him a light, nobody'll give him a light for his fag or nothin' . . . Well, he won't do it again, he won't do it again. I mean he puts his kettle on, on the stove of a morning, so they knock it off, don't they, you know, tek all his water out, put sand in, all this kind of thing (. . .) if he cum to the gaffer, 'Somebody's knocked me water over', or, er, 'They put sand in me cup' and all this business, 'Who is it then?'. 'I don't know who it is'. He'll never find out who it is.

The rejection of school work by 'the lads' and the omnipresent feeling that they know better is also paralleled by a massive feeling on the shopfloor, and in the working class generally, that practice is more important than theory. As a big handwritten sign, borrowed from the back of a matchbox and put up by one of the workers, announces on one shopfloor: 'An ounce of keenness is worth a whole library of certificates'. The shopfloor abounds with apocryphal stories about the idiocy of purely theoretical knowledge. Practical ability always comes first and is a *condition* of other kinds of knowledge. Whereas in middle class culture knowledge and qualifications are seen as a way of shifting upwards the whole mode of practical alternatives open to an individual, in working class eyes theory is riveted to particular productive practices. If it cannot earn its keep there, it is to be rejected. This is Spanksy's father talking at home. The fable form underlines the centrality and routinisation of this cultural view of 'theory'.

In Toll End Road there's a garage, and I used to work part-time there and . . . there's an elderly fellow there, been a mechanic all his life, and he must have been seventy years of age then. He was an old Hammertown professional, been a professional boxer once, an elderly chap and he was a practical man, he was practical, right? . . . and he told me this (. . .) I was talking to him, was talking about something like this, he says (. . .) 'This chap was all theory and he sends away for books about everything', and he says, 'Do you know', he says, 'he sent away for a book once and it came in a wooden box, and it's still in that box 'cos he can't open it'. Now that in't true, is it? But the point is true. That in't true, that didn't happen, but his point is right. He can't get at that box 'cos he don't know how to open the box! Now what's the good of that?

This can be seen as a clear and usually unremarked class function of knowledge. The working class view would be the rational one were it not located in class society, i.e. that theory is only useful insofar as it really does help to do things, to accomplish practical tasks and change nature. Theory is asked to be in a close dialectic with the material world. For the middle class, more aware of its position in a class society, however, theory is seen partly in its social guise of qualifications as the power to move up the social scale. In this sense theory is well worth having even if it is never applied to nature. It serves its purpose as the *means* to decide precisely which bit of nature one wants to apply it to, or even to choose not to apply it at all. Paradoxically, the working class distrust and rejection of theory comes partly from a kind of recognition, even in the moment that it oppresses, of the hollowness of theory in its social guise.

It is, of course, the larger class dimension which gives the working class counter-school culture its special edge and resonance in terms of style, its particular force of opposition and its importance as an experiential preparation for entry into working class jobs. Although all forms of institution are likely to breed their own informal accretions, and although all schools of whatever class always create oppositional cultures, it is the crucial conjunction of institutional opposition with a working class context and mode which gives the special character and significance to 'the lads'' culture.

REFERENCES

Taylor, F. 1972. *Scientific Management.* Westport, Conn.: Greenwood Press.

G.

Spontaneous Order

The top-down solution to the problem of social order described in the previous section addresses some of the weaknesses of solutions based on meaning, values, and norms. It raises its own set of difficulties, however. One criticism concerns its logical inconsistency (Parsons 1937, 89–94). If, as Hobbes assumes, individuals are rational egoists, then why would they ever act in the collective interest by establishing a coercive state? What is to stop each from withholding support from a central authority (by retaining their arms) so as to maintain their individual power? If everyone did so, however, then an effective state could never be established.[1]

The top-down solution has also generated substantive critiques. To be effective an authority may need to be more oppressive than people are willing to tolerate.[2] Enforcing rules may require more resources than any state can realistically command. Moreover, in many relatively ordered situations there simply is no central authority. Consider international relations, for example. How can nations resolve conflicts in the absence of a world government? Or consider relations among friends. No outside authority ensures their compliance with the rules of etiquette. Can self-interested individuals produce an orderly society without external authority?

Perhaps. In "Cosmos and Taxis," Friedrich von Hayek suggests that order need not necessarily be planned from above. Instead, it is possible for individ-

---

1. Parsons's criticism therefore anticipates arguments about the free-rider problem mentioned earlier in section C on the problem of social order. Also, see the section "Groups and Networks."

2. Too much policing (as in a police state) can also prove to be destabilizing and thus can lead ultimately to greater disorder.

uals pursuing their own interests to produce predictable systems. And because such systems incorporate the knowledge of many people, they may be preferable to those planned by a single individual. Thus, at least predictability can be achieved without a centralized authority.

But is this predictability necessarily accompanied by cooperation? That is, do stable expectations lead individuals to behave in ways that contribute to group welfare? Thomas Schelling's analysis of neighborhood racial segregation suggests that although interaction may produce predictable patterns of behavior, it does not necessarily increase social order. Schelling begins his argument by assuming that people do not live in racially segregated neighborhoods. Despite this, he shows that when all individuals pursue their own preferences, the outcome is segregation rather than integration. In this example, individual actions combine to produce predictable macro-level patterns. These patterns are not what people want, however. They contribute to neither individual nor group welfare. In Schelling's analysis, the unregulated interaction of rational egoists produces an outcome that is unintended—and unwanted—by all.

But other spontaneous order theorists make the claim that rational egoists *can* create social order in the absence of preexisting values, norms, and coercion. The most influential early statement of this view is found in Adam Smith's *The Wealth of Nations* (first published during the American Revolution). Smith borrows the notion that rational egoism could lead to social order from the maverick Dutch doctor Bernard Mandeville, author of *The Fable of the Bees; or Private Vices, Public Benefits*. In this text Mandeville claims to demonstrate

> that, neither the Friendly Qualities and kind Affections that are natural to Man, nor the real Virtues he is capable of acquiring by Reason and Self-Denial, are the Foundation of Society: but that what we call Evil in the World, Moral as well as Natural, is the grand Principle that makes us sociable Creatures, the solid Basis, the Life and Support of all Trades and Employments without Exception: That there we must look for the true Origin of all Arts and Sciences, and that the Moment Evil ceases, the Society must be spoiled, if not totally dissolved. (Mandeville [1723] 1924, 369)

In this statement, "evil" refers to selfishness. Smith agrees, arguing that "It is not from the benevolence of the butcher, the brewer or the baker, that we expect our dinner, but from their regard to their own interest. We address ourselves, not to their humanity, but to their self-love, and never talk to them of our own necessities but of their advantages" (see p. 258). For Smith, self-interest leads to cooperation, whereas for Hobbes and others, it produces conflict. How can this be? How can spontaneous order theorists make the same assumption of rational egoism but come to such different conclusions about social order?

Evidently, these theories must diverge in some way that has not yet been made explicit. A key difference lies in how the theorists view the social conditions in which people live. Recall that Hobbes sees the state of nature as a world in which people are relatively homogeneous—having the same desires and similar resources. Further, these resources are limited. There is a fixed supply over which individuals must compete. Like children's birthday parties where there is only so much cake to go around, the more that Jack eats, the less there is for Jill. This situation resembles a zero-sum game, where interaction invariably breeds conflict; thus, when one person wins, the other must lose.

Smith's argument, by contrast, suggests that this is not always the case. Instead, in "every improved society, people specialize. . . . the farmer is generally nothing but a farmer; the manufacturer, nothing but a manufacturer" (see p. 252). Thus individuals have different resources. The farmer has more wheat; the manufacturer has more cloth. Two things happen when there is such a division of labor. The first is that people can actually produce more than if they tried by themselves to produce everything—the wheat and cloth—that they needed. Smith provides an example of this dynamic by discussing how the division of labor leads to increased productivity. An individual working alone can produce only twenty pins a day, but if pin making is divided into many different operations, each performed by a specialized worker, then productivity increases by a factor of 240. Thus the division of labor allows the same number of people to accomplish much more work.

The second thing that happens is that people can use the surplus they produce to get other things they want. The farmer can use his wheat to purchase cloth; the manufacturer can use excess cloth to obtain wheat. "Every workman has a great quantity of his own work to dispose of beyond what he himself has occasion for; and every other workman being in exactly the same situation, he is enabled to exchange a great quantity of his own goods for a great quantity . . . of theirs." The result? "Universal opulence" and "general plenty" (see p. 256).

Thus, for Smith, social life is not necessarily like a group of children dividing up a birthday cake. Instead, it is potentially more like a team—when one member wins, the others do as well. Accordingly, social life can be a win-win proposition. In other words, it is analogous to a positive-sum rather than a zero-sum game. Peoples' interests are not necessarily opposed. As a result there is much less conflict and a greater potential for cooperation. And more cooperation, of course, means more social order.

But why do people exchange fairly? Why don't they just take what others give them and default on their end of the deal? Hobbes argues that people will not be able to enforce agreements with one another. Is there any reason to think that self-interested actors will be able to exchange without engaging in fraud?

In "The Evolution of Cooperation," Robert Axelrod provides an answer to this question. To develop his argument, he makes use of a new tool in social scientific research, the Prisoner's Dilemma.[3] The Prisoner's Dilemma offers researchers the possibility of studying the emergence of cooperation among strangers who are unable to communicate with one another. The game attempts to model something familiar to every fan of cops and robbers television shows. The cops hold two people suspected of having committed a crime. To obtain a conviction, they need to get at least one of the suspects to confess. To that end, each suspect is placed in a separate room. The cops offer a sweet deal to the first one to confess and promise to throw the book at the other. Jointly, the suspects are faced with four possible outcomes. If neither confesses, they

---

3. For an engaging discussion of the development of game theory in general, and of the Prisoner's Dilemma game in particular, see Nasar 1998. For an up-to-date survey of game-theoretical explanations of the emergence of norms, see Voss 2001.

get a light sentence. If both simultaneously confess, they each get longer prison terms. If only one confesses, he gets off scot-free.

If this game is played only once, then each suspect's optimal strategy is to confess. (No doubt, this is why the setup is used so frequently by the police!) Whereas this outcome is individually rational (each player gets the best outcome given that the other also confesses), it is collectively irrational (each would do better if neither confessed). Note that this outcome is analogous to Hobbes's state of nature. When everyone pursues their own interest, they are all unhappy. But if the game is played over an indefinite period with the same two players, cooperation can occur. This is because when people engage in repeated interactions, it is actually in their interest to cooperate. Thus in situations in which people interact many times, they may behave cooperatively—as Smith predicts. The welfare of the group is enhanced.

To demonstrate the relevance of these simple games for real-world outcomes, Axelrod shows (in the next reading) how cooperation emerged spontaneously on the battleground among French and German soldiers facing each other in the trenches of World War I. Other scholars continue to build on these ideas to understand a variety of empirical phenomena—from slime mold, to ants, to brains, to cities, to software (Johnson 2001). Their work highlights how stable patterns of large-scale behavior can emerge, as if by an invisible hand, from what appears to be the chaotic interaction of lower-level units. Under at least some conditions, the resulting patterns are "adaptive" and contribute to the welfare of the group.

REFERENCES

Johnson, Steven. 2001. *Emergence: The Connected Lives of Ants, Brains, Cities, and Software.* New York: Scribner's.

Mandeville, Bernard. [1723] 1924. *The Fable of the Bees; Or Private Vices, Publick Benefits.* Oxford: Clarendon Press.

Nasar, Sylvia. 1998. *A Beautiful Mind: A Biography of John Forbes Nash, Jr., Winner of the Nobel Prize in Economics, 1994.* New York: Simon and Schuster.

Parsons, Talcott. 1937. *The Structure of Social Action.* New York: McGraw-Hill.

Voss, Thomas. 2001. "Game-Theoretical Perspectives on the Emergence of Social Norms." In *Social Norms,* edited by Michael Hechter and Karl-Dieter Opp, 105–36. New York: Russell Sage Foundation.

19.

Cosmos and Taxis

FRIEDRICH A. HAYEK, 1976

THE CONCEPT OF ORDER

The central concept around which the discussion of this book will turn is that of order, and particularly the distinction between two kinds of order which we will provisionally call 'made' and 'grown' orders. Order is an indispensable concept for the discussion of all complex phenomena, in which it must largely play the role the concept of law plays in the analysis of simpler phenomena. There is no adequate term other than 'order' by which we can describe it, although 'system', 'structure' or 'pattern' may occasionally serve instead. The term 'order' has, of course, a long history in the social sciences,[1] but in recent times it has generally been avoided, largely because of the ambiguity of its meaning and its frequent association with authoritarian views. We cannot do without it, however, and shall have to guard against misinterpretation by sharply defining the general sense in which we shall employ it and then clearly distinguishing between the two different ways in which such order can originate.

By 'order' we shall thoughout describe *a state of affairs in which a multiplicity of elements of various kinds are so related to each other that we may learn from our acquaintance with some spatial or temporal part of the whole to form correct expectations concerning the rest, or at least expectations which have a good chance of proving correct.*[2] It is clear that every society must in this sense possess an order and that such an order will often exist without having been deliberately created. As has been said by a distinguished social anthropologist, 'that there

From *Law, Legislation, and Liberty*, vol. 1, by F. A. Hayek, 1982. Routledge.

1. It would seem that the currency of the concept of order in political theory goes back to St Augustine. See in particular his dialogue *Ordo* in J. P. Migne (ed) *Patrologiae cursus completus sec. lat.* 32/47 (Paris, 1861–2), and in a German version *Die Ordnung*, trans. C. J. Peel, fourth edition (Paderborn, 1966).

2. See L. S. Stebbing, *A Modern Introduction to Logic* (London, 1933), p. 228: 'When we know how a set of elements is ordered, we have a basis for inference.' See also Immanuel Kant, *Werke* (Akademie Ausgabe), *Nachlass*, vol 6, p. 669: 'Ordnung ist die Zusammenfügung nach Regeln.'

is some order, consistency and constancy in social life, is obvious. If there were not, none of us would be able to go about our affairs or satisfy our most elementary needs.'[3]

Living as members of society and dependent for the satisfaction of most of our needs on various forms of co-operation with others, we depend for the effective pursuit of our aims clearly on the correspondence of the expectations concerning the actions of others on which our plans are based with what they will really do. This matching of the intentions and expectations that determine the actions of different individuals is the form in which order manifests itself in social life; and it will be the question of how such an order does come about that will be our immediate concern. The first answer to which our anthropomorphic habits of thought almost inevitably lead us is that it must be due to the design of some thinking mind.[4] And because order has been generally interpreted as such a deliberate *arrangement* by somebody, the concept has become unpopular among most friends of liberty and has been favoured mainly by authoritarians. According to this interpretation order in society must rest on a relation of command and obedience, or a hierarchical structure of the whole of society in which the will of superiors, and ultimately of some single supreme authority, determines what each individual must do.

This authoritarian connotation of the concept of order derives, however, entirely from the belief that order can be created only by forces outside the system (or 'exogenously'). It does not apply to an equilibrium set up from within[5] (or 'endogenously') such as that which the general theory of the market endeavours to explain. A spontaneous order of this kind has in many respects properties different from those of a made order.

THE TWO SOURCES OF ORDER

The study of spontaneous orders has long been the peculiar task of economic theory, although, of course, biology has from its beginning been concerned with that special kind of spontaneous order which we call an organism. Only recently has there arisen within the physical sciences under the name of cy-

---

3. See E. E. Evans-Pritchard, *Social Anthropology* (London, 1951), p. 49.

4. See L. S. Stebbing, op. cit., p. 229: 'Order is most *apparent* where man has been at work.'

5. See J. Ortega y Gasset, *Mirabeau o el politico* (1927), in *Obras Completas* (Madrid, 1947), vol. 3, p. 603.

bernetics a special discipline which is also concerned with what are called self-organizing or self-generating systems.[6]

The distinction of this kind of order from one which has been made by somebody putting the elements of a set in their places or directing their movements is indispensable for any understanding of the processes of society as well as for all social policy. There are several terms available for describing each kind of order. The made order which we have already referred to as an exogenous order or an arrangement may again be described as a construction, an artificial order or, especially where we have to deal with a directed social order, as an *organization*. The grown order, on the other hand, which we have referred to as a self-generating or endogenous order, is in English most conveniently described as a *spontaneous order*. Classical Greek was more fortunate in possessing distinct single words for the two kinds of order, namely *taxis* for a made order, such as, for example, an order of battle,[7] and *kosmos* for a grown order, meaning originally 'a right order in a state or a community'.[8] We shall occasionally avail ourselves of these Greek words as technical terms to describe the two kinds of order.

It would be no exaggeration to say that social theory begins with—and has an object only because of—the discovery that there exist orderly structures which are the product of the action of many men but are not the result of human design. In some fields this is now universally accepted. Although there was a time when men believed that even language and morals had been 'invented' by some genius of the past, everybody recognizes now that they are the outcome of a process of evolution whose results nobody foresaw or designed. But in other fields many people still treat with suspicion the claim that the patterns of interaction of many men can show an order that is of nobody's deliberate making; in the economic sphere, in particular, critics still pour uncomprehending ridicule on Adam Smith's expression of the 'invisible hand' by which, in the language of his time, he described how man is led 'to promote an

---

6. See H. von Foerster and G. W. Zopf, Jr. (eds.), *Principles of Self-Organization* (New York, 1962) and, on the anticipation of the main conceptions of cybernetics by Adam Smith, cf. G. Hardin, *Nature and Man's Fate* (New York, 1961), p. 54; and Dorothy Emmet, *Function, Purpose and Powers* (London, 1958), p. 90.

7. See H. Kuhn, 'Ordnung im Werden und Zerfall', in H. Kuhn and F. Wiedmann (eds), *Das Problem der Ordnung* (Sechster Deutscher Kongress für Philosophie, Munich, 1960, publ. Meisenheim am Glan, 1962), especially p. 17.

8. See Werner Jaeger, *Paideia: The Ideals of Greek Culture,* trans. G. Highet, vol. 1, second edition (New York, 1945), p. 110. . . . See also the same author's 'Praise of law' in P. Sayre (ed.), *Interpretations of Modern Legal Philosophies: Essays in Honor of Roscoe Pound* (New York, 1947), especially p. 358. And ibid., p. 361.

end which was no part of his intentions'.[9] If indignant reformers still complain of the chaos of economic affairs, insinuating a complete absence of order, this is partly because they cannot conceive of an order which is not deliberately made, and partly because to them an order means something aiming at concrete purposes which is, as we shall see, what a spontaneous order cannot do.

We shall examine later . . . how that coincidence of expectations and plans is produced which characterizes the market order and the nature of the benefits we derive from it. For the moment we are concerned only with the fact that an order not made by man does exist and with the reasons why this is not more readily recognized. The main reason is that such orders as that of the market do not obtrude themselves on our senses but have to be traced by our intellect. We cannot see, or otherwise intuitively perceive, this order of meaningful actions, but are only able mentally to reconstruct it by tracing the relations that exist between the elements. We shall describe this feature by saying that it is an abstract and not a concrete order.

THE DISTINGUISHING PROPERTIES OF SPONTANEOUS ORDERS

One effect of our habitually identifying order with a made order or *taxis* is indeed that we tend to ascribe to all order certain properties which deliberate arrangements regularly, and with respect to some of these properties necessarily, possess. Such orders are relatively *simple* or at least necessarily confined to such moderate degrees of complexity as the maker can still survey; they are usually *concrete* in the sense just mentioned that their existence can be intuitively perceived by inspection; and, finally, having been made deliberately, they invariably do (or at one time did) *serve a purpose* of the maker. None of these characteristics necessarily belong to a spontaneous order or *kosmos*. Its degree of complexity is not limited to what a human mind can master. Its existence need not manifest itself to our senses but may be based on purely *abstract* relations which we can only mentally reconstruct. And not having been made it *cannot* legitimately be said to *have a particular purpose,* although our awareness of its existence may be extremely important for our successful pursuit of a great variety of different purposes.

Spontaneous orders are not necessarily complex, but unlike deliberate human arrangements, they may achieve any degree of complexity. One of our main contentions will be that very complex orders, comprising more particular facts than any brain could ascertain or manipulate, can be brought about only through forces inducing the formation of spontaneous orders.

9. Adam Smith, *Wealth of Nations,* edited by E. Cannan, vol. I, p. 421.

Spontaneous orders need not be what we have called abstract, but they will often consist of a system of abstract relations between elements which are also defined only by abstract properties, and for this reason will not be intuitively perceivable and not recognizable except on the basis of a theory accounting for their character. The significance of the abstract character of such orders rests on the fact that they may persist while all the particular elements they comprise, and even the number of such elements, change. All that is necessary to preserve such an abstract order is that a certain structure of relationships be maintained, or that elements of a certain kind (but variable in number) continue to be related in a certain manner.

Most important, however, is the relation of a spontaneous order to the conception of purpose. Since such an order has not been created by an outside agency, the order as such also can have no purpose, although its existence may be very serviceable to the individuals which move within such order. But in a different sense it may well be said that the order rests on purposive action of its elements, when 'purpose' would, of course, mean nothing more than that their actions tend to secure the preservation or restoration of that order. The use of 'purposive' in this sense as a sort of 'teleological shorthand', as it has been called by biologists, is unobjectionable so long as we do not imply an awareness of purpose of the part of the elements, but mean merely that the elements have acquired regularities of conduct conducive to the maintenance of the order—presumably because those who did act in certain ways had within the resulting order a better chance of survival than those who did not. In general, however, it is preferable to avoid in this connection the term 'purpose' and to speak instead of 'function'.

SPONTANEOUS ORDERS IN NATURE

It will be instructive to consider briefly the character of some spontaneous orders which we find in nature, since here some of their characteristic properties stand out most clearly. There are in the physical world many instances of complex orders which we could bring about only by availing ourselves of the known forces which tend to lead to their formation, and never by deliberately placing each element in the appropriate position. We can never produce a crystal or a complex organic compound by placing the individual atoms in such a position that they will form the lattice of a crystal or the system based on benzol rings which make up an organic compound. But we can create the conditions in which they will arrange themselves in such a manner.

What does in these instances determine not only the general character of the crystal or compound that will be formed but also the particular position of any one element in them? The important point is that the regularity of the conduct of the elements will determine the general character of the resulting order but not all the detail of its particular manifestation. The particular manner in which the resulting abstract order will manifest itself will depend, in addition to the rules which govern the actions of the elements, on their initial position and on all the particular circumstances of the immediate environment to which each of them will react in the course of the formation of that order. The order, in other words, will always be an adaptation to a large number of particular facts which will not be known in their totality to anyone.

We should note that a regular pattern will thus form itself not only if the elements all obey the same rules and their different actions are determined only by the different positions of the several individuals relatively to each other, but also, as is true in the case of the chemical compound, if there are different kinds of elements which act in part according to different rules. Whichever is the case, we shall be able to predict only the general character of the order that will form itself, and not the particular position which any particular element will occupy relatively to any other element.

Another example from physics is in some respects even more instructive. In the familiar school experiment in which iron filings on a sheet of paper are made to arrange themselves along some of the lines of force of a magnet placed below, we can predict the general shape of the chains that will be formed by the filings hooking themselves together; but we cannot predict along which ones of the family of an infinite number of such curves that define the magnetic field these chains will place themselves. This will depend on the position, direction, weight, roughness or smoothness of each of the iron filings and on all the irregularities of the surface of the paper. The forces emanating from the magnet and from each of the iron filings will thus interact with the environment to produce a unique instance of a general pattern, the general character of which will be determined by known laws, but the concrete appearance of which will depend on particular circumstances we cannot fully ascertain.

IN SOCIETY, RELIANCE ON SPONTANEOUS ORDER BOTH EXTENDS AND LIMITS OUR POWERS OF CONTROL

Since a spontaneous order results from the individual elements adapting themselves to circumstances which directly affect only some of them, and which in their totality need not be known to anyone, it may extend to circumstances so complex that no mind can comprehend them all. Consequently, the concept becomes particularly important when we turn from mechanical to such 'more highly organized' or essentially complex phenomena as we encounter in the realms of life, mind and society. Here we have to deal with 'grown' structures with a degree of complexity which they have assumed and could assume only because they were produced by spontaneous ordering forces. They in consequence present us with peculiar difficulties in our effort to explain them as well as in any attempt to influence their character. Since we can know at most the rules observed by the elements of various kinds of which the structures are made up, but not all the individual elements and never all the particular circumstances in which each of them is placed, our knowledge will be restricted to the general character of the order which will form itself. And even where, as is true of a society of human beings, we may be in a position to alter at least some of the rules of conduct which the elements obey, we shall thereby be able to influence only the general character and not the detail of the resulting order.

This means that, though the use of spontaneous ordering forces enables us to induce the formation of an order of such a degree of complexity (namely comprising elements of such numbers, diversity and variety of conditions) as we could never master intellectually, or deliberately arrange, we will have less power over the details of such an order than we would of one which we produce by arrangement. In the case of spontaneous orders we may, by determining some of the factors which shape them, determine their abstract features, but we will have to leave the particulars to circumstances which we do not know. Thus, by relying on the spontaneously ordering forces, we can extend the scope or range of the order which we may induce to form, precisely because its particular manifestation will depend on many more circumstances than can be known to us—and in the case of a social order, because such an order will utilize the separate knowledge of all its several members, without this knowledge ever being concentrated in a single mind, or being subject to those processes of deliberate coordination and adaptation which a mind performs.

In consequence, the degree of power of control over the extended and more complex order will be much smaller than that which we could exercise over a made order or *taxis*. There will be many aspects of it over which we will possess no control at all, or which at least we shall not be able to alter without interfering with—and to that extent impeding—the forces producing the spontaneous order. Any desire we may have concerning the particular position of individual elements, or the relation between particular individuals or groups, could not be satisfied without upsetting the overall order. The kind of power which in this respect we would possess over a concrete arrangement or *taxis* we would not have over a spontaneous order where we would know, and be able to influence, only the abstract aspects.

It is important to note here that there are two different respects in which order may be a matter of degree. How well ordered a set of objects or events is depends on how many of the attributes of (or the relations between) the elements we can learn to predict. Different orders may in this respect differ from each other in either or both of two ways: the orderliness may concern only very few relations between the elements, or a great many; and, second, the regularity thus defined may be great in the sense that it will be confirmed by all or nearly all instances, or it may be found to prevail only in a majority of the instances and thus allow us to predict its occurrence only with a certain degree of probability. In the first instance we may predict only a few of the features of the resulting structure, but do so with great confidence; such an order would be limited but may still be perfect. In the second instance we shall be able to predict much more, but with only a fair degree of certainty. The knowledge of the existence of an order will however still be useful even if this order is restricted in either or both these respects; and the reliance on spontaneously ordering forces may be preferable or even indispensable, although the order towards which a system tends will in fact be only more or less imperfectly approached. The market order in particular will regularly secure only a certain probability that the expected relations will prevail, but it is, nevertheless, the only way in which so many activities depending on dispersed knowledge can be effectively integrated into a single order.

SPONTANEOUS ORDERS RESULT FROM THEIR ELEMENTS OBEYING CERTAIN RULES OF CONDUCT

We have already indicated that the formation of spontaneous orders is the result of their elements following certain rules in their responses to their immediate environment. The nature of these rules still needs fuller examination, partly because the word 'rule' is apt to suggest some erroneous ideas, and partly because the rules which determine a spontaneous order differ in important respects from another kind of rules which are needed in regulating an organization or *taxis*.

On the first point, the instances of spontaneous orders which we have given from physics are instructive because they clearly show that the rules which govern the actions of the elements of such spontaneous orders need not be rules which are 'known' to these elements; it is sufficient that the elements actually behave in a manner which can be described by such rules. The concept of rules as we use it in this context therefore does not imply that such rules exist in articulated ('verbalized') forms, but only that it is possible to discover rules which the actions of the individuals in fact follow. To emphasize this we have occasionally spoken of 'regularity' rather than of rules, but regularity, of course, means simply that the elements behave according to rules.

That rules in this sense exist and operate without being explicitly known to those who obey them applies also to many of the rules which govern the actions of men and thereby determine a spontaneous social order. Man certainly does not know all the rules which guide his actions in the sense that he is able to state them in words. At least in primitive human society, scarcely less than in animal societies, the structure of social life is determined by rules of conduct which manifest themselves only by being in fact observed. Only when individual intellects begin to differ to a significant degree will it become necessary to express these rules in a form in which they can be communicated and explicitly taught, deviant behaviour corrected, and differences of opinion about appropriate behaviour decided. Although man never existed without laws that he obeyed, he did, of course, exist for hundreds of thousands of years without laws he 'knew' in the sense that he was able to articulate them.

What is of still greater importance in this connection, however, is that not every regularity in the behaviour of the elements does secure an overall order. Some rules governing individual behaviour might clearly make altogether impossible the formation of an overall order. Our problem is what kind of rules of conduct will produce an order of society and what kind of order particular rules will produce.

The classical instance of rules of the behaviour of the elements which will not produce order comes from the physical sciences: it is the second law of thermodynamics or the law of entropy, according to which the tendency of the molecules of a gas to move at constant speeds in straight lines produces a state for which the term 'perfect disorder' has been coined. Similarly, it is evident that in society some perfectly regular behaviour of the individuals could produce only disorder: if the rule were that any individual should try to kill any other he encountered, or flee as soon as he saw another, the result would clearly be the complete impossibility of an order in which the activities of the individuals were based on collaboration with others.

Society can thus exist only if by a process of selection rules have evolved which lead individuals to behave in a manner which makes social life possible. It should be remembered that for this purpose selection will operate as between societies of different types, that is, be guided by the properties of their respective orders, but that the properties supporting this order will be properties of the individuals, namely their propensity to obey certain rules of conduct on which the order of action of the group as a whole rests.

To put this differently: in a social order the particular circumstances to which each individual will react will be those known to him. But the individual responses to particular circumstances will result in an overall order only if the individuals obey such rules as will produce an order. Even a very limited similarity in their behaviour may be sufficient if the rules which they all obey are such as to produce an order. Such an order will always constitute an adaptation to the multitude of circumstances which are known to all the members of that society taken together but which are not known as a whole to any one person. This need not mean that the different persons will in similar circumstances do precisely the same thing; but merely that for the formation of such an overall order it is necessary that in some respects all individuals follow definite rules, or that their actions are limited to a certain range. In other words, the responses of the individuals to the events in their environment need be similar only in certain abstract aspects to ensure that a determinate overall order will result.

The question which is of central importance as much for social theory as for social policy is thus what properties the rules must possess so that the separate actions of the individuals will produce an overall order. Some such rules all individuals of a society will obey because of the similar manner in which their environment represents itself to their minds. Others they will follow spontaneously because they will be part of their common cultural tradition. But there will be still others which they may have to be made to obey, since, although it would be in the interest of each to disregard them, the overall order on which the success of their actions depends will arise only if these rules are generally followed.

In a modern society based on exchange, one of the chief regularities in individual behaviour will result from the similarity of situations in which most individuals find themselves in working to earn an income; which means that they will normally prefer a larger return from their efforts to a smaller one, and often that they will increase their efforts in a particular direction if the prospects of return improve. This is a rule that will be followed at least with sufficient frequency to impress upon such a society an order of a certain kind. But the fact that most people will follow this rule will still leave the character of the resulting order very indeterminate, and by itself certainly would not be sufficient to give it a beneficial character. For the resulting order to be beneficial people must also observe some conventional rules, that is, rules which do not simply follow from their desires and their insight into relations of cause and effect, but which are normative and tell them what they ought to or ought not to do.

We shall later have to consider more fully the precise relation between the various kinds of rules which the people in fact obey and the resulting order of actions. Our main interest will then be those rules which, because we can deliberately alter them, become the chief instrument whereby we can affect the resulting order, namely the rules of law. At the moment our concern must be to make clear that while the rules on which a spontaneous order rests, may also be of spontaneous origin, this need not always be the case. Although undoubtedly an order originally formed itself spontaneously because the individuals followed rules which had not been deliberately made but had arisen spontaneously, people gradually learned to improve those rules; and it is at least conceivable that the formation of a spontaneous order relies entirely on rules that were deliberately made. The spontaneous character of the resulting order must therefore be distinguished from the spontaneous origin of the rules on which it rests, and it is possible that an order which would still have to be described as spontaneous rests on rules which are entirely the result of deliberate design. In the kind of society with which we are familiar, of course, only some of the rules which people in fact observe, namely some of the rules of law (but never all, even of these) will be the product of deliberate design, while most of the rules of morals and custom will be spontaneous growths.

That even an order which rests on made rules may be spontaneous in character is shown by the fact that its particular manifestation will always depend on many circumstances which the designer of these rules did not and could not know. The particular content of the order will depend on the concrete circumstances known only to the individuals who obey the rules and apply them to facts known only to them. It will be through the knowledge of these individuals both of the rules and of the particular facts that both will determine the resulting order.

THE SPONTANEOUS ORDER OF SOCIETY IS MADE UP OF INDIVIDUALS AND ORGANIZATIONS

In any group of men of more than the smallest size, collaboration will always rest both on spontaneous order as well as on deliberate organization. There is no doubt that for many limited tasks organization is the most powerful method of effective co-ordination because it enables us to adapt the resulting order much more fully to our wishes, while where, because of the complexity of the circumstances to be taken into account, we must rely on the forces making for a spontaneous order, our power over the particular contents of this order is necessarily restricted.

That the two kinds of order will regularly coexist in every society of any degree of complexity does not mean, however, that we can combine them in any manner we like. What in fact we find in all free societies is that, although groups of men will join in organizations for the achievement of some particular ends, the co-ordination of the activities of all these separate organizations, as well as of the separate individuals, is brought about by the forces making for a spontaneous order. The family, the farm, the plant, the firm, the corporation and the various associations, and all the public institutions including government, are organizations which in turn are integrated into a more comprehensive spontaneous order. It is advisable to reserve the term 'society' for this spontaneous overall order so that we may distinguish it from all the organized smaller groups which will exist within it, as well as from such smaller and more or less isolated groups as the horde, the tribe, or the clan, whose members will at least in some respects act under a central direction for common purposes. In some instances it will be the same group which at times, as when engaged in most of its daily routine, will operate as a spontaneous order maintained by the observation of conventional rules without the necessity of commands, while at other times, as when hunting, migrating, or fighting, it will be acting as an organization under the directing will of a chief.

The spontaneous order which we call a society also need not have such sharp boundaries as an organization will usually possess. There will often be a nucleus, or several nuclei, of more closely related individuals occupying a central position in a more loosely connected but more extensive order. Such particular societies within the Great Society may arise as the result of spatial proximity, or of some other special circumstances which produce closer relations among their members. And different partial societies of this sort will often overlap and every individual may, in addition to being a member of the Great Society, be a member of numerous other spontaneous sub-orders or partial societies of this sort as well as of various organizations existing within the comprehensive Great Society.

Of the organizations existing within the Great Society one which regularly occupies a very special position will be that which we call government. Although it is conceivable that the spontaneous order which we call society may exist without government, if the minimum of rules required for the formation of such an order is observed without an organized apparatus for their enforcement, in most circumstances the organization which we call government becomes indispensable in order to assure that those rules are obeyed.

This particular function of government is somewhat like that of a maintenance squad of a factory, its object being not to produce any particular services or products to be consumed by the citizens, but rather to see that the mechanism which regulates the production of those goods and services is kept in working order. The purposes for which this machinery is currently being used will be determined by those who operate its parts and in the last resort by those who buy its products.

The same organization that is charged with keeping in order an operating structure which the individuals will use for their own purposes, will, however, in addition to the task of enforcing the rules on which that order rests, usually be expected also to render other services which the spontaneous order cannot produce adequately. These two distinct functions of government are usually not clearly separated; yet, as we shall see, the distinction between the coercive functions in which government enforces rules of conduct, and its service functions in which it need merely administer resources placed at its disposal, is of fundamental importance. In the second it is one organization among many and like the others part of a spontaneous overall order, while in the first it provides an essential condition for the preservation of that overall order.

In English it is possible, and has long been usual, to discuss these two types of order in terms of the distinction between 'society' and 'government'. There is no need in the discussion of these problems, so long as only one country is concerned, to bring in the metaphysically charged term 'state'. It is largely under the influence of continental and particularly Hegelian thought that in the course of the last hundred years the practice of speaking of the 'state' (preferably with a capital 'S'), where 'government' is more appropriate and precise, has come to be widely adopted. That which acts, or pursues a policy, is however always the organization of government; and it does not make for clarity to drag in the term 'state' where 'government' is quite sufficient. It becomes particularly misleading when 'the state' rather than 'government' is contrasted with 'society' to indicate that the first is an organization and the second a spontaneous order.

THE RULES OF SPONTANEOUS ORDERS AND THE RULES OF ORGANIZATION

One of our chief contentions will be that, though spontaneous order and organization will always coexist, it is still not possible to mix these two principles of order in any manner we like. If this is not more generally understood it is due to the fact that for the determination of both kinds of order we have to rely on rules, and that the important differences between the kinds of rules which the two different kinds of order require are generally not recognized.

To some extent every organization must rely also on rules and not only on specific commands. The reason here is the same as that which makes it necessary for a spontaneous order to rely solely on rules: namely that by guiding the actions of individuals by rules rather than specific commands it is possible to make use of knowledge which nobody possesses as a whole. Every organization in which the members are not mere tools of the organizer will determine by commands only the function to be performed by each member, the purposes to be achieved, and certain general aspects of the methods to be employed, and will leave the detail to be decided by the individuals on the basis of their respective knowledge and skills.

Organization encounters here the problem which any attempt to bring order into complex human activities meets: the organizer must wish the individuals who are to co-operate to make use of knowledge that he himself does not possess. In none but the most simple kind of organization is it conceivable that all the details of all activities are governed by a single mind. Certainly nobody has yet succeeded in deliberately arranging all the activities that go on in a complex society. If anyone did ever succeed in fully organizing such a society, it would no longer make use of many minds but would be altogether dependent on one mind; it would certainly not be very complex but extremely primitive—and so would soon be the mind whose knowledge and will determined everything. The facts which could enter into the design of such an order could be only those which were known and digested by this mind; and as only he could decide on action and thus gain experience, there would be none of that interplay of many minds in which alone mind can grow.

What distinguishes the rules which will govern action within an organization is that they must be rules for the performance of assigned tasks. They presuppose that the place of each individual in a fixed structure is determined by command and that the rules each individual must obey depend on the place which he has been assigned and on the particular ends which have been indicated for him by the commanding authority. The rules will thus regulate merely the detail of the action of appointed functionaries or agencies of government.

Rules of organization are thus necessarily subsidiary to commands, filling in the gaps left by the commands. Such rules will be different for the different members of the organization according to the different roles which have been assigned to them, and they will have to be interpreted in the light of the purposes determined by the commands. Without the assignment of a function and the determination of the ends to be pursued by particular commands, the bare abstract rule would not be sufficient to tell each individual what he must do.

By contrast, the rules governing a spontaneous order must be independent of purpose and be the same, if not necessarily for all members, at least for whole classes of members not individually designated by name. They must, as we shall see, be rules applicable to an unknown and indeterminable number of persons and instances. They will have to be applied by the individuals in the light of their respective knowledge and purposes; and their application will be independent of any common purpose, which the individual need not even know.

In the terms we have adopted this means that the general rules of law that a spontaneous order rests on aim at an abstract order, the particular or concrete content of which is not known or foreseen by anyone; while the commands as well as the rules which govern an organization serve particular results aimed at by those who are in command of the organization. The more complex the order aimed at, the greater will be that part of the separate actions which will have to be determined by circumstances not known to those who direct the whole, and the more dependent control will be on rules rather than on specific commands. In the most complex types of organizations, indeed, little more than the assignment of particular functions and the general aim will be determined by command of the supreme authority, while the performance of these functions will be regulated only by rules—yet by rules which at least to some degree are specific to the functions assigned to particular persons. Only when we pass from the biggest kind of organization, government, which as organization must still be dedicated to a circumscribed and determined set of specific purposes, to the overall order of the whole of society, do we find an order which relies solely on rules and is entirely spontaneous in character.

It is because it was not dependent on organization but grew up as a spontaneous order that the structure of modern society has attained that degree of complexity which it possesses and which far exceeds any that could have been achieved by deliberate organization. In fact, of course, the rules which made the growth of this complex order possible were initially not designed in expectation of that result; but those people who happened to adopt suitable rules developed a complex civilization which then often spread to others. To maintain that we must deliberately plan modern society because it has become so complex is therefore paradoxical, and the result of a complete misunderstanding of these circumstances. The fact is, rather, that we can preserve an order of such complexity not by the method of directing the members, but only indirectly by enforcing and improving the rules conducive to the formation of a spontaneous order.

We shall see that it is impossible, not only to replace the spontaneous order by organization and at the same time to utilize as much of the dispersed knowledge of all its members as possible, but also to improve or correct this order by interfering in it by direct commands. Such a combination of spontaneous order and organization it can never be rational to adopt. While it is sensible to supplement the commands determining an organization by subsidiary rules, and to use organizations as elements of a spontaneous order, it can never be advantageous to supplement the rules governing a spontaneous order by isolated and subsidiary commands concerning those activities where the actions are guided by the general rules of conduct. This is the gist of the argument against 'interference' or 'intervention' in the market order. The reason why such isolated commands requiring specific actions by members of the spontaneous order can never improve but must disrupt that order is that they will refer to a part of a system of interdependent actions determined by information and guided by purposes known only to the several acting persons but not to the directing authority. The spontaneous order arises from each element balancing all the various factors operating on it and by adjusting all its various actions to each other, a balance which will be destroyed if some of the actions are determined by another agency on the basis of different knowledge and in the service of different ends.

What the general argument against 'interference' thus amounts to is that, although we can endeavour to improve a spontaneous order by revising the general rules on which it rests, and can supplement its results by the efforts of various organizations, we cannot improve the results by specific commands that deprive its members of the possibility of using their knowledge for their purposes.

20.

Micromotives and Macrobehavior

THOMAS C. SCHELLING, 1978

A common occurrence among the Harvard faculty is the "dying seminar." Somebody organizes a group of twenty-five who are eager to meet regularly to pursue a subject of common interest. It meets at some hour at which people expect to be free. The first meeting has a good turnout, three-quarters or more, a few having some conflict. By the third or fourth meeting the attendance is not much more than half and pretty soon only a handful attend. Eventually the enterprise lapses, by consent among the few at a meeting or by the organizers' giving up and arranging no more.

The original members then express regret that it didn't work. Everybody is sorry that the others didn't find it worthwhile. The conclusion is drawn that the interest just wasn't there.

But it often looks as though the interest was there. The thing petered out in spite of interest. Nearly everybody, if asked, alleges that he'd have continued attending pretty regularly if enough others had cared enough to attend regularly enough to make it worthwhile.

Behind my building is a grassy area where a related social phenomenon—I think it is related—can be observed every autumn, as if it were an experiment. Somebody puts up the volleyball net, gathers a few friends, starts a game, and attracts a few more players. Then one of two things happens. By the second or third day, a pretty good crowd has gathered to play volleyball; people begin to get acquainted; there's discussion of what the best time to play is; there are by-standers willing to join the game; the enterprise is a success and may last until the snow comes. Or, it goes the way of the dying seminar—fun but not enough fun, because there are not enough people to generate the loyalty and enthusiasm that would keep the number large and the absentee rate small.

In a single day, I can encounter half a dozen occurrences that remind me of that volleyball game. At the busiest intersection in Cambridge, a few nimble pedestrians cross against the light and cars keep coming; more pedestrians

237

From *Micromotives and Macrobehavior* by Thomas C. Schelling, copyright © 1978 by W. W. Norton & Company, Inc. Used by permission of W. W. Norton & Company Inc.

hesitate, ready to join any surge of people into the street but not willing to venture ahead without safety in numbers. People look left and right—not to watch the traffic but to watch the other pedestrians! At some point several appear to decide that the flow of pedestrians is large enough to be safe and they join it, enlarging it further and making it safe for a few who were still waiting and who now join. Soon, even the timid join what has become a crowd. The drivers see they no longer have any choice and stop. At less busy intersections, smaller bands of pedestrians hesitate as a few of the adventurous step into the traffic, looking anxiously back to see who's following; too few to intimidate the traffic, and unable to get the troops out of the trenches behind them, the leaders fall back to the curb.

On the last day of class a few students, acting out of duty, politeness, or appreciation, begin to applaud hesitantly as the instructor gathers his materials to leave the room. If enough clap, the whole class may break into applause; if a few clap indecisively, it dwindles to an embarrassed silence. On all days except the last day of class, the instructor who keeps talking after the end of the hour notices that students, like the pedestrians at the curb, lean toward the door, shuffle, put books away, occasionally stand up, hoping to start enough of an exodus to keep any departing students from being conspicuous.

I walk across the lawn if that seems to be what others are doing; I sometimes double-park if it looks as though everybody is double-parked. I stay in line if everybody is standing politely in line, but if people begin to surge toward the ticket window I am alert to be—though never among the first—not among the last. If a few people get away with smoking in a no-smoking section, perhaps because the people who should tell them not to are momentarily preoccupied, so many others light up that the cause becomes hopeless and they are not even told to stop, or, if told, don't. Meanwhile, the newspapers report that certain old residential areas are deteriorating; they are deteriorating because the people who keep their homes attractive are leaving; they are leaving because the neighborhood is deteriorating because people like them are leaving because the neighborhood is deteriorating. . . . In some schools, the white pupils are being withdrawn because there are too few white pupils; as they leave, white pupils become fewer so that even those who didn't mind yesterday's ratio will leave at today's ratio, leaving behind still fewer, who may leave tomorrow. At other schools, black students, with what is reported to be the same motivation, are leaving because they find themselves too few for safety and comfort, and as they leave they aggravate the fewness for those they leave behind.

What is common to all of these examples is the way people's behavior depends on *how many* are behaving a particular way, or how much they are behaving that way—how many attend the seminar how frequently, how many play volleyball how frequently; how many smoke, or double-park; how many applaud and how loudly; how many leave the dying neighborhood and how many leave the school.

The generic name for behaviors of this sort is *critical mass*. Social scientists have adopted the term from nuclear engineering, where it is common currency in connection with atomic bombs. If radioactive decay occurs in a substance like uranium, neutrons are emitted that fly into space unless they hit other nuclei before they leave the mass of uranium, in which case they produce a couple of new neutrons that do the same thing. If the amount of uranium is small, each neutron traverses a small volume containing other atoms and, since most of the volume is "empty space" from a neutron's point of view, there is only a small amount of induced additional activity. If the amount of uranium is large, there is a greater likelihood that a neutron will produce two more neutrons rather than fly unobstructed into space. If there is enough uranium so that half the neutrons produce two others, the process is self-sustaining and a "critical mass" of uranium is said to be present. Any larger amount of uranium will lead each neutron to produce on the average more than one neutron: an explosive chain reaction occurs (as when each grain of gunpowder ignites other grains in an enclosed space) that could consume all the uranium (except that the mass of uranium may fly apart and halt the activity).

If we stick very close to the bomb analogy and deal only with a "mass" of people, about the only example I can think of is body warmth. One person standing alone radiates heat into space, two people reflect each other's heat, a roomful of people can keep each other warm, and if you pack enough people together, even in cold weather, they will overheat themselves.

But even with the atomic bomb, "mass" is not strictly correct. The density, purity, and shape of the uranium, as well as its mass, together with any reflective coating, will determine whether or not the lump "goes critical." Furthermore, mass is proportionate to the number of atoms, and *critical number* could have been equally apt.

For our purpose we can think of critical mass as shorthand for critical number, critical density, critical ratio, or in special cases like body heat and the production of carbon dioxide, actual mass. What all of the critical-mass models involve is some activity that is self-sustaining once the measure of that activity passes a certain minimum level. But whether the measure is the number of people engaged, or the number times the frequency or the length of time they engage in it, or the ratio of the number who do to the number who do not, or the amount of such activity per square foot or per day or per telephone extension, we can call it a "critical-mass" activity and a lot of people will know what we mean. By "activity" I specifically mean to include just being (or not being) someplace: if everybody will stay if enough others do, and the total number is more than "enough," everybody will stay; and everybody will go if not enough are present. Ratios rather than numbers may be involved if it is blacks and whites or men and women or English-speaking and French-speaking residing in a neighborhood or enrolling in a school or staying with some social event or political activity.

The variety of critical-mass models is great. In one version, people make their decision on the basis of actual numbers—being attracted to the majority party, volunteering on condition that twenty others do likewise, staying at a meeting if attendance is sufficient, or voting "guilty" on a jury's verdict. In some cases, it is not the number itself but some effect of the number that matters—it is the immunity in numbers that causes people to double park if everybody else is doing it, the noise level that causes people to raise their voices to be heard, or the grudging accommodation of automobile drivers that may make bicycling safer if enough people bicycle. And for some purposes, like those neutrons in the chain reaction, the activity may involve contact between individuals—if people pass along the rumors they've heard lately, the relevant population has to be large enough for somebody to meet somebody to tell it to pretty soon or the rumor, like an infectious disease, will die away rather than spread contagiously.

Again, some of the activities are continuous and reversible—you can walk home every evening after dark if enough other people do, and quit if it appears that not enough others are out walking. Some, like getting tattooed or committing suicide, are quite irreversible. Some are a single occurrence; you prefer to wear blue jeans to an official meeting unless most of the people are going to be more formally dressed. Some of the choices are binary—whether to pass on the right or the left; some are among multiple alternatives—which language to learn, to communicate with as many foreigners as possible. Sometimes the choice is on-off—whether or not to wear a tie; sometimes it is rate or intensity or frequency, as in deciding how loud to play your radio at the beach to drown out the other radios.

Though perhaps not in physical and chemical reactions, in social reactions it is typically the case that the "critical number" for one person differs from another's. You may dress formally if enough people do to keep you from being conspicuous, but I dress formally only if so many do that I would be conspicuous not to. You may be willing to enroll in a school in which the opposite sex outnumbers you no more than 3 or 4 to 1, but I may be unwilling to enroll in a school unless it is largely my own sex. You may work to support a candidate if there's any significant chance that she could win, somebody else only if her chances are better than anybody else's, and I only if I'm nearly certain that she is going to win.

The generic model therefore includes the case in which we all have the same critical point, as well as the case in which there are five of us who will show regularly for the seminar if as many as ten do; another five, for a total of ten, who will keep coming if fifteen do; thirty altogether for whom thirty is an adequate number; and fifty for whom forty is enough.

When people differ with respect to their cross-over points, there may be a large range of numbers over which, if that number of people were doing it, for a few but only a few among them that number wouldn't be big enough, while the rest would be content. When those few for whom the number is not enough drop out, they lower the number, and some more drop out, and so on all the way. The fact that in the end nobody is doing it does not give us any measure of *how many* satisfied participants were lacking at any point along the way.

In our dying seminar it could be that for any number present, two or three find it not large enough; when they drop out, another two or three find it not large enough and when they drop out, another two or three. The number along the way who, if they could be enticed or coerced into staying, would make the whole thing viable, may be small or large; the fact that it dies out completely does not tell us how near to being viable it was.

The model applies perfectly well to a situation in which some fraction of the population will engage in the activity independently of how many do, and some other fraction will not, independently of how many do. Consider the case of pass-fail grading in a law school. If the option of taking the course pass-fail (without a letter grade) is available to all students, it is usually observed that there are some who will elect pass-fail no matter how many others do, some who will elect letter grades no matter how many elect pass-fail, and an intermediate group who will elect pass-fail if enough do but will choose letter grades if pass-fail is uncommon. Notice that the first and second groups' behavior is independent of how the third group chooses, but not vice versa; the people whose behavior is uninfluenced nevertheless influence others. So we cannot just leave out of our analysis the two groups whose behavior is independently determined, and analyze only that group that displays the critical-mass phenomenon. If the two groups whose behavior is unconditional are small, there may be two sustainable outcomes: if all whose behavior is conditional are choosing pass-fail, the number (including the unconditional pass-fail choosers) is self-sustaining; and if the number choosing letter grades includes all those whose behavior is conditional, their letter-grade choice will be self-sustaining.

But there is another possibility. The unconditional—pass-fail students may be sufficient in numbers to induce some of the conditional choosers to elect pass-fail, who in turn are enough to induce some more, who in turn are enough to induce some more, and so on until all but the unconditional letter graders are electing pass-fail. In that case, there are not two self-sustaining outcomes—one with nearly everybody choosing pass-fail and the other with nearly everybody choosing letter grades—but a single ineluctable outcome. Critical mass is provided by the people whose behavior does not depend on numbers, and the chain reaction takes care of the rest.

Notice that the model itself does not tell us which outcome is preferable. There are at least three possibilities. First—and to clarify the point, let's suppose everybody's choice depends on how many choose pass-fail—it may be that everybody actually prefers pass-fail but feels uneasy about it unless enough others also choose it. Second, everybody may prefer letter grades but feel uneasy about it if most people choose pass-fail. Third, some may prefer pass-fail but feel insecure unless enough others choose it, while others prefer letter grades but feel uneasy unless enough others choose letter grades. The observed outcome may be one that everybody prefers, it may be one that nobody prefers, or it may be one that some prefer and others deplore.

So there may or may not be a unanimously preferred outcome. And even if one of the outcomes is unanimously chosen, we cannot infer that it is preferred from the fact that it is universally chosen. If everybody is on daylight saving or the metric system, or if everybody addresses women as Ms. or teachers by their first names, or everybody waits for the green light to cross at the intersection, I'll go along; if everybody feels the way I do, we'll all go along. But unless we smile or frown an observer cannot tell whether we go along joyfully or reluctantly. And, unless some of us smile and some of us frown, it may not be evident that some of us like it and some of us do not and that whichever is the custom we go along with it.

Two special terms have begun to come into currency to distinguish subclasses of critical-mass phenomena. One is *tipping*, and the other is *lemons*.

The lemons model is not only about a special kind of interdependent behavior, but has a name that illustrates it. The name is not an ancient idea or institution, like the commons, that has been newly appropriated for dramatic effect; it is not borrowed from nuclear physics or ecology or even horticulture. Nor did it just emerge through a consensual process of obscure origin. The name was picked by an economist because the "market for lemons" has interesting properties that can give insight into a variety of situations. And the lemons he had in mind are not the ones from which lemonade is made, but the kind that people drive.[1]

He argued that the seller of a used car knows whether or not it is a lemon; the buyer has to play the averages, knowing only that some cars are lemons but not whether the particular car he's buying is. Buyers will pay only a price that reflects the average frequency of lemons in the used-car crop. That average is a high price for a lemon but understates the worth of the better cars offered on the market. The owners of the better cars are reluctant to sell at a price that makes allowance for the lemons that other people are selling; so the better cars

1. Akerlof, George A., "The Market for 'Lemons': Quality Uncertainty and the Market Mechanism," *The Quarterly Journal of Economics,* 84 (August 1970), No. 3.

appear less frequently on the market and the average frequency of lemons increases. As customers learn this, they make a greater allowance for lemons in the price they're willing to pay. The cars of average quality in the previous market are now undervalued and their owners less willing to sell them. The percentage frequency of lemons continues to rise. In the end, the market may disappear, although institutional arrangements like guarantees, or the certification of cars by dealers who exploit a reputation for good cars, may keep the used-car market alive.

Akerlof generalized this model to a number of markets in which there is unequal information on the two sides—insurance companies know less than you do, usually, about whether you are accident prone, or susceptible to hereditary diseases, or are contemplating suicide. Life insurance rates for sixty-five-year-olds must allow for a large fraction who are not long for this world. And those who know they are healthy and have a family history of longevity and are exposed to few risks have to pay the same premium as the poorer risks; life insurance being unattractive at that price, few of them buy it. The average life expectancy of the customers goes down, the rates go up further, and the bargain now looks poor even to those of normal life expectancy. And so forth.

This process show[s] up in . . . the recruitment of "young" elderly people to an older persons' home. It is akin to, and sometimes coincides with, those situations in which the below average, or the above average, withdraw or won't join, causing some potential market or institution to unravel. Because people vary and because averages matter, there may be no sustainable critical mass; and the unravelling behavior, or initial failure to get the activity going at all, has much the appearance of a critical mass that is almost but not quite achieved. This is therefore a kindred but separate family of models.

I said that Akerlof's lemons model has a name that illustrates critical mass. "Lemons" appears to be over the hump and on its way to permanence in the language but in case it is not, maybe my readers can give it the boost it needs.

Tipping is a name that was first applied to neighborhood migration. It was observed that the entrance of a few members of a minority into a neighborhood often caused some among the formerly homogeneous population to leave, or to show signs of leaving. Their departure left openings, so more members of the minority could enter; the increase in new residents induced more of the old to leave, and so forth in the familiar process. Some of the departures might be motivated by the minority entrants who had already arrived, some by the belief that the process, once started, would continue, and some by the fear that they might soon be selling their houses in panic. Among early writers on the subject, the model was not explicit. The concept came to be applied to schools and school districts in the 1960s, racial minorities again being the stimulus and white-pupil-departure the phenomenon. The concept came to be applied to occupations, clubs and fraternities, medical schools and colleges, public beaches and tennis courts, restaurants, nightclubs and public parks.

It also became apparent that there was a complementary process of "tipping-in" as well as one of "tipping-out." Not only was the departure of a white population induced by the appearance of minorities, but minorities themselves would be more attracted the larger the minority colony and the faster its growth, with some minimum size required to get a self-sustaining influx started. For tipping-in as well as for tipping-out, part of the process may involve expectations—people do not wait until the alien colony exceeds their toleration before departing, nor do the minority entrants wait until comfortable numbers have been achieved, as long as they can foresee the numbers increasing with any confidence.

The tipping model is a special case—a broad class of special cases—of critical-mass phenomena. Its characteristics are usually that people have very different cross-over points; that the behavior involves place of residence or work or recreation or, in general, *being* someplace rather than *doing* something; that the critical numbers relate to two or more distinct groups, and each group may be separately tipping out or tipping in; and that the process involves conscious decisions and anticipations. It may be on a scale as small as the dining hall table that is abandoned by whites when blacks begin to sit there or as large as the white population of Rhodesia.

A SELF-FORMING NEIGHBORHOOD MODEL

Some vivid dynamics can be generated by any reader with a half-hour to spare, a roll of pennies and a roll of dimes, a tabletop, a large sheet of paper, a spirit of scientific inquiry, or, lacking that spirit, a fondness for games.

Get a roll of pennies, a roll of dimes, a ruled sheet of paper divided into one-inch squares, preferably at least the size of a checkerboard (sixty-four squares in eight rows and eight columns) and find some device for selecting squares at random. We place dimes and pennies on some of the squares, and suppose them to represent the members of two homogeneous groups—men and women, blacks and whites, French-speaking and English-speaking, officers and enlisted men, students and faculty, surfers and swimmers, the well dressed and the poorly dressed, or any other dichotomy that is exhaustive and recognizable. We can spread them at random or put them in contrived patterns. We can use equal numbers of dimes and pennies or let one be a minority. And we can stipulate various rules for individual decision.

For example, we can postulate that every dime wants at least half its neighbors to be dimes, every penny wants a third of its neighbors to be pennies, and any dime or penny whose immediate neighborhood does not meet these con-

```
# O # O # O
# O # O # O # O
O # O # O # O #
# O # O # O # O
O # O # O # O #
# O # O # O # O
O # O # O # O #
  O # O # O #
```

FIGURE 20.1

ditions gets up and moves. Then by inspection we locate the ones that are due to move, move them, keep on moving them if necessary and, when everybody on the board has settled down, look to see what pattern has emerged. (If the situation never "settles down," we look to see what kind of endless turbulence or cyclical activity our postulates have generated.)

Define each individual's neighborhood as the eight squares surrounding him; he is the center of a 3-by-3 neighborhood. He is content or discontent with his neighborhood according to the colors of the occupants of those eight surrounding squares, some of which may be empty. We furthermore suppose that, if he is discontent with the color of his own neighborhood, he moves to the nearest empty square that meets his demands.

As to the order of moves, we can begin with the discontents nearest the center of the board and let them move first, or start in the upper left and sweep downward to the right, or let the dimes move first and then the pennies; it usually turns out that the precise order is not crucial to the outcome.

Then we choose an overall ratio of pennies to dimes, the two colors being about equal or one of them being a "minority." There are two different ways we can distribute the dimes and the pennies. We can put them in some prescribed pattern that we want to test, or we can spread them at random.

Start with equal numbers of dimes and pennies and suppose that the demands of both are "moderate"—each wants something more than one-third of his neighbors to be like himself. The number of neighbors that a coin can have will be anywhere from zero to eight. We make the following specifications. If a person has one neighbor, he must be the same color; of two neighbors, one must be his color; of three, four, or five neighbors, two must be his color; and of six, seven, or eight neighbors, he wants at least three.

It is possible to form a pattern that is regularly "integrated" that satisfies everybody. An alternating pattern does it (Figure 20.1), on condition that we take care of the corners.

No one can move, except to a corner, because there are no other vacant cells; but no one wants to move. We now mix them up a little, and in the process empty some cells to make movement feasible.

```
 -  #  -  #  O  #  -  O          -  -  -  #  -  #  -  -
 #  #  #  O  -  O  #  O          -  -  -  -  -  -  -  -
 -  #  O  -  -  #  O  #          -  -  -  -  -  -  -  -
 -  O  #  O  #  O  #  O          -  -  #  -  #  -  #  -
 O  O  O  #  O  O  O  -          -  -  -  -  -  -  -  -
 #  -  #  #  #  -  -  O          #  -  -  -  -  -  -  -
 -  #  O  #  O  #  O  -          -  -  O  -  O  -  O  -
 -  O  -  O  -  -  #  -          -  -  -  -  -  -  -  -
```

FIGURE 20.2

There are 60 coins on the board. We remove 20, using a table of random digits; we then pick 5 empty squares at random and replace a dime or a penny with a 50-50 chance. The result is a board with 64 cells, 45 occupied and 19 blank. Forty individuals are just where they were before we removed 20 neighbors and added 5 new ones. The left side of Figure 20.2 shows one such result, generated by exactly this process. The #'s are dimes and the O's are pennies; alternatively, the #'s speak French and the O's speak English, the #'s are black and the O's are white, the #'s are boys and the O's are girls, or whatever you please.

The right side of Figure 20.2 identifies the individuals who are not content with their neighborhoods. Six #'s and three O's want to move; the rest are content as things stand. The pattern is still "integrated"; even the discontent are not without some neighbors like themselves, and few among the content are without neighbors of opposite color. The general pattern is not strongly segregated in appearance. One is hard-put to block out #-neighborhoods or O-neighborhoods at this stage. The problem is to satisfy a fraction, 9 of 45, among the #'s and O's by letting them move somewhere among the 19 blank cells.

Anybody who moves leaves a blank cell that somebody can move into. Also, anybody who moves leaves behind a neighbor or two of his own color; and when he leaves a neighbor, his neighbor loses a neighbor and may become discontent. Anyone who moves gains neighbors like himself, adding a neighbor like them to their neighborhood but also adding one of opposite color to the unlike neighbors he acquires.

I cannot too strongly urge you to get the dimes and pennies and do it yourself. I can show you an outcome or two. A computer can do it for you a hundred times, testing variations in neighborhood demands, overall ratios, sizes of neighborhoods, and so forth. But there is nothing like tracing it through for yourself and seeing the thing work itself out. In an hour you can do it several times and experiment with different rules of behavior, sizes and shapes of boards, and (if you turn some of the coins heads and some tails) subgroups of

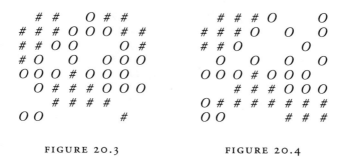

FIGURE 20.3   FIGURE 20.4

dimes and pennies that make different demands on the color compositions of their neighborhoods.

Chain Reaction

What is instructive about the experiment is the "unraveling" process. Everybody who selects a new environment affects the environments of those he leaves and those he moves among. There is a chain reaction. It may be quickly damped, with little motion, or it may go on and on and on with striking results. (The results of course are only suggestive, because few of us live in square cells on a checkerboard.)

One outcome for the situation depicted in Figure 20.2 is shown in Figure 20.3. It is "one outcome" because I have not explained exactly the order in which individuals moved. If the reader reproduces the experiment himself, he will get a slightly different configuration, but the general pattern will not be much different. Figure 20.4 is a replay from Figure 20.2, the only difference from Figure 20.3 being in the order of moves. It takes a few minutes to do the experiment again, and one quickly gets an impression of the kind of outcome to expect. Changing the neighborhood demands, or using twice as many dimes as pennies, will drastically affect the results; but for any given set of numbers and demands, the results are fairly stable.

All the people are content in Figure 20.3 and Figure 20.4. And they are more segregated. This is more than just a visual impression: we can make a few comparisons. In Figure 20.2 the O's altogether had as many O's for neighbors as they had #'s; some had more or less than the average, and 3 were discontent. For the #'s the ratio of #-neighbors to O-neighbors was 1:1, with a little colony of #'s in the upper left corner and 6 widely distributed discontents. After sorting themselves out in Figure 20.3, the average ratio of like to unlike neighbors for #'s and O's together was 2.3:1, more than double the original ratio. And it

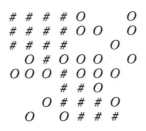

FIGURE 20.5

is about triple the ratio that any individual demanded! Figure 20.4 is even more extreme. The ratio of like to unlike neighbors is 2.8:1, nearly triple the starting ratio and four times the minimum demanded.

Another comparison is the number who had no opposite neighbors in Figure 20.2. Three were in that condition before people started moving; in Figure 20.3 there are 8 without neighbors of opposite color, and in Figure 20.4 there are 14.

What can we conclude from an exercise like this? We may at least be able to disprove a few notions that are themselves based on reasoning no more complicated than the checkerboard. Propositions beginning with "It stands to reason that . . ." can sometimes be discredited by exceedingly simple demonstrations that, though perhaps true, they do not exactly "stand to reason." We can at least persuade ourselves that certain mechanisms could work, and that observable aggregate phenomena could be compatible with types of "molecular movement" that do not closely resemble the aggregate outcomes that they determine.

There may be a few surprises. What happens if we raise the demands of one color and lower the demands of the other? Figure 20.5 shows typical results. Here we increased by one the number of like neighbors that a # demanded and decreased by one the number that an O demanded, as compared with Figure 20.3 and Figure 20.4. By most measures, "segregation" is about the same as in Figure 20.3 and Figure 20.4. The difference is in population densities: the O's are spread out all over their territory, while the #'s are packed in tight. The reader will discover, if he actually gets those pennies and dimes and tries it for himself, that something similar would happen if the demands of the two colors were equal but one color outnumbered the other by two or three to one. The minority then tends to be noticeably more tightly packed. Perhaps from Figure 20.5 we could conclude that if surfers mind the presence of swimmers less than swimmers mind the presence of surfers, they will become almost completely separated, but the surfers will enjoy a greater expanse of water.

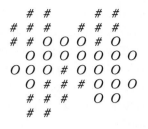

FIGURE 20.6

Is it "Segregated"?

The reader might try guessing what set of individual preferences led from Figure 20.2 to the pattern in Figure 20.6.

The ratio of like to unlike neighbors for all the #'s and O's together is slightly more than three to one; and there are 6 O's and 8 #'s that have no neighbors of opposite color. The result is evidently segregation; but, following a suggestion of my dictionary, we might say that the process is one of *aggregation,* because the rules of behavior ascribed both to #'s and to O's in Figure 20.6 were simply that each would move to acquire three neighbors of like color irrespective of the presence or absence of neighbors of opposite color. As an individual motivation, this is quite different from the one that formed the patterns in Figure 20.3 and Figure 20.4. But in the aggregate it may be hard to discern which motivation underlies the pattern, and the process, of segregated residence. And it matters!

The first impact of a display like this on a reader may be—unless he finds it irrelevant—discouragement. A moderate urge to avoid small-minority status may cause a nearly integrated pattern to unravel, and highly segregated neighborhoods to form. Even a deliberately arranged viable pattern, as in Figure 20.1, when buffeted by a little random motion, proves unstable and gives way to the separate neighborhoods of Figure 20.3 through Figure 20.6. These then prove to be fairly immune to continued random turnover.

For those who deplore segregation, however, and especially for those who deplore more segregation than people were seeking when they collectively segregated themselves, there may be a note of hope. The underlying motivation can be far less extreme than the observable patterns of separation. What it takes to keep things from unraveling is to be learned from Figure 20.2; the later figures indicate only how hard it may be to restore such "integration" as would satisfy the individuals, once the process of separation has stabilized. In Figure 20.2 only 9 of the 45 individuals are motivated to move, and if we could persuade them to stay everybody else would be all right. Indeed, the reader might exercise his own ingenuity to discover how few individuals would need to be invited into Figure 20.2 from outside, or how few individuals would need to be relocated in Figure 20.2, to keep anybody from wanting to move. If two lonely #'s join a third lonely #, none of them is lonely anymore, but the first will not move to the second unless assured that the third will arrive, and without some concert or regulation, each will go join some larger cluster, perhaps abandoning some nearby lonely neighbor in the process and surely helping to outnumber the opposite color at their points of arrival.

21.

The Division of Labor

ADAM SMITH, 1776

The greatest improvement in the productive powers of labour, and the greater part of the skill, dexterity, and judgement with which it is anywhere directed, or applied, seem to have been the effects of the division of labour.

The effects of the division of labour, in the general business of society, will be more easily understood by considering in what manner it operates in some particular manufactures. It is commonly supposed to be carried furthest in some very trifling ones; not perhaps that it really is carried further in them than in others of more importance: but in those trifling manufactures which are destined to supply the small wants of but a small number of people, the whole number of workmen must necessarily be small; and those employed in every different branch of the work can often be collected into the same work-house, and placed at once under the view of the spectator. In those great manufactures, on the contrary, which are destined to supply the great wants of the great body of the people, every different branch of the work employs so great a number of workmen that it is impossible to collect them all into the same workhouse. We can seldom see more, at one time, than those employed in one single branch. Though in such manufactures, therefore, the work may really be divided into a much greater number of parts than in those of a more trifling nature, the division is not near so obvious, and has accordingly been much less observed.

To take an example, therefore, from a very trifling manufacture; but one in which the division of labour has been very often taken notice of, the trade of the pin-maker; a workman not educated to this business (which the division of labour has rendered a distinct trade), nor acquainted with the use of the machinery employed in it (to the invention of which the same division of labour has probably given occasion), could scarce, perhaps, with his utmost industry, make one pin in a day, and certainly could not make twenty. But in the way in which this business is now carried on, not only the whole work is a peculiar trade, but it is divided into a number of branches, of which the greater

---

From Adam Smith, *The Wealth of Nations*.

part are likewise peculiar trades. One man draws out the wire, another straights it, a third cuts it, a fourth points it, a fifth grinds it at the top for receiving the head; to make the head requires three distinct operations; to put it on is a peculiar business, to whiten the pins is another; it is even a trade by itself to put them into the paper; and the important business of making a pin is, in this manner, divided into about eighteen distinct operations, which, in some manufactories, are all performed by distinct hands, though in others the same man will sometimes perform two or three of them. I have seen a small manufactory of this kind where ten men only were employed, and where some of them consequently performed two or three distinct operations. But though they were very poor, and therefore but indifferently accommodated with the necessary machinery, they could, when they exerted themselves, make among them about twelve pounds of pins in a day. There are in a pound upwards of four thousand pins of a middling size. Those ten persons, therefore, could make among them upwards of forty-eight thousand pins in a day. Each person, therefore, making a tenth part of forty-eight thousand pins, might be considered as making four thousand eight hundred pins in a day. But if they had all wrought separately and independently, and without any of them having been educated to this peculiar business, they could certainly not each of them have made twenty, perhaps not one pin in a day; that is, certainly, not the two hundred and fortieth, perhaps not the four thousand eight hundredth part of what they are at present capable of performing, in consequence of a proper division and combination of their different operations.

In every other art and manufacture, the effects of the division of labour are similar to what they are in this very trifling one; though, in many of them, the labour can neither be so much subdivided, nor reduced to so great a simplicity of operation. The division of labour, however, so far as it can be introduced, occasions, in every art, a proportionable increase of the productive powers of labour. The separation of different trades and employments from one another seems to have taken place in consequence of this advantage. This separation, too, is generally carried furthest in those countries which enjoy the highest degree of industry and improvement; what is the work of one man in a rude state of society being generally that of several in an improved one. In every improved society, the farmer is generally nothing but a farmer; the manufacturer, nothing but a manufacturer. The labour, too, which is necessary to produce any one complete manufacture is almost always divided among a great number of hands. How many different trades are employed in each branch of the linen and woollen manufactures, from the growers of the flax and the wool, to the bleachers and smoothers of the linen, or to the dyers and dressers of the cloth! The nature of agriculture, indeed, does not admit of so many subdivisions of labour, nor of so complete a separation of one business from another, as manufactures. It is impossible to separate so entirely the business of the grazier from that of the corn-farmer as the trade of the carpenter is commonly separated from that of the smith. The spinner is almost always a distinct person from the weaver; but the ploughman, the harrower, the sower of the seed, and the reaper of the corn, are often the same. The occasions for those different sorts of labour returning with the different seasons of the year, it is impossible that one man should be constantly employed in any one of them. This impossibility of making so complete and entire a separation of all the different branches of labour employed in agriculture is perhaps the reason why the improvement of the productive powers of labour in this art does not always keep pace with their improvement in manufactures. The most opulent nations, indeed, generally excel all their neighbours in agriculture as well as in manufactures; but they are commonly more distinguished by their superiority in the latter than in the former. Their lands are in general better cultivated, and having more labour and expense bestowed upon them, produce more in proportion to the extent and natural fertility of the ground. But this superiority of produce is seldom much more than in proportion to the superiority of labour and expense. In agriculture, the labour of the rich country is not always much more productive than that of the poor; or, at least, it is never so much more productive as it commonly is in manufactures. The corn of the rich country, therefore, will not always, in the same degree of goodness, come cheaper to market than that of the poor. The corn of Poland, in the same degree of goodness, is as cheap as that of France, notwithstanding the superior opulence and improvement of the latter country. The corn of France is, in the corn provinces, fully as good, and in most years nearly about the same price with the corn of England, though, in opulence and improvement, France is perhaps inferior to England. The corn-lands of England, however, are better cultivated than those of France, and the corn-lands of France are said to be much better cultivated than those of Poland. But though the poor country, notwithstanding the inferiority of its cultivation, can, in some measure, rival the rich in the cheapness and goodness of its corn, it can pretend to no such competition in its manufactures; at least if those manufactures suit the soil, climate, and situation of the rich country. The silks of France are better and cheaper than those of England, because the silk manufacture, at least under the present high duties upon the importation of raw silk, does not so well suit the climate of England as that of France. But the hardware and the coarse woollens of England are beyond all comparison superior to those of France, and much cheaper too in the same degree of goodness. In Poland there are said to be scarce any manufactures of any kind, a few of those coarser household manufactures excepted, without which no country can well subsist.

This great increase of the quantity of work which, in consequence of the division of labour, the same number of people are capable of performing, is owing to three different circumstances; first, to the increase of dexterity in every particular workman; secondly, to the saving of the time which is commonly lost in passing from one species of work to another; and lastly, to the invention of a great number of machines which facilitate and abridge labour, and enable one man to do the work of many.

First, the improvement of the dexterity of the workman necessarily increases the quantity of the work he can perform; and the division of labour, by reducing every man's business to some one simple operation, and by making this operation the sole employment of his life, necessarily increases very much the dexterity of the workman. A common smith, who, though accustomed to handle the hammer, has never been used to make nails, if upon some particular occasion he is obliged to attempt it, will scarce, I am assured, be able to make above two or three hundred nails in a day, and those too very bad ones. A smith who has been accustomed to make nails, but whose sole or principal business has not been that of a nailer, can seldom with his utmost diligence make more than eight hundred or a thousand nails in a day. I have seen several boys under twenty years of age who had never exercised any other trade but that of making nails, and who, when they exerted themselves, could make, each of them, upwards of two thousand three hundred nails in a day. The making of a nail, however, is by no means one of the simplest operations. The same person blows the bellows, stirs or mends the fire as there is occasion, heats the iron, and forges every part of the nail: in forging the head too he is obliged to change his tools. The different operations into which the making of a pin, or of a metal button, is subdivided, are all of them much more simple, and the dexterity of the person, of whose life it has been the sole business to perform them, is usually much greater. The rapidity with which some of the operations of those manufactures are performed, exceeds what the human hand could, by those who had never seen them, be supposed capable of acquiring.

Secondly, the advantage which is gained by saving the time commonly lost in passing from one sort of work to another is much greater than we should at first view be apt to imagine it. It is impossible to pass very quickly from one kind of work to another that is carried on in a different place and with quite different tools. A country weaver, who cultivates a small farm, must lose a good deal of time in passing from his loom to the field, and from the field to his loom. When the two trades can be carried on in the same workhouse, the loss of time is no doubt much less. It is even in this case, however, very considerable. A man commonly saunters a little in turning his hand from one sort of employment to another. When he first begins the new work he is seldom very keen and hearty; his mind, as they say, does not go to it, and for some time he rather trifles than applies to good purpose. The habit of sauntering and of indolent careless application, which is naturally, or rather necessarily acquired by every country workman who is obliged to change his work and his tools every half hour, and to apply his hand in twenty different ways almost every day of his life, renders him almost always slothful and lazy, and incapable of any vigorous application even on the most pressing occasions. Independent, therefore, of his deficiency in point of dexterity, this cause alone must always reduce considerably the quantity of work which he is capable of performing.

Thirdly, and lastly, everybody must be sensible how much labour is facilitated and abridged by the application of proper machinery. It is unnecessary to give any example. I shall only observe, therefore, that the invention of all those machines by which labour is so much facilitated and abridged seems to have been originally owing to the division of labour. Men are much more likely to discover easier and readier methods of attaining any object when the whole attention of their minds is directed towards that single object than when it is dissipated among a great variety of things. But in consequence of the division of labour, the whole of every man's attention comes naturally to be directed towards some one very simple object. It is naturally to be expected, therefore, that some one or other of those who are employed in each particular branch of labour should soon find out easier and readier methods of performing their own particular work, wherever the nature of it admits of such improvement. A great part of the machines made use of in those manufactures in which labour is most subdivided, were originally the inventions of common workmen, who, being each of them employed in some very simple operation, naturally turned their thoughts towards finding out easier and readier methods of performing it. Whoever has been much accustomed to visit such manufactures must frequently have been shown very pretty machines, which were the inventions of such workmen in order to facilitate and quicken their own particular part of the work. In the first fire-engines, a boy was constantly employed to open and shut alternately the communication between the boiler and the cylinder, according as the piston either ascended or descended. One of those boys, who loved to play with his companions, observed that, by tying a string from the handle of the valve which opened this communication to another part of the machine, the valve would open and shut without his assistance, and leave him at liberty to divert himself with his play-fellows. One of the greatest improvements that has been made upon this machine, since it was first invented, was in this manner the discovery of a boy who wanted to save his own labour.

All the improvements in machinery, however, have by no means been the inventions of those who had occasion to use the machines. Many improvements have been made by the ingenuity of the makers of the machines, when to make them became the business of a peculiar trade; and some by that of those who are called philosophers or men of speculation, whose trade it is not to do anything, but to observe everything; and who, upon that account, are often capable of combining together the powers of the most distant and dissimilar objects. In the progress of society, philosophy or speculation becomes, like every other employment, the principal or sole trade and occupation of a particular class of citizens. Like every other employment too, it is subdivided into a great number of different branches, each of which affords occupation to a peculiar tribe or class of philosophers; and this subdivision of employment in philosophy, as well as in every other business, improves dexterity, and saves time. Each individual becomes more expert in his own peculiar branch, more work is done upon the whole, and the quantity of science is considerably increased by it.

It is the great multiplication of the productions of all the different arts, in consequence of the division of labour, which occasions, in a well-governed society, that universal opulence which extends itself to the lowest ranks of the people. Every workman has a great quantity of his own work to dispose of beyond what he himself has occasion for; and every other workman being exactly in the same situation, he is enabled to exchange a great quantity of his own goods for a great quantity, or, what comes to the same thing, for the price of a great quantity of theirs. He supplies them abundantly with what they have occasion for, and they accommodate him as amply with what he has occasion for, and a general plenty diffuses itself through all the different ranks of the society.

Observe the accommodation of the most common artificer or day-labourer in a civilized and thriving country, and you will perceive that the number of people of whose industry a part, though but a small part, has been employed in procuring him this accommodation, exceeds all computation. The woollen coat, for example, which covers the day-labourer, as coarse and rough as it may appear, is the produce of the joint labour of a great multitude of workmen. The shepherd, the sorter of the wool, the wool-comber or carder, the dyer, the scribbler, the spinner, the weaver, the fuller, the dresser, with many others, must all join their different arts in order to complete even this homely production. How many merchants and carriers, besides, must have been employed in transporting the materials from some of those workmen to others who often live in a very distant part of the country! How many merchants and carriers, besides, how many ship-builders, sailors, sail-makers, rope-makers, must have been employed in order to bring together the different drugs made use of by the dyer, which often come from the remotest corners of the world! What a variety of labour, too, is necessary in order to produce the tools of the meanest of those workmen! To say nothing of such complicated machines as the ship of the sailor, the mill of the fuller, or even the loom of the weaver, let us consider only what a variety of labour is requisite in order to form that very simple machine, the shears with which the shepherd clips the wool. The miner, the builder of the furnace for smelting the ore, the seller of the timber, the burner of the charcoal to be made use of in the smelting-house, the brick-maker, the brick-layer, the workmen who attend the furnace, the mill-wright, the forger, the smith, must all of them join their different arts in order to produce them. Were we to examine, in the same manner, all the different parts of his dress and household furniture, the coarse linen shirt which he wears next his skin, the shoes which cover his feet, the bed which he lies on, and all the different parts which compose it, the kitchen-grate at which he prepares his victuals, the coals which he makes use of for that purpose, dug from the bowels of the earth, and brought to him perhaps by a long sea and a long land carriage, all the other utensils of his kitchen, all the furniture of his table, the knives and forks, the earthen or pewter plates upon which he serves up and divides his victuals, the different hands employed in preparing his bread and his beer, the glass window which lets in the heat and the light, and keeps out the wind and the rain, with all the knowledge and art requisite for preparing that beautiful and happy invention, without which these northern parts of the world could scarce have afforded a very comfortable habitation, together with the tools of all the different workmen employed in producing those different conveniences; if we examine, I say, all these things, and consider what a variety of labour is employed about each of them, we shall be sensible that, without the assistance and co-operation of many thousands, the very meanest person in a civilized country could not be provided, even according to what we very falsely imagine the easy and simple manner in which he is commonly accommodated. Compared, indeed, with the more extravagant luxury of the great, his accommodation must no doubt appear extremely simple and easy; and yet it may be true, perhaps, that the accommodation of a European prince does not always so much exceed that of an industrious and frugal peasant as the accommodation of the latter exceeds that of many an African king, the absolute master of the lives and liberties of ten thousand naked savages.

This division of labour, from which so many advantages are derived, is not originally the effect of any human wisdom, which foresees and intends that general opulence to which it gives occasion. It is the necessary, though very slow and gradual consequence of a certain propensity in human nature which has in view no such extensive utility; the propensity to truck, barter, and exchange one thing for another.

Whether this propensity be one of those original principles in human nature of which no further account can be given; or whether, as seems more probable, it be the necessary consequences of the faculties of reason and speech, it belongs not to our present subject to inquire. It is common to all men, and to be found in no other race of animals, which seem to know neither this nor any other species of contracts. Two greyhounds, in running down the same hare, have sometimes the appearance of acting in some sort of concert. Each turns her towards his companion, or endeavours to intercept her when his companion turns her towards himself. This, however, is not the effect of any contract, but of the accidental concurrence of their passions in the same object at that particular time. Nobody ever saw a dog make a fair and deliberate exchange of one bone for another with another dog. Nobody ever saw one animal by its gestures and natural cries signify to another, this is mine, that yours; I am willing to give this for that. When an animal wants to obtain something either of a man or of another animal, it has no other means of persuasion but to gain the favour of those whose service it requires. A puppy fawns upon its dam, and a spaniel endeavours by a thousand attractions to engage the attention of its master who is at dinner, when it wants to be fed by him. Man sometimes uses the same arts with his brethren, and when he has no other means of engaging them to act according to his inclinations, endeavours by every servile and fawning attention to obtain their good will. He has not time, however, to do this upon every occasion. In civilized society he stands at all times in need of the co-operation and assistance of great multitudes, while his whole life is scarce sufficient to gain the friendship of a few persons. In almost every other race of animals each individual, when it is grown up to maturity, is entirely independent, and in its natural state has occasion for the assistance of no other living creature. But man has almost constant occasion for the help of his brethren, and it is in vain for him to expect it from their benevolence only. He will be more likely to prevail if he can interest their self-love in his favour, and show them that it is for their own advantage to do for him what he requires of them. Whoever offers to another a bargain of any kind, proposes to do this. Give me that which I want, and you shall have this which you want, is the meaning of every such offer; and it is in this manner that we obtain from one another the far greater part of those good offices which we stand in need of. It is not from the benevolence of the butcher, the brewer, or the baker that we expect our dinner, but from their regard to their own interest. We address ourselves, not to their humanity but to their self-love, and never talk to them of our own necessities but of their advantages. Nobody but a beggar chooses to depend chiefly upon the benevolence of his fellow-citizens. Even a beggar does not depend upon it entirely. The charity of well-disposed people, indeed, supplies him with the whole fund of his subsistence. But though this principle ultimately provides him with all the necessaries of life which he has occasion for, it neither does nor can provide him with them as he has occasion for them. The greater part of his occasional wants are supplied in the same manner as those of other people, by treaty, by barter, and by purchase. With the money which one man gives him he purchases food. The old clothes which another bestows upon him he exchanges for other old clothes which suit him better, or for lodging, or for food, or for money, with which he can buy either food, clothes, or lodging, as he has occasion.

As it is by treaty, by barter, and by purchase that we obtain from one another the greater part of those mutual good offices which we stand in need of, so it is this same trucking disposition which originally gives occasion to the division of labour. In a tribe of hunters or shepherds a particular person makes bows and arrows, for example, with more readiness and dexterity than any other. He frequently exchanges them for cattle or for venison with his companions; and he finds at last that he can in this manner get more cattle and venison than if he himself went to the field to catch them. From a regard to his own interest, therefore, the making of bows and arrows grows to be his chief business, and he becomes a sort of armourer. Another excels in making the frames and covers of their little huts or movable houses. He is accustomed to be of use in this way to his neighbours, who reward him in the same manner with cattle and with venison, till at last he finds it his interest to dedicate himself entirely to this employment, and to become a sort of house-carpenter. In the same manner a third becomes a smith or a brazier, a fourth a tanner or dresser of hides or skins, the principal part of the clothing of savages. And thus the certainty of being able to exchange all that surplus part of the produce of his own labour, which is over and above his own consumption, for such parts of the produce of other men's labour as he may have occasion for, encourages every man to apply himself to a particular occupation, and to cultivate and bring to perfection whatever talent or genius he may possess for that particular species of business.

The difference of natural talents in different men is, in reality, much less than we are aware of; and the very different genius which appears to distinguish men of different professions, when grown up to maturity, is not upon many occasions so much the cause as the effect of the division of labour. The difference between the most dissimilar characters, between a philosopher and a common street porter, for example, seems to arise not so much from nature as from habit, custom, and education. When they came into the world, and for the first six or eight years of their existence, they were perhaps very much alike, and neither their parents nor play-fellows could perceive any remarkable difference. About that age, or soon after, they come to be employed in very different occupations. The difference of talents comes then to be taken notice of, and widens by degrees, till at last the vanity of the philosopher is willing to acknowledge scarce any resemblance. But without the disposition to truck, barter, and exchange, every man must have procured to himself every necessary and conveniency of life which he wanted. All must have had the same duties to perform, and the same work to do, and there could have been no such difference of employment as could alone give occasion to any great difference of talents.

As it is this disposition which forms that difference of talents, so remarkable among men of different professions, so it is this same disposition which renders that difference useful. Many tribes of animals acknowledged to be all of the same species derive from nature a much more remarkable distinction of genius, than what, antecedent to custom and education, appears to take place among men. By nature a philosopher is not in genius and disposition half so different from a street porter, as a mastiff is from a greyhound, or a greyhound from a spaniel, or this last from a shepherd's dog. Those different tribes of animals, however, though all of the same species, are of scarce any use to one another. The strength of the mastiff is not in the least supported either by the swiftness of the greyhound, or by the sagacity of the spaniel, or by the docility of the shepherd's dog. The effects of those different geniuses and talents, for want of the power or disposition to barter and exchange, cannot be brought into a common stock, and do not in the least contribute to the better accommodation and conveniency of the species. Each animal is still obliged to support and defend itself, separately and independently, and derives no sort of advantage from that variety of talents with which nature has distinguished its fellows. Among men, on the contrary, the most dissimilar geniuses are of use to one another; the different produces of their respective talents, by the general disposition to truck, barter, and exchange, being brought, as it were, into a common stock, where every man may purchase whatever part of the produce of the other men's talents he has occasion for.

22.

The Evolution of Cooperation

ROBERT AXELROD, 1984

Under what conditions will cooperation emerge in a world of egoists without central authority? This question has intrigued people for a long time. And for good.reason. We all know that people are not angels, and that they tend to look after themselves and their own first. Yet we also know that cooperation does occur and that our civilization is based upon it. But, in situations where each individual has an incentive to be selfish, how can cooperation ever develop?

The answer each of us gives to this question has a fundamental effect on how we think and act in our social, political, and economic relations with others. And the answers that others give have a great effect on how ready they will be to cooperate with us.

The most famous answer was given over three hundred years ago by Thomas Hobbes. It was pessimistic. He argued that before governments existed, the state of nature was dominated by the problem of selfish individuals who competed on such ruthless terms that life was "solitary, poor, nasty, brutish, and short" (Hobbes 1651/1962, p. 100). In his view, cooperation could not develop without a central authority, and consequently a strong government was necessary. Ever since, arguments about the proper scope of government have often focused on whether one could, or could not, expect cooperation to emerge in a particular domain if there were not an authority to police the situation.

Today nations interact without central authority. Therefore the requirements for the emergence of cooperation have relevance to many of the central issues of international politics. The most important problem is the security dilemma: nations often seek their own security through means which challenge the security of others. This problem arises in such areas as escalation of local conflicts and arms races. Related problems occur in international relations in the form of competition within alliances, tariff negotiations, and communal conflict in places like Cyprus.

The Soviet invasion of Afghanistan in 1979 presented the United States with a typical dilemma of choice. If the United States continued business as

From *The Evolution of Cooperation* by Robert Axelrod. Copyright © 1984 by Robert Axelrod. Reprinted by permission of Basic Books, a member of Perseus Books, L.L.C.

usual, the Soviet Union might be encouraged to try other forms of noncooperative behavior later on. On the other hand, any substantial lessening of United States cooperation risked some form of retaliation, which could then set off counter-retaliation, setting up a pattern of mutual hostility that could be difficult to end. Much of the domestic debate about foreign policy is concerned with problems of just this type. And properly so, since these are hard choices.

In everyday life, we may ask ourselves how many times we will invite acquaintances for dinner if they never invite us over in return. An executive in an organization does favors for another executive in order to get favors in exchange. A journalist who has received a leaked news story gives favorable coverage to the source in the hope that further leaks will be forthcoming. A business firm in an industry with only one other major company charges high prices with the expectation that the other firm will also maintain high prices—to their mutual advantage and at the expense of the consumer.

For me, a typical case of the emergence of cooperation is the development of patterns of behavior in a legislative body such as the United States Senate. Each senator has an incentive to appear effective to his or her constituents, even at the expense of conflicting with other senators who are trying to appear effective to *their* constituents. But this is hardly a situation of completely opposing interests, a zero-sum game. On the contrary, there are many opportunities for mutually rewarding activities by two senators. These mutually rewarding actions have led to the creation of an elaborate set of norms, or folkways, in the Senate. Among the most important of these is the norm of reciprocity—a folkway which involves helping out a colleague and getting repaid in kind. It includes vote trading but extends to so many types of mutually rewarding behavior that "it is not an exaggeration to say that reciprocity is a way of life in the Senate" (Matthews 1960, p. 100; see also Mayhew 1975).

Washington was not always like this. Early observers saw the members of the Washington community as quite unscrupulous, unreliable, and characterized by "falsehood, deceit, treachery" (Smith 1906, p. 190). In the 1980s the practice of reciprocity is well established. Even the significant changes in the Senate over the last two decades, tending toward more decentralization, more openness, and more equal distribution of power, have come without abating the folkway of reciprocity (Ornstein, Peabody, and Rhode 1977). As will be seen, it is *not* necessary to assume that senators are more honest, more generous, or more public-spirited than in earlier years to explain how cooperation based on reciprocity has emerged or proved stable. The emergence of cooperation can be explained as a consequence of individual senators pursuing their own interests.

The approach [here] is to investigate how individuals pursuing their own interests will act, followed by an analysis of what effects this will have for the system as a whole. Put another way, the approach is to make some assumptions about individual motives and then deduce consequences for the behavior of the entire system (Schelling 1978). The case of the U.S. Senate is a good example, but the same style of reasoning can be applied to other settings.

The object of this enterprise is to develop a theory of cooperation that can be used to discover what is necessary for cooperation to emerge. By understanding the conditions that allow it to emerge, appropriate actions can be taken to foster the development of cooperation in a specific setting.

The Cooperation Theory that is presented . . . is based upon an investigation of individuals who pursue their own self-interest without the aid of a central authority to force them to cooperate with each other. The reason for assuming self-interest is that it allows an examination of the difficult case in which cooperation is not completely based upon a concern for others or upon the welfare of the group as a whole. It must, however, be stressed that this assumption is actually much less restrictive than it appears. If a sister is concerned for the welfare of her brother, the sister's self-interest can be thought of as including (among many other things) this concern for the welfare of her brother. But this does not necessarily eliminate all potential for conflict between sister and brother. Likewise a nation may act in part out of regard for the interests of its friends, but this regard does not mean that even friendly countries are always able to cooperate for their mutual benefit. So the assumption of self-interest is really just an assumption that concern for others does not completely solve the problem of when to cooperate with them and when not to.

A good example of the fundamental problem of cooperation is the case where two industrial nations have erected trade barriers to each other's exports. Because of the mutual advantages of free trade, both countries would be better off if these barriers were eliminated. But if either country were to unilaterally eliminate its barriers, it would find itself facing terms of trade that hurt its own economy. In fact, whatever one country does, the other country is better off retaining its own trade barriers. Therefore, the problem is that each country has an incentive to retain trade barriers, leading to a worse outcome than would have been possible had both countries cooperated with each other.

This basic problem occurs when the pursuit of self-interest by each leads to a poor outcome for all. To make headway in understanding the vast array of specific situations which have this property, a way is needed to represent what is common to these situations without becoming bogged down in the details unique to each. Fortunately, there is such a representation available: the famous *Prisoner's Dilemma* game.

In the Prisoner's Dilemma game, there are two players. Each has two choices, namely cooperate or defect. Each must make the choice without knowing what the other will do. No matter what the other does, defection

		Column Player	
		Cooperate	*Defect*
Row Player	*Cooperate*	$R = 3$, $R = 3$ Reward for mutual cooperation	$S = 0$, $T = 5$ Sucker's payoff, and temptation to defect
	Defect	$T = 5$, $S = 0$ Temptation to defect and sucker's payoff	$P = 1$, $P = 1$ Punishment for mutual defection

NOTE: The payoffs to the row chooser are listed first.

FIGURE 22.1 The Prisoner's Dilemma

yields a higher payoff than cooperation. The dilemma is that if both defect, both do worse than if both had cooperated. This simple game will provide the basis for the entire analysis used in this book.

The way the game works is shown in Figure 22.1. One player chooses a row, either cooperating or defecting. The other player simultaneously chooses a column, either cooperating or defecting. Together, these choices result in one of the four possible outcomes shown in that matrix. If both players cooperate, both do fairly well. Both get *R,* the *reward for mutual cooperation.* In the concrete illustration of Figure 22.1 the reward is 3 points. This number might, for example, be a payoff in dollars that each player gets for that outcome. If one player cooperates but the other defects, the defecting player gets the *temptation to defect,* while the cooperating player gets the *sucker's payoff.* In the example, these are 5 points and 0 points respectively. If both defect, both get 1 point, the *punishment for mutual defection.*

What should you do in such a game? Suppose you are the row player, and you think the column player will cooperate. This means that you will get one of the two outcomes in the first column of Figure 22.1. You have a choice. You can cooperate as well, getting the 3 points of the reward for mutual cooperation. Or you can defect, getting the 5 points of the temptation payoff. So it pays to defect if you think the other player will cooperate. But now suppose that you think the other player will defect. Now you are in the second column of Figure 22.1, and you have a choice between cooperating, which would make you a sucker and give you 0 points, and defecting, which would result in, mutual punishment giving you 1 point. So it pays to defect if you think the other player will defect. This means that it is better to defect if you think the other player will cooperate, *and* it is better to defect if you think the other player will defect. So no matter what the other player does, it pays for you to defect.

So far, so good. But the same logic holds for the other player too. Therefore, the other player should defect no matter what you are expected to do. So you should both defect. But then you both get 1 point which is worse than the

3 points of the reward that you both could have gotten had you both cooperated. Individual rationality leads to a worse outcome for both than is possible. Hence the dilemma.

The Prisoner's Dilemma is simply an abstract formulation of some very common and very interesting situations in which what is best for each person individually leads to mutual defection, whereas everyone would have been better off with mutual cooperation. The definition of Prisoner's Dilemma requires that several relationships hold among the four different potential outcomes. The first relationship specifies the order of the four payoffs. The best a player can do is get T, the temptation to defect when the other player cooperates. The worst a player can do is get S, the sucker's payoff for cooperating while the other player defects. In ordering the other two outcomes, R, the reward for mutual cooperation, is assumed to be better than P, the punishment for mutual defection. This leads to a preference ranking of the four payoffs from best to worst as $T, R, P,$ and S.

The second part of the definition of the Prisoner's Dilemma is that the players cannot get out of their dilemma by taking turns exploiting each other. This assumption means that an even chance of exploitation and being exploited is not as good an outcome for a player as mutual cooperation. It is therefore assumed that the reward for mutual cooperation is greater than the average of the temptation and the sucker's payoff. This assumption, together with the rank ordering of the four payoffs, defines the Prisoner's Dilemma.

Thus two egoists playing the game *once* will both choose their dominant choice, defection, and each will get less than they both could have gotten if they had cooperated. If the game is played a known finite number of times, the players still have no incentive to cooperate. This is certainly true on the last move since there is no future to influence. On the next-to-last move neither player will have an incentive to cooperate since they can both anticipate a defection by the other player on the very last move. Such a line of reasoning implies that the game will unravel all the way back to mutual defection on the first move of any sequence of plays that is of known finite length (Luce and Raiffa 1957, pp. 94–102). This reasoning does not apply if the players will interact an indefinite number of times. And in most realistic settings, the players cannot be sure when the last interaction between them will take place. . . . [W]ith an indefinite number of interactions, cooperation can emerge. The issue then becomes the discovery of the precise conditions that are necessary and sufficient for cooperation to emerge.

. . . I will examine interactions between just two players at a time. A single player may be interacting with many others, but the player is assumed to be interacting with them one at a time. The player is also assumed to recognize another player and to remember how the two of them have interacted so far. This ability to recognize and remember allows the history of the particular interaction to be taken into account by a player's strategy.

A variety of ways to resolve the Prisoner's Dilemma have been developed. Each involves allowing some additional activity that alters the strategic interaction in such a way as to fundamentally change the nature of the problem. The original problem remains, however, because there are many situations in which these remedies are not available. Therefore, the problem will be considered in its fundamental form, without these alterations.

1. There is no mechanism available to the players to make enforceable threats or commitments (Schelling 1960). Since the players cannot commit themselves to a particular strategy, each must take into account all possible strategies that might be used by the other player. Moreover the players have all possible strategies available to themselves.

2. There is no way to be sure what the other player will do on a given move. This eliminates the possibility of metagame analysis (Howard 1971) which allows such options as "make the same choice as the other is about to make." It also eliminates the possibility of reliable reputations such as might be based on watching the other player interact with third parties. Thus the only information available to the players about each other is the history of their interaction so far.

3. There is no way to eliminate the other player or run away from the interaction. Therefore each player retains the ability to cooperate or defect on each move.

4. There is no way to change the other player's payoffs. The payoffs already include whatever consideration each player has for the interests of the other (Taylor 1976, pp. 69–73).

Under these conditions, words not backed by actions are so cheap as to be meaningless. The players can communicate with each other only through the sequence of their own behavior. This is the problem of the Prisoner's Dilemma in its fundamental form.

What makes it possible for cooperation to emerge is the fact that the players might meet again. This possibility means that the choices made today not only determine the outcome of this move, but can also influence the later choices of the players. The future can therefore cast a shadow back upon the present and thereby affect the current strategic situation.

But the future is less important than the present—for two reasons. The first is that players tend to value payoffs less as the time of their obtainment recedes into the future. The second is that there is always some chance that the players will not meet again. An ongoing relationship may end when one or the other player moves away, changes jobs, dies, or goes bankrupt.

For these reasons, the payoff of the next move always counts less than the payoff of the current move. A natural way to take this into account is to cumulate payoffs over time in such a way that the next move is worth some fraction of the current move (Shubik 1970). The *weight* (or importance) of the next move relative to the current move will be called w. It represents the degree to which the payoff of each move is discounted relative to the previous move, and is therefore a *discount parameter*.

The discount parameter can be used to determine the payoff for a whole sequence. To take a simple example, suppose that each move is only half as important as the previous move, making $w = 1/2$. Then a whole string of mutual defections worth one point each move would have a value of 1 on the first move, $1/2$ on the second move, $1/4$ on the third move, and so on. The cumulative value of the sequence would be $1 + 1/2 + 1/4 + 1/8$ . . . which would sum to exactly 2. In general, getting one point on each move would be worth $1 + w + w^2 + w^3$. . . . A very useful fact is that the sum of this infinite series for any w greater than zero and less than one is simply $1/(1-w)$. To take another case, if each move is worth 90 percent of the previous move, a string of 1's would be worth ten points because $1/(1-w) = 1/(1-.9) = 1/.1 = 10$. Similarly, with w still equal to .9, a string of 3 point mutual rewards would be worth three times this, or 30 points.

Now consider an example of two players interacting. Suppose one player is following the policy of always defecting (ALL D), and the other player is following the policy of TIT FOR TAT. TIT FOR TAT is the policy of cooperating on the first move and then doing whatever the other player did on the previous move. This policy means that TIT FOR TAT will defect once after each defection of the other player. When the other player is using TIT FOR TAT, a player who always defects will get T on the first move, and P on all subsequent moves. The *value* (or *score*) to someone using ALL D when playing with someone using TIT FOR TAT is thus the sum of T for the first move, wP for the second move, w^2P for the third move, and so on.

Both ALL D and TIT FOR TAT are strategies. In general, a *strategy* (or *decision rule*) is a specification of what to do in any situation that might arise. The situation itself depends upon the history of the game so far. Therefore, a strategy might cooperate after some patterns of interaction and defect after others. Moreover, a strategy may use probabilities, as in the example of a rule which is entirely random with equal probabilities of cooperation and defection on each move. A strategy can also be quite sophisticated in its use of the pattern of outcomes in the game so far to determine what to do next. An example is one which, on each move, models the behavior of the other player using a complex procedure (such as a Markov process), and then uses a fancy method of statistical inference (such as Bayesian analysis) to select what seems the best choice for the long run. Or it may be some intricate combination of other strategies.

The first question you are tempted to ask is, "What is the best strategy?" In other words, what strategy will yield a player the highest possible score? This is a good question, but . . . no best rule exists independently of the strategy being used by the other player. In this sense, the iterated Prisoner's Dilemma is completely different from a game like chess. A chess master can safely use the assumption that the other player will make the most feared move. This assumption provides a basis for planning in a game like chess, where the interests of the players are completely antagonistic. But the situations represented by the Prisoner's Dilemma game are quite different. The interests of the players are not in total conflict. Both players can do well by getting the reward, R, for mutual cooperation or both can do poorly by getting the punishment, P, for mutual defection. Using the assumption that the other player will always make the move you fear most will lead you to expect that the other will never cooperate, which in turn will lead you to defect, causing unending punishment. So unlike chess, in the Prisoner's Dilemma it is not safe to assume that the other player is out to get you.

In fact, in the Prisoner's Dilemma, the strategy that works best depends directly on what strategy the other player is using and, in particular, on whether this strategy leaves room for the development of mutual cooperation. This principle is based on the weight of the next move relative to the current move being sufficiently large to make the future important. In other words, the discount parameter, w, must be large enough to make the future loom large in the calculation of total payoffs. After all, if you are unlikely to meet the other person again, or if you care little about future payoffs, then you might as well defect now and not worry about the consequences for the future.

This leads to the first formal proposition. It is the sad news that if the future is important, there is no one best strategy.

> *Proposition 1.* If the discount parameter, w, is sufficiently high, there is no best strategy independent of the strategy used by the other player.

The proof itself is not hard. Suppose that the other player is using ALL D, the strategy of always defecting. If the other player will never cooperate, the best you can do is always to defect yourself. Now suppose, on the other hand, that the other player is using a strategy of "permanent retaliation." This is the strategy of cooperating until you defect and then always defecting after that. In that case, your best strategy is never to defect, provided that the temptation to defect on the first move will eventually be more than compensated for by the long-term disadvantage of getting nothing but the punishment, P, rather than the reward, R, on future moves. This will be true whenever the discount parameter, w, is sufficiently great. Thus, whether or not you should cooperate, even on the first move, depends on the strategy being used by the other player. Therefore, if w is sufficiently large, there is no one best strategy.

In the case of a legislature such as the U.S. Senate, this proposition says that if there is a large enough chance that a member of the legislature will interact *again* with another member, there is no one best strategy to use independently of the strategy being used by the other person. It would be best to cooperate with someone who will reciprocate that cooperation in the future, but not with someone whose future behavior will not be very much affected by this interaction (see, for example, Hinckley 1972). The very possibility of achieving stable mutual cooperation depends upon there being a good chance of a continuing interaction, as measured by the magnitude of w. As it happens, in the case of Congress, the chance of two members having a continuing interaction has increased dramatically as the biennial turnover rates have fallen from about 40 percent in the first forty years of the republic to about 20 percent or less in recent years (Young 1966, pp. 87–90; Polsby 1968; Jones 1977, p. 154; Patterson 1978, pp. 143–44).

However, saying that a continuing chance of interaction is necessary for the development of cooperation is not the same as saying that it is sufficient. The demonstration that there is not a single best strategy leaves open the question of what patterns of behavior can be expected to emerge when there actually is a sufficiently high probability of continuing interaction between two individuals.

Before going on to study the behavior that can be expected to emerge, it is a good idea to take a closer look at which features of reality the Prisoner's Dilemma framework is, and is not, able to encompass. Fortunately, the very simplicity of the framework makes it possible to avoid many restrictive assumptions that would otherwise limit the analysis:

1. The payoffs of the players need not be comparable at all. For example, a journalist might get rewarded with another inside story, while the cooperating bureaucrat might be rewarded with a chance to have a policy argument presented in a favorable light.

2. The payoffs certainly do not have to be symmetric. It is a convenience to think of the interaction as exactly equivalent from the perspective of the two players, but this is not necessary. One does not have to assume, for example, that the reward for mutual cooperation, or any of the other three payoff parameters, have the same magnitude for both players. As mentioned earlier, one does not even have to assume that they are measured in comparable units. The only thing that has to be assumed is that, for each player, the four payoffs are ordered as required for the definition of the Prisoner's Dilemma.

3. The payoffs of a player do not have to be measured on an absolute scale. They need only be measured relative to each other.

4. Cooperation need not be considered desirable from the point of view of the rest of the world. There are times when one wants to retard, rather than foster, cooperation between players. Collusive business practices are good for the businesses involved but not so good for the rest of society. In fact, most forms of corruption are welcome instances of cooperation for the participants

but are unwelcome to everyone else. So, on occasion, the theory will be used in reverse to show how to prevent, rather than to promote, cooperation.

5. There is no need to assume that the players are rational. They need not be trying to maximize their rewards. Their strategies may simply reflect standard operating procedures, rules of thumb, instincts, habits, or imitation (Simon 1955; Cyert and March 1963).

6. The actions that players take are not necessarily even conscious choices. A person who sometimes returns a favor, and sometimes does not, may not think about what strategy is being used. There is no need to assume deliberate choice at all.

The framework is broad enough to encompass not only people but also nations and bacteria. Nations certainly take actions which can be interpreted as choices in a Prisoner's Dilemma—as in the raising or lowering of tariffs. It is not necessary to assume that such actions are rational or are the outcome of a unified actor pursuing a single goal. On the contrary, they might well be the result of an incredibly complex bureaucratic politics involving complicated information processing and shifting political coalitions (Allison 1971).

Likewise, at the other extreme, an organism does not need a brain to play a game. Bacteria, for example, are highly responsive to selected aspects of their chemical environment. They can therefore respond differentially to what other organisms are doing, and these conditional strategies of behavior can be inherited. Moreover, the behavior of a bacterium can affect the fitness of other organisms around it, just as the behavior of other organisms can affect the fitness of a bacterium. . . .

For now the main interest will be in people and organizations. Therefore, it is good to know that for the sake of generality, it is not necessary to assume very much about how deliberate and insightful people are. Nor is it necessary to assume, as the sociobiologists do, that important aspects of human behavior are guided by one's genes. The approach here is strategic rather than genetic.

Of course, the abstract formulation of the problem of cooperation as a Prisoner's Dilemma puts aside many vital features that make any actual interaction unique. Examples of what is left out by this formal abstraction include the possibility of verbal communication, the direct influence of third parties, the problems of implementing a choice, and the uncertainty about what the other player actually did on the preceding move. . . . It is clear that the list of potentially relevant factors that have been left out could be extended almost indefinitely. Certainly, no intelligent person should make an important choice without trying to take such complicating factors into account. The value of an analysis without them is that it can help to clarify some of the subtle features of the interaction—features which might otherwise be lost in the maze of complexities of the highly particular circumstances in which choice must actually be made. It is the very complexity of reality which makes the analysis of an abstract interaction so helpful as an aid to understanding.

. . . [W]hat is a good strategy to employ if confronted with an iterated Prisoner's Dilemma[?] This exploration has been done in a novel way, with a computer tournament. Professional game theorists were invited to submit their favorite strategy, and each of these decision rules was paired off with each of the others to see which would do best overall. Amazingly enough, the winner was the simplest of all strategies submitted. This was TIT FOR TAT, the strategy which cooperates on the first move and then does whatever the other player did on the previous move. A second round of the tournament was conducted in which many more entries were submitted by amateurs and professionals alike, all of whom were aware of the results of the first round. The result was another victory for TIT FOR TAT! The analysis of the data from these tournaments reveals four properties which tend to make a decision rule successful: avoidance of unnecessary conflict by cooperating as long as the other player does, provocability in the face of an uncalled for defection by the other, forgiveness after responding to a provocation, and clarity of behavior so that the other player can adapt to your pattern of action.

These results from the tournaments demonstrate that under suitable conditions, cooperation can indeed emerge in a world of egoists without central authority. . . .

. . . [T]he basic approach is [that] seeing how individuals operate in their own interest reveals what happens to the whole group. This approach allows more than the understanding of the perspective of a single player. It also provides an appreciation of what it takes to promote the stability of mutual cooperation in a given setting. The most promising finding is that if the facts of Cooperation Theory are known by participants with foresight, the evolution of cooperation can be speeded up.

REFERENCES

Allison, Graham T. 1971. *The Essence of Decision*. Boston: Little, Brown.

Cyert, Richard M., and James G. March. 1963. *A Behavioral Theory of the Firm*. Englewood Cliffs, N. J.: Prentice-Hall.

Hinckley, Barbara. 1972. "Coalitions in Congress: Size and Ideological Distance." *Midwest Journal of Political Science* 26: 197–207.

Hobbes, Thomas. 1651/1962. *Leviathan*. New York: Collier Books.

Howard, Nigel. 1971. *Paradoxes of Rationality: Theory of Metagames and Political Behavior*. Cambridge, Mass.: MIT Press.

Luce, R. Duncan, and Howard Raiffal. 1957. *Games and Decisions*. New York: Wiley.

Matthews, Donald R. 1960. *U.S. Senators and their World*. Chapel Hill: University of North Carolina Press.

Mayhew, David R. 1975. *Congress: The Electoral Connection*. New Haven, Conn.: Yale University Press.

Ornstein, Norman, Robert L. Peabody, and David W. Rhode. 1977. "The Changing Senate: From the 1950s to the 1970s." In Lawrence C. Dodd and Bruce I. Oppenheimer, editors, *Congress Reconsidered*. New York: Praeger.

Patterson, Samuel. 1978. "The Semi-Sovereign Congress." In Anthony King, editor, *The New American Political System*. Washington, D.C.: American Enterprise Institute.

Polsby, Nelson. 1968. "The Institutionalization of the U.S. House of Representatives." *American Political Science Review* 62:144–68.

Schelling, Thomas C. 1978/1960. *The Strategy of Conflict*. Cambridge, Mass.: Harvard University Press.

Shubik, Martin. 1970. "Game Theory, Behavior, and the Paradox of Prisoner's Dilemma: Three Solutions." *Journal of Conflict Resolution* 14:181–94.

Simon, Herbert A. 1955. "A Behavioral Model of Rational Choice." *Quarterly Journal of Economics* 69:99–118.

Smith, Margaret Bayard. 1906. *The First Forty Years of Washington Society*. New York: Scribner's.

Taylor, Michael. 1976. *Anarchy and Cooperation*. New York: Wiley.

Young, James Sterling. 1966. *The Washington Community, 1800–1928*. New York: Harcourt, Brace and World.

23.

The Live-and-Let-Live System
in Trench Warfare in World War I

ROBERT AXELROD, 1984

Sometimes cooperation emerges where it is least expected. During World War
I, the Western Front was the scene of horrible battles for a few yards of territory. But between these battles, and even during them at other places along
the five-hundred-mile line in France and Belgium, the enemy soldiers often
exercised considerable restraint. A British staff officer on a tour of the trenches
remarked that he was

> astonished to observe German soldiers walking about within rifle range be-
> hind their own line. Our men appeared to take no notice. I privately made
> up my mind to do away with that sort of thing when we took over; such
> things should not be allowed. These people evidently did not know there was
> a war on. Both sides apparently believed in the policy of "live and let live."
> (Dugdale 1932, p. 94)

This is not an isolated example. The live-and-let-live system was endemic
in trench warfare. It flourished despite the best efforts of senior officers to stop
it, despite the passions aroused by combat, despite the military logic of kill or
be killed, and despite the ease with which the high command was able to repress any local efforts to arrange a direct truce.

This is a case of cooperation emerging despite great antagonism between
the players. As such, it provides a challenge for the application of [Coopera-
tion Theory]. In particular, the main goal is to use the theory to explain:

1. How could the live-and-let-live system have gotten started?

2. How was it sustained?

3. Why did it break down toward the end of the war?

4. Why was it characteristic of trench warfare in World War I, but of few
   other wars?

A second goal is to use the historical case to suggest how the original concepts and theory can be further elaborated.

From *The Evolution of Cooperation* by Robert Axelrod. Copyright © 1984 by Robert
Axelrod. Reprinted by permission of Basic Books, a member of Perseus Books, L.L.C.

Fortunately, a recent book-length study of the live-and-let-live system is available. This excellent work by a British sociologist, Tony Ashworth (1980), is based upon diaries, letters, and reminiscences of trench fighters. Material was found from virtually every one of the fifty-seven British divisions, with an average of more than three sources per division. To a lesser extent, material from French and German sources was also consulted. The result is a very rich set of illustrations that are analyzed with great skill to provide a comprehensive picture of the development and character of trench warfare on the Western Front in World War I. This chapter relies upon Ashworth's fine work for its illustrative quotes and for its historical interpretation.

While Ashworth does not put it this way, the historical situation in the quiet sectors along the Western Front was an iterated Prisoner's Dilemma. In a given locality, the two players can be taken to be the small units facing each other. At any time, the choices are to shoot to kill or deliberately to shoot to avoid causing damage. For both sides, weakening the enemy is an important value because it will promote survival if a major battle is ordered in the sector. Therefore, in the short run it is better to do damage now whether the enemy is shooting back or not. This establishes that mutual defection is *preferred* to unilateral restraint ($P > S$), and that unilateral restraint by the other side is even better than mutual cooperation ($T > R$). In addition, the reward for mutual restraint is preferred by the local units to the outcome of mutual punishment ($R > P$), since mutual punishment would imply that both units would suffer for little or no relative gain. Taken together, this establishes the essential set of inequalities: $T > R > P > S$. Moreover, both sides would prefer mutual restraint to the random alternation of serious hostilities, making $R > (T + S)/2$. Thus the situation meets the conditions for a Prisoner's Dilemma between small units facing each other in a given immobile sector.

Two small units facing each other across one hundred to four hundred yards of no-man's-land were the players in one of these potentially deadly Prisoner's Dilemmas. Typically, the basic unit could be taken to be the battalion, consisting of about one thousand men, half of whom would be in the front line at any one time. The battalion played a large role in the life of an infantryman. It not only organized its members for combat, but also fed, paid, and clothed them as well as arranged their leave. All of the officers and most of the other soldiers in the battalion knew each other by sight. For our purposes, two key factors make the battalion the most typical player. On the one hand, it was large enough to occupy a sufficient sector of the front to be "held accountable" for aggressive actions which came from its territory. On the other hand, it was small enough to be able to control the individual behavior of its men, through a variety of means, both formal and informal.

A battalion on one side might be facing parts of one, two, or three battalions on the other side. Thus each player could simultaneously be involved in several interactions. Over the course of the Western Front, there would be hundreds of such face-offs.

Only the small units were involved in these Prisoner's Dilemmas. The high commands of the two sides did not share the view of the common soldier who said:

> The real reason for the quietness of some sections of the line was that neither side had any intention of advancing in that particular district. . . . If the British shelled the Germans, the Germans replied, and the damage was equal: if the Germans bombed an advanced piece of trench and killed five Englishmen, an answering fusillade killed five Germans. (Belton Cobb 1916, p. 74)

To the army headquarters, the important thing was to develop an offensive spirit in the troops. The Allies, in particular, pursued a strategy of attrition whereby equal losses in men from both sides meant a net gain for the Allies because sooner or later Germany's strength would be exhausted first. So at the national level, World War I approximated a zero-sum game in which losses for one side represented gains for the other side. But at the local level, along the front line, mutual restraint was much preferred to mutual punishment.

Locally, the dilemma persisted: at any given moment it was prudent to shoot to kill, whether the other side did so or not. What made trench warfare so different from most other combat was that the same small units faced each other in immobile sectors for extended periods of time. This changed the game from a one-move Prisoner's Dilemma in which defection is the dominant choice, to an iterated Prisoner's Dilemma in which conditional strategies are possible. The result accorded with the theory's predictions: with sustained interaction, the stable outcome could be mutual cooperation based upon reciprocity. In particular, both sides followed strategies that would not be the first to defect, but that would be provoked if the other defected.

Before looking further at the stability of the cooperation, it is interesting to see how cooperation got started in the first place. The first stage of the war, which began in August 1914, was highly mobile and very bloody. But as the lines stabilized, nonaggression between the troops emerged spontaneously in many places along the front. The earliest instances may have been associated with meals which were served at the same times on both sides of no-man's land. As early as November 1914, a noncommissioned officer whose unit had been in the trenches for some days, observed that

> the quartermaster used to bring the rations up . . . each night after dark; they were laid out and parties used to come from the front line to fetch them. I

suppose the enemy were occupied in the same way; so things were quiet at that hour for a couple of nights, and the ration parties became careless because of it, and laughed and talked on their way back to their companies. (*The War the Infantry Knew* 1938, p. 92)

By Christmas there was extensive fraternization, a practice which the headquarters frowned upon. In the following months, direct truces were occasionally arranged by shouts or by signals. An eyewitness noted that:

In one section the hour of 8 to 9 A.M. was regarded as consecrated to "private business," and certain places indicated by a flag were regarded as out of bounds by the snipers on both sides. (Morgan 1916, pp. 270–71)

But direct truces were easily suppressed. Orders were issued making clear that the soldiers "were in France to fight and not to fraternize with the enemy" (*Fifth Battalion the Camaronians* 1936, p. 28). More to the point, several soldiers were courtmartialed and whole battalions were punished. Soon it became clear that verbal arrangements were easily suppressed by the high command and such arrangements became rare.

Another way in which mutual restraint got started was during a spell of miserable weather. When the rains were bad enough, it was almost impossible to undertake major aggressive action. Often ad hoc weather truces emerged in which the troops simply did not shoot at each other. When the weather improved, the pattern of mutual restraint sometimes simply continued.

So verbal agreements were effective in getting cooperation started on many occasions early in the war, but direct fraternization was easily suppressed. More effective in the long run were various methods which allowed the two sides to coordinate their actions without having to resort to words. A key factor was the realization that if one side would exercise a particular kind of restraint, then the other might reciprocate. Similarities in basic needs and activities let the soldiers appreciate that the other side would probably not be following a strategy of unconditional defection. For example, in the summer of 1915, a soldier saw that the enemy would be likely to reciprocate cooperation based on the desire for fresh rations.

It would be child's play to shell the road behind the enemy's trenches, crowded as it must be with ration wagons and water carts, into a bloodstained wilderness . . . but on the whole there is silence. After all, if you prevent your enemy from drawing his rations, his remedy is simple: he will prevent you from drawing yours. (Hay 1916, pp. 224–25)

Once started, strategies based on reciprocity could spread in a variety of ways. A restraint undertaken in certain hours could be extended to longer hours. A particular kind of restraint could lead to attempting other kinds of restraint. And most importantly of all, the progress achieved in one small sector of the front could be imitated by the units in neighboring sectors.

Just as important as getting cooperation started were the conditions that allowed it to be sustainable. The strategies that could sustain mutual cooperation were the ones which were provocable. During the periods of mutual restraint, the enemy soldiers took pains to show each other that they could indeed retaliate if necessary. For example, German snipers showed their prowess to the British by aiming at spots on the walls of cottages and firing until they had cut a hole (*The War the Infantry Knew* 1938, p. 98). Likewise the artillery would often demonstrate with a few accurately aimed shots that they could do more damage if they wished. These demonstrations of retaliatory capabilities helped police the system by showing that restraint was not due to weakness, and that defection would be self-defeating.

When a defection actually occurred, the retaliation was often more than would be called for by TIT FOR TAT. Two-for-one or three-for-one was a common response to an act that went beyond what was considered acceptable.

> We go out at night in front of the trenches. . . . The German working parties are also out, so it is not considered etiquette to fire. The really nasty things are rifle grenades. . . . They can kill as many as eight or nine men if they do fall into a trench. . . . But we never use ours unless the Germans get particularly noisy, as on their system of retaliation three for every one of ours come back. (Greenwell 1972, pp. 16–17)

There was probably an inherent damping process that usually prevented these retaliations from leading to an uncontrolled echo of mutual recriminations. The side that instigated the action might note the escalated response and not try to redouble or retriple it. Once the escalation was not driven further, it would probably tend to die out. Since not every bullet, grenade, or shell fired in earnest would hit its target, there would be an inherent tendency toward de-escalation.

Another problem that had to be overcome to maintain the stability of cooperation was the rotation of troops. About every eight days, a battalion would change places with another battalion billeted behind it. At longer intervals, larger units would change places. What allowed the cooperation to remain stable was the process of familiarization that the outgoing unit would provide for the incoming unit. The particular details of the tacit understandings with the enemy were explained. But sometimes it was quite sufficient for an old timer to point out to a newcomer that "Mr. Bosche ain't a bad fellow. You leave 'im alone; 'e'll leave you alone" (Gillon n.d., p. 77). This socialization allowed one unit to pick up the game right where the other left it.

Still another problem for the maintenance of stable cooperation was the fact that the artillery was much less vulnerable to enemy retaliation than was the infantry. Therefore, the artillery had a lesser stake in the live-and-let-live system. As a consequence, the infantry tended to be solicitous of the forward observers from the artillery. As a German artillery man noted of the infantry, "If they ever have any delicacies to spare, they make us a present of them, partly of course because they feel we are protecting them" (Sulzbach 1973, p. 71). The goal was to encourage the artillery to respect the infantry's desire to let sleeping dogs lie. A new forward observer for the artillery was often greeted by the infantry with the request, "I hope you are not going to start trouble." The best answer was, "Not unless *you* want" (Ashworth 1980, p. 169). This reflected the dual role of artillery in the maintenance of mutual restraint with the enemy: the passiveness when unprovoked, and the instant retaliation when the enemy broke the peace.

The high commands of the British, French, and German armies all wanted to put a stop to tacit truces; all were afraid that they sapped the morale of their men, and all believed throughout the war that a ceaseless policy of offense was the only way to victory. With few exceptions, the headquarters could enforce any orders that they could directly monitor. Thus the headquarters were able to conduct large battles by ordering the men to leave their trenches and risk their lives in charging the enemy positions. But between large battles, they were not able to monitor their orders to keep up the pressure. After all, it was hard for a senior officer to determine who was shooting to kill, and who was shooting with an eye to avoiding retaliation. The soldiers became expert at defeating the monitoring system, as when a unit kept a coil of enemy wire and sent a piece to headquarters whenever asked to prove that they had conducted a patrol of no-man's-land.

What finally destroyed the live-and-let-live system was the institution of a type of incessant aggression that the headquarters *could* monitor. This was the raid, a carefully prepared attack on enemy trenches which involved from ten to two hundred men. Raiders were ordered to kill or capture the enemy in his own trenches. If the raid was successful, prisoners would be taken; and if the raid was a failure, casualties would be proof of the attempt. There was no effective way to pretend that a raid had been undertaken when it had not. And there was no effective way to cooperate with the enemy in a raid because neither live soldiers nor dead bodies could be exchanged.

The live-and-let-live system could not cope with the disruption caused by the hundreds of small raids. After a raid neither side knew what to expect next. The side that had raided could expect retaliation but could not predict when, where, or how. The side that had been raided was also nervous, not knowing whether the raid was an isolated attack or the first of a series. Moreover, since raids could be ordered and monitored from headquarters, the magnitude of the retaliatory raid could also be controlled, preventing a dampening of the process. The battalions were forced to mount real attacks on the enemy, the retaliation was undampened, and the process echoed out of control.

Ironically, when the British High Command undertook its policy of raiding, it did not do so in order to end the live-and-let-live system. Instead, its initial goal was political, namely, to show their French allies that they were doing their part to harass the enemy. Their image of the direct effects of raiding was that it increased the morale of their own troops by restoring an offensive spirit and that it promoted attrition by inflicting more casualties on the enemy in the raids than the raiding troops themselves would suffer. Whether these effects on morale and casualty ratios were realized has been debated ever since. What is clear in retrospect is that the indirect effect of the raids was to destroy the conditions needed for the stability of the tacit restraints widely exercised on the Western Front. Without realizing exactly what they were doing, the high command effectively ended the live-and-let-live system by preventing their battalions from exercising their own strategies of cooperation based on reciprocity.

The introduction of raids completed the cycle of the evolution of the live-and-let-live system. Cooperation got a foothold through exploratory actions at the local level, was able to sustain itself because of the duration of contact between small units facing each other, and was eventually undermined when these small units lost their freedom of action. Small units, such as battalions, used their own strategies in dealing with the enemy units they faced. Cooperation first emerged spontaneously in a variety of contexts, such as restraint in attacking the distribution of enemy rations, a pause during the first Christmas in the trenches, and a slow resumption of fighting after bad weather made sustained combat almost impossible. These restraints quickly evolved into clear patterns of mutually understood behavior, such as two-for-one or three-for-one retaliation for actions that were taken to be unacceptable. The mechanisms of the evolution of these strategies must have been trial and error and the imitation of neighboring units.

The mechanisms for evolution involved neither blind mutation nor survival of the fittest. Unlike blind mutation, the soldiers understood their situation and actively tried to make the most of it. They understood the indirect consequences of their acts as embodied in what I call the echo principle: "To provide discomfort for the other is but a roundabout way of providing it for themselves" (Sorley 1919, p. 283). The strategies were based on thought as well as experience. The soldiers learned that to maintain mutual restraint with their enemies, they had to base that restraint on a demonstrated capability and willingness to be provoked. They learned that cooperation had to be based upon reciprocity. Thus, the evolution of strategies was based on deliberate rather than blind adaptation. Nor did the evolution involve survival of the fittest.

While an ineffective strategy would mean more casualties for the unit, replacements typically meant that the units themselves would survive.

The origins, maintenance, and destruction of the live-and-let-live system of trench warfare are all consistent with the theory of the evolution of cooperation. In addition, there are two very interesting developments within the live-and-let-live system which are new to the theory. These additional developments are the emergence of ethics and ritual.

The ethics that developed are illustrated in this incident, related by a British officer recalling his experience while facing a Saxon unit of the German Army.

> I was having tea with A Company when we heard a lot of shouting and went out to investigate. We found our men and the Germans standing on their respective parapets. Suddenly a salvo arrived but did no damage. Naturally both sides got down and our men started swearing at the Germans, when all at once a brave German got on to his parapet and shouted out "We are very sorry about that; we hope no one was hurt. It is not our fault, it is that damned Prussian artillery." (Rutter 1934, p. 29)

This Saxon apology goes well beyond a merely instrumental effort to prevent retaliation. It reflects moral regret for having violated a situation of trust, and it shows concern that someone might have been hurt.

The cooperative exchanges of mutual restraint actually changed the nature of the interaction. They tended to make the two sides care about each other's welfare. This change can be interpreted in terms of the Prisoner's Dilemma by saying that the very experience of sustained mutual cooperation altered the payoffs of the players, making mutual cooperation even more valued than it was before.

The converse was also true. When the pattern of mutual cooperation deteriorated due to mandatory raiding, a powerful ethic of revenge was evoked. This ethic was not just a question of calmly following a strategy based on reciprocity. It was also a question of doing what seemed moral and proper to fulfill one's obligation to a fallen comrade. And revenge evoked revenge. Thus both cooperation and defection were self-reinforcing. The self-reinforcement of these mutual behavioral patterns was not only in terms of the interacting strategies of the players, but also in terms of their perceptions of the meaning of the outcomes. In abstract terms, the point is that not only did preferences affect behavior and outcomes, but behavior and outcomes also affected preferences.

The other addition to the theory suggested by the trench warfare case is the development of ritual. The rituals took the form of perfunctory use of small arms, and deliberately harmless use of artillery. For example, the Germans in one place conducted "their offensive operations with a tactful blend of constant firing and bad shooting, which while it satisfies the Prussians causes no serious inconvenience to Thomas Atkins" (Hay 1916, p. 206).

Even more striking was the predictable use of artillery which occurred in many sectors.

So regular were they [the Germans] in their choice of targets, times of shooting, and number of rounds fired, that, after being in the line one or two
days, Colonel Jones had discovered their system, and knew to a minute
where the next shell would fall. His calculations were very accurate, and he
was able to take what seemed to uninitiated Staff Officers big risks, knowing
that the shelling would stop before he reached the place being shelled. (Hills
1919, p. 96)

The other side did the same thing, as noted by a German soldier commenting
on "the evening gun" fired by the British.

At seven it came—so regularly that you could set your watch by it. . . . It always had the same objective, its range was accurate, it never varied laterally or
went beyond or fell short of the mark. . . . There were even some inquisitive
fellows who crawled out . . . a little before seven, in order to see it burst.
(Koppen 1931, pp. 135–37)

These rituals of perfunctory and routine firing sent a double message. To
the high command they conveyed aggression, but to the enemy they conveyed
peace. The men pretended to be implementing an aggressive policy, but were
not. Ashworth himself explains that these stylized acts were more than a way
of avoiding retaliation.

In trench war, a structure of ritualised aggression was a ceremony where antagonists participated in regular, reciprocal discharges of missiles, that is,
bombs, bullets and so forth, which symbolized and strengthened, at one and
the same time, both sentiments of fellow-feelings, and beliefs that the enemy
was a fellow sufferer. (Ashworth 1980, p. 144)

Thus these rituals helped strengthen the moral sanctions which reinforced
the evolutionary basis of the live-and-let-live system.

The live-and-let-live system that emerged in the bitter trench warfare of
World War I demonstrates that friendship is hardly necessary for cooperation
based upon reciprocity to get started. Under suitable circumstances, cooperation can develop even between antagonists.

One thing the soldiers in the trenches had going for them was a fairly clear
understanding of the role of reciprocity in the maintenance of the cooperation. . . . [s]uch understanding by the participants is not really necessary for
cooperation to emerge and prove stable.

REFERENCES

Ashworth, Tony. 1980. *Trench Warfare, 1914–1918: The Live and Let Live System.* New York:
    Holmes and Meier.
Belton Cobb, G. 1916. *Stand to Arms.* London: Wells Gardner, Darton and Co.
Dugdale, G. 1932. *Langemarck and Cambrai.* Shrewsbury, U.K.: Wilding and Son.
The Fifth Battalion the Camaronians. 1936. Glasgow: Jackson & Co.

Gillon, S. n.d. *The Story of the 29th Division.* London: Nelson and Sons.

Greenwell, G. H. 1972. *An Infant in Arms.* London: Allen Lane.

Hay, Ian. 1916. *The First Hundred Thousand.* London: Wm. Blackwood.

Hills, J. D. 1919. *The Fifth Leicestershire 1914–1918.* Loughborough, U. K.: Echo Press.

Koppen, E. 1931. *Higher Command.* London: Faber and Faber.

Morgan, J.H. 1916. *Leaves from a Field Note Book.* London: Macmillan.

Rutter, Owen, editor. 1934. *The History of the Seventh (Services) Battalion: The Royal Sussex Regiment 1914–1919.* London: Times Publishing Co.

Sorley, Charles. 1919. *The Letters of Charles Sorley.* Cambridge: Cambridge University Press.

Sulzbach, H. 1973. *With the German Guns.* London: Leo Cooper.

The War the Infantry Knew. 1938. London: P. S. King.

H.
Groups and Networks

The bottom-up theories of social order discussed in the previous section have important policy implications. The most familiar is that the economy—and hence social order—is strengthened by promoting free markets rather than regulated ones. This view, known as economic liberalism, holds that tariffs and other government-imposed barriers to trade and government policies encouraging monopolies are all socially harmful. States that get out of the business of regulating markets therefore will have the greatest economic growth and social welfare.

But, as we've suggested, unregulated interaction does not necessarily lead to increased cooperation. And in fact, the liberal state that was built on Smithian premises (particularly, the mid-nineteenth-century British laissez-faire state) had a very short half-life (Polanyi 1943). Far from providing the rising tide that lifts all boats, the advent of free markets was accompanied by waves of economic depression and unemployment, by massive public health crises in the burgeoning cities, and by intense bouts of class conflict. These negative consequences of laissez-faire created a strong demand for renewed state intervention and economic regulation. By the end of the nineteenth century, state regulation had increased markedly in countries having different types of economies, political traditions, and ideologies. Indeed, the fact that all advanced capitalist countries today have adopted some form of welfare state constitutes a strong empirical critique of the invisible hand theory of social order. It appears, therefore, that unregulated, self-interested interactions may lead to chaos *or* to predictability *or* to cooperation. For spontaneous order theorists, one of the challenges is to identify the conditions under which interaction produces these different outcomes.

In general, the first four solutions to the problem of social order that we have described pay scant attention to social structure. Whereas they recognize the existence of individuals and the society as a whole, they have little to say about the nature of social organization within societies.[1] In fact, in all societies, people belong to a variety of groups—families, neighborhoods, churches, athletic clubs, businesses, and so forth. Order within these groups is related to order in the larger society, sometimes in complex ways. Group and network theories explicitly focus on structures of affiliation and their consequences for social order. They advance two basic arguments. One is that ties *across* groups increase order; the other is that ties *within* groups are key.[2]

Georg Simmel is noted for devoting some of the earliest attention to these issues. In "The Web of Group Affiliations," Simmel distinguishes between two different patterns of group affiliation. In the older pattern, characteristic of feudal Europe, group affiliations are concentric. That is, membership in one group implies membership in others. For example, if you live in Boston, you are simultaneously a "member" of the respective citizenries of Massachusetts, New England, and the United States. When groups are organized concentrically, individuals usually do not belong to groups outside the circle.

The modern form of group affiliation is quite different. By and large, modern groups are voluntary rather than compulsory. In consequence, for the first time in history, individuals are free to join socially heterogeneous groups. When groups are organized in this way, people may simultaneously be members of many groups. These multiple memberships create bridging ties across groups.[3]

Mark Granovetter's essay develops this idea and its implications more fully. Granovetter discusses two different kinds of social ties that can link individuals. Strong ties (such as those between family members and close friends) are

---

1. Even Marx and Engels, who typically are identified with structural explanations in sociology, tend to divide societies into classes. Within each class, however, they describe little differentiation.

2. See, for example, the cases discussed in Ostrom 1990.

3. The prevalence of such cross-cutting ties depends to a large extent on the number and size of groups in communities (Blau 1977).

time-intensive, emotional, intimate, and reciprocal. Weak ties (such as those between casual acquaintances), however, are fleeting, instrumental, and impersonal. Weak ties may not appear to contribute much to social order. But Granovetter argues that despite this intuition, these ties indeed are very important. Weak ties serve as bridges between socially homogeneous groups whose members ordinarily do not interact with one another. In contrast, strong ties tend to produce groups that are inward looking and hostile to outsiders. It follows that a complex society having a preponderance of strong ties is vulnerable to intergroup conflict and therefore to social disorder. In contrast, a society having a preponderance of weak ties has more intergroup relations and, as a result, greater levels of social order (Blau and Schwartz 1984).

That conflicting loyalties inhibit intergroup quarreling and thereby promote social order has been frequently demonstrated in ethnographic research, especially as carried out on stateless societies in Africa (Evans-Pritchard 1944). A classic example of this logic is found in norms mandating tribal exogamy. In most tribal societies, individuals are prohibited from marrying within their group. This norm compels individuals to seek mates from different tribal groups. The resulting marriages forge weak ties between different tribes. As the anthropologist Max Gluckman summarizes,

> Men can only belong to a large society through intermediate smaller groups, based on technical process, on personal association, on locality, on sectarian belief within a larger cult, and so forth. Schools which are organized in houses cutting across forms, and Universities which have colleges cutting across departments and faculties, exhibit more cohesion than amorphous schools and universities. Tight loyalties to smaller groups can be effective in strengthening a larger community if there are offsetting loyalties. The feud is, according to the dictionary, "a lasting state of hostility." There is no society which does not contain such states of hostility between its component sections; but provided they are redressed by other loyalties they may contribute to the peace of the whole. . . . Conflicting loyalties and divisions of allegiance tend to inhibit the development of open quarreling, and . . . the greater the division in one area of society, the greater is likely to be the cohesion in a wider range of relationships—provided that there is a general need for peace, and

FIGURE H.I *The Palm Beach Post* by Don Wright. © Tribune Media Services, Inc. All Rights Reserved. Reprinted with permission.

recognition of a moral order in which this peace can flourish. (Gluckman 1955, 24‒25)

Don Wright's cartoon (Figure H.1), inspired by events in the wake of the fall of the Taliban regime in Afghanistan, provides a humorous illustration of Gluckman's point.

Some of these ideas are foreshadowed in the writings of Ibn Khaldun, an Islamic scholar living in the fourteenth century (1332‒1406). Khaldun explores the structure of social life in desert society and its consequences for the maintenance of social order. In "Trust, Cohesion, and the Social Order," Ernest Gellner applies Khaldun's arguments to the problem of social order. Arid territories are unable to sustain agricultural cultivation; hence, people rely on herding to make a living.[4] Because livestock is moveable (unlike agricultural crops), it is easily stolen. Individuals therefore have a desire to protect their property.

---

4. Arid lands can support cultivation if they have the benefit of irrigation, but irrigation presupposes just the social order that we seek to explain.

This desire leads individuals "to gang up in a group, which in effect hangs up a notice saying: anyone who commits an act of aggression against any one of us must expect retaliation from us all, and not only will the aggressor himself be likely to suffer retaliation, but his entire group and all its members will be equally liable" (p. 311). This principle leads to a system of strong, self-policing tribal groups that defend themselves by threatening to retaliate indiscriminately against the individual members of any aggressor group.[5] Further, it provides an incentive for groups to police their own members so as not to provoke retaliation.

This system would seem to support the view that strong groups weaken the larger social order because they lead to intergroup conflict. But the relations among these groups are complex. To forestall a situation in which one powerful tribe becomes able to inflict unacceptable costs on others, tribal loyalties and coalitions must be impermanent. In such a system, groups are far from eternal enemies. Rather, they have continually changing connections to each other. This is partly because people can switch groups—what Gellner terms "treason" is acceptable. Patterns of alliances shift. This impermanence allows the system as a whole to remain in equilibrium, producing a fluid kind of order.

In addition to describing how the relations among groups promote order, Khaldun suggests that groups have a further impact—they produce rulers. Under conditions in which groups, rather than the government, provide protection, individuals learn to trust each other. They also become strong and self-reliant. By contrast, in cities, people depend on the government to produce order and have little trust in each other. But people who are weak and who cannot trust do not make fit rulers. Only those who have been made strong by the rigors of desert life are able to rule effectively. Thus, for Khaldun, independent groups operating outside of the jurisdiction of government are necessary because they produce individuals who have the capacity to rule and

---

5. For a more formal version of this argument, see Fearon and Laitin 1996.

therefore can contribute to the effective government essential for city life. Groups strengthen the state because they provide its rulers.

In Western societies, groups also contribute to a healthy state, although the mechanism is thought to be different. Alexis de Tocqueville is the first European scholar to emphasize the importance of voluntary groups for social order. In "Individualism and Free Institutions," Tocqueville explores the relation between democracy (and the free association it allows) and social order. Democracy makes rulers nervous because it gives freedom to citizens. Disadvantaged subjects may band together in hope of toppling the state and creating a more equitable political order. Despotic rulers, therefore, do everything in their power to prevent subjects from freely associating in groups.[6] But U.S. political institutions promote just such associations. How then does the United States manage to attain social order?

Tocqueville argues that freedom of association is no threat to social order but—on the contrary—a boon to it. This is because groups promote the value of cooperation. Voluntary associations essentially serve as schools for democratic decision making and the learning of the virtues and techniques of cooperation. According to Tocqueville,

> In their political associations the Americans, of all conditions, minds, and ages, daily acquire a general taste for association and grow accustomed to the use of it. There they meet together, they converse, they listen to one another, and they are mutually stimulated to all undertakings. They afterwards transfer to civil life the notions they have thus acquired and make them subservient to a thousand purposes. Thus it is by the enjoyment of a dangerous freedom that Americans learn the art of rendering the dangers of freedom less formidable. (see p. 327)

Without voluntary associations, people might never learn to behave cooperatively. With them, they become civic-minded. Thus for Tocqueville, groups

---

6. The current Chinese government's crackdown on the Falun Gong movement is a case in point.

help people to internalize prosocial values. Cooperative citizens, in turn, contribute to the economic and political life of a society.

Michael Hechter, Debra Friedman, and Satoshi Kanazawa take Tocqueville's basic insight and use it to look at two different types of groups—gangs and religious cults—and their effects on social order. However, whereas Tocqueville argues that groups help individuals to internalize cooperative values, Hechter, Friedman, and Kanazawa suggest that the principal effects groups have on social order is that they help enforce social norms.

If groups such as gangs or religious cults control their members, then the state does not have to. Group solidarity therefore enables states to shift the burden of control from police and other agents of government to group members themselves. Moreover, the resulting cost savings is greatest among the most deviant groups. The prospective members of a Presbyterian congregation are much less likely to threaten social order than are individuals attracted to groups made up of members who tend to occupy the fringes of society.

Thus groups that seem to be the strangest, but whose members do not engage in antisocial activities, contribute more to social order than do those considered to be in the mainstream. Solidary groups (Hechter 1987), like the Hare Krishna, contribute to order because they manage to keep their members busy, and therefore out of harm's way, but do not obligate them to engage in antisocial behavior.[7] When groups do encourage their members to engage in behaviors that harm others or threaten the power of the state—as did the Rajneeshees in Oregon—they attract the attention of the government, and its coercive power is directed against them. This argument shows that it is not only "good" groups like the PTA or the Junior League that contribute to order. Even deviant groups (as long they do not go too far) can contribute to order in the larger society.

Each of the arguments in this section points to the importance of understanding group and network structures. Some scholars emphasize the need for

---

7. Miller and Kanazawa (2000) use these ideas to explain why social order is greater in Japan than in the United States and other Western societies that have comparable occupational structures.

ties that provide bridges between groups. Others focus on ties within groups that allow for the transmission of cooperative values and for the enforcement of social norms. Both kinds of structures have implications for the maintenance of social order.

REFERENCES

Blau, Peter. 1977. *Inequality and Heterogeneity*. New York: Free Press.
Blau, Peter, and Joseph E. Schwartz. 1984. *Crosscutting Social Circles: Testing a Macrostructural Theory of Intergroup Relations*. Orlando, Fla.: Academic Press.
Evans-Pritchard, E. E. 1944. *The Nuer*. Oxford: Oxford University Press.
Fearon, James D., and David D. Laitin. 1996. "Explaining Interethnic Cooperation." *American Political Science Review* 90:715–35.
Gluckman, Max. 1955. *Custom and Conflict in Africa*. Oxford: Blackwell.
Hechter, Michael. 1987. *Principles of Group Solidarity*. Berkeley: University of California Press.
Miller, Alan S., and Satoshi Kanazawa. 2000. *Order by Accident: The Origins and Consequences of Conformity in Contemporary Japan*. Boulder, Colo., and Oxford: Westview Press.
Ostrom, Elinor. 1990. *Governing the Commons: The Evolution of Institutions for Collective Action*. Cambridge: Cambridge University Press.
Polanyi, Karl. 1943. *The Great Transformation*. Boston: Beacon Press.

24.

The Web of Group-Affiliations

GEORG SIMMEL, 1922

AFFILIATION WITH TWO GROUPS OF DIFFERENT TYPES

The unity of a group . . . grows out of a more primitive type, but need not always be of a more rational character. The consequences for the external position as well as for the internal make-up of the individual will have a special character if both types [of establishing unity] are founded upon equally deep-seated causes that lie beyond the control of the individual.

The Australian aborigines, whose cultural position is very primitive, live in small, rather close-knit tribes. But the entire population is divided into five *gentes* or totemic associations in such a way that members of the various gentes are found in each tribe and each gens extends over several tribes. Within the tribe the members of the same totemic association do not engage in collective action. Rather, the fact of their membership becomes an element in all other groups, however defined, and as such these members of the totemic association constitute an extended family. If in a fight between two hordes the members of the same totem meet, they avoid each other and seek out another opponent, which is likewise reported of the Mortlack Islanders. Sexual relations take place between men and women according to the conditions of the gentes, even though they are members of different tribes and have never met in any other way. Those wretched people are quite incapable of engaging in rational, collective action, properly so-called. But by belonging to two such sharply divided groups [the gens and the tribe] they must experience an enrichment of their lives, a tension and a doubling of their vitality, which they could probably not attain otherwise.

In modern family life a somewhat similar affiliation [with two divided groups] is often established by virtue of the solidarity among members of the same sex, though the content and the effect [of this affiliation] are of a very

Reprinted with the permission of The Free Press, an imprint of Simon & Schuster Adult Publishing Group, from *Conflict and the Web of Group Affiliations* by Georg Simmel, translated by Kurt H. Wolff and Reinhard Bendix. Copyright © 1955 by The Free Press; copyright renewed 1983 by Kurt H. Wolff.

different kind. For example, a mother's instincts will cause her to side with her son as her own kin on occasions when she is drawn into the disputes between himself and his wife. But on another occasion her instincts may cause her to take the side of her daughter-in-law as a member of her own sex. To belong to the same sex is one of the causes for collective action, which pervades social life perennially, and which intermingles with all other causes of collective action in the most varied ways and degrees. The fact that two persons are of the same sex will, as a rule, act as an organic and natural [cause of collective action] in contrast to which other causes [of collective action] have something of the individual, intentional, and conscious about them. However, in the case referred to, one may sense perhaps that the relationship between mother and son is the natural and effective one, while the solidarity of one woman with another is of a secondary and deliberate nature, which is more significant in an abstract than in an existential sense. Yet, to be of the same sex is sometimes a cause of solidarity, which is peculiar in the sense that it is primary, fundamental, and independent of all arbitrary decisions. Yet, this solidarity can become effective only through mediation, reflection and conscious striving. Hence, these much later and accidental causes function in fact as the first and unavoidable cause of group-formation.

ORGANIC AND RATIONAL CRITERIA OF GROUP-FORMATION

In relatively uncomplicated situations age groups may function as a sociological criterion and may become a basis of division for the entire group. Like the division between the sexes, age groups stand midway between the organic and the rational. For example, in Sparta around 200 B.C. political parties were designated as the elders, the young men, and the youngsters. Similarly, among different primitive peoples one finds men organized in age-groups, each of which has a special social significance and a special way of life. The basis of this solidarity is entirely personal and impersonal at the same time.

Obviously, age-groups provide such a basis of solidarity only when the culture is still without an extensive intellectual life. For this would immediately foster the unfolding of individual intellectual differences, of differences in the development of ideas, of political parties depending on ideologies. And as a result individuals of quite different age-groups would feel that they belong together. It is, indeed, this lack of an acquired education which is one of the reasons why youth as such shows a certain solidarity, why young people are attracted to one another much more so than are older people. Youths are often surprisingly indifferent towards each other's individuality.

The division by age-groups is a cause, though an extremely awkward cause, of group-formation, which combines personal and objective criteria. The organic and rational causes of group-formation, whose contrast is usually emphasized, are here brought together. A purely physiological aspect of individuals, their age, becomes a basis for joint action. Individuals are consciously brought together on this basis. Age is an entirely natural and personal fact which here works as a completely objective principle. It is understandable that this fact gains great importance for the social structure of primitive peoples, since age is relieved of all elements of caprice, since the fact of age is immediately apparent and as such readily determines one's outlook on life.

Group-affiliations which are formed according to objective criteria constitute a superstructure which develops over and above those group-affiliations which are formed according to natural, immediately given criteria. One of the simplest examples is the original cohesion of the family-group which is modified in such a way that the individual member introduces his family into other groups. One of the most complex examples is the "republic of scholars" which is in part an intellectual and in part a real association of all persons, who join in the pursuit of such a highly general goal as knowledge. In all other respects these scholars belong to the most varied groups—with regard to their nationality, their personal and special interests, their social position, and so on.

The period of the Renaissance demonstrated most clearly the power of intellectual and educational interests to bring together in a new community like-minded people from a large variety of different groups. Humanistic interests broke down the medieval isolation of social groups and of estates. They gave to people who represented the most diverse points of view and who often remained faithful to the most diverse occupations, a common interest in ideas and in knowledge. This common interest, whether one of active pursuit or of passive appreciation, cut across all previously established forms and institutions of medieval life. Humanism at that time entered the experience of all peoples and groups from the outside as something that was equally strange to all. And this very fact made it possible for Humanism to become a common area of interest for them all, or at any rate for certain people among them.

For example, the idea prevailed that all things famous belonged together. This is shown by the collections of biographies which began to appear in the 14th century. These biographies described in a single work people of excellence from many fields, whether they were theologians, or artists, statesmen or philologists. In their way, the secular rulers gave recognition to this new rank-order, which involved a new analysis and synthesis of social groups. Robert of Naples befriends Petrarch and makes him a gift of his own purple cape.

Two hundred years later this social action has shed its lyric guise and has assumed a more objective and strictly limited form. Francis I of France wanted to make that social group, which was concerned exclusively with the higher learning, completely independent and autonomous even in relation to the universities. These universities were charged with the education of theologians and jurists. But Francis I proposed a separate academy, whose members would devote themselves to investigation and teaching without having any practical purpose in mind. It was a consequence of this separation of what is intellectually significant from every other value that the Venetian Senate accompanied the extradition of Giordano Bruno with this letter to the Papal Court. Bruno was one of the worst heretics, it said, he had done the most reprehensible things, he had led a dissolute, even a devilish life. In other respects, however, he was one of the most distinguished intellects that could be imagined, a man of rare learning and spiritual greatness.

The restlessness and the adventurous spirit of the Humanists, their often unstable and unreliable character, were in keeping with the independence of the intellect, which was the central focus of their lives. This independence made them indifferent to all other obligations usually incumbent upon men. The individual humanist spent his life in a colorful variety of life-situations. This way of life was symbolic of the movement of Humanism, which embraced the poor scholar and the monk, the powerful General and the brilliant Duchess, in a single framework of intellectual interests. Thereby the way was opened for a most important, further differentiation of the social structure, though there are precedents for such a development in antiquity.

Criteria derived from knowledge came to serve as the basis of social differentiation and group-formation. Up to the Renaissance, social differentiation and group-formation had been based either on criteria of self-interest (economic, military, and political in a broad or narrow sense), or of emotion (religious), or of a mixture of both (familial). Now, intellectual and rational interests came to form groups, whose members were gathered from many other social groups. This is a striking example of the general trend, that the formation of groups, which has occurred more recently, often bears a rational character, and that the substantive purpose of these groups is the result of conscious reflection and intelligent planning. Thus, secondary groups, because of their rational formation, give the appearance of being determined by a purpose, since their affairs revolve around intellectually articulated interests.

MULTIPLE GROUP-AFFILIATIONS WHICH ARE NOT IN CONFLICT

The number of different social groups in which the individual participates is one of the earmarks of culture. The modern person belongs first of all to his parental family, then to his family of procreation and thereby also to the family of his wife. Beyond this he belongs to his occupational group, which often involves him in several interest-groups. For example, in an occupation that embraces both supervisory and subordinate personnel, each person participates in the affairs of his particular business, department office, etc., each of which comprises higher and lower employees. Moreover, a person also participates in a group made up of similarly situated employees from several, different firms. Then, a person is likely to be aware of his citizenship, of the fact that he belongs to a particular social class. He is, moreover, a reserve-officer, he belongs to a few clubs and engages in a social life which puts him in touch with different social groups. This is a great variety of groups. Some of these groups are integrated. Others are, however, so arranged that one group appears as the original focus of an individual's affiliation, from which he then turns toward affiliation with other, quite different groups on the basis of his special qualities, which distinguish him from other members of his primary group. His bond with the primary group may well continue to exist, like one aspect of a complex image, which retains its original time-space coordinates though the image itself has long since become established psychologically as an objective configuration in its own right.

During the Middle Ages the individual had certain typical opportunities of group-affiliation, over and above his citizenship in his community. The Hansa League was an association of cities, which permitted the individual to participate in a wide range of activities that not only extended beyond each individual city but far beyond the boundaries of the German Reich. Likewise, the medieval guilds were not organized in accordance with the jurisdiction of towns; instead, affiliation of the individual with the guild had no reference to his status as a citizen within a town but involved him in an organization extending throughout all of Germany. And journeymen-associations extended beyond the boundaries of the guilds, just as the guilds extended their jurisdiction beyond the boundaries of the towns.

These patterns [of group-affiliation] had the peculiarity of treating the individual as a member of a group rather than as an individual, and of incorporating him thereby in other groups as well. An association which is derived from the membership of other associations places the individual in a number of groups. But these groups do not overlap and the problems which they entail for the individual differ from the problems posed by the sociological constellations which will be discussed subsequently. Group-formation during the Middle Ages was inspired by the idea that only equals could be associated, however often the practice deviated from the theory. This idea obviously was connected with the completeness with which medieval man surrendered himself to his group-affiliation. Hence, cities allied themselves first of all with cities, monasteries with monasteries, guilds with related guilds. This was an extension of the equalitarian principle, even though in fact members of one corporate body may not have been the equals of members from an allied group. But as *members of a corporate body* they were equals. The alliance was valid only in so far as this was the case, and the fact that the members were individually differentiated in other respects was irrelevant. This way of doing things was extended to alliances between *different* groups, but these groups were regarded even then as equal powers within the new alliance. The individual as such was not a fact in such an alliance; hence his indirect participation in it did not add an individuating element to his personality. Nevertheless, as will be discussed later, this was the transitional step from the medieval type to the modern type of group-formation. The medieval group in the strict sense was one which did not permit the individual to become a member in other groups, a rule which the old guilds and the early medieval corporations probably illustrate most clearly. The modern type of group-formation makes it possible for the isolated individual to become a member in whatever number of groups he chooses. Many consequences resulted from this.

GROUP-AFFILIATIONS AND THE INDIVIDUAL PERSONALITY

The groups with which the individual is affiliated constitute a system of coordinates, as it were, such that each new group with which he becomes affiliated circumscribes him more exactly and more unambiguously. To belong to any one of these groups leaves the individual considerable leeway. But the larger the number of groups to which an individual belongs, the more improbable is it that other persons will exhibit the same combination of group-affiliations, that these particular groups will "intersect" once again [in a second individual]. Concrete objects lose their individual characteristics as we subsume them under a general concept in accordance with one of their attributes. And concrete objects regain their individual characteristics as other concepts are emphasized under which their several attributes may be subsumed. To speak Platonically, each thing has a part in as many ideas as it has manifold attributes, and it achieves thereby its individual determination. There is an analogous relationship between the individual and the groups with which he is affiliated.

A concrete object with which we are confronted has been called the synthesis of perceptions. And each object has a more enduring configuration, so to speak, the more various the perceptions are, which have entered into it. Similarly as individuals, we form the personality out of particular elements of life, each of which has arisen from, or is interwoven with, society. This personality is subjectivity par excellence in the sense that it combines the elements of culture in an individual manner. There is here a reciprocal relation between the subjective and the objective. As the person becomes affiliated with a social group, he surrenders himself to it. A synthesis of such subjective affiliations creates a group in an objective sense. But the person also regains his individuality, because his pattern of participation is unique; hence the fact of multiple group-participation creates in turn a new subjective element. Causal determination of, and purposive actions by, the individual appear as two sides of the same coin. The genesis of the personality has been interpreted as the point of intersection for innumerable social influences, as the end-product of heritages derived from the most diverse groups and periods of adjustment. Hence, individuality was interpreted as that particular set of constituent elements which in their quality and combination make up the individual. But as the individual becomes affiliated with social groups in accordance with the diversity of his drives and interests, he thereby expresses and returns what he has "received," though he does so consciously and on a higher level.

As the individual leaves his established position within *one* primary group, he comes to stand at a point at which many groups "intersect." The individual as a moral personality comes to be circumscribed in an entirely new way, but he also faces new problems. The security and lack of ambiguity in his former position gives way to uncertainty in the conditions of his life. This is the sense of an old English proverb which says: he who speaks two languages is a knave. It is true that external and internal conflicts arise through the multiplicity of group-affiliations, which threaten the individual with psychological tensions or even a schizophrenic break. But it is also true that multiple group-affiliations can strengthen the individual and reenforce the integration of his personality. Conflicting and integrating tendencies are mutually reenforcing. Conflicting tendencies can arise just because the individual has a core of inner unity. The ego can become more clearly conscious of this unity, the more he is confronted with the task of reconciling within himself a diversity of group-interests. The effect of marriage on both spouses is that they belong to several families; this has always been a source of enrichment, a way of expanding one's interests and relationships but also of intensifying one's conflicts. These conflicts may induce the individual to make internal and external adjustments, but also to assert himself energetically.

In primitive clan-organizations the individual would participate in several groups in such a way that he belonged to the kinship or totemic group of his mother, but also to the narrower, familial or local association of his father. Now these simple people are not equal to conflicts such as those just mentioned, which is basically due to the fact that they lack a firm awareness of themselves as personalities. With peculiar purposefulness these two kinds of association are therefore so differently arranged that they do not encroach upon each other. Relationships on the maternal side have a more ideal, spiritual nature, whereas on the paternal side they are real, material and directly effective. In the case of the Australian aborigines, i.e., the Hereros, and among many other hunting tribes, maternal kinship, and similarly the totemic association, do not constitute a basis for community-living. They have no effect on daily life, but only on festive occasions of deep significance, such as marriage ceremonies and ceremonies occasioned by death and blood revenge. The last of these has an ideal, abstract character in the lives of the primitive peoples. The totemic association is transmitted through maternal descent and, therefore, it is often scattered through many tribes and hordes. It is held together only by common taboos on food and common ceremonials, and particularly by means of special names and special symbols on weapons. On the other hand, the paternal kinship-relations encompass all of daily life, waging war, alliances, inheritance, hunting, and so on. They do not have these taboos and symbols and do not need them, because the bond of a community in one locality and the convergence of their direct interests provide the basis for a sense of group-cohesion. At this stage, each connection which is not local usually assumes a more ideal character. It is the sign of a higher social development that group-cohesion can transcend local ties and yet be thoroughly realistic and concrete. But if the individual in a primitive tribe belongs to both the paternal-local group and to the maternal clan, these groups must be separated from each other in terms of the distinctly concrete or distinctly abstract values which they embody. Given the undifferentiated character of the primitive mind, this separation is a precondition for the possibility that the same individual belongs to both groups.

25.

The Strength of Weak Ties

MARK S. GRANOVETTER, 1973

A fundamental weakness of current sociological theory is that it does not relate micro-level interactions to macro-level patterns in any convincing way. Large-scale statistical, as well as qualitative, studies offer a good deal of insight into such macro phenomena as social mobility, community organization, and political structure. At the micro level, a large and increasing body of data and theory offers useful and illuminating ideas about what transpires within the confines of the small group. But how interaction in small groups aggregates to form large-scale patterns eludes us in most cases.

I will argue, in this paper, that the analysis of processes in interpersonal networks provides the most fruitful micro-macro bridge. In one way or another, it is through these networks that small-scale interaction becomes translated into large-scale patterns, and that these, in turn, feed back into small groups.

Sociometry, the precursor of network analysis, has always been curiously peripheral—invisible, really—in sociological theory. This is partly because it has usually been studied and applied only as a branch of social psychology; it is also because of the inherent complexities of precise network analysis. We have had neither the theory nor the measurement and sampling techniques to move sociometry from the usual small-group level to that of larger structures. While a number of stimulating and suggestive studies have recently moved in this direction (Bott 1957; Mayer 1961; Milgram 1967; Boissevain 1968; Mitchell 1969), they do not treat structural issues in much theoretical detail. Studies which do so usually involve a level of technical complexity appropriate to such forbidding sources as the *Bulletin of Mathematical Biophysics*, where the original motivation for the study of networks was that of developing a theory of

Reprinted with the permission of The University of Chicago, from "The Strength of Weak Ties," *American Journal of Sociology* 78(6):1360–80, by Mark Granovetter. Copyright © 1973 The University of Chicago Press.

This paper originated in discussions with Harrison White, to whom I am indebted for many suggestions and ideas. Earlier drafts were read by Ivan Chase, James Davis, William Michelson, Nancy Lee, Peter Rossi, Charles Tilly, and an anonymous referee; their criticisms resulted in significant improvements.

neural, rather than social, interaction (see the useful review of this literature by Coleman [1960]; also Rapoport [1963]).

The strategy of the present paper is to choose a rather limited aspect of small-scale interaction—the strength of interpersonal ties—and to show, in some detail, how the use of network analysis can relate this aspect to . . . social cohesion. . . . While the analysis is essentially qualitative, a mathematically inclined reader will recognize the potential for models; mathematical arguments, leads, and references are suggested mostly in footnotes.

THE STRENGTH OF TIES

Most intuitive notions of the "strength" of an interpersonal tie should be satisfied by the following definition: the strength of a tie is a (probably linear) combination of the amount of time, the emotional intensity, the intimacy (mutual confiding), and the reciprocal services which characterize the tie. Each of these is somewhat independent of the other, though the set is obviously highly intracorrelated. Discussion of operational measures of and weights attaching to each of the four elements is postponed to future empirical studies. It is sufficient for the present purpose if most of us can agree, on a rough intuitive basis, whether a given tie is strong, weak, or absent.

Consider, now, any two arbitrarily selected individuals—call them A and B—and the set, $S = C, D, E, \ldots$, of all persons with ties to either *or* both of them. The hypothesis which enables us to relate dyadic ties to larger structures is: the stronger the tie between A and B, the larger the proportion of individuals in S to whom they will *both* be tied, that is, connected by a weak or strong tie. This overlap in their friendship circles is predicted to be least when their tie is absent, most when it is strong, and intermediate when it is weak.

The proposed relationship results, first, from the tendency (by definition) of stronger ties to involve larger time commitments. If A-B and A-C ties exist, then the amount of time C spends with B depends (in part) on the amount A spends with B and C, respectively. (If the events "A is with B" and "A is with C" were independent, then the event "C is with A and B" would have probability equal to the product of their probabilities. For example, if A and B are together 60% of the time, and A and C 40%, then C, A, and B would be together 24% of the time. Such independence would be less likely after than before B and C became acquainted.) If C and B have no relationship, common strong ties to A will probably bring them into interaction and generate one. Implicit here is Homans's idea that "the more frequently persons interact with one another, the stronger their sentiments of friendship for one another are apt to be" (1950, p. 133).

The hypothesis is made plausible also by empirical evidence that the stronger the tie connecting two individuals, the more similar they are, in various ways (Berscheid and Walster 1969, pp. 69–91; Bramel 1969, pp. 9–16; Brown 1965, pp. 71–90; Laumann 1968; Newcomb 1961, chap. 5; Precker 1952). Thus, if strong ties connect *A* to *B* and *A* to *C*, both *C* and *B*, being similar to *A*, are probably similar to one another, increasing the likelihood of a friendship once they have met. Applied in reverse, these two factors—time and similarity—indicate why weaker *A-B* and *A-C* ties make a *C-B* tie less likely than strong ones: *C* and *B* are less likely to interact and less likely to be compatible if they do.

The theory of cognitive balance, as formulated by Heider (1958) and especially by Newcomb (1961, pp. 4–23), also predicts this result. If strong ties *A-B* and *A-C* exist, and if *B* and *C* are aware of one another, anything short of a positive tie would introduce a "psychological strain" into the situation since *C* will want his own feelings to be congruent with those of his good friend, *A*, and similarly, for *B* and *his* friend, *A*. Where the ties are weak, however, such consistency is psychologically less crucial. (On this point see also Homans [1950, p. 255] and Davis [1963, p. 448].)

Some direct evidence for the basic hypothesis exists (Kapferer 1969, p. 229 n.; Laumann and Schuman 1967; Rapoport and Horvath 1961; Rapoport 1963). This evidence is less comprehensive than one might hope. In addition, however, certain inferences from the hypothesis have received empirical support. Description of these inferences will suggest some of the substantive implications of the above argument.

WEAK TIES IN DIFFUSION PROCESSES

To derive implications for large networks of relations, it is necessary to frame the basic hypothesis more precisely. This can be done by investigating the possible triads consisting of strong, weak, or absent ties among *A, B,* and any arbitrarily chosen friend of either or both (i.e., some member of the set *S,* described above). A thorough mathematical model would do this in some detail, suggesting probabilities for various types. This analysis becomes rather involved, however, and it is sufficient for my purpose in this paper to say that the triad which is most *unlikely* to occur, under the hypothesis stated above, is that in which *A* and *B* are strongly linked, *A* has a strong tie to some friend *C,* but the tie between *C* and *B* is absent. This triad is shown in Figure 25.1. To see the consequences of this assertion, I will exaggerate it in what follows by supposing that the triad shown *never* occurs—that is, that the *B-C* tie is always present (whether weak or strong), given the other two strong ties. Whatever

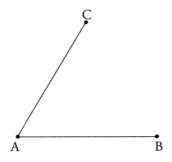

FIGURE 25.1 Forbidden Triad

results are inferred from this supposition should tend to occur in the degree that the triad in question tends to be absent.

Some evidence exists for this absence. Analyzing 651 sociograms, Davis (1970, p. 845) found that in 90% of them triads consisting of two mutual choices and one nonchoice occurred less than the expected random number of times. If we assume that mutual choice indicates a strong tie, this is strong evidence in the direction of my argument.[1] Newcomb (1961, pp. 160–65) reports that in triads consisting of dyads expressing mutual "high attraction," the configuration of three strong ties became increasingly frequent as people knew one another longer and better; the frequency of the triad pictured in Figure 25.1 is not analyzed, but it is implied that processes of cognitive balance tended to eliminate it.

The significance of this triad's absence can be shown by using the concept of a "bridge"; this is a line in a network which provides the *only* path between two points (Harary, Norman, and Cartwright 1965, p. 198). Since, in general, each person has a great many contacts, a bridge between A and B provides the only route along which information or influence can flow from any contact of A to any contact of B, and, consequently, from anyone connected *indirectly* to A to anyone connected indirectly to B. Thus, in the study of diffusion, we can expect bridges to assume an important role.

Now, if the stipulated triad is absent, it follows that, except under unlikely conditions, *no strong tie is a bridge.* Consider the strong tie *A-B:* if A has another strong tie to C, then forbidding the triad of Figure 25.1 implies that a tie exists between C and B, so that the path *A-C-B* exists between A and B; hence, *A-B* is not a bridge. A strong tie can be a bridge, therefore, *only if* neither party to it has any *other* strong ties, unlikely in a social network of any size (though

---

1. This assumption is suggested by one of Davis's models (1970, p. 846) and made explicitly by Mazur (1971). It is not obvious, however.

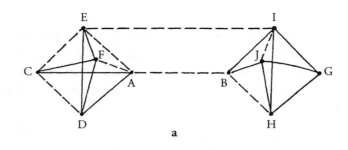

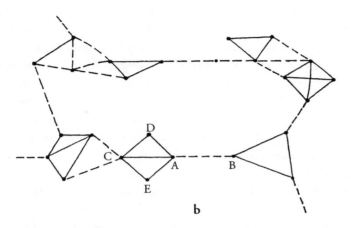

FIGURE 25.2 Local Bridges. a. Degree 3. b. Degree 13.

———— strong tie   – – – weak tie

possible in a small group). Weak ties suffer no such restriction, though they are certainly not automatically bridges. What is important, rather, is that all bridges are weak ties.

In large networks it probably happens only rarely, in practice, that a specific tie provides the *only* path between two points. The bridging function may nevertheless be served *locally*. In Figure 25.2a, for example, the tie *A-B* is not strictly a bridge, since one can construct the path *A-E-I-B* (and others). Yet, *A-B* is the shortest route to *B* for *F, D,* and *C.* This function is clearer in Figure 25.2b. Here, *A-B* is, for *C, D,* and others, not only a local bridge to *B*, but, in most real instances of diffusion, a much more likely and efficient path. Harary et al. point out that "there may be a distance [length of path] beyond which it is not feasible for *u* to communicate with *v* because of costs or distortions entailed in each act of transmission. If *v* does not lie within this critical distance, then he will not receive messages originating with *u*" (1965, p. 159). I will refer to a tie as a "local bridge of degree *n*" if *n* represents the shortest path between its two points (other than itself), and *n* > 2. In Figure 25.2a, *A-B* is a local bridge of degree 3, in 25.2 *b*, of degree 13. As with bridges in a highway system, a local bridge in a social network will be more significant as a connection between two sectors to the extent that it is the only alternative for many people—that is, as its degree increases. A bridge in the absolute sense is a local one of infinite degree. By the same logic used above, only weak ties may be local bridges.

Suppose, now, that we adopt Davis's suggestion that "in interpersonal flows of most any sort the probability that 'whatever it is' will flow from person *i* to person *j* is (*a*) directly proportional to the number of all-positive (friendship) paths connecting *i* and *j*; and (*b*) inversely proportional to the length of such paths" (1969, p. 549). The significance of weak ties, then, would be that those which are local bridges create more, and shorter, paths. Any given tie may, hypothetically, be removed from a network; the number of paths broken and the changes in average path length resulting between arbitrary pairs of points (with some limitation on length of path considered) can then be computed. The contention here is that removal of the average weak tie would do more "damage" to transmission probabilities than would that of the average strong one.

Intuitively speaking, this means that whatever is to be diffused can reach a larger number of people, and traverse greater social distance (i.e., path length), when passed through weak ties rather than strong. If one tells a rumor to all his close friends, and they do likewise, many will hear the rumor a second and third time, since those linked by strong ties tend to share friends. If the motivation to spread the rumor is dampened a bit on each wave of retelling, then the rumor moving through strong ties is much more likely to be limited to a few cliques than that going via weak ones; bridges will not be crossed.

WEAK TIES AND COMMUNITY ORGANIZATION

. . . I would like to develop my argument further by analyzing, in this section, why some communities organize for common goals easily and effectively whereas others seem unable to mobilize resources, even against dire threats. The Italian community of Boston's West End, for example, was unable to even *form* an organization to fight against the "urban renewal" which ultimately destroyed it. This seems especially anomalous in view of Gans's description of West End social structure as cohesive (1962).

Variations in culture and personality are often cited to explain such anomalies. Gans contrasts "lower"-, "working"-, and "middle"-class subcultures, concluding that only the last provides sufficient trust in leaders and practice in working toward common goals to enable formation of an effective organization. Thus, the working-class West End could not resist urban renewal (pp. 229–304). Yet, numerous well-documented cases show that *some* working-class communities have mobilized quite successfully against comparable or lesser threats (Dahl 1961, pp. 192–99; Keyes 1969; Davies 1966, chap. 4).[3] I would suggest, as a sharper analytical tool, examination of the network of ties comprising a community to see whether aspects of its structure might facilitate or block organization.

Imagine, to begin with, a community completely partitioned into cliques, such that each person is tied to every other in his clique and to none outside. Community organization would be severely inhibited. Leafletting, radio announcements, or other methods could insure that everyone was *aware* of some nascent organization; but studies of diffusion and mass communication have shown that people rarely *act* on mass-media information unless it is also transmitted through personal ties (Katz and Lazarsfeld 1955; Rogers 1962); otherwise one has no particular reason to think that an advertised product or an organization should be taken seriously. Enthusiasm for an organization in one clique, then, would not spread to others but would have to develop independently in *each one* to ensure success.

The problem of trust is closely related. I would propose that whether a person trusts a given leader depends heavily on whether there exist intermediary personal contacts who can, from their own knowledge, assure him that the leader is trustworthy, and who can, if necessary, intercede with the leader or his lieutenants on his behalf. Trust in leaders is integrally related to the *capacity to predict and affect their behavior.* Leaders, for their part, have little motivation to be responsive or even trustworthy toward those to whom they have no direct or indirect connection. Thus, network fragmentation, by reducing drastically the number of paths from any leader to his potential followers, would inhibit trust in such leaders. This inhibition, furthermore, would not be entirely irrational.

Could the West End's social structure really have been of this kind? Note first that while the structure hypothesized is, by definition, extremely fragmented, this is evident only at a macroscopic level—from an "aerial view" of the network. The local phenomenon is cohesion. (Davis [1967] also noted this paradox, in a related context.) An analyst studying such a group by participant observation might never see the extent of fragmentation, especially if the cliques were not earmarked by ethnic, cultural, or other visible differences. In the nature of participant observation, one is likely to get caught up in a fairly restricted circle; a few useful contacts are acquired and relied on for introduction to others. The "problem of entry into West End society was particularly vexing," Gans writes. But eventually, he and his wife "were welcomed by one

---

3. This point was brought to my attention by Richard Wolfe.

of our neighbors and became friends with them. As a result they invited us to many of their evening gatherings and introduced us to other neighbors, relatives and friends. . . . As time went on . . . other West Enders . . . introduced me to relatives and friends, although *most* of the social gatherings at which I participated were those of our *first* contact and their circle" (1962, pp. 340–41; emphasis supplied). Thus, his account of cohesive groups is not *inconsistent* with overall fragmentation.

Now, suppose that all ties in the West End were either strong or absent, and that the triad of Figure 25.1 did not occur. Then, for any ego, all his friends were friends of one another, and all their friends were ego's friends as well. Unless each person was strongly tied to *all* others in the community, network structure did indeed break down into the isolated cliques posited above. (In terms of Davis's mathematical treatment, the overall network was "clusterable," with unique clusters [1967, p. 186].) Since it is unlikely that anyone could sustain more than a few dozen strong ties, this would, in fact, have been the result.

Did strong ties take up enough of the West Enders' social time to make this analysis even approximately applicable? Gans reported that "sociability is a routinized gathering of a relatively unchanging peer group of family members and friends that takes place several times a week." Some "participate in informal cliques and in clubs made up of unrelated people. . . . In number, and in the amount of time devoted to them, however, these groups are much less important than the family circle" (1962, pp. 74, 80). Moreover, two common sources of weak ties, formal organizations and work settings, did not provide them for the West End; organization membership was almost nil (pp. 104–7) and few worked within the area itself, so that ties formed at work were not relevant to the community (p. 122).

Nevertheless, in a community marked by geographic immobility and life-long friendships (p. 19) it strains credulity to suppose that each person would not have known a great many others, so that there would have been *some* weak ties. The question is whether such ties were bridges. If *none* were, then the community would be fragmented in exactly the same way as described above, except that the cliques would then contain weak as well as strong ties. (This follows, again, from Davis's analysis of "clusterability," with strong and weak ties called "positive" and absent ones "negative" [1967].) Such a pattern is made plausible by the lack of ways in the West End to *develop* weak ties other than by meeting friends of friends (where "friend" includes relatives)—in which case the new tie is automatically not a bridge. It is suggested, then, that for a community to have many weak ties which bridge, there must be several distinct ways or contexts in which people may form them. The case of Charlestown, a working-class community which successfully organized against the urban renewal plan of the same city (Boston) against which the West End was powerless, is instructive in this respect: unlike the West End, it had a rich organizational life, and most male residents worked within the area (Keyes 1969, chap. 4).

In the absence of actual network data, all this is speculation. The hard information needed to show either that the West End was fragmented or that communities which organized successfully were not, and that both patterns were due to the strategic role of weak ties, is not at hand and would not have been simple to collect. Nor has comparable information been collected in *any* context. But a theoretical framework has, at least, been suggested, with which one could not only carry out analyses post hoc, but also *predict* differential capacity of communities to act toward common goals. A rough principle with which to begin such an investigation might be: the more local bridges (per person?) in a community and the greater their degree, the more cohesive the community and the more capable of acting in concert. Study of the origins and nature (strength and content, for example) of such bridging ties would then offer unusual insight into the social dynamics of the community.

CONCLUSION

The major implication intended by this paper is that the personal experience of individuals is closely bound up with larger-scale aspects of social structure, well beyond the purview or control of particular individuals. Linkage of micro and macro levels is thus no luxury but of central importance to the development of sociological theory. Such linkage generates paradoxes: weak ties, often denounced as generative of alienation (Wirth 1938) are here seen as indispensable to individuals' opportunities and to their integration into communities; strong ties, breeding local cohesion, lead to overall fragmentation. Paradoxes are a welcome antidote to theories which explain everything all too neatly.

The model offered here is a very limited step in the linking of levels; it is a fragment of a theory. Treating only the *strength* of ties ignores, for instance, all the important issues involving their content. What is the relation between strength and degree of specialization of ties, or between strength and hierarchical structure? How can "negative" ties be handled? Should tie strength be developed as a continuous variable? What is the developmental sequence of network structure over time?

As such questions are resolved, others will arise. Demography, coalition structure, and mobility are just a few of the variables which would be of special importance in developing micro-macro linkage with the help of network analysis; how these are related to the present discussion needs specification. My contribution here is mainly, then, exploratory and programmatic, its primary purpose being to generate interest in the proposed program of theory and research.

REFERENCES

Berscheid, E., and E. Walster. 1969. *Interpersonal Attraction.* Reading, Mass.: Addison-Wesley.

Boissevain, J. 1968. "The Place of Non-Groups in the Social Sciences." *Man* 3 (December): 542–56.

Bott, Elizabeth. 1957. *Family and Social Networks.* London: Tavistock.

Bramel, D. 1969. "Interpersonal Attraction, Hostility and Perception." In *Experimental Social Psychology,* edited by Judson Mills. New York: Macmillan.

Brown, Roger. 1965. *The Mobile Professors.* Washington, D.C.: American Council on Education.

Coleman, J. S. 1960. "The Mathematical Study of Small Groups." In *Mathematical Thinking in the Measurement of Behavior,* edited by H. Solomon. Glencoe: Free Press.

Coleman, J. S., E. Katz, and H. Menzel. 1966. *Medical Innovation: A Diffusion Study.* Indianapolis: Bobbs-Merrill.

Dahl, Robert. 1961. *Who Governs?* New Haven, Conn.: Yale University Press.

Davies, J. C. 1966. *Neighborhood Groups and Urban Renewal.* New York: Columbia University Press.

Davis, James A. 1963. "Structural Balance, Mechanical Solidarity and Interpersonal Relations." *American Journal of Sociology* 68 (January): 444–62.

———. 1967. "Clustering and Structural Balance in Graphs." *Human Relations* 20 (May): 181–87.

———. 1970. "Clustering and Hierarchy in Interpersonal Relations." *American Sociological Review* 35 (October): 843–52.

Davis, James A., and S. Leinhardt. 1971. "The Structure of Positive Interpersonal Relations in Small Groups." In *Sociological Theories in Progress,* vol. 2, edited by J. Berger, M. Zelditch, and B. Anderson. Boston: Houghton-Mifflin.

Gans, Herbert. 1962. *The Urban Villagers.* New York: Free Press.

Harary, F., R. Norman, and D. Cartwright. 1965. *Structural Models.* New York: Wiley.

Heider, F. 1958. *The Psychology of Interpersonal Relations.* New York: Wiley.

Homans, George. 1950. *The Human Group.* New York: Harcourt, Brace & World.

Kapferer, B. 1969. "Norms and the Manipulation of Relationships in a Work Context." In *Social Networks in Urban Situations,* edited by J. C. Mitchell. Manchester: Manchester University Press.

Katz, E., and P. Lazarsfeld. 1955. *Personal Influence.* New York: Free Press.

Keyes, L. C. 1969. *The Rehabilitation Planning Game.* Cambridge, Mass.: M.I.T. Press.

Laumann, Edward. 1968. "Interlocking and Radial Friendship Networks: A Cross-sectional Analysis." Mimeographed. Ann Arbor: University of Michigan.

Laumann, Edward, and H. Schuman. 1967. "Open and Closed Structures." Paper prepared for the 1967 ASA meeting. Mimeographed.

Mayer, Adrian. 1966. "The Significance of Quasi-Groups in the Study of Complex Societies." In *The Social Anthropology of Complex Societies,* edited by M. Banton. New York: Praeger.

Milgram, Stanley. 1967. "The Small-World Problem." *Psychology Today* 1 (May): 62–67.

Mitchell, J. Clyde. 1969. *Social Networks in Urban Situations.* Manchester: Manchester University Press.

Newcomb, T. M. 1961. *The Acquaintance Process.* New York: Holt, Rinehart & Winston.

Precker, Joseph. 1952. "Similarity of Valuings as a Factor in Selection of Peers and Near

Authority Figures." *Journal of Abnormal and Social Psychology* 47, suppl. (April): 406–14.

———. 1963. "Mathematical Models of Social Interaction." In *Handbook of Mathematical Psychology*, vol. 2, edited by R. Luce, R. Bush, and E. Galanter. New York: Wiley.

Rapoport, A., and W. Horvath. 1961. "A Study of a Large Sociogram." *Behavioral Science* 6:279–91.

Rogers, Everett. 1962. *Diffusion of Innovations*. New York: Free Press.

Wirth, Louis. 1938. "Urbanism as a Way of Life." *American Journal of Sociology* 44 (July): 1–24.

26.

Trust, Cohesion, and the Social Order

ERNEST GELLNER, 1987

There is one point at which the conventional Hobbesian and the Ibn Khal-dunian visions of the basis of social order are diametrically opposed. On the whole, the advantage lies with Ibn Khaldun.

The Hobbesian problem arises from the assumption that anarchy, absence of enforcement, leads to distrust and social disintegration. We are all familiar with the deductive model which sustains and re-enforces that argument, but there is a certain amount of interesting empirical evidence which points the other way. The paradox is: it is precisely anarchy which engenders trust or, if you want to use another name, which engenders social cohesion. It is effective government which destroys trust. This is a basic fact about the human condition, or at any rate about a certain range of real human conditions. It is the basic premise of Ibn Khaldun's sociology, which happens to be the greatest and most accurate analysis of traditional Muslim society.

The argument is that anarchy engenders trust and government destroys it; or, put in a more conventional way, that anarchy engenders cohesion. In this case, we have both an argument *and* an empirical illustration. The claim that anarchy engenders cohesion is well sustained empirically, but it can also be sustained by theoretical considerations. There is a powerful model which lends support to this contention. The model is constructed with the help of a number of factors actually corresponding to the realities prevailing in an important part of the world.

To begin with, assume the absence of any strong central authority. Secondly, add the ecological conditions which prevail in the arid zone, and which impel large and significant proportions of its inhabitants towards pastoralism. Thirdly, acknowledge the diffusion of a certain level of expectation concerning what life is meant to be like. The importance of this will emerge in due course. One might even reduce these factors to two, in so far as weak government can itself be seen as a corollary of pastoralism. Shepherds are hard to govern, because their wealth is on the hoof and they can easily escape author-

Reprinted with the permission of Basil Blackwell from "Trust, Cohesion and the Social Order," by Ernest Gellner. In *Trust: Making and Breaking Cooperative Relations,* edited by Diego Gambetta. Copyright © Basil Blackwell Ltd 1988. All rights reserved.

ity. Their mobility makes it possible to avoid taxation, to raid, and to elude oppression.

If you take these three points and work out the implications, the result is that those living on such terms cannot manage without cohesion. The argument runs: pastoralism implies that the major part of wealth is on the hoof. This means that it is easy to move it, but it also makes it easy to perform acts of robbery. Pastoral work is not labour intensive. Looking after 400 sheep is not very much harder than looking after 200 sheep. But pastoralism *is* defence intensive. What the shepherd does is protect the flock from jackals, hyenas, wolves, and above all from other shepherds. And the prospects of economic growth are very remarkable: all a shepherd needs to do in order to double his wealth is ambush another shepherd.

This is quite different from the relationship between agricultural sedentary producers, who can steal the harvest but cannot easily steal the fields. If they wish to enslave the people they defeat, they land themselves with grave problems of labour management. So the appeal of aggression for agricultural producers is much less, unless they are effectively centralized and can monopolize the means of coercion, and possess the machinery for controlling the subjugated population. But for a shepherd, the temptation to rob is very strong, immediate and unconditional, *and there is only one effective means of protecting oneself against this kind of aggression.*

This method is to gang up in a group, which in effect hangs up a notice saying: anyone who commits an act of aggression against any one of us must expect retaliation from us all, and not only will the aggressor himself be likely to suffer retaliation, but his entire group and all its members will be equally liable. And this notice is in effect posted by the very culture which pervades pastoral societies. It constitutes the code of honour which is familiar to all. So the gangs themselves do not need literally to put an announcement in the press or even on their tent. The culture, or specifically the obligation of feud which is inherent in it, does it for them.

To recapitulate: because these groups are mobile and live in difficult terrain, they are very difficult to tax. Consequently there is no government, there being no resources to sustain it. Because there is no government, the groups have to look after themselves: hence they are strong, and government is weak or absent. The argument is a kind of circle, but it reflects a self-perpetuating social reality. Once this kind of system is established, it manifests itself as the highly characteristic arid zone pattern of strong, self-policing, self-defending, politically participating groups, generally known as tribes. They defend themselves by the threat of indiscriminate retaliation against the group of any aggressor. Hence they also police themselves and their own members, for they do not wish to provoke retaliation. Inside each such group, order is maintained by a similar mechanism: the group itself divides into sub-groups which each exercise restraint over the others.

This is a teleological or 'functional' argument, of course, open to the objection that the *need* for the cohesion of social groups will not automatically engender that cohesion. In the absence of a designer and creator, the favourite logical substitutes are our old friends, natural selection and rational foresight. Presumably each of them operates, though no one really knows in what proportion. All one does know is that a system corresponding to this model—a system of mutually supportive or, in the language of the present discussion, of mutually *trusting* 'kinsmen'—is conspicuously present, or was traditionally present. The 'kinsmen' need not literally be such, of course, but they do tend to be cohesive, which is a shorthand way of saying that, on the whole, they trust each other.

The argument runs thus: a single shepherd can protect himself against ambush by another shepherd only by ganging up with (say) 20 similar shepherds, and hanging out the invisible but unmistakable sign threatening retaliation against any group whose members attack any one member of the first group. Thereby the other group is forced to police and restrain its own members. This argument *applies at all levels of size*. It can be repeated at the level of the unit itself: any single such herding camp of 20 members is extremely vulnerable to any coalition of others, and the only way it can protect itself is by *also* becoming part of a coalition. The coalition itself may have to be part of a meta-coalition, and so on. The result of all this is the very characteristic 'nesting' of similar units. The similarity is vertical as well as lateral: larger units resemble their own subgroup, just as groups resemble their 'peers' on the same level of size.

These units display a number of features: above all, they have a very high military participation ratio (see Andreski 1954). Basically, all adults take part in violence. They also have a high political participation ratio. All heads of households take part in assemblies. The same is true of culture. As a Kazakh scholar writing in Russian once put it, every member of the tribe is simultaneously senator, judge, juryman, minstrel, and poet of his society (see Tolybekov 1959). Both culture and political participation are evenly diffused.

This of course makes these societies very attractive objects of romanticization by vicarious populists from other societies. But there are other, and seemingly paradoxical, cultural features that should not be overlooked. One of them is this: although they are cohesive, they are also very treacherous. Treason is built into the working of such a society and its culture and, if carried out properly and in due form, no stigma attaches to it. This kind of society could not possibly function without treason. Treason within it performs the same role that price changes perform in a market society. It helps to maintain equilibrium through realignment. Just as a rise or fall in price ideally redirects resources to the point at which they are optimally deployed, so a realignment—treason, if you will—restores balance to the segmentary tribal world. An outnumbered clan C1, unable to hold its own within tribe T1, will leave T1 and join T2. Alternatively, members of T1, if they do not wish to see themselves weakened by such a loss, will arrange an internal adjustment in numbers to ensure that C1 henceforth is on reasonably equal terms with C2 or C3.

The balancing of units requires a certain equality of size. But the accidents of birth and health and so on ensure that the groups do not in fact maintain such a neat balance of reasonably equal size. Adjustments have to be made, and a rough equilibrium maintained. The adjustments *can* of course occur through dramatic forms of betrayal, but the interesting thing is that treason can also be heavily institutionalized and ritualized. An individual or group wishing to attach itself to a new and larger grouping does so by means of a ritual. This imposes a shame compulsion on the receiving group, which cannot honourably refuse the request.

What the system does require is that people's membership of groups be very clearly defined and visible *at any given time*. The feud, that is to say genetic revenge against a whole category of people, can only work if you know who falls within a given group and who does not. In Berber customary law, there is a rule that if homicide takes place, the *ten* closest agnates are immediately at risk, because they are equally 'culpable', even though they had nothing to do with the initial act and provocation. Supposing a cousin of mine commits a murder, and I truthfully proclaim that I am eleventh in order of proximity (the eleventh claimant to his inheritance, in other words), would this protect me? This question of mine was considered extremely funny. The actual number is not to be taken literally; there is no safety in arithmetic. But the membership of the group has to be clear, and indeed it *is* clear.

None the less, you *can* change your membership. There is nothing dishonourable about changing your group membership, which of course means changing your obligation to feud, and the risk of being a victim of feud, and the participation in giving or receiving blood money. It is done simply by making a public sacrifice—and it has to be public, that being the whole point of it—to another group, which thereafter is actually obliged to accept you. The same act takes you *out* of your previous group. Such reallocation, as long as it is clear and public, is perfectly honourable.

Similarly, the feuds between these kinds of groups do not always lead to actual violence. They can be settled by collective oath. And there it is perfectly honourable, in fact it is held to be pious, to let down your side if you are not convinced of the rightness of its cause. What you are *said* to be doing is showing that your fear of the supernatural is greater than your loyalty to the clan.

GELLNER

313

In practice, what you are probably doing is assessing that, in this case, it is better to let your side down, because victory at the oath might provoke too strong a coalition against it. Better pay blood money than involve ourselves in a conflict which may end badly. But, very significantly, such caution can be expressed as piety, so that in a sense morality militates against unconditioned cohesion. By reallocating yourself, by refusing to testify with your segment, you can risk splitting the group and so bring about realignment. The equilibrium-restoring mechanism works, but the calculation can be camouflaged as piety and reverence.

All this is coherent with certain well-known features of segmentary society. The great cult of hospitality, combined with a tendency to attack people, simply reflects a situation in which a stranger must be made into either an ally or an enemy. Either entertain a stranger or attack him (or perhaps both). The intermediate attitude of indifferent neutrality is not present in the logic of the situation. The result is a series of groups which are both cohesive and fragile, which perpetuate themselves by means of loyalty, and adjust to new realities by treason, whether formalized, pious, or sudden.

So far, I have been sketching features of the society which follow from its internal organization; they would apply to any tribal or segmentary society, irrespective of whether it is locked into a wider cultural unit, endowed with a literate civilization. So far, there is nothing specifically Muslim.

The other half of Ibn Khaldun's sociology of trust or cohesion, and of their absence, is that urban life is incompatible with trust and cohesion. Urban lineages and groups exist in name only, but Ibn Khaldun considers them to constitute a kind of sociological fraud. Urban populations may invoke a common ancestor, and say that they are of 'the house of such and such', but this is fraudulent because they are not in fact cohesive. They do not act as real corporate groups; they will not fight and feud together, and they will not defend themselves jointly. The very fact that they are urban means that they accept governmental authority, so that the vicious or beneficial circle (whichever way you look at it), which otherwise engenders cohesion and indeed also intermittent treason, does not operate amongst *them*. They are not allowed, by effective government, to act as corporate and violent bodies. They are atomized by their economic specialisms and political dependence. They have no effective groups they could betray.

Why need there be any cities, with their atomized and uncohesive, trustless populations? It is not entirely clear whether this is inherent in ecology or in culture. The standard of living to which the populations in the arid zone have long become accustomed, in the course of the last three millennia perhaps, is such that it assumes artisan production and trade. Unlike, say, East African nomads, the pastoral and rural populations of the arid zone are habituated to a certain level of equipment, from saddles and stirrups and tent equipment to decorations and carpets. But cultural equipment also counts; they also recognize, revere, and internalize a religion which involves literacy. Their entire military, productive, and cultural machinery presupposes large clusterings of artisans, plus some scribes, and the complementation of ecological diversity by trade. In brief, it presupposes *cities*.

The city is comprised of specialists. A specialist has no cousins; or rather, he does not have politically *effective* cousins. Cousin specialists stick to their lasts and do not easily combine in these self-defending, self-administering rural groups. At most, they occasionally meld into rather ephemeral urban *frondes*. They need peace to pursue their trade, and they accept oppression as the price of peace. A significant aspect of tribal culture, on the other hand, is that it despises the specialist, even (or especially) when it needs him—and even, interestingly enough, when he is held to be morally elevated. Tribesmen overtly and unambiguously despise the artisans, butchers, blacksmiths, and so on, who live amongst them, but they are also somewhat ambivalent about the religious arbitration specialists who in a sense are above them, and whom they nominally revere, not without irony.

There is an Algerian saying there is always a snake in a *zawiya*. The tribesmen look up to the holy men but they also laugh at them. Specialists *as such*, of any kind, are morally suspect. I was told in the central High Atlas that any clan which acquires the reputation of special wisdom is *therefore* deprived of the vote in tribal elections. Excellence of any kind is a form of specialization and that precludes full citizenship. The unspecialized human being constitutes the moral norm. It is he who can lose himself in a solitary unit, and gladly accept collective responsibility. By contrast, the specialists of the towns, for whom specialization is of the essence, are politically castrated and incapable of cohesion, and hence of self-government. Consequently they are also incapable of governing others.

The corollaries of this situation are worked out by Ibn Khaldun in a rather teleological but nevertheless perfectly accurate model. Given that the society as a whole needs a level of production and trade which presupposes urban centres, and given that urban centres (clusters of specialists) are quite incapable of social cohesion and hence of political and military effectiveness, what is to be done? What is done is that the tribes provide cities with rulers: the state is the gift of the tribe to the city. Economically, the tribe needs the city: politically, the city needs the tribe.

The city is made up of a market (artisans and traders), a mosque, and the citadel. The rulers in the citadel are the people who acquired the capacity or the tendency to trust each other, and hence to be cohesive, *by being ungoverned*. If you wish to govern, you must never have submitted to government yourself. Only the ungoverned condition of the savannah, desert, and mountain, engenders the kind of tribal group whose members trust each other and display cohesion.

This and this alone makes such groups capable both of government and self-government. Consequently, from time to time, some of them occupy the citadel. Once they are there, and this of course is the best known part of Ibn Khaldun's theory, they gradually lose that very cohesion they acquired when they were ungoverned, and which enabled them to rule. In his schematized version, this takes about three or four generations. They lose it in the process of governing and of benefiting from the privileges of government. After four generations or so, they are replaced by a new wave of as yet uncorrupted tribesmen, and so on forever and ever. It is a system of rotating corporate elites, in which the personnel changes but the structure remains the same. The city provides the tribesmen with the technical and cultural equipment on which they have come to rely: the tribesmen, or rather some of them, provide the city with government and defence, whilst the rest of the tribes govern themselves, and also constitute the permanent threat which keeps the city subservient to its temporary and rotated rulers.

REFERENCES

Andreski, S. 1954. *Military Organization and Society.* London: Routledge and Kegan Paul.
Ibn Khaldun. 1958. *The Muqaddima,* trans. F. Rosenthal. London: Routledge and Kegan Paul.
Tolybekov, S. E. 1959. *Obshtestvenno-ekonomicheskii stroi Kazakhov v XVII–XIX vekakh* (Socio-economic structure of the Kazakhs in the 17th–19th centuries). Alma-Ata.

27.

Individualism and Free Institutions

ALEXIS DE TOCQUEVILLE, 1848

HOW THE AMERICANS COMBAT INDIVIDUALISM
WITH FREE INSTITUTIONS

Despotism, which in its nature is fearful, sees the most certain guarantee of its own duration in the isolation of men, and it ordinarily puts all its care into isolating them. There is no vice of the human heart that agrees with it as much as selfishness: a despot readily pardons the governed for not loving him, provided that they do not love each other. He does not ask them to aid him in leading the state; it is enough that they do not aspire to direct it themselves. He calls those who aspire to unite their efforts to create common prosperity turbulent and restive spirits, and changing the natural sense of words, he names those who confine themselves narrowly to themselves good citizens.

Thus the vices to which despotism gives birth are precisely those that equality favors. These two things complement and aid each other in a fatal manner.

Equality places men beside one another without a common bond to hold them. Despotism raises barriers between them and separates them. It disposes them not to think of those like themselves, and for them it makes a sort of public virtue of indifference.

Despotism, which is dangerous in all times, is therefore particularly to be feared in democratic centuries.

It is easy to see that in these same centuries men have a particular need of freedom.

When citizens are forced to be occupied with public affairs, they are necessarily drawn from the midst of their individual interests, and from time to time, torn away from the site of themselves.

Reprinted with the permission of The University of Chicago, from *Democracy in America*, by Alexis de Tocqueville, edited, translated, and with an introduction by Harvey C. Mansfield and Delba Winthrop. Copyright © 2000 by The University of Chicago. All rights reserved.

317

From the moment when common affairs are treated in common, each man perceives that he is not as independent of those like him as he at first fancied, and that to obtain their support he must often lend them his cooperation.

When the public governs, there is no man who does not feel the value of public benevolence and who does not seek to capture it by attracting the esteem and affection of those in the midst of whom he must live.

Several of the passions that chill and divide hearts are then obliged to withdraw to the bottom of the soul and hide there. Haughtiness dissimulates; content does not dare come to light. Selfishness is afraid of itself.

Under a free government, since most public functions are elective, men who by the loftiness of their souls or the restiveness of their desires are cramped in private life, feel every day that they cannot do without the populace surrounding them.

It then happens that through ambition one thinks of those like oneself, and that often one's interest is in a way found in forgetting oneself. I know that one can object to me here with all the intrigues that arise in an election, the shameful means the candidates often make use of, and the calumnies their enemies spread. These are occasions for hatred, and they present themselves all the more often as elections become more frequent.

These evils are undoubtedly great, but they are passing, whereas the goods that arise with them stay.

The longing to be elected can momentarily bring certain men to make war on each other, but in the long term this same desire brings all men to lend each other a mutual support; and if it happens that an election accidentally divides two friends, the electoral system brings together in a permanent manner a multitude of citizens who would have always remained strangers to one another. Freedom creates particular hatreds, but despotism gives birth to general indifference.

The Americans have combated the individualism to which equality gives birth with freedom, and they have defeated it.

The legislators of America did not believe that, to cure a malady so natural to the social body in democratic times and so fatal, it was enough to accord to the nation as a whole a representation of itself; they thought that, in addition, it was fitting to give political life to each portion of the territory in order to multiply infinitely the occasions for citizens to act together and to make them feel every day that they depend on one another.

This was wisely done.

The general affairs of a country occupy only the principal citizens. They assemble in the same places only from time to time; and as it often happens that afterwards they lose sight of each other, lasting bonds among them are not established. But when it is a question of having the particular affairs of a district regulated by the men who inhabit it, the same individuals are always in contact and they are in a way forced to know each other and to take pleasure in each other.

Only with difficulty does one draw a man out of himself to interest him in the destiny of the whole state, because he understands poorly the influence that the destiny of the state can exert on his lot. But should it be necessary to pass a road through his property, he will see at first glance that he has come across a relation between this small public affair and his greatest private affairs, and he will discover, without anyone's showing it to him, the tight bond that here unites a particular interest to the general interest.

Thus by charging citizens with the administration of small affairs, much more than by leaving the government of great ones to them, one interests them in the public good and makes them see the need they constantly have for one another in order to produce it.

One can capture the favor of a people all at once by a striking action; but to win the love and respect of the populace that surrounds you, you must have a long succession of little services rendered, obscure good offices, a constant habit of benevolence, and a well-established reputation of disinterestedness.

Local freedoms, which make many citizens put value on the affection of their neighbors and those close to them, therefore constantly bring men closer to one another, despite the instincts that separate them, and force them to aid each other.

In the United States, the most opulent citizens take much care not to isolate themselves from the people; on the contrary, they constantly come close to them, they gladly listen to them and speak to them every day. They know that the rich in democracies always need the poor, and that in democratic times one ties the poor to oneself more by manners than by benefits. The very greatness of the benefits, which brings to light the difference in conditions, causes a secret irritation to those who profit from them; but simplicity of manners has almost irresistible charms: their familiarity carries one away and even their coarseness does not always displease.

At first this truth does not penetrate the minds of the rich. They ordinarily resist it as long as the democratic revolution lasts, and they do not accept it immediately even after this revolution is accomplished. They willingly consent to do good for the people, but they want to continue to hold them carefully at a distance. They believe that is enough; they are mistaken. They would thus ruin themselves without warming the hearts of the population that surrounds them. It does not ask of them the sacrifice of their money, but of their haughtiness.

One would say that in the United States there is no imagination that does not exhaust itself in inventing the means of increasing wealth and satisfying the needs of the public. The most enlightened inhabitants of each district constantly make use of their enlightenment to discover new secrets appropriate to increasing the common prosperity; and when they have found any, they hasten to pass them along to the crowd.

When examining up close the vices and weakness often displayed in America by those who govern, one is astonished at the growing prosperity of the people—and one is wrong. It is not the elected magistrate who makes American democracy prosper; but it prospers because the magistrate is elective.

It would be unjust to believe that the patriotism of the Americans and the zeal that each of them shows for the well-being of his fellow citizens have nothing real about them. Although private interest directs most human actions, in the United States as elsewhere, it does not rule all.

I must say that I often saw Americans make great and genuine sacrifices for the public, and I remarked a hundred times that, when needed, they almost never fail to lend faithful support to one another.

The free institutions that the inhabitants of the United States possess and the political rights of which they make so much use recall to each citizen constantly and in a thousand ways that he lives in society. At every moment they bring his mind back toward the idea that the duty as well as the interest of men is to render themselves useful to those like them; and as he does not see any particular reason to hate them, since he is never either their slave or their master, his heart readily leans to the side of benevolence. One is occupied with the general interest at first by necessity and then by choice; what was calculation becomes instinct; and by dint of working for the good of one's fellow citizens, one finally picks up the habit and taste of serving them.

Many people in France consider equality of conditions as the first evil and political freedom as the second. When they are obliged to submit to the one, they strive at least to escape the other. And I say that to combat the evils that equality can produce there is only one efficacious remedy: it is political freedom.

ON THE USE THAT THE AMERICANS MAKE OF ASSOCIATION IN CIVIL LIFE

I do not wish to speak of those political associations with the aid of which men seek to defend themselves against the despotic action of a majority or against the encroachments of royal power. I have already treated this subject elsewhere. It is clear that if each citizen, as he becomes individually weaker and consequently more incapable in isolation of preserving his freedom, does not learn the art of uniting with those like him to defend it, tyranny will necessarily grow with equality.

Here it is a question only of the associations that are formed in civil life and which have an object that is in no way political.

The political associations that exist in the United States form only a detail in the midst of the immense picture that the sum of associations presents there.

Americans of all ages, all conditions, all minds constantly unite. Not only do they have commercial and industrial associations in which all take part, but they also have a thousand other kinds: religious, moral, grave, futile, very general and very particular, immense and very small; Americans use associations to give fêtes, to found seminaries, to build inns, to raise churches, to distribute books, to send missionaries to the antipodes; in this manner they create hospitals, prisons, schools. Finally, if it is a question of bringing to light a truth or developing a sentiment with the support of a great example, they associate. Everywhere that, at the head of a new undertaking, you see the government in France and a great lord in England, count on it that you will perceive an association in the United States.

In America I encountered sorts of associations of which, I confess, I had no idea, and I often admired the infinite art with which the inhabitants of the United States managed to fix a common goal to the efforts of many men and to get them to advance to it freely.

I have since traveled through England, from which the Americans took some of their laws and many of their usages, and it appeared to me that there they were very far from making as constant and as skilled a use of association.

It often happens that the English execute very great things in isolation, whereas there is scarcely an undertaking so small that Americans do not unite for it. It is evident that the former consider association as a powerful means of action; but the latter seem to see in it the sole means they have of acting.

Thus the most democratic country on earth is found to be, above all, the one where men in our day have most perfected the art of pursuing the object of their common desires in common and have applied this new science to the most objects. Does this result from an accident or could it be that there in fact exists a necessary relation between associations and equality?

Aristocratic societies always include within them, in the midst of a multitude of individuals who can do nothing by themselves, a few very powerful and very wealthy citizens; each of these can execute great undertakings by himself.

In aristocratic societies men have no need to unite to act because they are kept very much together.

Each wealthy and powerful citizen in them forms as it were the head of a permanent and obligatory association that is composed of all those he holds in dependence to him, whom he makes cooperate in the execution of his designs.

In democratic peoples, on the contrary, all citizens are independent and weak; they can do almost nothing by themselves, and none of them can oblige those like themselves to lend them their cooperation. They therefore all fall into impotence if they do not learn to aid each other freely.

If men who live in democratic countries had neither the right nor the taste to unite in political goals, their independence would run great risks, but they could preserve their wealth and their enlightenment for a long time; whereas if they did not acquire the practice of associating with each other in ordinary life, civilization itself would be in peril. A people among whom particular persons lost the power of doing great things in isolation, without acquiring the ability to produce them in common, would soon return to barbarism.

Unhappily, the same social state that renders associations so necessary to democratic peoples renders them more difficult for them than for all others.

When several members of an aristocracy want to associate with each other they easily succeed in doing so. As each of them brings great force to society, the number of members can be very few, and, when the members are few in number, it is very easy for them to know each other, to understand each other, and to establish fixed rules.

The same facility is not found in democratic nations, where it is always necessary that those associating be very numerous in order that the association have some power.

I know that there are many of my contemporaries whom this does not embarrass. They judge that as citizens become weaker and more incapable, it is necessary to render the government more skillful and more active in order that society be able to execute what individuals can no longer do. They believe they have answered everything in saying that. But I think they are mistaken.

A government could take the place of some of the greatest American associations, and within the Union several particular states already have attempted it. But what political power would ever be in a state to suffice for the innumerable multitude of small undertakings that American citizens execute every day with the aid of an association?

It is easy to foresee that the time is approaching when a man by himself alone will be less and less in a state to produce the things that are the most common and the most necessary to his life. The task of the social power will therefore constantly increase, and its very efforts will make it vaster each day. The more it puts itself in place of associations, the more particular persons, losing the idea of associating with each other, will need it to come to their aid: these are causes and effects that generate each other without rest. Will the public administration in the end direct all the industries for which an isolated citizen cannot suffice? and if there finally comes a moment when, as a consequence of the extreme division of landed property, the land is partitioned infinitely, so that it can no longer be cultivated except by associations of laborers, will the head of the government have to leave the helm of state to come hold the plow?

The morality and intelligence of a democratic people would risk no fewer dangers than its business and its industry if the government came to take the place of associations everywhere.

Sentiments and ideas renew themselves, the heart is enlarged, and the human mind is developed only by the reciprocal action of men upon one another.

I have shown that this action is almost nonexistent in a democratic country. It is therefore necessary to create it artificially there. And this is what associations alone can do.

When the members of an aristocracy adopt a new idea or conceive a novel sentiment, they place it in a way next to themselves on the great stage they are on, and in thus exposing it to the view of the crowd, they easily introduce it into the minds or hearts of all those who surround them.

In democratic countries, only the social power is naturally in a state to act like this, but it is easy to see that its action is always insufficient and often dangerous.

A government can no more suffice on its own to maintain and renew the circulation of sentiments and ideas in a great people than to conduct all its industrial undertakings. As soon as it tries to leave the political sphere to project itself on this new track, it will exercise an insupportable tyranny even without wishing to; for a government knows only how to dictate precise rules; it imposes the sentiments and the ideas that it favors, and it is always hard to distinguish its counsels from its orders.

This will be still worse if it believes itself really interested in having nothing stir. It will then hold itself motionless and let itself be numbed by a voluntary somnolence.

It is therefore necessary that it not act alone.

In democratic peoples, associations must take the place of the powerful particular persons whom equality of conditions has made disappear.

As soon as several of the inhabitants of the United States have conceived a sentiment or an idea that they want to produce in the world, they seek each other out; and when they have found each other, they unite. From then on, they are no longer isolated men, but a power one sees from afar, whose actions serve as an example; a power that speaks, and to which one listens.

The first time I heard it said in the United States that a hundred thousand men publicly engaged not to make use of strong liquors, the thing appeared to me more amusing than serious, and at first I did not see well why such temperate citizens were not content to drink water within their families.

In the end I understood that those hundred thousand Americans, frightened by the progress that drunkenness was making around them, wanted to provide their patronage to sobriety. They had acted precisely like a great lord who would dress himself very plainly in order to inspire the scorn of luxury in simple citizens. It is to be believed that if those hundred thousand men had lived in France, each of them would have addressed himself individually to the government, begging it to reverse the cabarets all over the realm.

There is nothing, according to me, that deserves more to attract our regard than the intellectual and moral associations of America. We easily perceive the political and industrial associations of the Americans, but the others escape us; and if we discover them, we understand them badly because we have almost never seen anything analogous. One ought however to recognize that they are as necessary as the first to the American people, and perhaps more so.

In democratic countries the science of association is the mother science; the progress of all the others depends on the progress of that one.

Among the laws that rule human societies there is one that seems more precise and clearer than all the others. In order that men remain civilized or become so, the art of associating must be developed and perfected among them in the same ratio as equality of conditions increases.

RELATIONS BETWEEN CIVIL ASSOCIATIONS AND POLITICAL ASSOCIATIONS

There is only one nation on earth where the unlimited freedom to associate for political views is used daily. That same nation is the only one in the world whose citizens have imagined making a continuous use of the right of association in civil life, and have come in this manner to procure for themselves all the goods that civilization can offer.

Among all the peoples where political association is prohibited, civil association is rare.

It is hardly probable that this is the result of an accident; and one ought rather to conclude that a natural and perhaps necessary relation exists between these two types of association.

By chance, some men have a common interest in a certain affair. It is a question of a commercial undertaking to direct, of an industrial operation to conclude; they meet each other and unite; in this manner they familiarize themselves little by little with association.

The more the number of these small common affairs increases, the more do men, even without their knowing it, acquire the ability to pursue great ones in common.

Civil associations therefore facilitate political associations; but, on the other hand, political association singularly develops and perfects civil association.

In civil life, each man can, if he must, fancy that he is in a state of self-sufficiency. In politics he can never imagine it. When a people has a public life, the idea of association and the desire to associate with each other are therefore presented daily to the minds of all citizens: whatever natural repugnance men have for acting in common, they will always be ready to do it in the interest of a party.

Thus politics generalizes the taste for and habit of association; it makes a crowd of men who would otherwise have lived alone desire to unite, and teaches the art of doing it.

Politics not only gives birth to many associations, it creates vast associations.

In civil life it is rare that the same interest naturally attracts many men toward a common action. Only with much art can one come to create [an interest] like this.

In politics, the occasion offers itself at every moment. For it is only in large associations that the general worth of associations is manifest. Individually weak citizens do not get in advance a clear idea of the force they can acquire in uniting; for them to understand it, one must show it to them. Hence it is that it is often easier to assemble a multitude for a common goal than a few men; a thousand citizens cannot see the interest they have in uniting; ten thousand perceive it. In politics, men unite for great undertakings, and the advantage they derive from association in important affairs teaches them in a practical manner the interest they have in aiding each other in lesser ones.

A political association draws a multitude of individuals outside themselves at the same time; however separated they are naturally by age, mind, fortune, it brings them together and puts them in contact. They meet each other once and learn to find each other always.

One can be engaged in most civil associations only by risking a portion of one's patrimony; so it is for all industrial and commercial companies. When men are still little versed in the art of associating and they are ignorant of the principal rules, they dread, in associating in this manner for the first time, paying dearly for the experience. Therefore they would rather be deprived of a powerful means of success than risk the dangers that accompany it. But they hesitate less to take part in political associations, which appear to them to be without peril, because in them they do not risk their money. Now, they cannot take part in those associations for a long time without discovering how to maintain order among a great number of men and with what procedure one succeeds in getting them to advance in accord and methodically toward the same goal. They learn to submit their will to that of all the others and to subordinate their particular efforts to the common action—all things it is no less necessary to know in civil associations than in political associations.

Political associations can therefore be considered great schools, free of charge, where all citizens come to learn the general theory of associations.

Even if political association did not directly serve the progress of civil association, one would still do harm to the latter in destroying the former.

When citizens can only associate in certain cases, they regard association as a rare and singular procedure and they scarcely ever dare to think of it.

When they are allowed to associate freely in all things, in the end they see in association the universal, and so to speak the unique, means of which men can make use to attain the different ends they propose for themselves. Each new need immediately awakens the idea of it. The art of association then becomes, as I said above, the mother science; all study it and apply it.

When certain associations are forbidden and others permitted, it is difficult to distinguish in advance the first from the second. When in doubt, one abstains from all, and a sort of public opinion is established that tends to make one consider any association whatsoever as a bold and almost illicit undertaking.[1]

It is therefore a chimera to believe that the spirit of association, compromised on one point, will be left to develop with the same vigor on all others, and that it will suffice to permit men to execute certain undertakings in common for them to hasten to attempt it. When citizens have the ability and the habit of associating for all things, they will as willingly associate for small ones as for great. But if they can only associate for small ones, they will not even have the desire and the capacity to do so. In vain will you allow them entire freedom to engage in common in their trade: they will use only half-heartedly the rights that are granted them, and after you are exhausted by efforts to turn them away from forbidden associations, you will be surprised at not being able to persuade them to form permitted associations.

I do not say that there cannot be civil associations in a country where political association is prohibited; for men can never live in society without engaging in some common undertaking. But I maintain that in a country like this, civil associations will always be very few in number, weakly conceived, unskillfully conducted, and that they will never embrace vast designs or will fail when they want to execute them.

This naturally leads me to think that freedom of association in political matters is not as dangerous for public tranquility as is supposed, and that it could happen that after having shaken up the state for some time, it would consolidate it.

In democratic countries, political associations form so to speak the only powerful particular persons who aspire to regulate the state. So governments

---

1. That is above all true when it is the executive power that is charged with permitting or forbidding associations according to its arbitrary will.

When the law is limited to prohibiting certain associations and leaves to the courts the care of punishing those who disobey, the evil is much less great: each citizen then knows almost in advance what to count on; he judges for himself in some way before his judges do, and avoiding forbidden associations, he turns to permitted associations. It is thus that all free peoples have always understood that one could restrain the right of association. But if it happened that the legislator charged one man with sorting out in advance which are the dangerous and useful associations and left him free to destroy the seed of all associations or to let them spring up, no one being able to foresee in advance in which case one can associate and in which one must abstain, the spirit of association would be wholly stricken with inertia. The first of these two laws attacks only certain associations; the second is addressed to society itself and hurts it. I conceive that an acknowledged government may have recourse to the first, but I recognize in no government the right to bring on the second.

in our day consider these kinds of association with the same eye that the kings of the Middle Ages regarded the great vassals of the crown: they feel a sort of instinctive horror of them and combat them at every encounter.

They have, on the contrary, a natural benevolence toward civil associations because they have readily discovered that, instead of directing the minds of citizens toward public affairs, these serve to distract them and, engaging them more and more in projects that cannot be accomplished without public peace, turn them away from revolutions. But they do not take note that political associations multiply civil associations and facilitate them enormously, and in avoiding a dangerous evil, they deprive themselves of an efficacious remedy. When you see Americans associate freely every day for the goal of making a public opinion prevail, of elevating a statesman to the government, or of taking away power from someone, you have trouble comprehending that men so independent do not fall into license at every moment.

If you come, on the other hand, to consider the infinite number of industrial undertakings that are pursued in common in the United States, and if you perceive Americans on all sides working without relaxation in the execution of some important and difficult design that the least revolution could confound, you easily conceive why people so well occupied are not tempted to trouble the state or to destroy a public repose from which they profit.

Is it enough to perceive these things separately, or must one not discover the hidden knot that binds them? It is within political associations that Americans of all conditions, of all minds, and of all ages get the general taste for association daily and familiarize themselves with its use. There they see each other in great number, speak to each other, understand each other, and in common become animated for all sorts of undertakings. Afterwards, they carry into civil life the notions they have acquired and make them serve a thousand uses.

It is therefore while enjoying a dangerous freedom that Americans learn the art of rendering the perils of freedom less great.

If one chooses a certain moment in the existence of a nation, it is easy to prove that political associations trouble the state and paralyze industry; but should one take the whole life of a people, it will perhaps be easy to demonstrate that freedom of association in political matters is favorable to the well-being and even to the tranquillity of citizens.

I said in the first part of this work: "Unlimited freedom of association cannot be confused with the freedom to write: the former is at once less necessary and more dangerous. A nation can set bounds for it without ceasing to be master of itself; it sometimes must do that to continue to be such." And further on I added: "One cannot conceal from oneself that unlimited freedom of association in political matters is, of all freedoms, the last that a people can tolerate. If it does not make it fall into anarchy, it makes it so to speak touch it at each instant."

Thus, I do not believe that a nation is always so much a master as to allow citizens the absolute right to associate in political matters, and I even doubt that there is any country, in any period, in which it would not be wise to set bounds for freedom of association.

Such and such a people, it is said, cannot maintain peace within itself, inspire respect for the laws, or found a lasting government if it does not confine the right of association within narrow limits. Such goods are doubtless precious, and I conceive that to acquire them or preserve them a nation consents to impose great hindrances temporarily; but still it is good for it to know precisely what these goods cost it.

If to save the life of a man one cuts off his arm, I understand it; but I do not want someone to assure me that he is going to show himself as adroit as if he were not one-armed.

28.

The Attainment of Social Order in Heterogeneous Societies

MICHAEL HECHTER, DEBRA FRIEDMAN, and SATOSHI KANAZAWA, 1992

Two quite different theoretical traditions have emerged to account for social order. The first tradition, which is most popular among rational choice theorists, emanates from Hobbes. Its central idea is that order results from a large number of independent decisions to transfer individual rights and liberties to a coercive state in return for its guarantee of security for persons and their property, as well as its establishment of mechanisms to resolve disputes. The transfer of these various individual rights and liberties to the state does not in and of itself produce order, however, because individuals still have an incentive to disrupt order when they can profit by doing so. No state has sufficient resources to maintain order solely via policing; this is why Weber invoked the famous concept of *legitimacy*.

The second tradition, which is most popular among sociologists, emanates from Aristotle and is echoed by Rousseau, Durkheim, Parsons, and their contemporary followers. It views the ultimate source of social order as residing not in external controls but in a concordance of specific values and norms that individuals somehow have managed to internalize. In this tradition, the attainment of order generally is not considered problematic in socially and culturally homogeneous societies, for in these settings the internalized values and norms will tend to be common to all. Now this contention is controversial (for a critique, see Hechter and Kanazawa 1993), but even if it is granted, how then is it possible to account for order in heterogeneous societies—those that encompass a variety of different normative orientations? In such settings, internalization is likely to sow the seeds of conflict rather than order.

. . . [W]e briefly outline the problematic nature of social order in heterogeneous societies and propose that the attainment of local order helps provide a solution. Because order is more easily explained in small homogeneous groups than in large heterogeneous ones, much is to be gained theoretically by reducing the global problem to a local one. Our argument is that the members

From James S. Coleman and Thomas J. Fararo, eds., *Rational Choice Theory: Advocacy and Critique,* pp. 79–97, copyright © 1992 by Sage Publications, Inc. Reprinted by permission of Sage Publications, Inc.

of social groups can be expected to produce local order to satisfy their own private ends, and once produced, this local order, regardless of its normative content, often contributes to the production of global order. One counterintuitive implication of this argument is that *the more deviant the normative content of the local order, the greater its relative contribution to global order.*

In tacit recognition that global order rests, at least in part, on the local order produced in deviant social groups, we expect the state to tolerate the existence and parochial activities of social groups of any normative orientation unless they threaten the state as an autonomous and ultimate power broker or impose negative externalities on people who have sufficient resources to persuade the authorities to protect them. The argument is illustrated by discussions of the divergent fates of a number of cults and urban street gangs and by some evidence of the state's tolerance of vice.

THE PROBLEM OF SOCIAL ORDER IN HETEROGENEOUS SOCIETIES

To understand variations in social order among homogeneous societies requires an appreciation of factors that permit one society to exercise social control more efficaciously than another (Hechter and Kanazawa 1993). Although social control mechanisms remain operative in heterogeneous societies, one major difference makes the attainment of social order somewhat more difficult to capture analytically in these societies. The principal threat to social order in homogeneous societies emanates from individuals alone (because all groups in such societies will tend to share common norms and values), but in heterogeneous societies, threats to social order may emanate from groups, as well as from individuals.

The array of normative orientations in a homogeneous society is centered around a single mean, with a relatively small variance. Two quite different types of heterogeneous societies exist, however. One type is distinguished from homogeneous societies only in degree: Whereas still only a single mean exists, the distribution is much wider around that mean. A second type of heterogeneous society is characterized by its polymodal character. Whereas the second type of heterogeneity is qualitatively different from homogeneity, the first type is distinguished from it only by degree. The first type characterizes societies of immigration, such as the United States. The second type characterizes societies of amalgamation, such as the Soviet Union. In this chapter, we shall be concerned solely with the dynamics underlying social order in the first (unimodal) type of heterogeneous society.

All groups, even deviant ones, must produce social order locally to benefit their own group's solidarity. The production of local order creates a largely unintended by-product for large societies: social order on a global scale. States free-ride on the production of local order, particularly that produced by deviant groups. Local order always will contribute to global order, regardless of the norms of local groups, as long as the production of order or the failure to produce it does not consume state resources.

The deviance of a group turns out to be a rather poor predictor of whether it contributes to global order. Groups whose normative orientation diverges from that of the center but whose members do not engage in activities that create threats or externalities contribute more to global order than those whose normative orientation is closer to that of the center.

Regardless of their normative orientation, groups contribute to global order by regulating the behavior of their members. In order to provide themselves with jointly produced goods that provide the rationale for group formation and maintenance, members establish production and allocation norms and enforce them through monitoring and sanctioning mechanisms (Hechter 1987). Participation in groups regulates the behavior of members by demanding their compliance with group norms. Members of every group thus have a private interest in contributing to that group's solidarity and are willing to expend control resources to attain that solidarity. The mere regulation of behavior, for whatever end, represents a contribution to global order (given the exceptions noted above) even though this contribution is a by-product.

Consider, for instance, the Hare Krishna, a group that attracts and serves those who tend to be peripheral members of the society: individuals who are not in school, gainfully employed, or in traditional family arrangements. It is not the aim of the leadership of the Hare Krishna to get their members to finish school, take a job, or form traditional family units. Nonetheless, members are far from free to do as they wish: The obligations required of them are considerable (see the description of their rigorous daily schedule in Daner [1976, pp. 39–44] and Rochford [1985, pp. 13–18]). Members are consumed by the demands of the group, and although the group explicitly intends to provide an alternative to mainstream norms, that their members are compelled to satisfy corporate obligations limits their ability to engage in other, potentially antisocial, activities.

Yet groups that mobilize members who occupy the margins of society provide an even greater—albeit an unintended—service to the larger society. Individuals who are able to negotiate the social mainstream have the greatest opportunity to affiliate with multiple groups and therefore to establish the ties that regulate their behavior. The farther from the mainstream people are, the less their opportunity to join groups; *hermits* by definition are individuals who face the fewest social constraints on their behavior.

It follows, therefore, that Presbyterian church congregations—made up of people who work, people who have children, and the elderly—make a less important contribution to global order than do the congregations of the Nation of Islam, who draw their members disproportionately from African-Americans, the poor, the young, and the dispossessed. Were these two congregations disbanded simultaneously, threats to global order would be less likely to come from the Presbyterian congregations than from the Islamic ones, not because of a difference in norms but because of a difference in the number of ties that bind.

Groups cannot be classified, then, as either deviant or not for the purposes of understanding when they will contribute to global order. Yet the practice of classifying groups by their norms persists. This is because global order, like its local counterpart, is produced by monitoring and sanctioning mechanisms. *Monitoring* entails the collection and analysis of information, and *norms* often are regarded as a signalling device that economize on information: Threats to social order are thought to come less often from mainstream groups than from deviant ones.

Although it may well be the case that groups equally distant from the modal normative orientation of a society are subject to similar levels of monitoring, we will argue that they are not subject to similar levels of sanctioning. Were normative orientation the only concern for agencies of social control, we should expect no differences in sanctioning. Yet as we will demonstrate, sanctioning varies widely among comparably deviant groups. Sanctioning is reserved for groups whose members threaten the state as an autonomous and ultimate power broker or impose negative externalities on people with sufficient resources to persuade the authorities to protect them.

Like de Tocqueville ([1848] 1945, p. 119), we see global order as the product of group solidarities at lower levels of aggregation. Because global order is a collective good, however, no group can be expected to contribute directly to its provision. Our argument avers that global order is achieved as an unintended by-product of the efforts that members of social groups make in getting one another to comply with group-specific obligations through their social control efforts.[1]

Our argument extends beyond this. Whereas previous discussions regard social order as the product of the solidarities of groups that share many norms and values in common, such uniformity is not necessary to produce order at the global level. To illustrate this, we turn to a comparison of two normatively similar deviant groups—Hare Krishna and Rajneesh—and ask

---

1. This conclusion is the exact inverse of that averred by theorists of mass society (such as Arendt 1958, Part 3), who argued that the stability of states increased as the solidarity of their constituent social groups waned.

under what conditions the apparatus of state control will be brought to bear on their activities.

DETERMINANTS OF STATE INTERVENTION: THE CASES OF HARE KRISHNA AND RAJNEESH

Both Hare Krishna and Rajneesh were direct imports from India that belonged to the "neo-Hindu" tradition. Both movements are well outside of the Judeo-Christian tradition, and their normative status in the American society is marginal, at best. Both were led and brought into the United States by a charismatic leader, and both count mostly peripheral (although from white, middle-class background [Rochford 1985, pp. 46–57]) members of American society among their devoted followers. Despite these many similarities, these groups have had completely different fates in the United States, and the two factors identified above (threats to state autonomy and the imposition of negative externalities on resourceful others) hint at the reason why.

Hare Krishna emerged in the United States after the arrival of Swami Bhaktivedanta in New York in 1966 (Poling and Kenney 1986, p. 7); he established the International Society for Krishna Consciousness (ISKCON) and began to attract followers at his first temple on Second Avenue. In four years (1966–70), ISKCON grew from 1 temple with 16 initiated disciples to 30 temples, 35 initiated disciples, and 347 ministerial students (*Krsna Consciousness Handbook* 1970, pp. 98–105).[2]

While the Rajneesh movement in central Oregon had origins similar to Hare Krishna, its short history in the United States provides a notable contrast. Like Hare Krishna, Rajneesh began in 1981 following the arrival in the United States of its leader, Bhagwan Shree Rajneesh, but the movement came to its demise in 1985 with his deportation from the country. What accounts for its quick demise?

---

2. Although the Hare Krishna movement experienced a major crisis after the death of Swami in 1977 (Rochford 1985, Chap. 9), it has not faced any external intervention by the state. On occasion, outside deprogrammers hired by the parents of ISKCON members have kidnapped and deprogrammed some members in order to return them to their parents. In such cases, however, ISKCON has successfully prosecuted the deprogrammers and parents in criminal court for kidnapping and other First Amendment violations by claiming that it represents a genuine religious tradition (Poling and Kenney 1986, p. 10). State tolerance for ISKCON exists to such a high extent that, in Gainesville, Florida, ISKCON operated a Food For Life program that provided 2,400 meals a month for the urban poor, *with a HUD grant of $20,000*. As its own financial measure, ISKCON sold the official T-shirt of the Hare Krishna Food For Life Program for $7.75.

First, unlike Hare Krishna, the Rajneesh movement presented a threat to the autonomy of the state. It first took over political control of the small village of Antelope, Oregon, near their commune, and changed its name to Rajneesh (Carter 1990, p. xv). Then it successfully petitioned to incorporate the commune as another city, Rajneeshpuram (Price 1985, p. 19). Now two municipalities were under complete political control of this religious movement, in violation of the separation of church and state. Rajneeshees maintained their own police force ("Peace Force") whose leaders were trained by the Oregon Police Academy (Carter 1990, p. 92). They built their own airport, with three DC-3 planes in their Air Rajneesh fleet (Price 1985, pp. 25–6), and their free public transportation system was second in size only to Portland's in the state of Oregon (Androes 1986, p. 52). They also constructed and maintained a municipal water system conservatively estimated as capable of serving a population of 50,000 (Androes 1986, p. 53). The Rajneeshees increasingly took on and over usual governmental functions, and the public services they provided were often better and more efficient than those provided by other municipalities in Oregon.[3]

Of course, no state (neither the state of Oregon nor the government of the United States) could tolerate any large social group, whatever its normative orientation, that threatened to become a sovereign state within its borders (cf. Arrington 1958 on the conflict between the Mormons of Utah, who had a similar aspiration, and the United States government in an earlier era).

Second, in its attempt to gain sovereignty, the Rajneesh movement and its activities imposed a host of negative externalities on its neighbors, who felt "intimidated, threatened, and slandered" (Carter 1990, p. xvii). At the outset, the movement had different effects on different people:

> Many locals appear to have reacted primarily to Rajneesh dominance and control moves, while other opponents were clearly offended by what they saw as immorality and the challenge to their religious traditions. The environmentalist group pursued the threat to its traditional "preservationist" goals as

---

3. The purpose of this seemed to emanate from Bhagwan's aspirations, formulated at an earlier time in India, to create a self-sufficient "new society" that was independent of the host culture and thus fell outside of its political jurisdiction. With all of its institutions in place, the Oregon commune seemed very close to fulfillment of his dream. "The term 'new society' had become more than a metaphor for sannyasin [Rajneeshees] by 1982. The ranch provided sufficient isolation for members to see themselves as independent of outside institutions, effectively *a sovereign state*. The illusion of total autonomy developed quite naturally from the increasing completeness of their institutions (agriculture, finance, medical services) and the separation from outside definitions of reality (an internal press, video and audio productions, limited and controlled outside contact)" (Carter 1990, p. 158 [emphasis added]).

well as gains in regional popularity accruing from its opposition to an unpopular group. (Carter 1990, p. 130)

Some people were adversely affected by the movement's aggressive expansion to adjacent communities. Those who owned land across the river from the commune thus were among the strongest opponents (Carter 1990, pp. 133–4). When the followers eventually took over the nearby small village of Antelope, 32 of the original 49 inhabitants were forced to relocate, and those who stayed were continually harassed by the "Peace Force" (Carter 1990, p. 93). With the political takeover of the Antelope village government, the Rajneeshees also made some changes in the local public school system (Carter 1990, pp. 181–2). These changes forced the local school children to be bussed 50 miles to Madras, Oregon. The quiet way of life to which the prior residents had been accustomed was suddenly disrupted by intruders.

Religious fundamentalists in Oregon were alarmed when a "meditation center" established in Antelope suddenly changed its name to Rajneesh International Foundation and was officially categorized as a church (Carter 1990, p. 140). Furthermore, 1000 Friends of Oregon, a regional environmentalist group, was concerned with the Rajneesh's violation of county land-use plans when the followers began building non-farm-related buildings outside of the designated Urban Growth Boundaries (Carter 1990, pp. 139–40).

Eventually all these groups in the local communities united in their opposition to Rajneesh. As the opposition became increasingly organized, the Rajneeshees took a more militant stance and made further moves to alienate and threaten the local residents. One of these counterproductive moves was to treat Antelope as a "hostage town":

> Over the course of the year, the Rajneesh council of Antelope raised taxes and fees, hired security services from the Rajneeshpuram "Peace Force," and took control of the Antelope school. The increased taxes imposed some burden on retirees (most of whom left); the Peace Force instituted intimidating surveillance of locals; and the public school controversy broadened the base of public opposition. At one point, Rajneesh leaders offered to "trade" Antelope for a bill officially recognizing Rajneeshpuram. They would withdraw from Antelope to the ranch if the legislature would sanction their incorporated city. (Carter 1990, p. 167)[4]

The confrontation with locals escalated over time:

---

4. Elsewhere the Rajneeshees also employed this tactic of raising the cost of living to drive people out. When they purchased the Martha Washington women's hotel in Portland for $1.5 million, they immediately raised the rent from $285 per month to $750 per month, effectively dislodging prior residents. The hotel then was used almost exclusively by devotees in transit to Rajneeshpuram (Carter 1990, p. 170).

Additional housing was acquired [in Antelope] and a campaign was begun to discomfit remaining locals. Milne [a Rajneeshee who was later excommunicated for ideological differences] reports instructions to sannyasin to hold loud, all-night parties near the residences of others and to offend locals with public displays of affection. . . . Milne reports several confrontations with locals when he took pictures of their homes in Antelope and dwellings in other parts of the state to document the part-time nature of their residency in Antelope. He also notes that his film "documentation" was intended to intimidate and harass these residents. (Carter 1990, p. 150)

The Rajneesh Peace Force stopped and occasionally searched non-Rajneeshees traveling on county roads in and around newly incorporated Rajneeshpuram. All access to the city was tightly controlled by these armed security guards (Carter 1990, pp. 182–3).

Toward the end of the conflict, the Rajneeshees resorted to criminal tactics (for which some of their leaders were later convicted). They set fire to the field of a rancher near Antelope who refused to sell land to the group. And they poisoned Jefferson County District Attorney Michael Sullivan when he became alienated from the movement despite his earlier extended attempt to negotiate accommodation between the Rajneeshees and the locals (Carter 1990, pp. 198–200).

Local residents responded with equally strong, if legal, measures; they filed numerous lawsuits against the commune leaders and members. The assault on the Rajneesh movement eventually involved the federal government. In December 1982, the INS denied Bhagwan's application for permanent residency (Carter 1990, p. 163), and ultimately he was deported from the United States after pleading guilty to two counts of making false statements to federal INS officials. He was charged with 1 count of conspiracy and 34 counts of making false statements to a federal official. Under a plea bargain, Bhagwan was fined $400,000, given a 10-year suspended sentence, "allowed" to depart the country "voluntarily," and placed on probation for 5 years. Other leaders of the movement were charged similarly and pleaded guilty for such felonies as attempted murder and first-degree arson (Carter 1990, pp. 235–40).

The divergent histories of Hare Krishna and Rajneesh illustrate our earlier contention that the state tolerates the activities of deviant social groups as long as they do not threaten its exclusive exercise of power and do not impose negative externalities on others with collective action potential.

True, Hare Krishna devotees often accost people at airports and other public places (Rochford 1985, Chap. 7). The negative externalities the Hare Krishna impose on such people, however, are different from those the Rajneeshees imposed on Oregonians in two crucial respects. The occasional harassment of people at an airport hardly compares in magnitude or seriousness to the political takeover of an entire municipality or attempted murder. More important, victims of Hare Krishna harassment at an airport do not know one another (and thus have no social closure [Coleman 1988, 1990]); hence they have little potential to engage in collective action. In contrast, the Rajneesh movement adversely affected long-term residents of Antelope and other central Oregon communities who knew each other very well; these victims could pool their resources to combat their intruders collectively, and this is what they did.

Had Rajneesh not so obviously challenged the state and imposed negative externalities on resourceful actors, it might have survived to enjoy the same kind of parasitic relationship with the state that Hare Krishna seems to enjoy. Such relationships between the state and alternative social groups are parasitic because these groups enjoy the tolerance and even implicit support of the state for their deviant activities (as with the HUD grant to ISKCON), and in turn the state can farm out some of its responsibilities to produce and maintain global order to its constituent groups. (The mayors of New York and San Francisco once commended ISKCON for its total ban on drugs among its members [Daner 1976, p. 60].) Because most Americans regard both Hare Krishna and Rajneesh as deviant cult organizations, and most of the internal values, norms, and practices of both are equally incongruent with the values and norms of American society at large, their deviance alone explains nothing of the state's differential treatment of these two groups.

Nonetheless it may be argued that although the followers of Rajneesh were clearly marginal members of society, even if they were deprived of membership in this kind of group, they would be unlikely to engage in activities that would threaten global order. It is even the case, perhaps, that they were more likely to do so as members of Rajneesh than if they were left to their own devices. It would seem plausible that groups whose members are wont to engage in illegal behavior when left on their own are even more likely to do so when organized into a collectivity.[5] Urban street gangs appear to be the prime example; made up of disadvantaged youth with little to lose, they seem to be the principal threat to social order in the contemporary United States.

Gangs allow us to distinguish among groups on the edge. Because our proposition is that the state enjoys as a by-product the control mechanisms that social groups institute for their own purposes, those whose control mechanisms impose net negative externalities on society will not be tolerated, for

---

5. LeBon (1899) was the first to suggest that members of a crowd are less restrained by social conventions and therefore more likely to engage in antisocial behavior than nonmembers.

they produce social *dis*order. No state countenances groups that challenge its monopoly of the means of violence and its role as ultimate power broker in civil society. Instances of social disorder will be acknowledged, however, let alone redressed, only if they affect individuals who have the capacity to engage in collective action on their own behalf.

These criteria should be important in explaining differential police harassment of deviant groups. Because the state always has extremely limited control capacity, it can only enforce the legal code selectively. The police are more likely to turn a blind eye to illegal activities of groups that contribute to global order (like gambling parlors in New York's Chinatown) than those that threaten it (like crack-dealing gangs in Watts).[6] Several excellent studies of urban gangs shed light on these issues.

SAINTS, ROUGHNECKS, GUARDIAN ANGELS, AND 37 URBAN STREET GANGS: AN ALTERNATIVE INTERPRETATION

In a classic study, Chambliss (1973) observed two youth gangs in Hanibal High School over the course of 2 years. The Saints were an upper-middle-class gang, while the members of the Roughnecks came from lower-class families. Despite the fact that both gangs engaged in delinquent activities, the community, the school, and the police consistently regarded the Saints as "good, upstanding, nondelinquent youths with bright futures" but the Roughnecks as "tough, young criminals who were headed for trouble" (Chambliss 1973, p. 28). Over the course of the study, none of the eight Saints even so much as received a traffic ticket. In contrast, each of the six Roughnecks was arrested at least once; several of them were arrested a number of times and spent at least one night in jail. If the Saints and Roughnecks were equally delinquent, what accounts for the differential police treatment of the two gangs?

Chambliss's answer was a typical interactionist one. The influential upper-middle-class parents of the Saints (and others like them) were able to exert subtle pressure on the police to disregard their children's delinquent acts as harmless pranks and the occasional sowing of wild oats, while the powerless lower-class parents of the Roughnecks (and others like them) were unable to do so. Further, the rich Saints had access to their own cars, which allowed them to travel to nearby Big City to commit their delinquent acts, an option that the poor Roughnecks, who owned no cars, did not have. The Saints' upper-middle-class appearance and demeanor also biased the police's percep-

---

6. Yet since successful prosecution of criminal behavior usually requires evidence held by community members, if such evidence is collectively withheld, the police will be powerless to act on their intentions (Jankowski 1991).

tion of their behaviors in their favor. Chambliss argues that the local Hanibal residents perceived the seriousness of the delinquent acts committed by the Saints and the Roughnecks quite differently because of their different class backgrounds, and this distorted perception led to the unequal treatment of the two youth gangs by the police.

Our argument suggests a different interpretation. Differential police treatment may have been a result of the amount of negative externalities imposed by these two youth gangs and of the kinds of people who were adversely affected. Despite the fact that "in sheer number of illegal acts, the Saints were the more delinquent" (Chambliss 1973, p. 29), their delinquent acts created very few negative externalities for local community members.

> [The Saints] simply viewed themselves as having a little fun and who, they would ask, was really hurt by it? The answer had to be no one, although this fact remains one of the most difficult things to explain about the gang's behavior. Unlikely though it seems, in two years of drinking, driving, carousing and vandalism no one was seriously injured as a result of the Saints' activities. (Chambliss 1973, p. 26)

"The Saints were more continuously engaged in delinquency but their acts were not for the most part costly to property" (Chambliss 1973, p. 29); in contrast, the Roughnecks' delinquent acts were. They frequently stole from local stores and other students at school. "The thefts ranged from very small things like paperback books, comics and ballpoint pens to expensive items like watches" (Chambliss 1973, p. 27). Apart from occasional theft of gasoline, the only things the Saints stole were wooden barricades and lanterns from construction sites and road repair areas, which belonged to no private citizens. The Saints abandoned most of these stolen items, and these could thus later be recovered (Chambliss 1973, p. 29).

The Saints and the Roughnecks also had differential propensities toward violence. "The Roughnecks were more prone to physical violence" while "the Saints never fought" (Chambliss 1973, p. 29). The Roughnecks' fighting activities were frequent and often involved other members of the local community. It appears that the Roughnecks imposed more negative externalities on others both in their property crimes and violent crimes.

Moreover, on those rare occasions when the Saints' delinquent acts did impose some negative externalities, they hardly ever affected the local Hanibal residents, who knew the boys well, but instead were directed against the residents of Big City, who did not know them. In contrast, all of the Roughnecks' delinquent acts took place in Hanibal because they did not have access to cars. So while the Big City driver who drove into a hole in the road deliberately left unmarked by the Saints did not know who the pranksters were (Chambliss 1973, p. 25), the teacher whom one of the Roughnecks threatened to beat up and who had to hide under the desk in order to escape him had no illusion about the identity of the delinquent boy (Chambliss 1973, p. 28). Because the Saints' pranks affected the anonymous people of metropolitan Big City, who knew neither the boys' identities nor each other, they could not pool their resources to deal with the Saints' delinquency. In contrast, the Roughnecks' victims were mostly the local residents, who knew both the boys and each other very well. They were thus able to band together and deal with the Roughnecks' delinquency collectively.

No doubt the Saints were able to commit their pranks on strangers in Big City because they had cars, which their upper-middle-class status afforded; in that sense, their class position, which Chambliss emphasizes, is an important factor in this story. The unequal treatment of the two gangs by the police, however, may have happened *independent* of their class position *if* their respective delinquent acts affected, as they did, different segments of the society. With their nice cars, influential parents, and polite demeanor, the Saints may have been arrested anyway had some of their pranks actually resulted in some injuries and/or affected members of the local community, who could act collectively.

Our interpretation is reinforced by a new ethnographic study of 37 urban street gangs in New York, Los Angeles, and Boston. Noting that street gangs have been a feature of the American urban landscape for at least a century, Jankowski (1991) attributes their persistence to interdependence between gangs and their local communities (see also Suttles 1968, pp. 6–9, 189–229). The principal benefits that gangs provide their communities are two. The first is welfare: Through their participation in the underground economy (dealing drugs, running prostitution, and so forth), gangs produce wealth for their members, and this wealth also is available to meet some community needs. The second is security: Gangs are a local militia that protects neighborhood residents and small businesses from external predators far more effectively than the police. In return for these goods, members of the community provide the gang with social approval, a license to recruit their children, and—most important—a safe haven from the authorities. Most of the violence committed by gangs is strategic—designed to capture new territory—and is hardly ever directed against community members.[7] The most successful gangs (those with

---

7. This is why the local order that is invariably produced by urban street gangs usually does not contribute to global order. Because a gang's ability to produce local order ultimately rests on territorial expansion, this leads to a high risk of violent conflict with the gangs that control the coveted territory. As this violence often imposes negative externalities on resourceful actors, it tends to attract police attention and to consume public resources.

what Jankowski terms *vertical/hierarchical* organization) regulate their members' behavior by punishing those who engage in random violence that is unsanctioned by the leadership. Gangs who fail to keep their members from preying on the community are denied the community's safe haven and soon unravel.

Yet another variation on this theme is provided by a close examination of the Guardian Angels, who fit the standard definition of a gang but who are openly tolerated by the police. Despite their status as modern vigilantes (Kenney 1987) and their well-known propensity toward violence and extralegal activities (Reinecke 1982; Pileggi 1980; Cordts 1981), no chapter has come under concerted police control (Kenney 1987). One answer might be their sense of themselves as upholding the law, and their ability to communicate that to the general public. Yet these claims would be unlikely to convince police in the face of behavioral evidence to the contrary.

Instead state tolerance may be due to the inefficacy of the Guardian Angels: They do surprisingly little that affects others either positively or negatively. For instance, the Guardian Angels actually interrupted crimes and made arrests in only 258 instances in the entire nation after 3 years of active operation (Newport 1982, p. 10). It seems that the negative externalities that they impose on others are limited enough to account for police inattention despite their obvious similarity to other urban gangs.

STATE TOLERANCE OF VICE

If the state tacitly recognizes the positive contributions of deviant social groups toward global order and tolerates their existence as long as they do not challenge its authority or impose negative externalities on resourceful others, it follows that the formal legal status of social groups in and of itself does not affect how the state treats these groups. In particular, the police should be especially tolerant of groups that explicitly engage in "victimless crimes" (such as prostitution, gambling, drug use) unless these groups challenge the state's monopoly on violence and/or impose negative externalities on resourceful actors.

James Q. Wilson (1968) underscores these points in a study of police behavior in eight United States communities. Wilson argues that the primary function of patrol officers on the beat is the maintenance of public order rather than strict enforcement of the letter of the law. The police operate to emphasize public order over law enforcement and tolerate some vice in order to maintain order mostly because city officials, to whom the police chief is responsible, recognize, as we do, the important role that some deviant groups perform in the overall production of social order.

The city administration [of Albany, NY] has changed its policy on vice slowly but in accordance with what it thinks public opinion expects. The Gut [the red-light district in Albany] was once defended by officials who felt that it kept the "riff-raff" in one place; no decent citizen would be offended unless he went there looking for action, in which case he could hardly complain. Toward the end, however, it was receiving too much unfavorable publicity. Most of the honky-tonks and brothels torn down by the governor did not reopen. (Wilson 1968, p. 240)

A Democratic leader in Albany tells one of Wilson's interviewers:

There was gambling in the Stone Age, there's gambling today, there will be gambling when your grandchildren are as old as I am. I can't see enforcing a law against nature. Anyway, there's never been any gang murders or stuff like goes on in New York as a result of gambling and prostitution. The gamblers up here are nice people, otherwise; they're businessmen. (Wilson 1968, p. 245)

The implication in this politician's comment is that if "gang murders or stuff like goes on in New York as a result of gambling and prostitution" were to occur, then the government would act swiftly to close down these operations.

Further, some city officials seem to recognize that deviant groups are especially likely to regulate the behavior of marginal individuals:

A high city official told an interviewer that "Nobody wants to eliminate all of the gambling and prostitution, *especially among the Negroes*. We feel that some of it has to go on, but it should be kept down and under control." After the charges made by the Negro minister at the February 1967 council meeting, the city announced that gambling and prostitution had been shut down. Some arrests were made, in fact, but privately a high city official told an interviewer afterwards that the city was not "closed tight"; he explained that "We couldn't close the place down totally *with the minority group that we have here* [emphasis added]—we have to allow some safety valve." (Wilson 1968, pp. 245–6)

Incidentally a wave of burglaries and the murder of a businessman in the area led to both the charges by the minister and the city's action ostensibly to crack down on gambling and prostitution—serious negative externalities as a result of otherwise tolerated vice operations (Wilson 1968, p. 244).

Wilson's research indicates that, at least in some American cities in the 1960s, the police treated some forms of "victimless crimes" in accordance with the argument in this chapter. Further, the police attitude toward vice operations seems to reflect the opinions of the municipal officials that these operations have important implications for the production of order, especially for peripheral members of the society (such as African-Americans in the context of the mid-1960s United States).

Order in heterogeneous national societies is enhanced by the existence of large numbers of relatively small groups that are unable to command control over resources that threaten the unique position of the state. Competition among groups for resources and members is likely to be advantageous from the standpoint of the production of global order.

The normative orientation of these groups matters not: The greater the number of groups that attract the membership of those on the margin of society, the better.

Still a question remains: Instead of fostering association among peripheral individuals, why not try to buy their loyalty through transfers and state entitlements? In a relatively heterogeneous society, this solution would be both politically infeasible and prohibitively expensive. Yet for a more important theoretical reason this kind of state co-optation is unlikely to be effective. Entitlements tend to decrease global order when they come from the state, because then citizens become dependent on an entity—the state—that necessarily has relatively weak control capacity. Entitlements increase global order only when they come from social groups—as they do, for example, in Japan—because then people are dependent on entities that have relatively great control capacity.

Global order therefore is enhanced by freedom of association, especially at the margins of society. The most efficacious way to produce global order is to strengthen the conditions for the production of local solidarity.

REFERENCES

Androes, Louis C. 1986. "Cultures in Collision: The Rajneesh Search for Community." *Communities* 71–72:49–54.

Arendt, Hannah. 1958. *The Origins of Totalitarianism.* New York: World.

Arrington, Leonard. 1958. *Great Basin Kingdom: An Economic History of the Latter-Day Saints.* Cambridge, Mass.: Harvard University Press.

Carter, Lewis F. 1990. *Charisma and Control in Rajneeshpuram: The Role of Shared Values in the Creation of a Community.* Cambridge: Cambridge University Press.

Chambliss, William J. 1973. "The Saints and Roughnecks." *Transaction: Social Science and Modern Society* 11:24–31.

Coleman, James S. 1988. "Social Capital in the Creation of Human Capital." *American Journal of Sociology* 94:S95–S120.

———. 1990. *Foundations of Social Theory.* Cambridge, Mass.: Harvard University Press.

Cordts, Michael. 1981. "I Was a Guardian Angel." *Chicago Sun Times,* November 8.

Daner, Francine Jeanne. 1976. *The American Children of Krsna: A Study of the Hare Krsna Movement.* New York: Holt, Rinehart and Winston.

Hechter, Michael. 1987. *Principles of Group Solidarity.* Berkeley: University of California Press.

Hechter, Michael, and Satoshi Kanazawa. 1993. "Group Solidarity and Social Order in Japan." *Journal of Theoretical Politics* 5:455–493.

Jankowski, Martín Sánchez. 1991. *Islands in the Street: Gangs and American Urban Society.* Berkeley: University of California Press.

Kenney, Dennis Jay. 1987. *Crime, Fear, and the New York City Subways: The Role of Citizen Action.* New York: Praeger.

Krsna Consciousness Handbook: For the Year 484, Caitanya Era. 1970. Boston: ISKCON Press.

Le Bon, Gustave. 1899. *The Crowd.* London: Unwin.

Newport, John Paul, Jr. 1982. "Opinion on Angels: A Devil of a Division." *Fort Worth Star Telegram,* March 21, pp. 1–10a.

Pileggi, Nicholas. 1980. "The Guardian Angels: Help—or Hype?" *New York Magazine.* 24(November):14–19.

Poling, Tommy H., and J. Frank Kenney. 1986. *The Hare Krishna Character Type: A Study of the Sensate Personality.* Lewiston: Edwin Mellen.

Price, Marie Daly. 1985. "Rajneeshpuram and the American Utopian Tradition." (Discussion Paper No. 87.) Syracuse University, Department of Geography.

Reinccke, William. 1982. "Marching with the Avenging Angels." *Today/Philadelphia Inquirer,* January 31, p. 1.

Rochford, Jr., E. Burke. 1985. *Hare Krishna in America.* New Brunswick, NJ: Rutgers University Press.

Suttles, Gerald D. 1968. *The Social Order of the Slum: Ethnicity and Territory in the Inner City.* Chicago: University of Chicago Press.

de Tocqueville, Alexis. [1848] 1945. *Democracy in America,* edited by Phillips Bradley. New York: Knopf.

Wilson, James Q. 1968. *Varieties of Police Behavior: The Management of Law and Order in Eight Communities.* Cambridge, Mass.: Harvard University Press.

I.
Conclusion

It is time to take stock. This volume has delineated five solutions to the problem of social order—meaning, values and norms, power and authority, spontaneous order, and groups and networks. The solutions identify a variety of causal factors and different mechanisms that link these causal factors to social order. These differences are reflected in the key issues addressed by each solution and in their varying implications for social policy.

Table 1 provides a summary of each theoretical approach. Of course, this summary is overly simplified. It describes the three kinds of mechanisms deemed responsible for order only in broad strokes. It also highlights the questions that each of the theories leaves begging. Research that is relevant to the problem of social order is both interdisciplinary and multidisciplinary. Because it is carried out across the social sciences, the selections in this book come from sociologists, political scientists, economists, psychologists, and anthropologists. The range of empirical evidence about social order is vast: it can be gleaned from the study of crime and deviance, religion, the family, social movements, organizations, politics, and many other topics. The varying mechanisms and assumptions about actors that appear in the theories described here often underlie competing explanations of various social phenomena. They are also implicated in many of the political debates of the day.

Understanding the various solutions to the problem of order therefore provides a foundation for thinking about social issues more generally. This understanding is relevant not only in academia but in the broader world as well. As people argue about welfare, the environment, crime policy, or ways to protect citizens from terrorist threats, they usually advert to implicit theories about why the divorce rate is changing, why people commit crimes, how

TABLE I

Summary of Theoretical Approaches

SOLUTIONS AND AND PROPONENTS	CAUSAL FACTORS	KEY ISSUES	MECHANISMS	REMAINING QUESTIONS
Meaning Marx Durkheim Fleck Mead Cohen and Vandello	Shared meaning	How are shared meanings produced?	S: Social and physical environment affects meaning. B: Shared meaning leads to individuals coordinating their behavior. T: Coordinated individual behaviors aggregate to produce social order.	Why do people behave in ways counter to their individual interests? How do meaning and interests intersect to affect action? People may share meanings, but does this mean they will act in a prosocial manner? Under what conditions is coordination cooperative?
Values and Norms Freud Durkheim Horne Goffman Fehr and Gächter	Shared values and norms	How do values and norms emerge? What makes values and norms effective?	S: Behavioral consequences lead to normative rules. S: Social environment leads to internalization of values and/or interest in enforcing norms. B: Internalization and external enforcement foster cooperative behavior. T: Cooperative individual behaviors aggregate to produce social order.	What accounts for the content of values? Under what conditions are values and norms prosocial or antisocial? How do different situations affect the interpretation of norms? Why are values and norms sometimes effective and sometimes not?
Power and Authority Hobbes Marx Engels Weber Willis	Central authority	How does a central authority emerge? What makes it effective?	S: Social structure leads to conflicts of interest. B: Conflicts of interest lead to demand for government. T: Demand for government leads to formation of government. S: Government increases the negative consequences of anti-social behavior and/or tries to instill a sense of its legitimacy.	Why do self-interested individuals agree to government control? How are the resources necessary to exercise control provided? Are there sufficient resources? Under what conditions are governments successful at instilling a sense of legitimacy?

Approach / Authors	Key concept	Question	Mechanisms	Research question
			B: These costs and sense of legitimacy discourage individual deviance and encourage prosocial behavior. T: Cooperative individual behaviors aggregate to produce social order.	Under what conditions are costs and legitimacy sufficient to induce self-interested individuals to change their behavior in accordance with government demands?
Spontaneous Order Hayek Schelling Smith Axelrod	Interdependence	Can unregulated individuals produce an orderly society?	S: Interdependence leads to interest in interacting cooperatively. B: This interest leads individuals to interact cooperatively. T: Interactions between individuals lead to macro-level patterns of behavior.	Under what conditions do individual action and interaction lead to chaos, coordination, and/or cooperation?
Groups and Networks Simmel Granovetter Gellner Tocqueville Hechter, Friedman, and Kanazawa	Group solidarity and structure of network ties	How do groups influence behavior of members? How can groups be influenced by the larger society?	S/B: A group controls members through values and norms (see mechanisms for values and norms). S/B: The state punishes antisocial groups or rewards prosocial groups (see mechanisms for power and authority). T: Group prosocial behavior aggregates to produce social order. OR S: Network ties (within group, and cross-cutting) affect individual information, perceptions of group members, and leaders, social values, etc. B: These internal states affect individual propensity to go along with the group or the larger society. T: Individual action that contributes to the larger society aggregates to produce social order.	What determines if these values and norms are prosocial or antisocial? What is the relation between values, norms, and law? What is the optimal mix of horizontal and vertical ties? What is the optimal mix of within-group and across-group ties?

NOTE: S, situational mechanism; B, behavioral mechanism; T, transformational mechanism individuals react to welfare, and so forth. Their policy preferences tend to reflect these implicit theories. And of course, their arguments, like those of academics, rest on (also, mostly implicit) assumptions about situational, behavioral, and transformational mechanisms. Likewise, as we interact with others, we too make assumptions, on the basis of simplified theories, about how people work and operate.

Each theory treats different aspects of social order as problematic. Meaning theories, for example, maintain that order cannot exist unless individuals have the ability to coordinate their activities. Because this ability rests on a foundation of shared concepts and beliefs, meaning theories emphasize the importance of understanding the processes by which meanings come to be shared. The obstacles to social order are institutions and practices that impede interpersonal communication. Hence, meaning theorists would be dubious of policies like bilingual education in multicultural societies such as the United States.

Proponents of power and authority theories would take a very different view of these matters. They would point out that although shared concepts and beliefs indeed may facilitate cooperation (as the meaning theories hold), by no means do such factors preclude conflict. For example, the most common site of conflict in complex societies is the household—the first suspects in murder investigations typically are family members—but this is precisely the group with the best prospect of developing shared concepts and beliefs. Regardless of the common meanings that people might attach to social phenomena, power and authority theories regard self-interested behavior as the principal obstacle to the attainment of social order. As such, the problem of deterring free riding looms large. Among the policy implications of these theories is investment in police and other agents of law enforcement, such as the Internal Revenue Service. Meaning and power and authority theories identify distinct causes and mechanisms, and have different policy implications. Similar differences can be found between all the theories.

At this point, we do not have sufficient evidence to determine with certainty which of the five solutions is most useful in particular circumstances.

Each theory provides important insights and understanding into a very complex problem. (Recall what the theoretical physicist said about sociology at the beginning of this book.) At the same time, each also raises further questions. Accordingly, research on social order continues. Scholars extend existing theoretical arguments and seek to determine their limits. They explore if and how different solutions may be combined to provide more satisfactory explanations. Contemporary research builds on these five types of solutions to develop new theories of social order. And the empirical implications of these new theories are tested against observations taken from a variety of settings in the real world.

When we think about social issues, concrete events are usually foremost in our minds. Murder rates increase or decrease. The average income rises or falls. Urban riots wax and wane. Such phenomena can only be explained, however, if we think about them in more abstract terms. Sometimes, we direct our focus to abstract issues—how to achieve freedom and equality, how to provide security and civil rights, or how to produce economic growth and social justice. To assess arguments about both kinds of issues, we must move between abstract theoretical concepts and concrete empirical situations. Responsible thinking about social issues demands the kinds of skills that are emphasized by this volume.

At the beginning of this book, we suggested that when reading social theory, it is useful to try to identify the causal relations (causes and outcomes) and causal mechanisms that explain an outcome. Making these distinctions is also essential when we assess empirical research, evaluate the arguments of policy makers, or develop our own explanations. Even though it takes more time, this kind of analysis is well worth the effort. Doing so contributes to our understanding of an argument, along with its strengths and weaknesses. If we can identify the causal relations and mechanisms in an explanation (often this is no easy task), we are in a much better position to evaluate it. We will be less likely to be convinced by talk that sounds plausible but that has little analytical substance. We may also find that we have something to contribute to the debate. In addition, when the structure of an explanation is clear, we are better able to think about the implications it might have in different circumstances. Further, the kind of evidence that would be necessary to test a theory becomes more readily apparent.

This book does more than simply provide substantive information about the problem of social order. It also emphasizes the importance of analyzing social explanations—identifying causal relations and causal mechanisms. It argues that theory is not just something to learn about in a vacuum, not simply a course taken to fulfill curricular requirements. Rather, theory matters because it has implications for research as well as for our capacity to understand the social world. We trust that this reader has helped you to appreciate the problem of social order and the various solutions that have been advanced to explain it. But more important, we hope that, in attaining a greater understanding of this problem, you will have improved your ability to think about theory and to apply this theoretical awareness to the social forces that impinge on your own life.

INDEX

351

Freedom, political, 326–28
Free riding, 151, 155–57
French Revolution, 59
Freud, Sigmund, 93–94
Friedman, Debra, 289
Friendliness, and violence, 80–82
Friends of Oregon, 335

Gächter, Simon, 99
Games: and social development, 69–70; theories as, 12
Gangs, 337–41
Gans, Herbert, 304–6
Gellner, Ernest, 286–87
Generality, in theory, 11, 13
Generalized other, 65–72; and social control, 66; society as, 65
Genital mutilation, female, 134
George, Stefan, 199–200
Gluckman, Max, 285
Goethe, Johann Wolfgang von, 111
Goffman, Erving, 99
Government: versus associations, 322–23; democratic, 317–28; despotic, 317; leadership in, 315–16; regulation by, 283; role in society of, 232–33; tolerance of deviant religious groups by, 332–37; tolerance of gangs by, 337–41; tolerance of vice by, 341–42; and trust, 310, 311
Granovetter, Mark, 284–85
Groups, 284–90; affiliation effects of, 291–98; conflicting loyalties in, 285–86; in democratic societies, 317–28; local and global order in, 329–43; and social order in heterogeneous societies, 330–31; strong or weak ties in, 299–307; trust in, 310–16
Guardian Angels, 341
Guilt, 104–11; two origins of, 107
Gumplowicz, Ludwig, 63–64

Habits, versus organized self, 72
Happiness: and desire, 167; instinctual versus civilized, 104; social limits and, 121
Hare Krishna, 289, 331, 333, 336–37
Hayek, Friedrich A., 216–17
Hechter, Michael, 289
Hegel, G. W. F., 179, 233

Henry VIII, 18
Heterogeneous societies: social order in, 329–31; types of, 330
History, theory in, 13
Hobbes, Thomas, 28; on cooperation, 261; on social organization, 310; on state authority, 159–60
Homans, George, 4, 5, 300
Honor, cultures of, see Cultures of honor
Horne, Christine, 98, 99
Humanism, 293–94

Idealism, critique of, 50–51
Identification: of child with authority, 108; of individual with group, 67–68
Immigration and Naturalization Service (INS), 336
Individual: desires of, 118–20; and group affiliations, 296–98; physical versus cultural needs of, 114; role of social limits for, 120–23; social integration and, 112–17; society's influence over, 53–59; society's role in developing, 65–72. See also Self-interest
Individualism, and suicide, 112–17
Inivisible hand theory, 283
Instinctual renunciation, 107–9
Instrumental rationality, 17–18, 22, 23–24
Insults, 73–90; meaning of, 79–80; role in culture of honor of, 75, 76
Integration, racial, 243–44
Integration, social, see Social integration
International politics, and cooperation, 261–62
International Society for Krishna Consciousness (ISKCON), 333, 337
Interpersonal ties, 300–307
Intervention, economic, 235–36, 283
Invisible hand theory, 223–24, 283

Jerusalem, Wilhelm, 63
Justice, Hobbes on, 174

Kahan, Dan, 85
Kanazawa, Satoshi, 289
Kepler, Johannes, 62
Kernan, Thomas, 83, 89
Khaldun, Ibn, 286, 287, 310, 315, 316

Pin-making, 251–52
Police, 180
Politeness, and violence, 80–82
Positive-sum game, 219
Power: legitimation of, 183–203; of the state, 179–82; state of nature and, 166–78. *See also* Authority
Prisoner's Dilemma, 219–20, 263–71; applicability of, 269–71; applied to trench warfare, 274–75; assumptions underlying, 265; fundamental form of, 266; strategy in, 267–71; time factor in, 266–67
Productive activities: and development of consciousness, 50–51; as distinctively human, 49; as origin of meaning, 45; and social structure, 50
Property: and aggression, 102–3; state protection of, 181
Proudhon, Pierre-Joseph, 162–63
Public behavior, 140–50
Public force, 180
Public-spiritedness, 33, 35
Punishment, altruistic, 151–57
Purpose, spontaneous order and, 224, 225

Rajneesh, Bhagwan Shree, 333, 336
Rajneesh (group), 289, 333–37
Rational choice theory, 329
Rational egoism, 19; and social order, 31
Reason, Hobbes' definition of, 166–67
Reed, John, 87, 89
Regulation, government, 235–36, 283
Religion: Hobbes on, 169–70; and moral consciousness, 57; and moral power of society, 52–59; totemism, 52–53
Respect, for society, 53–54
Revolutionary epochs, 56–57
Rights, of nature, 174–77
Roughnecks, 338–40
Rousseau, Jean-Jacques, 62
Rules: commands versus, 235–36; as destructive of order, 229; implicitness in spontaneous order of, 228–29; as productive of order, 229–31; of spontaneous versus made orders, 233–36

Sacred versus profane reality, 58–59

Saints, 338–40
Sanctioning: costs and benefits of, 135–36; organizational effectiveness and, 136–37
Schelling, Thomas, 217
School, *see* Counter-school culture
Science: as dependent on opinion, 55–56; social nature of, 60–64. *See also* Social science, versus natural science
Segregation, critical-mass models and, 248–50
Self-consciousness, society's role in developing, 66–67, 72
Self development: group contribution to, 71–72; two stages of, 68–69
Self-forming neighborhood model, 244–50
Self-interest: and cooperation, 217–18, 261–71; and division of labor, 258–59
Senate, cooperation in, 262, 268–69
Shepherds, 310–11
Shopfloor culture, 212–15
Simmel, Georg, 284
Situational mechanisms, 16–17
Skinner, Cornelia Otis, 149
Smith, Adam, 217–19, 223–24
Smith, Joseph, 197
Social action, types of, 22–24
Social behavior, Hobbes on, 167–70
Social contracts, 177–78
Social integration: collapse of, 116–17; and individual happiness, 112–13; and suicide, 4, 6–7
Social limits: characteristics of, 120–22; crisis in, 123–24; economic sphere and, 124–27; and individual happiness, 121
Social order: absence of, 33–43; in ants, 27–28; components of, 29–31; degrees of, 29; as focus of sociology, xii–xiv; in heterogeneous societies, 329–43; problem of, 27; relationship to violence of, 87–89
Social science, versus natural science, 9, 12, 46
Social structure, *see* Groups
Society: compared to divine, 53–59; as generalized other, 65; influence over individual of, 53–59, 120–23; role in self development of, 65–72; stimulation of emotion in, 56–57